# Rugby For Dummies, 2nd Edition

D0939880

## Key Rugby Terms

**Line-out:** Looks somewhat like a jump-ball in basketball, with bo[...] other, but one team then throws the ball down the middle of the [...] the ball, or a player carrying it, has gone out of bounds.

**Maul:** Occurs when a player carrying the ball is held by one or m[...], and one or more of the ball-carrier's teammates bind on the ball-carrier. All the players involved are on their feet and moving toward a goal line. Open play has ended.

**Ruck:** One or more players from each team, who are on their feet and in contact, close around the ball on the ground. Once a ruck has been formed, players can't use their hands to get the ball, only their feet.

**Scrum:** A contest for the ball involving eight players who bind together and push against the other team's assembled eight for possession of the ball. Scrums restart play after certain minor infractions.

## Rugby Tournaments at a Glance

| Tournament | Description | Participants |
|---|---|---|
| Rugby World Cup | Held every four years to crown the World Champion | 20 qualifying nations |
| Six Nations Championship | Annual international championship of Northern Hemisphere | England, Scotland, Wales, Ireland, France, and Italy |
| Tri Nations Series | Annual international championship of Southern Hemisphere | Australia, New Zealand, and South Africa |
| Churchill Cup | Annual international series designed to improve North American rugby competitiveness | Canada, England Saxons, New Zealand Maori, Scotland A, Ireland A, and the United States |
| Super 14 | Annual Southern Hemisphere interprovincial championship | **Australia:** Brumbies, Reds, Waratahs, Western Force; **New Zealand:** Blues, Chiefs, Crusaders, Highlanders, Hurricanes; **South Africa:** Bulls, Cats, Cheetahs, Sharks, Stormers |
| Heineken Cup | Annual European interprovincial/club championship | Varies every year by finish in domestic competition. **England:** Gloucester, Leicester, London Wasps, London Irish, Northampton, Sale; **Wales:** Cardiff, Llanelli, Neath/Swansea; **Scotland:** Borders, Edinburgh; **Ireland:** Leinster, Munster, Ulster; **Italy:** Calvisano, Parma, Treviso; **France:** Agen, Biarritz, Bourgoin, Castres, Perpignan, Stade Français, Toulouse |

# Rugby For Dummies®, 2nd Edition

## A Team on the Attack

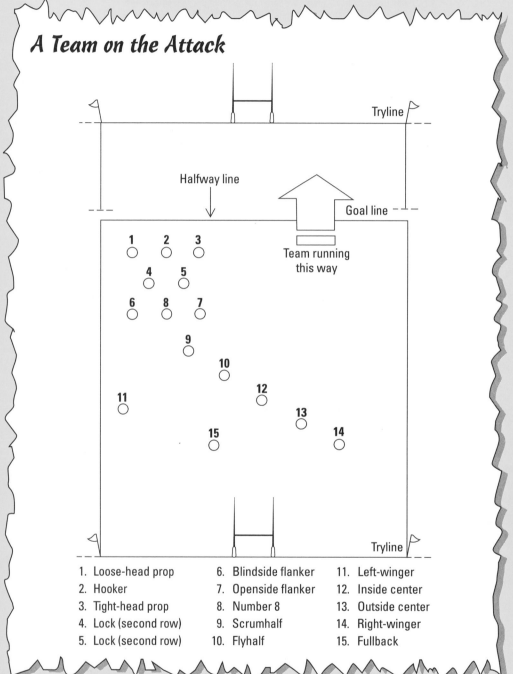

Tryline

Halfway line

Goal line

Team running this way

Tryline

| 1. Loose-head prop | 6. Blindside flanker | 11. Left-winger |
|---|---|---|
| 2. Hooker | 7. Openside flanker | 12. Inside center |
| 3. Tight-head prop | 8. Number 8 | 13. Outside center |
| 4. Lock (second row) | 9. Scrumhalf | 14. Right-winger |
| 5. Lock (second row) | 10. Flyhalf | 15. Fullback |

## For Dummies: Bestselling Book Series for Beginners

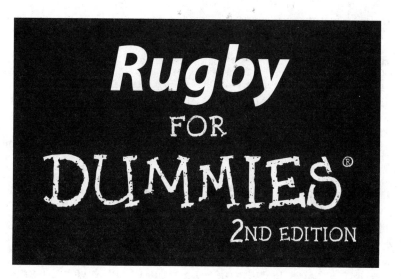

# Rugby
## FOR
# DUMMIES®
### 2ND EDITION

by Mathew Brown
Patrick Guthrie
Greg Growden

BICENTENNIAL
1807
WILEY
2007
BICENTENNIAL

John Wiley & Sons Canada, Ltd.

**Rugby For Dummies,® 2nd Edition**

Published by
**John Wiley & Sons Canada, Ltd.**
6045 Freemont Boulevard
Mississauga, ON L5R 4J3
www.wiley.com

For general information on John Wiley & Sons Canada, Ltd., including all books published by Wiley Publishing Inc., please call our warehouse, Tel. 1-800-567-4797. For reseller information, including discounts and premium sales, please call our sales department, Tel. 416-646-7992. For press review copies, author interviews, or other publicity information, please contact our marketing department, Tel. 416-646-4584, Fax 416-236-4448.

For authorization to photocopy items for corporate, personal, or educational use, please contact in writing The Canadian Copyright Licensing Agency (Access Copyright). For an Access Copyright license, visit www.accesscopyright.ca or call toll free 1-800-893-5777.

Library and Archives Canada Cataloguing in Publication Data

Brown, Matthew (Matthew Timothy)
Rugby for dummies / by Matthew Brown, Patrick Guthrie,
Greg Growden. — 2nd ed.

Includes index.
ISBN 978-0-470-15327-7

1. Rugby football. I. Guthrie, Patrick, 1962- II. Growden, Greg III. Title.

GV945.B76 2007          796.333          C2007-902522-6

Printed in Canada

1 2 3 4 5 TRI 11 10 09 08 07

WILEY

# About the Authors

**Mathew Brown** is America's foremost rugby writer. From 1999 to 2004 he wrote a weekly rugby column for Fox Sports.com, was a producer of *Championship Rugby,* and also hosted and produced the Fox Sports World *Rugby Report* and tended bar at *The Rugby Club*. Since 2005 he has been the rugby producer for MediaZone Rugby and writes the weekly Brownie's Best of the Weekend and Brownie's Weekend Preview columns. Brown began his rugby career at Occidental College, has been a member of various clubs from Missoula to Riga, played international rugby for Latvia, and has coached at the collegiate and club level.

**Patrick Guthrie** pioneered the delivery of rugby programming to North Americans. He produced more than 700 rugby television shows including *Championship Rugby* and *The Rugby Club* for the International Channel, FOX Sports International, ESPN, ESPNU, and Versus from 1995 to 2007. Mr. Guthrie is the Executive Producer of the USA Sevens from 2003–07 and Churchill Cup in 2006. He was instrumental in launching the MediaZone Rugby broadband service worldwide and has been Director of Rugby at MediaZone.com since 2005. A former member of the USA Rugby Board of Directors from 2003 to 2006, he currently serves on the USA Rugby Congress.

**Greg Growden** is one of Australia's best-known sports writers. He began writing about rugby union in 1981, and since 1987 has been the chief rugby writer for the *Sydney Morning Herald*. He is also a regular on New Zealand television rugby shows.

Greg's other books include *A Wayward Genius: The Fleetwood Smith Story* and *Gold, Mud 'N Guts, The Incredible Tom Richards: Footballer, War Hero, Olympian.*

# Dedication

This book is dedicated to rugby and all who have ever played, watched, or enjoyed it. The sport has been the driving force in both our lives and we're hopeful that this attempt to enlighten the uninitiated will bring a greater audience to this fascinating and wonderful game.

—Mathew Brown and Patrick Guthrie

# Authors' Acknowledgments

Thanks to Train and Vandy for getting me started and to Godfree for instilling in me a deep and abiding love for the game. Thanks to all of the teammates I've ever played with from the Blackshirts, Oxy Olde Boys, Powell River, All-Maggots, Miesnieks, Exiles, Vail, Flies, Tsunami, and many more over the years. Special thanks to Guthrie for convincing me to join him on the quest to expand the rugby audience and to Jan for giving me the opportunity to immerse myself even more fully in the worldwide game. Thanks to Reid for keeping me housed and my family for putting up with me forever and understanding how important this sport is to me.

—Mathew Brown

My father comes first for his support, love, and recognition early on that I was on a crusade to grow the game, no matter the personal costs. Special thanks to Bo Kelly for his trust and financial backing to get the whole project started. Kudos to Bob Watkins, Ed Hagerty, and Dennis Storer for being my three wise men. Thanks also to Jan Steenkamp for sharing my dream of building a global home for the game. But most of all, thanks to the Oxy Olde Boys, Kev, Yauch, and Brownie in particular for introducing me to my life's great passion.

—Patrick Guthrie

## Publisher's Acknowledgments

We're proud of this book; please send us your comments through our online registration form located at www.dummies.com/register/.

Some of the people who helped bring this book to market include the following:

**Acquisitions, Editorial, and Media Development**

**Editor:** Robert Hickey

**Copy Editor:** Kelli Howey

**Cover photography:** Russell Cheyne/ Stone Collection/Getty Images

**Illustrations:** Paul Lennon, Adrian So

**Anniversary logo design:** Richard J. Pacifico

**Cartoons:** Rich Tennant (www.the5thwave.com)

**Composition Services**

**Publishing Services Director:** Karen Bryan

**Project Manager:** Elizabeth McCurdy

**Project Coordinator:** Lindsay Humphreys

**Graphics:** Stacie Brooks, Kim Monteforte, Heidy Lawrence Associates

**Layout:** Claudia Bell, Carl Byers, Alicia B. South

**Proofreader:** Laura Albert, Aptara

**Indexer:** Belle Wong

### Photo Credits:

Fig 8-2: Getty Images/Daniel Berehulak; Fig 9-2: Getty Images/John Gichigi; Fig 9-3: Getty Images/ Clive Brunskill; Fig 10-3:Sport the Library/Action Photos Rugby Union; Fig 10-4: Sport the Library: Tom Putt; Fig 10-6: Newspix/Mark Evans; Fig 10-8, 13-1, 15-1, 17-2, 23-2, Fig 15-2: courtesy Kevin Roberts; Fig 15-3: courtesy of Jen Doan, USA Rugby; Fig 16-1: Dave Stephenson (www.lumina photo.com); Fig 16-2: courtesy of Chuck Bruce; Fig 16-3: courtesy of Pat Sayer; Fig 17-1: Dave Stephenson (www.luminaphoto.com); Fig 21-1: International Rugby Academy; Fig 22-1: Sport the Library; Fig 23-1: Doug Crosse; Fig 23-3: Dave Stephenson (www.luminaphoto.com)

---

**John Wiley & Sons Canada, Ltd.**

    **Bill Zerter,** Chief Operating Officer

    **Jennifer Smith,** Vice President and Publisher, Professional & Trade Division

**Publishing and Editorial for Consumer Dummies**

    **Diane Graves Steele,** Vice President and Publisher, Consumer Dummies

    **Joyce Pepple,** Acquisitions Director, Consumer Dummies

    **Kristin A. Cocks,** Product Development Director, Consumer Dummies

    **Michael Spring,** Vice President and Publisher, Travel

    **Kelly Regan,** Editorial Director, Travel

**Publishing for Technology Dummies**

    **Andy Cummings,** Vice President and Publisher, Dummies Technology/General User

**Composition Services**

    **Gerry Fahey,** Vice President of Production Services

    **Debbie Stailey,** Director of Composition Services

# Contents at a Glance

Introduction ...................................................................1

## Part I: Rugby: Roots, Boots, and All.............................7

Chapter 1: Rugby's Beginnings, Allure, and a Basic Overview ..............9

Chapter 2: The Basics ...........................................................19

Chapter 3: Grab Your Rugby Gear ..........................................33

## Part II: Getting Down and Dirty.................................45

Chapter 4: Location, Location, Location: Positions on the Pitch...............47

Chapter 5: Laying Down the Laws ..............................................65

Chapter 6: Understanding the Fundamentals ...............................77

Chapter 7: Playing the Game....................................................97

Chapter 8: The Art of Scrummaging.........................................113

Chapter 9: Line-outs: Restarting from Touch ...............................127

Chapter 10: Individual Skills...................................................143

Chapter 11: Tactics and Teamwork.............................................167

Chapter 12: Talented Training ................................................183

## Part III: Welcome to the Oval Planet.........................195

Chapter 13: The World Cup.....................................................197

Chapter 14: The International Calendar .....................................213

Chapter 15: North American Rugby ..........................................227

Chapter 16: Amateur Rugby in North America...............................241

Chapter 17: Collegiate, High School, and Youth Rugby in North America.....249

## Part IV: Coaching and Refereeing .............................257

Chapter 18: Coaching...........................................................259

Chapter 19: Coaching Certification and Advancement ....................271

Chapter 20: Managing the Game — The Referee............................279

## Part V: Following the Game: The Informed Fan............287

Chapter 21: Get Your Game — Rugby on TV.................................289

Chapter 22: Spectating and Staying in Touch with Rugby News ............297

## Part VI: The Part of Tens .............................309

Chapter 23: The Ten Greatest North American Players ...............................311

Chapter 24: The Ten Best Rugby Moments....................................................319

Chapter 25: Ten Peculiar Facts about Rugby.................................................327

## Appendix A: U.S. and Canada Tests....................337

## Appendix B: Glossary ......................................351

## Index ..............................................................365

# Table of Contents

*Introduction* ..................................................................... 1

About This Book.............................................................................1
Conventions Used in This Book ...................................................2
Why You Need This Book...............................................................2
How This Book Is Organized.........................................................2
    Part I: Rugby: Roots, Boots, and All ....................................2
    Part II: Getting Down and Dirty............................................2
    Part III: Welcome to the Oval Planet ...................................3
    Part IV: Coaching and Refereeing.........................................3
    Part V: Following the Game: The Informed Fan....................3
    Part VI: The Part of Tens .......................................................3
    The Appendixes......................................................................4
Icons Used in This Book.................................................................4
Where to Go from Here...................................................................5

*Part 1: Rugby: Roots, Boots, and All* .......................... 7

**Chapter 1: Rugby's Beginnings, Allure, and a Basic Overview** ......9

Rugby's Roots — The Birth of the Game ....................................9
    The mythical pick-up of William Webb Ellis........................10
    A century of amateurism.......................................................11
How the Game Is Played...............................................................11
    The field.................................................................................11
    The scoring ...........................................................................12
    The gear.................................................................................12
Understanding the Essentials of the Game................................13
    Puzzling out the positions....................................................13
    Grasping the laws of the game.............................................14
    Scoping out skills, tactics, and training..............................14
Rugby's a Worldwide Game .........................................................15
    An international affair............................................................15
    North America gets into the action......................................16
Coaching and Refereeing..............................................................16
Keeping Informed about the Game .............................................17

**Chapter 2: The Basics** ...................................................19

Figuring Out the Field ..................................................................19
    Dimensions of the playing area ...........................................19
    What do all those lines mean?..............................................20
    Recognizing the goalposts and flags....................................22

Understanding the Scoring System.....................................23
   Scoring a try...........................................................23
   Awarding a penalty try ..........................................24
   Converting a try....................................................24
   Kicking penalty goals ............................................26
   Drop-kicking goals ................................................26
Timekeeping on the Field ...............................................27
   When the clock runs and when it stops ................28
   When someone's injured........................................28
   When the TMO is looking at play ..........................28
   When the hooter sounds ........................................28
Introducing the Players..................................................29
   Taking up position ................................................29
   Positions by the numbers .....................................30
   The reserves .........................................................31

**Chapter 3: Grab Your Rugby Gear** . . . . . . . . . . . . . . . . . . . . . . . . . **.33**
Getting It Together: The Essentials of the Kit Bag .........33
   Having a ball..........................................................34
   Kicking in with a kicking tee .................................35
   Miscellaneous kit items ........................................36
Getting the Gear .............................................................36
   Rugby jerseys........................................................37
   Rugby shorts .........................................................37
   Booting up.............................................................38
   Socking it to you ...................................................39
Protecting Your Assets ...................................................40
   Choosing protective equipment ...........................40
   Avoiding serious injury.........................................42
   Knowing what's barred on the pitch......................43

**Part II: Getting Down and Dirty .....................................45**

**Chapter 4: Location, Location, Location: Positions on the Pitch** . . . .**47**
A Place for Everyone .......................................................47
Playing the Numbers Game...............................................48
Fearless Forwards ..........................................................50
   Getting in tight with the tight five .......................51
   Facing off in the front row ....................................52
   The second row: Exerting in the engine room....................55
   The back-row forwards: Breaking loose with the loosies ..............56
Get to the Back of the Line...............................................58
   Passing and pestering for profit: The scrumhalf....................58
   Feeling footloose and fancy-free: The flyhalf .....................59
   Mastering the midfield: Centers ...........................60

Running wild out wide: The wings ....................................................62
Roaming the range: The fullback........................................................62

**Chapter 5: Laying Down the Laws** ...........................**65**
The Laws of the Game ........................................................................65
The IRB writes the law........................................................................66
The laws are dynamic and ever-changing.........................................67
Reading the law book.........................................................................68
Building up your knowledge ..............................................................68
Introducing the Match Officials............................................................70
The referee: The one with the whistle ..............................................70
Touch judges: The ones with the flags ............................................71
The substitution official: The one with the numbers .....................72
The TMO: The one with the video screen ..........................................73
Recognizing the Referee's Signals ....................................................73

**Chapter 6: Understanding the Fundamentals** ....................**77**
The Object of the Game......................................................................78
Running, Passing, and Kicking.............................................................79
Running....................................................................................................79
Passing....................................................................................................79
Kicking ....................................................................................................79
What Can Go Wrong?............................................................................81
Knock-on.................................................................................................81
Forward pass ........................................................................................82
The Tackle Law — Where Football Ends, Rugby Begins .....................82
The tackle situation and continuity ..................................................83
The tackled player................................................................................83
The tackler .............................................................................................84
Tackling no-no's ...................................................................................84
The Advantage Law — When Play Stops and When It Continues............85
Observing the Offside Law....................................................................87
In general play .....................................................................................87
From set pieces .....................................................................................90
At tackles, rucks, and mauls ..............................................................91
Playing Foul............................................................................................92
Obstruction ...........................................................................................92
Unfair play ............................................................................................93
Repeated infringements.......................................................................93
Misconduct............................................................................................93
Taking penalties ...................................................................................94
Kicking at goal......................................................................................94
Kicking for touch ................................................................................94
Choosing a scrum.................................................................................95
Taking it quick......................................................................................95
Free kicks...............................................................................................95

**Chapter 7: Playing the Game** ................................ **97**

Getting Started ................................................98
Kickoffs to begin each half ...............................98
Restarts after scores and 22s...........................100
The Tackle Situation ..........................................101
The tackled player.........................................102
The tackler ................................................102
What happens next?.......................................103
Breaking Down the Breakdown ................................103
Tackle, Ruck, or Maul?........................................104
Roughing It in the Rucks .....................................104
Rucking rules .............................................106
Directing the ruck.........................................108
Working the pick-and-go ..................................108
Mastering the Maul ...........................................109
Mauling laws .............................................110
Directing the maul ........................................111
Stopping the maul ........................................112

**Chapter 8: The Art of Scrummaging** ....................... **113**

Scrum Is Not Synonymous with Mayhem .....................113
Sections of the Scrum.........................................115
The front row .............................................115
The second row ...........................................117
The back row .............................................117
The ninth forward — The scrumhalf ......................118
Engagement...................................................119
The put-in ................................................120
The contest for possession ...............................120
Laws at Scrumtime............................................121
Binding and releasing.....................................121
Collapsing.................................................122
Driving in and up .........................................122
Feeding....................................................123
Strategic Scrummaging........................................123
Attacking from the scrum..................................123
Wheeling the scrum .......................................124
Getting a shove on.........................................125
Pushing it over the edge...................................126

**Chapter 9: Line-outs: Restarting from Touch** .....................**127**

When Does a Line-out Occur? ................................128
Where Does a Line-out Take Place? ..........................128
Directly into touch ........................................129
Indirectly into touch ......................................129

Who Gets the Throw-in?................................................................130
Lining Up for a Line-out.............................................................131
 Forming a line-out...............................................................132
 Calling the play.....................................................................132
 Throwing in the ball............................................................134
 Taking the throw..................................................................135
Starring Roles in a Line-out......................................................136
 Jumpers and lifters..............................................................136
 The receiver..........................................................................138
 Movement in the line-out...................................................138
Talking Tactics Down the Line..................................................139
 Peeling off.............................................................................139
 Throwing to the front..........................................................139
 Setting up the maul.............................................................140
 Quick off the top.................................................................140
Things You Can't Do ..................................................................140
Taking It Quick............................................................................141

**Chapter 10: Individual Skills** . . . . . . . . . . . . . . . . . . . . . . . . . . . . . . .**143**
Running Rampant........................................................................144
 Receiving a pass on the run..............................................145
 Side-stepping the tackler....................................................145
 Curving into the swerve......................................................146
 Fending off forcibly.............................................................147
 Going into a hit and spin....................................................148
 Doing the goose step..........................................................148
 Throwing the dummy...........................................................149
Passing with Panache................................................................149
 Bringing tactics into play....................................................150
 Spiral pass............................................................................151
 Cut-out pass.........................................................................152
 Lob pass...............................................................................153
 Pop pass...............................................................................153
 Dive pass..............................................................................154
 Scrumhalf pass....................................................................154
Kicking Cleverly..........................................................................154
 Spiral punt kick....................................................................155
 Up and under.......................................................................156
 Chip kick...............................................................................157
 Grubber kick.........................................................................158
 Drop kick..............................................................................159
 Goal kicking.........................................................................160
Tackling Tough............................................................................162
 Front-on driving tackle........................................................163
 Side-on tackle......................................................................165
 Tackle from behind..............................................................165

         Ball-and-all tackle ...................................................................166
         Stationary tackle......................................................................166
         Ankle tap...................................................................................166

**Chapter 11: Tactics and Teamwork** ............................**167**
     Creating a Game Plan.........................................................................168
         Understanding your team's strengths and weaknesses.................168
         Analyzing the opponent ...........................................................172
     Weathering the Conditions ...............................................................174
         Adapting to inclement weather ...............................................175
         Playing the pitch.......................................................................175
     Deciding on a Game Plan....................................................................176
     Attacking Artistically .........................................................................177
         Launching an effective attack ..................................................178
         Breaking through ......................................................................178
     Defending Devilishly ...........................................................................179
         Coordinating the defense .........................................................179
         Blocking the advance: Defensive systems ..............................179
         Commitment and trust ..............................................................182

**Chapter 12: Talented Training** ...................................**183**
     Getting Match Fit.................................................................................183
         Warming up and having a good stretch....................................184
         Stretching for performance......................................................185
         Developing a fitness program ..................................................187
     Psyching Up for a Stellar Performance.............................................190
     Eating Your Way to Victory ................................................................191
         Choosing a balanced diet .........................................................192
         Taking in fuel .............................................................................192
         Choosing your supplements carefully.....................................193

*Part III: Welcome to the Oval Planet* ...........................*195*

**Chapter 13: The World Cup** ......................................**197**
     The Crown Jewel of Rugby..................................................................197
     The Origins and History of the Rugby World Cup ...........................198
         1987 World Cup — Australia and New Zealand ......................199
         1991 World Cup — Great Britain, Ireland, and France...............199
         1995 World Cup — South Africa ..............................................199
         1999 World Cup — Wales, England, Scotland,
             Ireland, and France..............................................................200
         2003 World Cup — Australia .....................................................200
         2007 World Cup — France, Wales, and Scotland .......................201
     Qualification and Finals Tournaments .............................................201

North Americans in the World Cup........................................203
    Fighting Eagles.....................................................203
    Competing Canadians ...........................................203
Mammoths and Minnows .................................................204
Great World Cup Moments ...............................................205
    Australia versus England — 2003 final .................205
    South Africa versus New Zealand — 1995 final .....206
    Australia versus South Africa — 1999 Semifinal #1 .....206
    New Zealand versus France — 1999 Semifinal #2 .........207
Other Cups on the World Stage .........................................208
    Sevens World Cup...................................................208
    Women's Rugby World Cup .....................................209
    The Under-21 Rugby World Cup ..............................210
    The Under-19 World Championships........................211

**Chapter 14: The International Calendar** .........................**213**
How the Game Is Organized...............................................213
    Rugby's rulers — The IRB ......................................214
    National unions.......................................................214
    Provincial unions....................................................215
    Local unions ...........................................................215
The Powers That Be..........................................................216
    Where tradition is king — The Six Nations .............216
    South versus North — The SANZAR home tests.........217
    The battle of the Big Three — The Tri Nations .......217
    North versus south — The Fall tests .......................219
    The British & Irish Lions .........................................219
    The Barbarian Football Club..................................220
    The World Sevens Series ........................................221
Interprovincial and Provincial Rugby................................221
    The sensational Super 14 .......................................222
    The Heineken Cup overfloweth ...............................222
    The Celtic scene .....................................................223
    The Air New Zealand Cup.........................................224
    The South African ABSA Currie Cup ........................225
    The English domestic scene ...................................225
    The Top 14...............................................................226

**Chapter 15: North American Rugby** .............................**227**
Checking Out Rugby in the United States ...........................227
    Origins and Olympic gold........................................228
    Formation and reformation of USA Rugby ...............229
    Soaring with the Eagles .........................................232
    Eagles atop the world: Women's rugby ...................234
    Sevens ....................................................................235

Investigating Rugby in Canada ................................................235
    The birth of Rugby Canada ........................................236
    Canadian women on the rise ....................................237
    Canadian National Women's League ........................238
    Sevens ..........................................................................238
Going Global: North American Internationals ...............238
    Barclays Churchill Cup ..............................................239
    North America 4 .........................................................239

**Chapter 16: Amateur Rugby in North America** ..................**241**

Clubbing with the Yanks ................................................241
    The USA Rugby Super League....................................243
    USA Club Championships ...........................................245
Considering the Canadian Club Scene ...........................246
    The Rugby Canada Super League..............................246
    Canadian National Championships ...........................247

**Chapter 17: Collegiate, High School,
and Youth Rugby in North America** ..........................**249**

Playing the American Collegiate Game ..........................249
Starting Young: High School and Youth Rugby in the U.S.A. .........251
    High school championships........................................252
    Youth rugby..................................................................253
Canadian Collegiate Championships ..............................255
High School and Youth Rugby in Canada .......................255
    High school rugby ......................................................256
    Youth rugby..................................................................256

*Part IV: Coaching and Refereeing* ..............................*257*

**Chapter 18: Coaching** .....................................................**259**

Grand Obsession: The Making of a Good Coach...................260
    Improving skill levels ................................................260
    Getting your team fighting fit....................................261
    Motivating your team..................................................261
Coaching Safety ................................................................262
    Keeping your players safe ..........................................262
    False assumptions and the truth about injuries in rugby...........263
Tackling a Tough Job ........................................................264
Deciding Whether Coaching Is for You............................266
You're Not Alone: Support Staff.......................................267
    Coaching: Assistant coach .........................................267
    Coaching: Defense coach ...........................................268
    Managing the team ......................................................268
    Training the team ........................................................269

Massaging the players: The physiotherapist.................................269
Calling on the team doctor.......................................................269

**Chapter 19: Coaching Certification and Advancement . . . . . . . . . . .271**
Coaching Accreditation in the U.S. ...............................................271
Looking at the Coach Development Program...............................272
Getting certified.....................................................................272
Coach Training in Canada.............................................................273
The International Rugby Academy ................................................273
Coaching Hatchlings to Eagles ....................................................274
Nurturing the youth................................................................274
Having an oval ball in high school ...........................................275
Corralling collegians ..............................................................275
Catering to the clubs..............................................................276

**Chapter 20: Managing the Game — The Referee . . . . . . . . . . . . . . .279**
The Responsibility of the Whistle................................................279
Knowledge..............................................................................280
Consistency.............................................................................280
Communication ......................................................................280
Temperament..........................................................................281
Fitness....................................................................................282
Becoming a Ref in the States .......................................................282
Getting started........................................................................282
Moving up...............................................................................283
Reaching the top .....................................................................284
Picking Up the Whistle Up North.................................................284

**Part V: Following the Game: The Informed Fan ............287**

**Chapter 21: Get Your Game — Rugby on TV . . . . . . . . . . . . . . . . . .289**
The History of Rugby on TV in North America...............................289
Rugby on Television in the U.S.A. ................................................290
Rugby on Television in Canada ....................................................291
Speaking the Language.................................................................292
Rugby's TV jargon glossary......................................................292
Marvelous Mextedisms.............................................................293
The best of the commentators .................................................294

**Chapter 22: Spectating and Staying in Touch with Rugby News . . .297**
Finding a Match to Watch .............................................................297
Blending In with the Crowd .........................................................298
Following rugby etiquette ........................................................298
Dressing for the occasion.........................................................299
Spectating across North America..............................................300

Going to watch a test match ...............................................300
The club experience.............................................................301
Sounding like a rugby expert .............................................302
Touring Overseas ...........................................................................302
Learning More about the Game......................................................303
North American magazines ..................................................303
Rugby matches on the Web...................................................305
Rugby news in cyberspace...................................................305
North American focus ..........................................................307
IRB and union Web sites .....................................................307

## Part VI: The Part of Tens .................................309

### Chapter 23: The Ten Greatest North American Players ..........311

Gareth Rees.............................................................................311
Dan Lyle..................................................................................312
Al Charron...............................................................................313
Dave Hodges...........................................................................314
Mike James.............................................................................314
Brian Vizard............................................................................314
Patty Jervey ............................................................................315
Jen Crawford...........................................................................315
Gillian Florence.......................................................................315
Heather Moyse .......................................................................316
Honorable Mentions ..............................................................316

### Chapter 24: The Ten Best Rugby Moments ...................319

Top Five Around the World............................................................319
The greatest test ever .........................................................319
The 2003 World Cup final ....................................................320
Barbarians versus New Zealand 1973.................................321
The Bulls win the Super 14..................................................322
1995 World Cup final ...........................................................323
Top Five North American Moments................................................323
Women's Rugby World Cup final 1991 ................................324
Canada versus France 1994..................................................324
U.S. Olympians versus France (1920 and 1924)..................324
Wales versus Canada 1993 ..................................................325
Canada versus Argentina 2005.............................................325

### Chapter 25: Ten Peculiar Facts about Rugby ..................327

Rugby Attracts Some Surprising People ........................................327
Unlikely Lads Can Make It to the Top...........................................328

Siblings Like to Battle It Out Together ........................................329
Players Injure Themselves in Bizarre Ways ...............................330
Rugby Players Hate to Cancel Games..........................................330
Rugby Is Played in Extreme Weather and in Strange Locations............331
Players Score in Unorthodox Ways..............................................332
Sometimes Officials Make Unofficial Calls ................................333
Rugby Blunders into Multicultural Minefields .........................333
If It's Going to Happen, It'll Happen on Tour ...........................334

*Appendix A: U.S. and Canada Tests* ..........................*337*

*Appendix B: Glossary*................................................*351*

*Index*............................................................................*365*

# Introduction

**W**elcome to *Rugby For Dummies*, 2nd Edition. This book is your introduction to a sport that has attracted a passionate following around the world for more than a century, but is just now exploding in popularity in the United States and Canada. As rugby devotees ourselves, we understand the natural appeal of the sport and why you feel the need to find out more about it.

Rugby is the world's third-most popular team sport and is played in more than a hundred countries. The nonstop action is breathtaking as the athletes confront each other over 80 minutes of gut-wrenching competition.

Although it was first introduced here more than 133 years ago, up until very recently rugby was a mystery to most North Americans. In the past few years rugby has made the transition from being a totally amateur game to a fully professional sport. This revolutionary development has increased the fitness of the players, sped up the game, and created a vastly more entertaining, television-friendly product that is growing by leaps and bounds all across North America.

This book is intended to help parents, players, coaches, and their families get acquainted with the basic elements of this fantastic game. We hope this book lifts the veil of mystery that has shrouded the sport and enables you to appreciate both the excitement on the field and the camaraderie off it that makes rugby truly unique.

## About This Book

*Rugby For Dummies* includes all the information you need to get started in the sport, whether you want to be a player, coach, or spectator. It's the first comprehensive guide to all things rugby and was written specifically for a North American audience. Plenty of foreign books talk about rugby, but to our knowledge (and we know it all!) this is the only one that explains the game in terms that Americans and Canadians can easily understand.

We've made ease of access and cross-referencing a priority at all times, so you can use this book to quickly locate a specific topic, find the information you're looking for, and get on with your life.

# Conventions Used in This Book

Rugby has its own language, so to help you understand what we're talking about we've made a point of putting rugby jargon in *italics* and then defining those terms right away. If we missed one here or there, however, and you encounter a term you're not familiar with, check the glossary in Appendix B.

# Why You Need This Book

If you tried to figure out rugby on your own, it would take you at least a decade of constantly watching, playing, asking questions, and absorbing the atmosphere for you to get a good feel for the game. We know, because that's how we did it. Until we wrote this book there was no easy way to access and assimilate all the information needed to gain a solid understanding of the game — other than personal experience through trial and error.

Whatever your reasons for reading this book — whether you're barely acquainted with the game or possess a wealth of knowledge about it — *Rugby For Dummies* answers your questions and increases your understanding of the sport.

# How This Book Is Organized

This book is organized into six parts. Each of the parts covers a major aspect of the game.

## Part I: Rugby: Roots, Boots, and All

The first chapter tells why rugby is a unique sport and gives you a preview of all the information that's contained throughout the book. Then we cover the basics of the field, explain the scoring system, and take a quick look at all the positions. To prevent you from showing up unprepared, we also list all the gear you need to play.

## Part II: Getting Down and Dirty

The second course is the meat-and-potatoes portion of this book. First, we explain the various responsibilities and skills needed to play all 15 positions.

Second, we introduce the laws of the game and the match officials, which leads to an explanation of the object of the game, what happens after a tackle, and the concepts of offside and foul play. Then we discuss the differences among tackles, rucks, and mauls. Next, we analyze scrums and line-outs. We then shift gears to address the individual skills of running, passing, kicking, and tackling, and finish off with a look at tactics and training for rugby.

## Part III: Welcome to the Oval Planet

This part spans the globe to survey the annual calendar of provincial, inter-provincial, and international competitions. We move next to the Rugby World Cup and the International Rugby Board's (IRB) stable of events. Then we move back closer to home with a look at the USA National Team — the Eagles, followed by a look at the pride of Rugby Canada — the Canadian National Team. We conclude with a tour of the heart and soul of North American rugby — the club game.

## Part IV: Coaching and Refereeing

Part IV covers the full spectrum of coaching — from the minis to the Super League — and explains how you can become a certified coach. The refereeing section reviews the responsibility of the ref and what you need to do to become one so that we can address the current shortage of whistle-blowers.

## Part V: Following the Game: The Informed Fan

The fifth part brings joy to your household, as we lay out when and where you can watch rugby on TV and on the Internet. We survey the various channels and Web sites and tell you what's on tap so you can watch rugby across North America. Next, we tell you how you can find a local match to attend. In order to satisfy your thirst for more knowledge, we also detail all the rugby-related magazines, books, and places on the Web to access rugby information.

## Part VI: The Part of Tens

In the sixth part we offer three top ten lists. The first provides our ten best North American players. The second covers the ten best rugby moments of all time. The third list conveys ten peculiar facts about the oval game.

## *The Appendixes*

Finally, we've included two appendixes for easy access to information you're likely to need. Appendix A includes the USA Rugby and Rugby Canada test records. Appendix B contains a handy glossary of rugby terms for your edification.

# *Icons Used in This Book*

To help you navigate your way through this book, seven icons appear in the margins. The icons point you to a particular type of information, depending on your needs. The icons mean the following:

This icon indicates useful information for players looking to improve their skills. Even if you're not a player, they'll help you understand what players are trying to accomplish and elevate your knowledge and enjoyment.

This symbol is used when we offer advice to coaches. All of these suggestions have worked for us in our coaching experience, so we hope you'll find them useful and we encourage you to give us feedback.

Whenever we use a word or phrase that is unique to rugby speak, we employ this icon to identify the term and then define it.

This icon indicates a technical discussion is underway. You can skip this information if you want to, because it isn't necessary for an understanding of the basics. If you do read it, though, your rugby expertise goes up a few notches.

Whenever safety is an issue, we use this symbol to alert you of the potential risk and then explain how to minimize or avoid harm.

When you see this icon, get buckled in for an entertaining tale from your author's vast reservoir of rugby exploits, recounted from his unique rugby-centric perspective of the universe.

When you find this icon, remember that your author has been at the forefront of bringing rugby to the North American audience for a dozen years and has, by necessity, become a self-educated expert in everything related to the game.

# *Where to Go from Here*

So now you're ready to start your incredible journey into the world's most amazing game. Where you go from here depends on your experience and the type of information you're looking for. If you've got no clue at all, start at the beginning and enjoy the ride. If you have a question about a particular phase of play, head directly to that chapter and get the answers you need.

Regardless of where you begin, we're confident that by the time you reach the end of your trip through these pages, you'll see the light and share our love for the game they play in heaven. Welcome to the rugby family!

# Part I
# Rugby: Roots, Boots, and All

The 5th Wave                    By Rich Tennant

# In this part . . .

To make you feel comfortable about everything rugby, this part provides an introduction to the game and lays out the basic parameters of the sport.

To start, we tell you why rugby is so awesome and one of the most widely played sports around the world. We explain what's required to win, describe how the scoring system works, show the field on which the game is played, and spell out what goes on during a match. Finally, we tell you what gear you'll need to have when you show up for that first training session.

# Chapter 1

# Rugby's Beginnings, Allure, and a Basic Overview

*In This Chapter*

▶ Exploring rugby's illustrious past

▶ Understanding how the game is played

▶ Boning up on rugby's laws

▶ Going around with world with rugby

▶ Calling the shots with coaches and referees

▶ Staying in touch with the rugby world

*W*hy do millions of fans around the globe watch 30 players chase an oval ball on a field of grass as if the world would end if they missed one pass, kick, or tackle? Because they're hooked on rugby, a game of passion that's full of action, excitement, beauty, unpredictable moments and dramatic resolutions on the field, and unique camaraderie off it. When played by the best exponents of the game, rugby union satisfies the soul like nothing else.

## Rugby's Roots — The Birth of the Game

The game gets its name from Rugby, a town in England's Midlands, where it was first played at Rugby School. The legend goes that in 1823, a schoolboy by the name of William Webb Ellis first picked up the ball in the middle of a soccer game and ran with it, thereby breaking the old rules and setting the stage for an entirely new game (see the following section for the creation of this myth).

What is true is that the game was popularized and the rules codified at Rugby School. Its alumni spread it throughout Britain to other schools and universities like Oxford and Cambridge, and eventually to the far reaches of the British Empire.

### *The mythical pick-up of William Webb Ellis*

William Webb Ellis was indeed a student at Rugby School in 1823, but that's about as much historical fact as can be determined about him regarding his invention of the game of rugby. In reality, years after his death in 1872 the myth was created for a specific purpose — so the upper classes in England could justify their control of the game. Around the time the story was concocted, rugby was in the throes of a great battle between amateurism and professionalism that would eventually split the sport into two different codes.

## Reasons why rugby is so awesome

We've been collectively around the game from club to international level for almost forty years, and have observed the following truths about the game. Here are the reasons we think rugby is the best sport in the world:

✔ **Anyone can play rugby.** The game does not discriminate — rich or poor, male or female, young or old, every person can enjoy this fantastic game.

✔ **There's a position for everyone.** Whether you are 7 feet tall or 5 feet tall, 100 pounds or 300 pounds, fleet as a cheetah or slow as an ox, an appropriate position exists for every body type.

✔ **Rugby players share a global bond.** The game is played in more than 100 countries, but its devotees nevertheless belong to a select group. No rugby player is ever without a friend as long as another rugby player is nearby.

✔ **Everyone participates fully.** Although there are 15 different positions, each player has to possess a skill set that includes running with the ball, passing, tackling, rucking, mauling, and kicking.

✔ **Rugby has a unique ethos on the field.** Rugby is a hard, aggressive game that attracts fierce competitors. Regardless of the intensity, however, gentlemanly conduct is expected of all participants and you won't find the sort of trash-talking that pollutes most other professional sports in North America.

✔ **Rugby has a unique ethos off the field.** The same players who do their best to legally smash each other for 80 minutes during a match will always shake hands and share a beverage and a chat afterward. Whether at a club game or the highest international level, socializing with the opposition is mandatory.

✔ **Rugby tests athleticism and courage.** Fast running, towering kicking, and fearless tackling are all elements of the game that challenge players to reach their athletic potential in the face of danger.

✔ **Rugby is easy to follow.** Although it looks chaotic at first, rugby is easy to understand and appreciate when you become familiar with a few simple principles of play.

✔ **Rugby people are cool.** Rugby brings together a gregarious, intelligent, diverse group of characters who are fun to be around.

✔ **Rugby has a proud history.** While it is new to many North Americans, rugby has a long and storied tradition of competitive excellence, fair play, and sporting spirit that transcends the game itself.

Ellis' posthumous anointment as father of the game was a significant event in that battle and his name lives on today as the embodiment of the sport's crowning achievement, the William Webb Ellis Cup, which is awarded to the winner of the quadrennial World Cup (see Chapter 13 for more about the World Cup).

## A century of amateurism

From its beginnings at English public schools, rugby was definitely an elitist pursuit that actively discouraged and prohibited the payment of players. In 1895, after the Rugby Football Union (RFU) refused to allow clubs to compensate players for missing work to play the game, 22 clubs broke away from the union to form the Northern Football Union. This forerunner of professional rugby league eventually adopted its own set of rules and began paying players — something rugby union wouldn't do for another century.

Up until the 1990s, rugby union was a strictly amateur sport. While there were obviously numerous cases of cushy jobs, special treatment, and under-the-table payments, rugby administrators in both hemispheres diligently ferreted out cases of direct pay for play and banned those who were caught. Making the jump to rugby league meant no further involvement in union at any level.

That this prohibition against remuneration outlasted even the Olympic movement's similar rule is a testament to the amount of control the game's conservative governors exerted over a worldwide sport. By 1995, the pressures of money and television had become too great and, under threat of losing the best players to league or upstart union competitions, the powers that be capitulated and the sport entered a new era of professionalism.

# How the Game Is Played

At first glance rugby can look very complicated. Its field is covered in a myriad of lines and populated by 30 players running around and performing seemingly disjointed actions while wearing a variety of accouterments. Don't fear, though — a little bit of explanation will clear up exactly where they are, what they're doing, and what they're wearing.

## The field

Rugby is played on a grass field measuring 100 meters long by no more than 70 meters wide (109.4 yards long by 76.5 yards wide). At each end of the field there are goalposts on the goal line and an in-goal area that varies by venue but is usually between 10 and 22 meters long (10.9 yards to 24.1 yards). (All measurements in this book and in rugby are given in meters.)

Lots of lines are marked on a rugby field. The most important ones are the following:

- ✔ **Goal lines:** Players have to reach these lines in order to score.

- ✔ **22-meter lines:** These lines are vital, because they influence where play restarts after the ball is kicked out from behind them.

- ✔ **Halfway line:** This is where play starts after every score.

We talk more about the field — and all its other lines — in Chapter 2.

## The scoring

The aim of rugby is to score more points than the opposition. This is done in four different ways:

- ✔ The most valuable play is to score a *try,* which means touching the ball down in the opponent's in-goal or on their goal line. Doing so is worth five points and earns that team the right to attempt a conversion kick.

- ✔ A conversion kick is worth an additional two points. The conversion kick is taken from a spot in line with where the ball was originally grounded, so it's better to score as close to the posts as possible.

- ✔ Penalties for various infractions can be used to take a kick at goal, which is worth three points.

- ✔ A *dropped goal,* which occurs when the player drops the ball on the ground and then kicks it just as it bounces, is worth three points if it goes through the uprights.

We cover scoring in greater detail in Chapter 2.

## The gear

In the old days rugby players wore boots, socks, jerseys, and maybe a bit of tape. The laws have changed over the years to allow much more safety gear. In the modern era it's not uncommon for players to wear padded headgear, compression shorts, light padding under their jerseys to protect shoulders and ribs, and, of course, mouth guards. Chapter 3 lets you know what's legal to wear and what's not.

# Understanding the Essentials of the Game

Like most sports that didn't originate in North America, at first glance rugby can be difficult to comprehend because of the large number of players involved, the seemingly random calls of the referee, and the wide variety of strategies employed by different teams to score points and get wins. To help you begin your journey toward a complete understanding of the game, in the following sections we outline who all the players are, explain what the referee is generally looking for during the match, and spell out the basic skills required to be successful on the pitch.

## Puzzling out the positions

A rugby team has 15 positions. Each one wears a specific number and has individual responsibilities:

- 1 and 3 are the props
- 2 is the hooker
- 4 and 5 are the locks
- 6 and 7 are the flankers
- 8 is, conveniently enough, the eightman

This group is collectively referred to as the pack or the forwards.

A rugby team has another group as well — the backs or back line.

- 9 is the scrumhalf
- 10 is the flyhalf
- 11 and 14 are the wings
- 12 and 13 are the inside and outside centers
- 15 is the fullback

To get a feel for what each player is charged with doing on the rugby pitch, see Chapter 4.

## Grasping the laws of the game

Rugby is governed by laws, not rules. The laws of the game are designed to produce an entertaining and free-flowing contest for possession in an attempt to score the most points. Twenty-two laws cover all aspects of the field, the players, and the match officials. The referee, helped by two touch judges, is the sole judge of fact and law during a match.

The laws are constantly evolving and are the same all over the world wherever the game is played. Chapter 5 details where the laws come from and also shows pictures of all the different referee signals to help you figure out what's going on the very first time you watch a match.

In general the laws governing play are straightforward about what's allowed, but three crucial parts can be somewhat confusing: the tackle situation, advantage, and offsides:

✔ In a nutshell, when a tackle is made in rugby the requirements are that the tackler releases the tacklee and that the tacklee releases the ball so that players who are on their feet can use it.

✔ Advantage simply means that when one team makes an error the other team can try to capitalize on it, instead of the referee immediately stopping the action. If they can't, play restarts where the original mistake took place.

✔ Specific offsides laws exist for different phases of play, but essentially you can't be involved if you are in front of a teammate who last played the ball or are behind the ball when the opposition has it.

Chapter 6 explicates all the intricacies of the game and will have you understanding like an expert in no time.

## Scoping out skills, tactics, and training

The four basic skills necessary for any rugby player to excel at the game are running, passing, kicking, and tackling. In Chapter 10 we explain how to execute each skill including doing the goose step with ball in hand, throwing the cut-out pass, making a grubber kick, and pulling off a ball-and-all tackle. (And while these names may seem slightly humorous to you now, when they're explained within the context of play they'll make perfect sense.)

Plenty of rugby teams are filled with great athletes who never get to hoist trophies in triumph, either because they don't have the right game plan or they aren't employing the correct tactics in accordance with their abilities. Rugby coaches have lots of options open to them as far as strategy is concerned, but the most important thing for them to do if they want to win is to select an overall structure that fits their players' strengths. Either that or go out and get players who can play the type of game the coach envisions! Chapter 11 looks at the various ways to attack and defend in order to create a winning team.

Rugby has always been a physical game, but since the advent of the professional era the strength and speed of the participants have grown by leaps and bounds. That growth has been achieved not just through more time in the weight room and on the track but also by adhering to better diets and mental preparation regimes. Chapter 12 features all the necessary elements to get ready to play the game including warming up, stretching, developing a rugby fitness program, and managing intake of food and fluids.

# Rugby's a Worldwide Game

Rugby is played all over the planet by everyone from little kids to millionaire athletes. What binds them together in one collective embrace is passion for the game. More than any other sport, rugby is about tradition, lifestyle, and a gentlemanly ethos. Whether you're interested in watching the professional game abroad or playing for your local third-division club, rugby offers an entertaining spectacle or years of athletic enjoyment that can't be matched.

## An international affair

The Rugby World Cup is a relatively new tournament, having made its debut in 1987. Just 20 years later, it's by far the most important event in the minds of fans — and of national unions, who go all out to win it every four years. So far only New Zealand, Australia (twice), South Africa, and England have managed to lift the William Webb Ellis trophy. Chapter 13 delves deeply into the origins and history of the World Cup (including sections on the U.S.'s and Canada's participation), plus gives loads of info on all the other International Rugby Board (IRB) World Cup competitions from Women's to Sevens.

The World Cup may be a newcomer on the global sporting scene but rugby's international tradition goes back to 1871, when England and Scotland squared off in the first test match. The international calendar is chock-full of exciting action from both hemispheres with the Six Nations Championship and Tri Nations Series supplemented by annual tours of the top countries to each other's home turf. The interprovincial and provincial scenes are every bit as entertaining, with the Super 14, Heineken Cup, Magners League, Guinness Premiership, Top 14, Air New Zealand Cup, and Currie Cup providing nearly year-round action. Chapter 14 gives an overview of all these international, interprovincial, and provincial tournaments.

## North America gets into the action

North Americans are relative newcomers to the sport of rugby, but both Canada and the United States are passionate about the game. In Chapter 15 we provide the lowdown on their respective histories and detail how the national governing bodies are organized on both sides of the border.

Before you can earn your international call-up, you need to play some club rugby. In Chapter 16, we survey the amateur club game across North America. Over the past ten years, the most encouraging development in North America has been the rapid growth of the sport at the youth, high school, and collegiate levels, a trend we examine in Chapter 17.

# Coaching and Refereeing

Other than the players themselves, the two next-most-important jobs in rugby are the referee and the coach. Neither is an easy assignment, nor one to be taken lightly. In our experience, coaching can be one of the most satisfying (and sometimes frustrating) things you can do.

There's nothing that compares to the feeling of watching your charges artfully deploy your brilliant game plan with devastating effect, complete with the knowledge that you were the one who devised and implemented the whole plan of attack! When that happens, the unavoidable pains of being a coach seem a distant memory — at least until the next training session.

Chapter 18 talks about the what it takes to be a good coach and outlines the various other support roles available to those who want to be involved in the sport. Chapter 19 details the different procedures to become a coach in the U.S. and Canada, as well as provides some background about what's entailed in doing so at various levels of the game.

The most important person at any rugby match is the referee — without his presence the game would evolve into a giant wrestling match and tempers would certainly flare out of control. Although the referee is always respected by the players on the field — and if not, he's got the power to effect change — the job is still a tough one. The laws of the game don't protect him from criticism by spectators — or, at higher levels, from media scrutiny. In other words, refereeing isn't for everyone but it is for a select knowledgeable and confident few who dearly love the game as much as if not more than the players they adjudicate. Chapter 20 provides the pathway to taking up the whistle in Canada and the United States.

# Keeping Informed about the Game

Rugby used to be a purely local affair, but in today's globally interconnected, media-driven world it's possible to watch the sport wherever you are, whether you live in a rugby-mad country or not. Chapter 21 takes all the guesswork out of the process for you with a handy guide to watching rugby on TV. Chapter 22 delves into the Internet and provides a plethora of Web sites to keep you up-to-date on your favorite country, competition, team, or player. Plus we list our favorite books and magazines that will give you the real flavor of the sport. We also give you advice about how to actually go see a rugby match in person, where you'll be able to soak up the positive atmosphere that makes rugby such a unique endeavor.

# Chapter 2

# The Basics

. . . . . . . . . . . . . . . . . . . . . . . . . . . . . . . . . . . . . . . . . . . . . . . . . . . .

*In This Chapter*

▶ Finding your way around the rugby pitch

▶ Keeping score

▶ Keeping time on the field

▶ Meeting the team

. . . . . . . . . . . . . . . . . . . . . . . . . . . . . . . . . . . . . . . . . . . . . . . . . . . .

*L*ike most things in life, you need to understand the basics before you can really appreciate rugby. Whether you're a complete newcomer, have had some exposure to the sport, or are a full-fledged expert, the material we cover in this chapter will help you get that much more familiar with the ins and outs of the game.

In this chapter we describe the playing field, outline how points are scored, explain timekeeping, and describe the positions of the players.

# Figuring Out the Field

Rugby is primarily played on a grass field, although sand, clay, dirt, and artificial surfaces are permitted provided they're not dangerous. A permanently hard surface, such as asphalt or cement, is prohibited. The place where rugby is played is variously referred to as the field of play, the playing field, the ground, and the pitch, but they all refer to the same place, which is shown in Figure 2-1.

## Dimensions of the playing area

Rugby players do battle on the playing area. The playing area comprises the field of play and two in-goal areas.

- **The field of play:** The area where the bulk of the action takes place is referred to as the *field of play*. It measures no more than 100 meters long by no more than 70 meters wide (109.4 yards long by 76.5 yards wide). The field of play does not include the touchlines or the in-goal areas at either end of the ground (see Figure 2-1).

- **The in-goal areas:** At each end of the playing area are the *in-goal areas*, which must be between 10 and 22 meters long and 70 meters wide (10.9 yards to 24.1 yards long and 76.5 yards wide). The in-goal areas include the goal lines, but not the touch-in-goal or dead-ball lines.

- **The playing area:** This includes both the *field of play* and the two *in-goal* areas. The touchlines, touch-in-goal lines, and dead-ball lines are not part of the playing area.

## What do all those lines mean?

Like most newcomers, when we began playing rugby the field markings were an indecipherable mystery of seemingly random chalk marks. The rugby pitch has numerous lines marked on it — confusing at first, but after you know what all the lines mean and comprehend their strategic importance your overall understanding of the game will be significantly enhanced. Keep reading and you'll understand in five minutes what it took us five years to figure out! Here's a rundown of the lines and what they signify:

- **Halfway line:** The *halfway line* is a solid line that marks the center of the field, and is where the game starts. Play is also restarted at the halfway line after successful tries, drop goals, or penalty goals. One of the objectives in rugby is to spend as much time as possible in the opponent's half of the field (see Figure 2-1).

- **10-meter line:** Two broken *10-meter lines* are placed 10 meters on either side of the halfway line. When a team kicks off, the ball must reach this line for the kick to be legal.

---

## Basic rugby terminology

Before launching into the specifics of the pitch, a couple of key rugby terms require definition. A *scrum* is used to restart play after certain minor infractions. The scrum is a contest for the ball involving eight players who bind together and push against the other team's assembled eight for possession of the ball. A *line-out* is used to restart play after the ball, or a player carrying it, has gone out of bounds. The line-out looks somewhat like a jump ball in basketball, with both teams lining up opposite each other, with one team throwing the ball down the middle of the tunnel.

✔ **22-meter line:** Two solid *22-meter lines* are located 22 meters out from each goal line. Drop-outs, a specific kind of restart (discussed in more detail in Chapter 7), are taken from behind the 22-meter line. The 22-meter line is also crucial in positional play (see Chapter 9 to learn how the 22-meter line affects the kicking game).

✔ **Goal line:** The *goal line,* also called the *tryline,* is a solid line that delineates the beginning of the in-goal areas. There are two goal lines, one at either end of the field of play, which players must reach to successfully score a try.

✔ **Dead-ball line:** The line beyond the in-goal area at each end of the pitch is the *dead-ball line.* When the ball touches or goes over this line the ball is considered "dead," or out of play.

✔ **Touchline:** The two solid lines that run from goal line to goal line are the *touchlines* — just like the sidelines in football, but called touchlines because when the ball contacts the line or the ground beyond them it's considered to be *in touch,* which means out of bounds (see Chapter 9 for more on the touchlines).

✔ **Touch-in-goal line:** The *touch-in-goal line* is the continuation of the touchline between the goal line and the dead-ball line.

Grasping the meaning of the principal lines described above allows newcomers to follow the flow of play. However, some other broken lines and dash lines in Figure 2-1 remain unaccounted for.

✔ **5-meter line:** The *5-meter line* is a broken line that runs from one tryline to the other, parallel to the touchlines. It marks the front of the line-out and the minimum distance a line-out throw must travel (see Chapter 9 for more line-out particulars).

✔ **Dash lines:** Dash lines are 1 meter in length and provide reference points for both referees and players. There are three different types of dash lines:

• **15-meter dash line:** Seven dash lines are located 15 meters in and parallel to both touchlines. The dash lines intersect the goal lines, the 22-meter lines, the 10-meter lines, and the halfway line. They define the back of the line-out, and also where scrums and penalties are taken after line-out infringements (see Chapter 8 for more on scrums and Chapter 9 for more on line-outs).

• **5-meter dash line:** Six 5-meter dash lines are positioned 5 meters in front of and parallel to each tryline. They are placed in from each touchline at 5 and 15 meters, and one in front of each goalpost. The dashes mark the minimum distance from the defending team's tryline, where a scrum or line-out can be set or a penalty can be taken.

• **Halfway dash line:** This is a half-meter-long dash that intersects the halfway line at midfield. It's the spot where kickoffs and restarts are supposed to originate — even though most kickers will cheat a meter or two sideways in either direction.

Dead-ball line

Tryline

5-meter line

22-meter line

Touchline/
sideline

5-meter
line

5-meter
line

10-meter line

The halfway line

Not more
than 100
meters
(109.4
yards)

10-meter line

15-meter
dash line

15-meter
dash line

22-meter line

Goalposts and
crossbar

Post
with
flag

5-meter line

Tryline

In-goal area not more than
22 meters (24.1 yards) or less
than 10 meters (10.9 yards)

Dead-ball line

Not more than 70 meters
(76.5 yards)

**Figure 2-1:**
The rugby
playing
enclosure.

## Recognizing the goalposts and flags

Old-time football fans will immediately recognize the H-shaped structures at
either end of the pitch — the goalposts situated at each end of the field of
play, directly on the tryline. The uprights must be 5.6 meters (6.12 yards)
apart with a *crossbar* (the horizontal beam between the goalposts) measuring
3 meters (3.28 yards) above the ground. The minimum height of the goalposts is 3.4 meters (3.71 yards) above the crossbar. As a safety precaution,
the goalposts have to be covered with padding to prevent injury if players
crash into them. The pads also provide great advertising opportunities for
sponsors!

There are 14 flags on the rugby pitch. Four of the flags mark the intersections of the dead-ball and touch-in-goal lines. These flags rarely come into play, as they mark the extreme corners of the field.

Another four flags mark the three-way intersection of the goal lines, touchlines, and touch-in-goal lines. These flags are not part of the in-goal areas, so players who make contact with any of them during play are out of bounds. Use of these flags is under review by the International Rugby Board (IRB), and they may be eliminated entirely in 2008. Although it may seem self-evident, the game of rugby is meant to be played within the boundaries with limited exceptions (see Chapter 9 for the times when you're allowed to play from out-of-bounds areas).

The remaining six flags are also outside the playing area, positioned 2 meters beyond the touchline, at the 22-meter and halfway lines.

# Understanding the Scoring System

Football developed from rugby, so if you understand touchdowns, extra points, and field goals, getting a handle on rugby's scoring system is a breeze. How points are accumulated in rugby has evolved over the last hundred years, with the addition of awarding points for tries and conversions. Long ago, scoring a try didn't result in points — it just earned the right to attempt a kick at goal. The modern system encourages teams to score tries over simply kicking penalties.

There are five ways to tally points in rugby. The ease or difficulty of achieving each of them plays a crucial role in strategic decision making by players and coaches. When you understand what the five ways are, your enjoyment of the game really takes off as you come to appreciate what the players are doing at crucial moments on the field.

## Scoring a try

Scoring a try is the quickest way to amass the most points in rugby. A try is the *pièce de résistance* of rugby, similar to scoring a touchdown in football. In fact, rugby is where the term "touchdown" came from, because the ball must actually be touched down for a try to be awarded. A try is scored when the ball is grounded by an offensive player in the in-goal area, on the tryline itself, or on rare occasions against the goalpost padding.

To signal a try, the referee raises an arm and blows the whistle at the spot where the ball came into contact with the turf (see Chapter 5 for a complete list of all the referee signals). The exact place is important because it determines where the conversion kick can be taken from (see "Converting a try" later in this chapter).

A try is worth five points, which is the highest number of points a rugby team can score at one time.

## Awarding a penalty try

The awarding of a penalty try is one of the most contentious and misunderstood aspects of rugby, usually because of when and why it occurs. A *penalty try* must be awarded if the referee believes the defending team committed a penalty that prevented the attacking team from scoring a try that would probably otherwise have been scored. This gives the referee plenty of latitude to negate cynical or desperate acts of cheating by awarding points to override what happened on the field. This unique license to rectify the impact of unsportsmanlike conduct is in keeping with the gentlemanly ethos of the game.

When a penalty try is awarded, the referee runs beneath the crossbar in the center of the goalposts, raises an arm, and blows the whistle.

Just like a normal try, the attacking team receives five points, but also gets to attempt the conversion as if the try had been scored in the most advantageous position under the posts.

## Converting a try

After a try or penalty try is awarded, the attacking team has the chance to add a further two points to the scoreboard by kicking a *conversion*. The referee marks the place where the try was scored and then the *goal kicker* can tee up the ball anywhere along a line parallel to the touchline, out from where the ball was grounded. In other words, if the try was scored 5 meters (5.46 yards) from the sideline, then the conversion must be taken 5 meters (5.46 yards) from the sideline. (Figure 2-1 shows the sideline.)

Usually the goal kicker takes the ball back as far as he needs to get a better angle in order to improve his chances of making the kick.

Another reason for taking the kick from farther away is that on a conversion, the opposition may charge the kicker and block his attempt. The defending team must stand on or behind the goal line until the kicker begins to approach the ball — then they're allowed to rush the kicker.

The goal kicker places the ball on either a specially constructed kicking tee or on a mound of hand-sculpted sand. A *kicking tee* is a small plastic device that's placed on the ground and holds the rugby ball upright. Making a sand castle is the old-fashioned way but, unfortunately for silica aficionados, it's rarely seen anymore. Andre Pretorius, who plays in South Africa for the Lions and the Springboks, is the last big-name kicker to use sand.

Goal kickers have their own unique routines for kicking goals, including how many steps they take, where they aim, and how they position the rest of their body (see Figure 2-2). This used to be a long and drawn-out process that interrupted the flow of the game and wasted time. To speed up play, after the 1999 Rugby World Cup the IRB imposed a one-minute time limit for conversions and penalties, which begins when the kicker receives the tee from the sidelines. Gone are the days when a game consisted of a never-ending series of interminable stoppages for penalties and conversions, punctuated by short bursts of actual rugby.

If the conversion kick flies through the uprights, the touch judges raise their flags and the referee blows the whistle. (See Chapter 5 for more on touch judges, the match officials who use signal flags to assist the referee.)

Conversion kicks are worth two points. Thus, a "converted" try is worth seven points in total: five for the try plus two for the conversion. If the goal kicker misses, the team gets only the five points for the try.

**Figure 2-2:** Preparing to take a penalty kick.

## Kicking penalty goals

If the referee determines that a team has broken one of the laws of the game, a penalty can be awarded to the other side. The non-offending team can choose among several options of how best to utilize the resulting possession. One of those choices is to kick a penalty goal.

The referee signals a penalty by blowing the whistle and raising an arm in the direction of the team to whom the penalty has been awarded (there's a diagram of all the penalty signals in Chapter 5). Next, that team's captain has to make a decision. If the captain chooses to kick at goal, the kicker places the ball on the spot where the penalty occurred, or anywhere on a direct line behind it, just like a conversion. Unlike a conversion, however, the defending team is not allowed to rush the kicker at any time while a penalty kick is being attempted.

A successful penalty goal is worth three points.

## Drop-kicking goals

A *dropped goal* (also called a *drop goal, drop kick,* or *droppie*) is different than a conversion or penalty kick because it takes place while the ball is in play. A drop goal involves a player dropping the ball and trying to kick it between the poles just after it hits the ground, as shown in Figure 2-3. (We discuss the finer points of the drop kick in Chapter 10.)

---

### The importance of a specialist goal kicker

In the modern era, having an outstanding goal kicker on your team is of paramount importance. Goal kickers are immensely valuable because their skills are so often called upon during the match when one player or another has committed any one of the indiscretions that result in a penalty. If you have a reliable goal kicker, your team can be outscored in the try department but still win the match because you've kicked enough penalties.

In the 2003 World Cup the boot of England fly-half Jonny Wilkinson was instrumental in his country's triumph. In the knockout stage of the competition England was outscored in tries by 5 to 2 but were able to come away with the trophy because Wilkinson accounted for 62 of England's 72 points, kicking 16 penalties, 4 drop goals, and 1 conversion.

Since their World Cup triumph England has slumped to as low as sixth in the world rankings. This is at least partially attributable to Jonny Wilkinson being unable to play for long stretches because of numerous injuries, robbing England of their greatest scoring threat.

**Figure 2-3:**
Scoring a drop goal with a drop kick requires a lot of skill and excellent timing.

Slotting a drop goal is a clever maneuver that most teams don't utilize. Drop kicks are rare because they require perfect timing and lots of practice to properly execute.

If the ball passes between the goalposts and above the crossbar, the team earns three points.

# Timekeeping on the Field

Play is divided into two halves. Each half is 40 minutes, with a 10-minute half-time in between. The referee has the power to extend play to make up for time lost because of injuries or delays. This is called *injury time* and is entirely up to the referee's discretion. Unlike most other clock-governed sports, the referee is the official timekeeper. When the referee determines that all time has expired he blows the whistle to signal the end of the match, which is called *fulltime*.

## When the clock runs and when it stops

The 40 minutes in each half is running time, not elapsed time. In rugby the clock counts up rather than down, beginning at the kickoff. Running time stops for injured players to be quickly treated or removed from the pitch, occasionally for water when it's really hot, for players' clothing to be replaced, and for times when the referee wants to speak with the respective captains, the individual players, the touch judges, or the television match official (TMO).

## When someone's injured

Stopping the clock for injury or continuing to play is another decision made by the referee. If a player can be quickly treated, most refs will allow a slight delay in the game. Special dispensation and a little extra recovery time is afforded front-row players if a scrum or line-out is required to restart play (see Chapters 8 and 9 for more on scrums and line-outs). The referee also has the option of letting the match continue while a player receives treatment, if the player isn't in the way. For serious injuries, time stops until medical personnel can remove the player from the pitch.

## When the TMO is looking at play

The TMO is the equivalent of instant replay in football. In selected leagues and international competitions, if the match is produced for television the referee has the option of checking with a fellow official who can review various angles the referee didn't see (see Chapter 5 for the TMO's scope and responsibilities). When the referee and the TMO are communicating, running time is off.

## When the hooter sounds

The *hooter* — or *horn* or *siren* — is a relatively new addition to most professional rugby stadiums. By keeping track of when the referee's time is running and when it isn't, the stadium timekeeper sounds the hooter when 40 minutes of running time has expired in each half. The hooter does not mean the end of the match, and play can continue after it sounds. It's more like a signal to players and fans that time is almost up. In many cases, the next time the ball goes dead, the referee will blow the whistle to signal fulltime (the end of the match).

# Introducing the Players

Rugby is one of the few sports that caters to all sorts of body shapes and sizes. A photograph of a rugby team often looks as if one specimen of every human body type has been assembled at the same spot, at the same time, to provide an illustration for an anthropological study.

A quick scan of any team out at training is proof that everyone can play the game. Within every team, the tall, the small, the fat, the skinny, and everyone in between can find a position that suits them.

## Taking up position

Each *squad* or *side* — the group of players who make up a rugby team — comprises 22 players. This includes the 15 who start the match plus the 7 reserves. The starting 15 take the pitch at the beginning of the match and the 7 reserves sit on the sideline in case of injury or tactical changes.

While most of the positions involve specialized skills, that doesn't mean players are stuck in the same position for the rest of their rugby lives. Players often move around throughout their careers, especially if their body shapes change with age. In this section, we give you a brief overview of the positions on a rugby team. We discuss the positions in more detail in Chapter 4.

The 15 players who start the game are divided into 8 forwards (also referred to as the *pack*), and 7 backs (commonly called the *back line*). The forwards are primarily responsible for winning the ball and the backs are charged with doing something positive when they get it. An old oval adage says the forwards decide who wins a match and the backs decide by how much.

Regardless of position, however, every rugby player must possess a basic set of skills. Each player must be able to tackle opposition ball-carriers, catch the ball, run with it, and competently pass it.

## Positions by the numbers

The 15 starters on a rugby side all wear specific numbers on their jerseys to designate their position. Even among English speakers, some of the names of the individual positions vary depending on where you are in the world (we cover these name variations in detail in Chapter 4), but the following terms are the most generally recognized:

- **Loose-head prop (jersey number 1):** A big, strong player who is responsible for scrumming in the front row and lifting the jumpers in the line-out.

- **Hooker (jersey number 2):** This front-rower actually hooks the ball with his foot at scrumtime, hence the name; plus, he or she usually does the throwing at line-outs.

- **Tight-head prop (jersey number 3):** The rock upon which the scrum is built, he has to be the strongest and most technically proficient player in the pack.

- **Locks (jersey numbers 4 and 5):** Locks form the second row in the scrum and are normally used as line-out jumpers and restart takers because of their superior height and reliable hands. Some teams number their locks according to left or right, others by seniority, or simply preference of the players for a specific number.

- **Blindside flanker (jersey number 6):** This player must be powerful and make an impact in contact on offense and defense. He must have excellent ball-handling skills.

- **Openside flanker (jersey number 7):** This is usually the most dynamic and best defensive player on the team, responsible for making critical tackles, creating turnovers, and ranging all over the pitch.

- **Number 8 (jersey number 8):** The number 8 (or eightman) plays a crucial role on the team. This player directs and controls the scrum from the rear and is often a pivotal link between the forwards and the backs.

- **Scrumhalf (jersey number 9):** Also known as the halfback, this player must be compact and quick, with excellent passing skills and the ability to operate in tight quarters.

- **Flyhalf (jersey number 10):** This is the player who runs the show on offense either by running, passing, or kicking the ball.

- **Wings (jersey numbers 11 and 14):** Two of the fastest players on the pitch, the wings must be able to kick and play good positional defense. Which side the two wings play on is usually decided by kicking ability and side-stepping preference.

- **Inside center (jersey number 12):** This is a physical player with quickness and power running the ball, and no fear when tackling.

- **Outside center (jersey number 13):** The outside center is a creative runner and ball-handler with very good speed and solid defensive skills.

- **Fullback (jersey number 15):** This is the back-line general. This player must possess excellent tactical knowledge, have a strong leg for kicking, be an attack-oriented runner, and be the last line of defense.

## The reserves

Players who don't start the match but come on as replacements or substitutes are called *reserves*. The reserves sit near the field of play ready to go on at any time. Coaches can replace players who are injured, make tactical changes to combat a threat posed by the opposition, or simply remove a player who is tiring or having a poor game. Each reserve has the same basic designated role as the players they replace. Wearing the jersey numbers 16 to 22, they are as follows:

- **Reserve hooker (jersey number 16):** The hooker replacement has to be able to come off the bench and hit the line-out jumpers with minimal warm-up.

- **Reserve prop (jersey number 17):** This player needs to be able to cover for both the tight-head and loose-head props.

- **Reserve forward (jersey number 18):** This player can be used to cover either lock position.

- **Reserve forward (jersey number 19):** This player can provide backup for all three back-row forward positions (the flankers or the number 8).

- **Reserve scrumhalf (jersey number 20):** This reserve is a specialized scrumhalf replacement.

- **Reserve back (jersey number 21):** This player can usually replace either the inside or outside center.

- **Reserve back (jersey number 22):** The second reserve back is used to provide backup for the wings or the fullback.

Of the seven backup players who sit on the *reserve bench* (the name given to the place the replacement players sit), three are specialist positions: the hooker, the prop, and the scrumhalf. For a scrum, an injured prop or hooker must be replaced by another suitably trained prop or hooker, not by just any player filling in, because of the particular technique, strength, and experience required to safely compete in the front row.

Officials are deeply concerned about the risk of serious injury to front-rowers if a scrum is incorrectly set, or injury to someone who doesn't have the ability to withstand the pressure coming through from the opposition. Safety on all levels has improved in recent years, with a greater emphasis on injury prevention (player safety is discussed further in Chapter 18).

Clever use of the reserve bench can often mean the difference between winning and losing a match, particularly if it's going right down to the wire. With the faster and fitter game of rugby being played these days, the reserve bench has become a vital part of every coach's arsenal.

Bringing on players from the reserve bench for tactical reasons is now a well established practice in the professional game. It has changed the way coaches select their 22-person squad and their strategy throughout. Fresh players are brought on as impact players, usually in the second half, to try to take advantage of a tiring opposition. This doesn't mean a team gets an unfair advantage — the opposition also has the chance to use fresh legs whenever required.

Being a reserve is a tough assignment in rugby, especially if the conditions are foul. Sitting on the sidelines while your teammates do battle is never easy and is even more difficult when you have to be ready to join the fray at any moment.

Each player on the reserve bench is there for a specific reason. Whenever you're in the reserves you have to stay focused on how the game is unfolding. It's important to watch the players you're likely to replace and see what's working and what's not against the opposition. The key is to be mentally switched-on and ready to get stuck-in right away should the need arise.

# Chapter 3

# Grab Your Rugby Gear

. . . . . . . . . . . . . . . . . . . . . . . . . . . . . . . . . . . . . . . . . . . . .

## In This Chapter

▶ Putting your kit bag together

▶ Looking like a rugby player

▶ Protecting yourself from injury

. . . . . . . . . . . . . . . . . . . . . . . . . . . . . . . . . . . . . . . . . . . . .

**R**ugby is often referred to as football without pads. Of course that's not true, but it does highlight one of the main advantages of rugby — that you don't need to break the bank buying all those expensive football pads, helmets, and uniforms to outfit your team or yourself for action. All you need is a jersey, some shorts, a mouth guard, a pair of cleats, and a ball, and you're on your way to playing the game.

In this chapter, we describe the necessary items to pack into your bag, as well as some extra stuff you may consider worthwhile — in rugby circles, your gear is collectively referred to as your kit, which you lug around in your kit bag. Next, we discuss the important issue of personal safety while playing rugby and the precautions you can take to protect yourself on the pitch.

## Getting It Together: The Essentials of the Kit Bag

A strong, yet lightweight, sports bag is essential to carry your rugby kit around in. The bag should be big enough to hold a rugby jersey, socks, shorts, boots, football, and towel, plus a change of clothing. Bag sizes vary, but look for one that's larger than a normal gym bag — you'll soon have it stuffed to capacity. Try to find a bag that has a separate pocket for your valuables and has a waterproof compartment, either on the outside or the inside, where you can stuff your muddy socks, shorts, and boots.

Before you rush out and purchase a kit bag, inquire whether your team has bags for sale. Many clubs periodically order personalized team bags, sometimes to commemorate tours or championship seasons — it's the ultimate in sophisticated rugby luggage!

## Having a ball

A rugby ball is oval, not round. It can be made of leather or a strong synthetic material and consists of four panels. Some balls are designed to be easier to grip when playing in muddy or wet conditions. The ball used in youth rugby is slightly smaller than the one for adults. Whatever your age, though, it's important you train with the same size ball you play with in a game.

A rugby ball is the first item any aspiring rugby player buys. Even though rugby clubs usually have an abundance of balls, it's still a smart idea to have one to practice with on your own. Coaches recommend you get a ball in your hands as often as possible so you can practice your kicking, passing, catching, and handling skills.

Finding a rugby ball in a sporting goods store in North America is more serendipity than certainty. Your best bet is to order a ball online from one of the many online rugby stores.

The dimensions of a rugby ball are as follows:

- **Length:** 280–300 millimeters (11–12 inches)
- **Circumference (end to end):** 760–790 millimeters (30–31 inches)
- **Circumference (width):** 580–620 millimeters (23–24 inches)
- **Weight:** 400–440 grams (14.5–15.5 ounces)
- **Air pressure:** 0.67–0.70 kilograms per square centimeter, or 9½–10 pounds per square inch

Maintaining the proper air pressure is important. Make sure your ball has enough give in it for you to push your fingers in slightly at one end. A softer ball is easier to catch, handle, and pass, and is therefore better suited for training purposes.

You'll find two categories of rugby balls:

- A *match ball* is usually a rock-hard, top-of-the-line rugby ball. Match balls are well balanced to pass, kick, and punt consistently. You'll pay $50 US or more for a match-quality ball. Don't bother buying a match ball to kick around the neighborhood.

✔ A *training ball* is virtually the same as a match ball but is less expensive and should be used for practicing. Although a training ball isn't as good as a match ball, it's perfectly fine for your needs and is much more affordable. The average training ball costs about $30 US.

## Kicking in with a kicking tee

Over the last few years, the introduction of kicking tees has made life a lot easier for goal kickers. This small plastic apparatus is placed on the ground and holds the ball upright, as shown in Figure 3-1. A kicking tee holds a rugby ball in the same way as a golf tee holds a golf ball when a golfer prepares to hit a drive. In rugby, it's used when a team attempts to kick a conversion or a penalty goal (the scoring system is explained in Chapter 2).

**Figure 3-1:**
Placing the ball at the correct angle on the kicking tee.

Kicking tees are quicker and less messy than the old method of kicking off a hand-sculpted mound of sand or dirt: Players used to have to wait for a ball boy to run onto the pitch with a sand bucket, wait for the goal kicker to build a sandcastle, wait for the goal kicker to be satisfied with his work, and wait for the kicker to place the ball on top of his castle, check the wind and gauge the distance one last time, and finally kick it.

It's not compulsory to use a kicking tee, because some players still prefer sand. Try both and see what's most comfortable for you.

Different goal kickers like to place the ball on the kicking tee at different angles, depending on their kicking style — the kicking tee caters to all the different variations.

Not every player on the team has to own a kicking tee, especially if you have no interest in goal kicking. However, if you want to kick for goal, a kicking tee is a must-have on your shopping list. You won't use your own tee in a game because clubs have plenty of them, but you'll need a kicking tee to practice with. Your club may even let you have one of their spares, particularly if you start kicking match-winning penalties or conversions.

Kicking tees are a one-time purchase, usually costing between $10 and $20, and can be found online and in selected sports shops.

## Miscellaneous kit items

If you're lucky, your club will sell team bags, hats, T-shirts, jackets, and warm-up outfits. There's nothing like showing up for a match with the whole squad decked out in matching outfits. Even if you get thumped by 100 points, you'll look good, improve team morale, and make a much-needed contribution to the club's treasury.

To heighten your experience, consider a few more handy items to toss into your kit bag for use on match day. To supplement the team's medical kit, bring some plastic bandages and antibiotic ointment to treat the minor cuts and scrapes that are inevitable if you've played hard enough. Bring a roll of white cloth athletic tape to keep your ears fully attached to your head and for other running repairs. Invest in a pair of good sunglasses, a wide-brimmed hat, and sandals to wear after the match, while you root your second-side teammates to victory from the sideline.

# Getting the Gear

The International Rugby Board (IRB) in Dublin, Ireland, sets the standards for rugby union regulations. The IRB allows for pads made of soft, thin material to be incorporated into an undergarment or jersey, provided the pads cover the shoulder and collarbone only. No part of the pads can be thicker than 1 centimeter when uncompressed, or have a density of more than 45 kilograms per cubic meter.

## Rugby jerseys

Rugby jerseys can be short- or long-sleeved, and they have traditionally featured a full collar. They're made of thick cotton, or synthetic fibers, which tend to breathe more than other materials. Because rugby involves tackling and binding onto one another it's important to wear a jersey that won't be easily destroyed by the constant aggression.

Game-day rugby jerseys are usually supplied by the club, but you'll need your own to wear at practice. You can purchase a proper rugby jersey for about $40 US, which should get you through your first season of play.

Your jersey needs to be sturdy enough to withstand the punishment, so don't make the mistake of buying a department store knockoff.

## Rugby shorts

Like the jersey, rugby shorts must be able to withstand punishment. Most rugby shorts have pockets, but you can find some varieties without them. Generally, you want a pair of shorts that are thick enough to last (and provide some protection to sensitive areas) and don't give your opponents too much to hold on to.

New players usually have to obtain their own shorts. The color and style are determined by the club you play for. There may even be two different colors, for games at home and away. Different brands fit differently — over the years we've found that Canterbury (New Zealand) and Barbarian (Canada) shorts are the most durable and comfortable available.

Make sure the shorts you buy are comfortable and not too tight or too loose. If anything, go bigger rather than smaller. We also recommend you buy shorts with a drawstring in the waistband to ensure they remain snugly in place around your waist. It's hard enough tackling an opponent without your efforts being impeded by a pair of shorts heading south. Moreover, if you're a line-out jumper (see Chapter 9 to see if you'll soon be launched to new heights), you'll be lifted by your shorts — so they better be fastened well or you'll get a serious wedgie.

Rugby shorts are usually priced between $20 and $35 US. They can be purchased online, in Canterbury clothing shops, or at specialty sporting goods stores.

## Booting up

Of all your rugby equipment, footwear is probably the most important. A perfectly good rugby game can be ruined by the discomfort caused by a pair of ill-fitting boots. If your feet aren't happy, brace yourself for an uncomfortable afternoon on the pitch.

Rugby boots (or cleats) are similar to soccer shoes or football cleats, but the studs need to be circular and otherwise meet IRB specifications. You can wear football cleats for rugby, but you'll need to remove the toe stud for them to be legal.

Forwards' boots are generally mid- to high-cut with different stud patterns designed for the rigors of scrumming and close-in work. Backs' boots are more often low-cut — built for speed and easy direction change. It doesn't really matter if you're a forward or a back — it's more important that you buy the boots that are most comfortable on your feet.

The first rule of *boot law* is to make certain that your boots fit snugly around your feet, side to side and heel to toe, to prevent blisters caused by friction. Boots should be comfortable and have the required traction on the pitch.

The best place to buy boots is online or, if you're one of the geographically fortunate few, at a rugby shop in your area. Also keep in mind that at most large rugby tournaments you'll find vendors offering their wares. Take the opportunity to try on a variety of makes and models to find the boots that are just right for your feet. When you've found the right fit, you'll have more confidence ordering online.

When you buy a new pair of boots, walk around in them for a while to get comfortable before practice — and never use a brand-new pair for a match! At your first training session with new boots, apply a little petroleum jelly inside the boot along the back of the heel and above your toes to prevent blisters.

Although rugby boots range widely in price, you'll find good reliable brands that start at $50 US. Although a lot of rugby gear is available at fairly low prices, please don't economize in the boot department — cheap can be very painful and take all the fun out of the game.

When heading off to the game, always remember to check your kit bag to ensure that your boots are included. If you forget your socks, jersey, or even your shorts there's usually someone on the team that can lend you his or hers — but if you leave your boots behind and wear a teammate's that don't fit you'll be cursing your forgetfulness with every step. When it comes to rugby players and boots, when you find a pair that fits right there's no limit to what you'll do to keep them in action.

## The boots that wouldn't die

My first real rugby boots were Patrick Parcs that I bought at the OMBAC tournament in 1988. They lasted for eight seasons, thanks to several rolls of duct tape. After about two years, the boots separated from the soles, so before each match I would carefully tape them together on my feet and then cut them off after the final whistle. I loved those boots because they were phenomenally comfortable and perfectly molded to my feet. I took a lot of grief from both teammates and opponents over my silver footwear, but I didn't care, because they were the ideal fit. Sadly, they met their end in Missoula, Montana, in 1995 after a particularly wet Maggotfest when I left them on a friend's porch to dry. (See Chapter 16 for a full description of the exploits at the Maggotfest.) His girlfriend, now wife, threw them away, not understanding how anyone could be so attached to such ragged and dilapidated footwear. It was a crushing blow and it took me seven more years to forgive her and to find another pair of boots that fit as well. Today, I play in a pair of Canterbury Mokos that I also love and will be wearing for many years to come.

## *Socking it to you*

Rugby socks are similar to soccer socks and are worn to the knee. Soccer socks from any sporting goods store will get you started until you can purchase your game socks from your club — just make sure they stretch up slightly above your knee, enabling you to roll the top over to just below the knee.

PLAYER TIP

Make certain each sock has an elasticized band near the top so it stays up during the match. Socks dangling around your ankles are not a recommended fashion statement. If your socks have a propensity to sink to half-mast, get a couple of short lengths of shoelace and tie a piece around each sock just below the knee and then fold the top of the sock over. Don't tie it too tightly or you'll impede the flow of blood to your legs, which could give you cramps or cause your lower legs to turn blue, wither, and eventually fall off. Old-style rugby socks used to be secured in this way before the advent of elastic (your coauthors still keep theirs up the old-fashioned way).

Depending on the club you play with, you may be supplied with rugby socks to ensure you're wearing the right club colors. If not, the club can tell you where to buy the right pair. Socks are not expensive and the type for players at club level are available at sports shops starting at about $4 a pair.

## Finding gear in North America

In North America, you can get gear in three ways. If you happen to live close to one of the few rugby supply houses, consider yourself lucky. For the vast majority of rugby players, your best options are to buy online (or by mail order) or attend one of the many annual tournaments where rugby retailers set up mobile stores to display their wares. Other than mouth guards, don't expect to find proper rugby gear at your local sporting goods store — and, whatever you do, don't try to adapt football, hockey, or other sports' pads for use in rugby.

One of the best places to start outfitting yourself online is at WorldRugbyShop.com (www. worldrugbyshop.com). Your local sports shop may have two or three models of football or soccer cleats that can work okay for rugby, but WorldRugbyShop.com has a dazzling array of real rugby boots. They have two separate categories of boots designed for either soft or firm fields, with 50 soft-ground choices and an incredible inventory of 299 firm-ground models to choose from. They also carry a comprehensive selection of jerseys, balls, bags, technical videos, and official team jerseys for virtually every national team and most of the overseas professional teams. (You can also find protective gear of every shape and size that you'll learn about next, but now were getting ahead of ourselves.)

# Protecting Your Assets

After you experience the joy of playing rugby you're likely to regard the myriad bumps and bruises as badges of courage, and come to enjoy the horrified reactions of family, friends, and co-workers who cringe at the sight of your occasional black eyes and minor facial stitches. Despite temporary trivial cosmetic alterations to your visage, rugby is actually very safe, considering the fact it is a full-contact sport.

In Chapter 18, we address safety and the truth about injuries in rugby. Here, we detail the variety of protective clothing available to lessen your chances of getting hurt.

## Choosing protective equipment

In recent years, the increased emphasis on safety has led the IRB to approve the use of more and more articles of protective gear. Responding to the challenge and commercial opportunity, manufacturers have improved existing devices to protect teeth and have developed new products to lessen the impact of collisions. Below is a list of the most widely used safety items.

Before you buy headgear or shoulder pads, make sure they comply with IRB specifications. The IRB has strict standards for rugby gear, and manufacturers must have their products approved by an IRB testing house. When an item is approved, it's given an approval number and the garment label is marked with the IRB logo and the words "Approved Clothing." Don't get too intimidated by all this IRB stuff. When buying protective gear, check the packaging to see if the product is approved for use.

- **Mouth guards:** Almost all professional players wear mouth guards to protect their teeth from wayward fists, boots, or bodies. Mouth guards are an essential piece of protective gear and anyone who takes the pitch at any level should always wear one. Most sporting goods stores stock mouth guards for football, and they can be molded at home to fit your teeth by following the directions on the package. Compared to the cost of dental reconstruction, a guard is a worthwhile investment at less than $5 US.

- **Headgear:** Regardless of whether you're a forward or a back, if you feel more comfortable or confident wearing padded headgear you shouldn't hesitate to use it. Headgear must be made of soft and thin material, and the IRB has set standards for what is legal. Look for the IRB logo to be sure that your headgear is approved for use. Good, comfortable, reputable brands can be purchased for between $35 and $75 US.

- **Shoulder pads and vests**: Shoulder pads and padded vests, as shown in Figure 3-2, provide rugby players with shoulder, collar bone, and chest protection. Those made with Lycra allow more air circulation and dry more quickly. They also come in various sizes, so you can choose the amount of padding you're comfortable with. Some are short, covering mainly the upper chest and shoulders. Others are long and will protect the entire torso as well as biceps. Female rugby players should look for vests that are designed for women. These vests are longer and have more padding for chest protection. The IRB states that these chest pads can be made of soft, thin material, as long as no part of the pad is thicker than 1 centimeter when uncompressed. Keep in mind that shoulder protection alone won't prevent injury — you need to use good technique at all times during contact sports. Vests are generally priced at around $50 US, but can be more expensive if they have special features.

- **Sports bras:** Most female rugby players also wear sports bras to reduce breast pain and limit movement. No specific bra is designed for rugby players (yet), but it's important to find one that provides good support and protection. Sports bras help to protect women as long as they fit properly. If you've never purchased a sports bra before, it's a good idea to get measured by an expert so you can get the right one. A good sports bra will cost around $30 US.

✔ **Compression shorts**: These are worn under your rugby shorts to provide extra protection and support. They also help prevent and repair hamstring and groin injuries. The shorts are usually made of thick Lycra or cotton, allowing for maximum airflow. Prices vary, but a good pair shouldn't cost more than $25 US.

✔ **Jock straps:** As an alternative to compression shorts, jock straps provide support for men who prefer the more traditional method of protection. These can be found at any sporting goods store and cost about $10 US.

**Figure 3-2:**
Shouldering
the load
with
protective
shoulder
pads.

## Avoiding serious injury

Although mouth guards, headgear, and shoulder pads offer some protection if you're hit in a certain spot, they don't guarantee a totally pain-free experience.

The best way to avoid serious injury is to play hard and at full throttle every minute you're on the pitch: "The half-hearted are the first to get hurt" is an old adage. Your club will teach you how to take other precautions, such as tackling safely and falling properly.

Rugby administrators are on the side of the player, instituting numerous laws to protect those on the pitch from serious injury. The referee is also required to stop any play that he or she determines to be dangerous and where a player may get hurt.

## Jewelry removal

After some offhand comments in support of women's rugby fueled by being awarded a beer mug for occasionally helping out the women's team plus the consumption of ample liquid refreshment at my club's end-of-the-season banquet a few years back, I found myself coaching the Occidental College Women's team the next fall, which I had supposedly agreed to do at said party. The experience was fantastic overall, but one aspect was definitely different from my own collegiate days on the pitch — the abundance of jewelry in all forms. In my day, the occasional earring or class ring would hastily be removed just before kickoff and tossed to the sideline. With the Oxy women at the beginning of the 21st century, it meant unscrewing multiple earrings, nose studs, tongue studs, belly rings, and pieces of jewelry from unmentionable areas. This was a process that usually took a good 15 minutes or so, even longer with the more heavily accessorized players. Regardless of its decorative value or strategic placement, *all* jewelry had to come off because metal is a serious safety hazard on the pitch.

Don't hesitate to use any form of protection allowed by the IRB. Ignore any nonsense about forwards who wear shoulder vests and headgear being cowards — try telling that to All Blacks Captain Richie McCaw or Springbok Victor Matfield who both wear protective gear. Like so many other professional players, they choose to wear it — and if you've ever stood next to either one of them, you know that whatever they want to wear is A-Okay with us.

## Knowing what's barred on the pitch

You need to take note of things that are not allowed on the rugby pitch. For safety reasons, players cannot wear or take onto the pitch:

- Anything contaminated with blood
- Anything sharp or abrasive
- Anything containing buckles, clips, rings, hinges, zippers, screws, or bolts
- Jewelry, such as rings or earrings
- Communication devices, such as two-way radios tucked into rugby boots
- Shorts with padding sewn into them

In addition, players aren't allowed to have any toe cleats on the soles of their boots, nor are players allowed to wear gloves onto the pitch, other than the fingerless variety. If you wear a knee brace that's reinforced with metal parts, you'll need to pick up a soft brace to play rugby.

Referees are required to examine both teams before the game to ensure players are not equipped with anything that may be dangerous. Part of this inspection is the boot check — when the referee looks at both teams' boots for worn-down studs or other prohibited items.

# Part II
# Getting Down and Dirty

# In this part . . .

It's time to get serious and find out exactly what's required to play the game. In this part, we start off by listing the various positions and outlining the skills you need to be a star. We then explain the laws of the game so you know what's legal and what's not. We also detail the object of the game and then demystify the scrum, rugby's signature formation that's used to restart play. Then we cover the lineout, and finish this part with a chat about training smart to win.

# Chapter 4

# Location, Location, Location: Positions on the Pitch

## In This Chapter

▶ Defining the role of each player

▶ Playing by numbers

▶ Scrapping in the scrum

▶ Making every position count

*W*hen 30 strapping rugby players all take the field at once, there's a rush of beef to rival the greatest cattle stampede. To the rugby-watching novice, it can look like total confusion. But don't despair. Rugby has a major advantage over a lot of other sports — the number on each player's back actually determines the exact position he or she plays.

In this chapter, we help you sort out which number goes with which player and what the person is trying to do in the game.

## A Place for Everyone

Rugby is an equal-opportunity game. Whether you're 5 feet tall or 7 feet tall, 100 pounds, 300 pounds, or anywhere in between, there's a place for you on a rugby team. If you want to play rugby, it will be easier to decide which position best suits you if you understand the typical characteristics and role on the team of each player.

A *side* is made up of 15 players — 8 forwards and 7 backs. The forwards (known collectively as the *pack*) have the primary role of winning the ball, while the backs are responsible for doing something productive with it. Generally, the bigger you are the more likely you'll become a forward; the faster you are the more likely you'll become a back.

Regardless of position, every rugby player needs a basic set of skills. Everyone on the team plays both offense and defense throughout the match. This means that the shortest player and the tallest, the lightest and the heaviest, all must be able to perform various duties such as tackling, catching, carrying the ball, and passing it when necessary.

## Playing the Numbers Game

Unlike American football, where the players' numbers are individually selected within a certain range for each position, and baseball, where numbers are essentially random, rugby union uses specific jersey numbers to identify each position on the field. In this regard, rugby is spectator-friendly. On the field, the players who start the game are numbered from 1 to 15, and the reserves are numbered from 16 to 22 (check out Chapter 2 for more about reserves).

Jersey numbers indicate the position each player occupies on the team. Numbers also let spectators, players, and coaches know who to cheer for when something wonderful happens. At the same time, everyone, including the referees and touch judges, can identify who is to blame if something goes wrong. When you're clear about the designated role and responsibilities of the player in each position, you'll be able to pick the stars from the slugs.

### A quick word on rucking and mauling

Before we discuss the responsibilities of the respective positions, a quick primer is in order to explain rucks and mauls. A ruck usually forms after a tackle is made when two or more players who are on their feet come into contact over the ball on the ground. The goal is to compete for possession by driving over the ball and using your feet to move it back to your side. A maul, in contrast, requires a minimum of three players and occurs when a player carrying the ball is held by one or more opponents and one or more of his teammates bind onto the ball-carrier who has the ball in hand off the ground. In a maul, everyone must be on his feet.

Figure 4-1 shows the forwards and backs in typical scrum attacking formation. It may be helpful to refer to this figure often while you're reading about each of the positions.

**Figure 4-1:** The forwards and backs getting ready to attack.

| | | |
|---|---|---|
| 1. Loose-head prop | 6. Blindside flanker | 11. Left-winger |
| 2. Hooker | 7. Openside flanker | 12. Inside center |
| 3. Tight-head prop | 8. Number 8 | 13. Outside center |
| 4. Lock (second row) | 9. Scrumhalf | 14. Right-winger |
| 5. Lock (second row) | 10. Flyhalf | 15. Fullback |

## What's in a name: Positions around the world

Rugby originated in England in the early to mid-1800s and has spread throughout the world over the last couple of centuries. As such, the game has developed on similar but somewhat divergent paths, depending upon where you are in the world. One of the byproducts of these unique threads of evolution is reflected in the proliferation of different position names. Although most of the positions on the rugby pitch have standardized names all over the English-speaking world, a few regional variations that can be confusing crop up in certain countries.

Terms that are interchangeable with the standard nomenclature and are not specific to any country or region include:

- Scrumhalf — halfback, inside half

- Flyhalf — pivot, first receiver, outside half

- Lock — second-rower

- Flanker — wing forward, breakaway, break

- Flankers and the number 8 — loose forwards, or loosies

Names that are a product of regional variation include:

New Zealand:

- Flyhalf — halfback, first five-eighth

- Inside Center — second five-eighth

- Outside Center — center, center three-quarter

- Wing — three-quarter

United Kingdom and Ireland:

- Flyhalf — standoff, outhalf

South Africa:

- Flankers — numbers are reversed

- Openside — wears jersey number 6

- Blindside — wears jersey number 7

- Eightman — eighthman

# Fearless Forwards

Eight players make up the forwards (or pack) of a rugby team — two props, the hooker, two locks, two flankers, and the number 8. This group's main goal is to win possession of the ball. These players are usually the heavyweights of the team, using their bulk and strength to try to overpower their opponents. Forwards can be broken up into three groups: front-rowers, second-rowers, and the back row.

## *Getting in tight with the tight five*

The *tight five* is the group of players who wear the jerseys numbered 1 to 5. This group consists of the three front-row players (tight-head prop, hooker, and loose-head prop — or "front-rowers" collectively) and the two second-row players (two locks, or "second-rowers" collectively) who line up behind them. The tight five forms the core of the pack. The group's main function is to keep the scrum steady and productive in the hope that when the ball is placed in the scrum it ends up in their team's possession. After a minor infringement occurs, the three front-rowers bind together and are joined by the two second-rowers (plus the three back-rowers) to compete for possession of the ball in a *scrum*.

A *scrum* is the term used for the interlocking formation of the team where the forwards' arms are around each others' shoulders, their knees are bent, and their heads are down. As shown in Figure 4-2, all eight players bind together and face their opponents. Both units then come together on the referee's call (four parts — crouch, touch, pause, engage), creating a tunnel in the middle. The ball is put in this tunnel by the scrumhalf and both teams' hookers attempt to channel it back to the rear of their own scrum with their feet. This is one of the signature elements of rugby and is used to restart play after an infraction. A scrum is over when the ball has been released from the web of players and is in play (see Chapter 8 for more details on the scrum).

**Figure 4-2:**
Forming a scrum, ready to compete for the ball.

Picture those wildlife documentaries where two huge rams slam together and head-butt each other for supremacy of the herd and you've got some idea of what goes on when a scrum is engaged. Brute force and strength are only half the battle. Proper, usually hard-learned technique will invariably prevail over simple bulk in the tight five. Understanding play is a little bit easier if you take the tight five positions one by one. We'll start by explaining the function of the three front-rowers (tight-head prop, hooker, and loose-head prop), and follow by talking about the two second-rowers (the locks).

## Facing off in the front row

The front row is easy to pick out: the loose-head prop wears the number 1 jersey; the hooker wears number 2; and the tight-head prop wears number 3. Don't panic — we explain these unusual names in the next few paragraphs. (Remember, the location of these players is outlined in Figure 4-1.)

The front-rowers form the platform upon which the whole team is built. These three players must be uncompromising, technically sound, and committed to doing whatever it takes to win the battle up front. If the front-rowers are weak or off their game, the team is at risk of collapsing.

Front-rowers take enormous pride in their scrummaging technique and revel in the fact that it's literally the only head-to-head confrontation in the game. Other rugby players may make jokes about props' less-than-svelte physiques, but there's also a huge amount of respect involved in the ribbing because everyone loves playing behind a solid front row.

You won't find many flashy or cocky front-rowers, but they believe they're the three most important rugby players on the field and in many respects they're right.

### Propping up: Tight-heads and loose-heads

The *props* are the players who wear numbers 1 and 3. They can be found on either side of the hooker in the front row. Because props take most of the physical impact in the scrum, they must possess superior upper and lower body strength.

The term "prop" comes from the fact that these two players "prop up" the hooker when the scrumhalf (more about this position later in the chapter) puts the ball into the scrum. Figure 4-3 shows the scrumhalf putting the ball in at the scrum and the hooker being supported by his loose-head and tight-head props.

**Figure 4-3:**
The scrumhalf putting the ball in at the scrum.

The words "loose" and "tight" simply describe how the props are positioned in the actual formation of the scrum. Because of the alignment of the scrum, the loose-head prop has his head outside the scrum and can see what the others are doing. The tight-head prop, however, positions his head between the opposition's hooker and loose-head prop. In other words, the loose-head has no other head to his left, whereas the tight-head's noggin is sandwiched between two opposing players' heads (we talk more specifically about scrums in Chapter 8).

Don't be discouraged if it takes some time to tell the difference between a tight-head and a loose-head prop. The best way to remember exactly who is who is that the loose-head is on the left-hand side of the scrum and the tight-head is on the right-hand side of the scrum. The way to remember this is that "tight" rhymes with "right."

Tight-head props and loose-head props have exactly the same aim, though their techniques are different. The tight-head is the anchor of the scrum, requiring enormous strength to keep the scrum straight and intact. The loose-head is more of a technician, using different tricks to give his team an advantage in winning the ball.

## Technique beats athleticism

Years ago there was a beautiful annual rugby tournament on the polo grounds at Pebble Beach in Monterey, California. A few years after I took up the game my team, the Oxy Olde Boys, was scheduled to play a side from Sacramento that was made up mostly of Pacific Islander players. As we watched them warm up in their sweats prior to kickoff, all of us focused on one particular athlete who was about 6'2", 225 pounds, incredibly fast, and looked menacing in his athleticism and obvious strength. A long ponytail and a glowering countenance completed the effect. Somebody eventually muttered what everyone was thinking: "Who is going to have to play directly against that guy?" As the other team took off their jackets just before kickoff, I saw the number 3 on his back, indicating that he was a tight-head and would be opposite me, a loose-head, in the scrum. As

luck would have it, that must have been his very first outing in the front row because I had my way with him, relentlessly bending him every which way, lifting him off the ground (that was before it was made illegal for safety reasons), driving him mercilessly backward at each scrum, and generally making his life miserable to the point where he eventually took to trying to punch me as a means of self-preservation. The thumping he took in the scrums totally negated his effectiveness in the rest of play as well. At the time I was still a relatively inexperienced prop but I had the basics down and was therefore miles ahead of this newcomer — and it showed on the pitch. Rugby is a game where physical attributes are important but technical proficiency is even more significant, and nowhere is that more true than in the front row.

Props are crucial performers at the *line-out* (a line-out is how play is restarted when the ball has been taken out over the sideline or kicked into touch; we discuss line-outs in detail in Chapter 9), because they're required to lift their teammates at exactly the right time and place. This takes excellent footwork, timing, quickness, and strength. They're also prized defenders who take on other hard-charging forwards in tight quarters. In attack, one of a prop's main tasks is to drive defenders back a few yards whenever they touch the ball; the occasional long run is a bonus, not a requirement.

### Highlighting the hooker

In between the two props is the *hooker,* who wears the number 2 jersey. This is the most versatile of the three front-row positions. The hooker is seen around the field more often because this position has a wider range of responsibility. The hooker needs to have superior hand–eye and foot–eye coordination, flexibility, agility, upper body strength, and quickness. Powerful legs are also an asset.

At the scrum, the hooker is supported by his two props, enabling him to hang suspended over the scrum opening. When the scrumhalf puts the ball into the tunnel between the feet of the opposing front rows, the hooker is required to "strike" at the ball with his foot, guiding it back toward the feet of the players in the second and back rows so that his team gets possession.

The hooker must also be right on his game at every line-out, because he has the tough task of throwing the ball in and making sure that it's on target to one of the line-out jumpers. Because line-outs are used to initiate play more than any other restart, it's imperative that a hooker is able to accurately hit his jumpers on a consistent basis.

Hookers can make or break their reputation based on their ability as a line-out thrower. The ranks of former internationals are littered with hookers who were great in every other aspect of the game, but couldn't regularly maintain possession at the line-out with their throws. If throwing isn't one of your strengths, then this probably isn't the position for you.

The hooker is often expected to function as an extra loose forward, so he must be a courageous tackler and able to provide a link between forwards and backs in support play.

## The second row: Exerting in the engine room

The second row of the tight five is made up by the two *locks,* who wear numbers 4 and 5. This pair is referred to as the *engine room* because this is where the power is generated in a scrum. While the front row sets the platform, the locks drive it forward — or keep it from being driven backward.

Locks are typically tall, athletic players with strong backs and powerful legs. These two (who often look like they got lost on the way to an NBA game) are the players who are lifted high in the air to catch the ball tossed in by the hooker in a line-out. Because of their height, they're also usually the two key ball-takers on kickoffs. Simply being tall isn't enough — locks also need to have good hands, balance, and coordination in the air. The ideal lock will have legs like springs and hands like glue.

Most locks either have athletic tape wrapped around their heads or they wear protective headgear. This is done to prevent their ears from chafing when they pack down in the scrum.

Locks are the workhorses of the pack. They bind to each other and the props in front of them to attain the cohesion required to ensure that the scrum stays stable and doesn't collapse. This position generally requires someone tall and sturdy enough to not snap in two when pressure is applied in the scrum.

A truly great second-rower is almost superhuman. While a second-rower may have a physique that at first sight doesn't look as if it belongs on a rugby field, he needs to be an outstanding ball-carrier, have tremendous agility, and be an enforcer on defense.

# The back-row forwards: Breaking loose with the loosies

The back row consists of the players in jersey numbers 6, 7, and 8 (blindside flanker, openside flanker, and the number 8). Collectively, these players are referred to as the "loose forwards" (or loosies), because they're the first players to break away from the formation when the scrum ends. An excellent back-row combination is vital for a successful team because the three players are involved in so much of the game, creating numerous opportunities and thwarting many of the opposition's tactics.

These three players must be strong, quick off the mark, agile, and fearless in order to effectively tackle, carry the ball, and compete for possession.

## Foraging with the flankers

The primary role of the two *flankers* is to tackle everything that moves and to steal the ball whenever possible. Flankers are built like football linebackers, with excellent quickness, agility, strength, and courage. These players are willing to sacrifice their bodies in a mission to gain possession of the ball and prevent their opponents from doing so.

The terms "openside" and "blindside" refer to which side of the scrum the flankers line up on. A scrum is usually set up on either side of the field, with open field on one side and the sideline on the other. The openside flanker joins the scrum beside the open field. The blindside flanker joins the side of the scrum closest to the sideline. The flankers bind to the locks' bodies on the "flanks" of the scrum, switching from one side of the scrum to the other depending on field position.

### Toughing it on the blindside

The *blindside flanker* (number 6) has to be industrious. Along with the number 8, he is usually the second or third to arrive at the breakdown. He must be an outstanding defender, particularly as many opposing teams attempt to attack down the blindside from a scrum. The blindside flanker has to always be mindful of this and be ready to cut off this option immediately with a devastating tackle. Usually, he is also required to be the third major line-out jumper. And, like the number 8, the blindside flanker must also be one of the real hard men in the team, and take on the enforcer's role if need be.

# The best in the business — Richie McCaw

New Zealand's Richie McCaw exemplifies all the skills, athleticism, and rugby IQ needed to excel on the openside. He's big and strong at 6'2", 218 pounds, and has tremendous quickness and agility, plus the stamina to maintain a high work rate for the entire 80 minutes. His greatest asset, however, is his command of the subtleties of the breakdown. Along with Australia's George Smith, he's the best in the world at contesting for possession after a tackle occurs. He draws a couple of penalties every game because he always plays right on the edge of the law. He more than makes up for his infractions by regularly producing multiple turnovers. As teams get better at maintaining continuity on offense through multiple phases, having a player on your team who can create turnovers in general play each game is a huge advantage. One of the main reasons why New Zealand is the number-one ranked team in the world is because they have Richie McCaw wearing number 7.

Discipline is a critical component of this flanker's makeup, because if he can't regulate his emotions and behavior his actions will often get him in trouble. A flanker's mantra should be controlled aggression in search of and maintenance of possession. Flankers also need superior handling skills to support other ball-carriers and must be ready to transfer the ball in any situation.

### Patrolling the openside

The *openside flanker* is usually the smaller and speedier of the two because he patrols a greater amount of field. His prime aim is to be the first to the ball wherever it is on the pitch. He has to be quick to arrive at the scene after a tackle has occurred so he can wrestle the ball away from the opposition on defense before others get there and the ruck forms (see Chapter 7 for more on the intricacies of the ruck). For offensive support, the openside must reach the breakdown first to make sure that possession is maintained if his teammate is stopped by a defender.

The good and not-so-good things that openside flankers do are often obscured by the heaps of bodies on the ground where they put in a substantial amount of their work. They fight and tussle for the ball whenever there's a chance to take it away, but must also know when to give up the struggle for possession to avoid a penalty. If they're good enough to pilfer the ball without upsetting the referee, they're worth their weight in gold. A good openside must have a perfect knowledge of rugby law and be able to adapt to individual referees' interpretations and commands.

### Piloting the pack at the number 8

The pack leader is the *number 8,* who, not surprisingly, wears the number 8 jersey. The ideal number 8 is shorter than the locks and taller than the flankers, with a bit more bulk to smash through opposing defensive lines. This position usually goes to the most skillful and savvy forward because so much of the match happens around him; he is often the first to receive the ball from scrums, line-outs, and in open play. He has responsibilities all over the field, so he has to make his presence felt from sideline to sideline.

From any scrum, the number 8, working in tandem with the scrumhalf and flyhalf (we explain the roles of these players later in this chapter), decides how the team initiates the attack or structures its defense. If the team is attacking, the number 8 must decide, as the ball arrives at his feet, whether to run with it, pass it to the scrumhalf, or protect the scrumhalf while he plays the ball.

A good number 8 always knows exactly what the opposition is up to and seizes any opportunity to take the ball forward himself if he believes he can expose a defensive weakness by making a quick run from the base of the scrum. He basically has to be anywhere and everywhere, always thinking and anticipating the flow of the game to stay near the ball, especially when there is a breakdown in play.

# Get to the Back of the Line

The seven remaining players, who wear jersey numbers 9 to 15, are often referred to collectively as the "back line" (not to be confused with the back row of the forwards).

Like in football, where the linemen do all the dirty work in the trenches and the quarterback, running backs, and receivers get all the glory, in rugby an old oval adage says that the forwards win the ball and the backs win the game. A team with great backs and mediocre forwards will find itself starved of ball to work with. The opposite will produce plenty of possession, but few chances to attack and score. To play winning rugby, you need 15 players totally committed to their roles and each other.

## Passing and pestering for profit: The scrumhalf

The *scrumhalf* wears number 9, and is the border collie of the team. This is the team's organizer, who commands the forwards, directing their movements at ruck and maul time. Scrumhalves are usually the smallest players on the field and must have exceptional balance, be lightning-quick, and have superior passing skills. The very best scrumhalves are considered part of the pack by admiring forwards.

The scrumhalf's main aim is to be the team distributor. Because he is supposed to be one step away from everything that's happening, he is the one who usually distributes the ball from the scrums, line-outs, rucks and mauls, and whenever there is any form of breakdown in play. (We discuss the scrumhalf's passing skills in Chapter 10.)

The scrumhalf must be agile, intensely courageous, and the best passer on the team. The scrumhalf upholds communication between the forwards and the backs, and constantly urges the scrum on to greater heights, directing the rolling maul and calling for runners to take it up hard off of rucks. The scrumhalf usually works in tandem with the flyhalf, and the pair decides on the best attack and defensive options (for more about game tactics, see Chapter 9). When you see the scrumhalf and flyhalf making weird hand signals, or cupping their hands around the mouth so that they won't be heard by the opposition, it means they're calling plays for the next phase of attack and something interesting is about to occur.

A scrumhalf has to be able to kick over the top to both relieve and impose pressure. On defense a scrumhalf has to repeatedly tackle much bigger players, so his technique must be exemplary.

## Feeling footloose and fancy-free: The flyhalf

The *flyhalf* wears number 10 and is the chief playmaker on the team, making the big decisions that often determine whether a team wins or loses. He is usually the player with the best combination of tactical acumen, kicking ability, and distribution skills.

The flyhalf is sometimes called the pivot because so much turns on what the player does. The flyhalf dictates the flow and style of the team's game plan, determining whether the team adopts a running game, relies instead on midfield kicking, or uses forward power to grind out a victory. (Chapter 11 discusses the flyhalf's role in devising winning tactics.) The rest of the back line has to be on the same wavelength as the flyhalf. He generally calls the various moves and plays, and chooses who will be chasing his variety of kicks downfield. In this sense he is very much like a quarterback in football, deciding where the ball is going and to whom. On most teams, the flyhalf is also the first-choice goal kicker, but not always.

A flyhalf of any note must have a very cool demeanor and an ability to think clearly under pressure. He also needs to possess good all-around skills, because every one of those skills is usually put to the test. Flyhalf is a very demanding position, but it's also one of the most rewarding in the game.

## Mastering the midfield: Centers

While both are called *centers,* the players wearing numbers 12 (inside center) and 13 (outside center) fulfill slightly different roles. The aim remains the same: trying to elude their opponents so that they can set up tries. Typically, centers have excellent kicking, passing, and handling skills, and can deliver a mean tackle.

### Attacking from the inside out

Number 12 is the *inside center,* the player who stands closest in attack to the flyhalf (number 10) and who often acts as a back-up flyhalf, being the second midfield organizer of the attack. In simple terms, the main goal of the inside center is to keep attacks in some sort of formation by providing the link between the flyhalf and the outer backs.

A good inside center must be dependable, able to straighten the attack when required, and fearless in all facets of play. Few players touch the ball more often than the inside center, so he needs to have exceptional ball-handling skills and a tough hide to know when exactly to pass, when to run, or when to try to mix it up a bit with a "chip kick" (we explain kicking skills in Chapter 10). Most importantly, he cannot drop the ball, especially as he is invariably playing in a confined area with opponents hovering all around him. He has to be the coolest of customers with great hands. Centers are more likely to be drawn into rucks than other backs, so they should have more highly developed skills in this area.

Like the flyhalf, the inside center often has to decide whether to straighten the attack by running directly upfield with the ball, or to push the attack wider by passing to either the outside center or the fullback. He often plays a "battering ram" role in running the ball hard into the opposition's defensive line, plowing into defenders, and challenging them to tackle him. Ideally, he's strong enough to maintain the appropriate body position in the tackle so that his teammates have a better chance to recycle the ball — the quicker the better! (We talk about running with the ball and tackling in Chapter 10.)

On the defensive side of the ball, the inside center's job is to stop his opposite number from breaking through the line. Missed head-up tackles by inside centers are anathema to any coach's defensive stratagem. This means taking on a speedy, aggressive runner, built like himself, over and over during the course of 80 minutes.

## The world's best center — Brian O'Driscoll

Irish center Brian O'Driscoll is the best number 13 in the world. The Irish captain is a talismanic player, inspiring his Leinster and Ireland teammates to greater heights with his intensity and ability to create something out of nothing with ball in hand.

O'Driscoll possesses a wide variety of skills on both sides of the ball. He is a ferocious tackler and plays like a loose forward at the breakdown, stealing ball and hitting rucks like a Mack truck. It's as a ball-carrier, though, where O'Driscoll really shines. He is one of the planet's most feared attackers who can chip through or over with a deft boot, beat defenders with incredible moves, outrun them with exceptional pace, or draw multiple defenders and then offload to his support runners.

O'Driscoll is Ireland's all-time leading tryscorer, and despite numerous injuries over the years has amassed 74 caps for his country. In 2005 he became the first Irishman to captain the British & Irish Lions on tour since 1983.

### Attacking from the outside in

Number 13 is the *outside center,* who is generally the faster of the two centers and, along with the wings, is among the team's more important attacking players. The prime aim of the outside center is to set up teammates playing outside him, in particular the fullback and wings. This usually involves luring the opposition's defense into pursuing him and, through that, creating enough room to throw what must be a perfectly timed pass, putting a teammate through the opposition's defensive line. But he must also have the attacking instinct to know when to attack the line himself — and have faith in his own speed to get him through. The outside center is the player who tries to ruin the opposition's defensive pattern by providing an unpredictable attacking spark.

The outside center usually has more space to work with than the inside center. Many tries have been achieved after a number 13 has broken his way through the opposition defense and then put his wing or fullback over the goal line with a precise kick into the corner of the field, well behind the opposition defense. (Shown in Figure 4-1, the goal line is the line on or over which the attacking team must ground the ball in order to score a try.)

Just as important, the outside center must also be one of the best defenders, especially as a fast-running fullback is usually charging at him with ball in hand. This is no position for the fainthearted.

To be successful, the two centers must work together. Good chemistry between this pair is an important element of a rugby team's dynamics. Centers who work well together are able to read each other's intentions without giving them away — like bridge partners or old married couples.

# Running wild out wide: The wings

Each team has two *wings*. Number 11 is the left wing and number 14 is the right wing. When facing the defenders, the left wing is on the left-hand side of the team and the right wing is on the right-hand side.

Wings have to be the fastest players on the team, possessing extraordinary acceleration and the ability to beat their opponents and then out-sprint them to the tryline. Wings need to be fast in attack and able to work well in a limited amount of space; they also need to be furious in defense, especially when the attack is focused on the outer reaches of the field.

The demands of playing on the left and right wing are basically the same. However, who plays on which wing is usually determined by which foot a player prefers to kick with, or if he has a better left- or right-footed *side-step* (side-stepping is where you dart off in a different direction than that anticipated by the opposition; we discuss it further in Chapter 10).

Wings are regarded as the "glory boys" of the team, whose primary function is to finish off attacking moves and score heaps of tries. On any team, they should be the most prolific tryscorers, because their teammates devote so much of their energies into putting them in a perfect position to get over the opposition's tryline.

# Roaming the range: The fullback

The *fullback* wears the number 15 jersey and has more freedom to roam than any other player on the pitch. The fullback's prime responsibility is to be the last line of defense to prevent tries. Fullbacks are generally well-rounded rugby players. They must be able to catch the opposition's high kicks during attacks, or become the extra player in an attack.

The fullback has to have a kicking leg on him equal to that of the flyhalf because he will invariably be forced to clear the ball from deep in his own territory. Accuracy in kicking is paramount, because if his kick doesn't find touch he has to chase it down and put his teammates on-side before they can participate again (we cover the complexities of the offside law in Chapter 6).

A good fullback is like a chess player who uses intuition to anticipate what's going to happen a few moves ahead and then gets himself into the right place to deal with it. The best fullbacks also use their skills to predict their opponents' next move and counter before the other side can react.

When the opposition has the ball, the fullback has to know where and when to join in the team's defensive line, to ensure that the correct number of players are in the right spots to stop the opposition from scoring. This can mean joining the defensive line between the centers, or among the forwards, to fill any gaps that may occur. Or it can mean placing himself in a strategic position behind the defensive line so he is in the right spot to catch a clearing kick from the opposition, or even a chip kick, which is aimed at turning around and disorienting his side.

Forwards and the midfield attackers have relatively defined areas of ground to work in and cover. However, the fullback, as the team's "gatekeeper," has a lot of territory to patrol.

A fullback's normal position on the pitch is standing several meters behind his attacking line. This means he usually has half the pitch to cover, and even more when his own side is close to the opposition's tryline. So it's important that he knows how to cover that area. No other player on the pitch is on his own so often without the support of a teammate. It's a demanding position, which explains why a good fullback is so vital to a team's prospects of winning. It also explains why this is probably the most stressful position on the field — the fullback is the last tackler, and if he misses not only is his entire team let down but also the other side gets five points!

### Surprising the enemy

A fullback can really make his mark on attack. Because he's relatively free to move about the field, the fullback should be used as the surprise attack weapon — he can pop up anywhere and everywhere on the pitch. A running fullback radically improves the attacking prowess of any back line, particularly if he is able to read a play, knowing when it's time to hit the line at pace or to join the line to create the extra man.

The aim of most rugby attacks is to create an overlap where the attacking team has more players than the defensive line in front of them. The fullback can create that overlap if he chooses to enter the back line either near the centers or wings at an opportune moment.

### Defusing bombs

In addition to being a sure tackler and intuitive attacker, the fullback needs to be cool under pressure. To break up their attacking patterns, or to take advantage of wet or windy conditions, teams often kick high balls to test the fullback. A *high ball* (or an *up and under*) is a kick from the opposition that's aimed downfield, traveling high in the air, usually 20 to 30 meters above the heads of the players. It takes great intestinal fortitude for the number 15 to maintain total concentration when fielding the ball, all the while knowing that tacklers are bearing down on him. The ball usually swirls in the air and is often tricky to catch, making it a fullback's nightmare.

The fullback is usually the first opposing player a team tests. If he's not up to the task of fielding the high ball, you can be sure his opponents will target him and keep applying pressure. If the fullback mishandles the ball, the attacking side usually gains serious ground, if not a try.

# Chapter 5

# Laying Down the Laws

· · · · · · · · · · · · · · · · · · · · · · · · · · · · · · · · · · · · · · ·

## In This Chapter

▶ Learning where the laws come from

▶ Meeting the match officials

▶ Understanding the referee's signals

· · · · · · · · · · · · · · · · · · · · · · · · · · · · · · · · · · · · · · ·

**R**ugby is a game governed by laws rather than rules — rules are imposed to regulate behavior, whereas laws are implemented to achieve a desired result. In the case of rugby, the laws are designed to produce a free-flowing game during which two teams score as many points as possible, with the team that scores more being declared the winner.

Arguing about interpretations and discussing the laws of the game is a noble pastime that takes place in pubs, clubhouses, and rugby grounds all over the world. In this chapter we introduce you to the laws by telling you where they come from and how they've evolved. We explain how you can get a copy of the coveted law book, and we detail the responsibilities of the people who are charged with running the game on the pitch from start to finish.

## The Laws of the Game

Twenty-two laws cover every aspect of how the game is played on the field. From how the pitch is laid out and marked, to what happens in the in-goal area, the laws of the game encompass all the information necessary to allow the game to be played. (A separate set of regulations involves how the sport itself is governed.) While regional variations may develop in terms of style and technique in playing the game, the laws at the senior level are exactly the same whether the match is the World Cup Final or a third-division match in a less-developed country. (Laws for younger rugby players are age-appropriate for safety reasons; see Chapter 17.) Rugby is a centrally administered sport, which means that the International Rugby Board (IRB) decides on the laws and controls when and if they are to be changed.

## The International Rugby Board (IRB)

The IRB, founded in 1886, is the world-governing and law-making body for the game of rugby. The Executive Council meets twice a year and consists of the eight founding nations — Scotland, Ireland, Wales, England, Australia, New Zealand, South Africa, and France. Each founding nation has two seats. Argentina, Canada, Italy, and Japan each have one seat on the Council, as does FIRA-AER (the International Amateur Rugby Federation — European Rugby Association). The day-to-day business of the Board is conducted by a professional staff of more than 40, the majority of whom are based in Dublin. Rugby is played by men and women and boys and girls in more than a hundred countries across five continents. The IRB has 95 member Unions, 20 Associates, and 6 Regional Associations.

## The IRB writes the law

Until the 21st century there were 28 laws, many of which overlapped in a mishmash of repetitive jargon. Fortunately, the IRB saw the detrimental effect this was having on the development of the game, and simplified the jumble quite a bit by consolidating the essential knowledge into 22 laws with far less repetition and a lot more clarity. While still seemingly daunting to the rugby novice, the newer version of the laws has been instrumental in producing some of the finest examples of rugby matches ever played in just the last few years.

The IRB does not make lighthearted changes for the sake of seeing bigger numbers on the scoreboard, but instead has a detailed process for updating the law book. Pursuant to the organization's bylaws, a Laws Committee is empowered to consider changes proposed by the individual unions that make up the IRB, to recommend changes and amendments to those submissions, and to clarify real-life situations that occur during the course of each year. In this way, the IRB can respond to trends in the game happening around the world and also prevent harmful alterations that detract from the overall spirit of the laws. From time to time, the IRB will authorize the application of experimental laws in prescribed matches to test whether or not they would benefit the sport. The IRB also continually amends the language of the law book to clarify points of confusion without making material changes. The next major revision of the laws is due in 2008, after the conclusion of the 2007 Rugby World Cup.

# *The laws are dynamic and ever-changing*

If you were to pick up a law book from the early days of the game it would be pretty unrecognizable in content compared to today's version. Rugby did not start like basketball did, with a complete set of laws handed down from on high. What happened was that the early attempts at codification reflected what was already occurring on the pitch. As the game spread throughout the world, modifications were instituted to ensure continuity.

Over the years many laws have been changed to promote specific strategic objectives, to rein in wayward practitioners of dubious techniques, and to correct imbalances in the way offense and defense interact. The best way to understand this process is to take a close look at a specific law relating to one part of the line-out that has undergone radical changes in the last few years.

The line-out is a means of restarting play after the ball has gone into touch, or out of bounds. One team throws the ball in as both teams' jumpers are lifted to precarious heights in an attempt to gain possession and produce a quick ball for the back line to use. Line-outs have become an intricately choreographed phase that requires coordinated timing from everyone involved. But it wasn't always so.

Until 1999, lifting in the line-out was done surreptitiously under the guise of supporting the jumper, who had to rely on good old-fashioned vertical leaping ability and natural height to secure the throw-in. There was also a lot more contact between the two teams and fewer clean takes that allowed the ball to be spun out wide in a hurry. When the law changed and lifting was brought into the open, a whole new set of skills had to be learned and the sport of rugby gained by highlighting its enormous collective capacity for ingenuity and the athleticism of its players. As of this writing no serious advocates are calling for a return to the older, slower, less exciting incarnation of the line-out law.

Of course, unintended consequences always accompany any change, and lifting was no exception. If lifting was legal in line-outs, then why not on restart kicks? It's now common to see jumpers positioned at various points on the pitch with an individual lifter ready to propel them skyward in hopes of cleanly fielding the kick. This has also made the game more interesting and put more strategic emphasis on what was a neglected area of play.

Then, some coach or player somewhere had the bright idea of lifting jumpers to snatch penalty and conversion kicks out of the air before they could clear the crossbar. It actually worked a few times over a couple of seasons but proved too much for the traditionalists at the IRB, so the Laws Committee deemed that it contravened the spirit of the law governing penalties (a viewpoint we both agree with), and added an amendment that made the practice illegal. This episode demonstrates how the laws are evolving with the game but never at the expense of the all-important ethos of the sport.

## Reading the law book

We played rugby for many years before ever actually holding a copy of the laws in our hands and daring to look inside. Because we didn't know any better we spent years believing incorrect interpretations and committing penalties for unknown reasons, which generally limited our effectiveness for our teams. Knowledge of the laws came from older, more experienced players who spouted knowingly about "hands in the ruck," "offside at the tackle," and other vague terms. In retrospect, what we heard varied from almost right to completely wrong.

Delving into the law book opened up a whole new world. Referees' calls that previously seemed unfathomable were suddenly made clear. Confidence soared at the breakdown where strength and technique were supplemented with an almost magical sense of knowledge. Our enjoyment of the game expanded exponentially as the mysterious shield of ignorance surrounding referees' decisions melted away.

Our advice for any aspiring rugby player, coach, referee, or fan is to get a copy of the laws and dig in. Versions can be downloaded from the Internet, but it's best to go to the IRB's official Web site (www.irb.com) so you know the version is up-to-date. Getting your hands on a hard copy is a little more difficult, but not impossible (see Chapter 3 for a full list of options).

## Building up your knowledge

You don't have to spend long days and nights poring over the laws — far from it. However, an hour or two going through the main points of the law is time well spent. You'll begin to have a better understanding of what the referee is doing on the pitch if you've done your homework. In fact, you're more likely to know what's going on than some of the players, many of whom, sad to say, don't have a clue what the referee is going on about.

A good way to familiarize yourself with the laws in action is to focus on the referee during a game. Watch his every move and try to figure out why he makes the decisions he does. Through close observation, you'll get to know the various signals and recognize the types of play that lead to important decisions (all 45 of the referee signals are found later in this chapter).

## Don't hide behind your law book

A few years back, after a hard-fought match between my club, the Oxy Olde Boys RFC, and San Luis Obispo RFC, both sides gathered at the reception to take in some grub, liquid refreshment, and good old-fashioned rugby camaraderie. As the evening wore on, the match referee felt compelled to vehemently defend one particularly questionable call (the first and only sending-off of my coauthor) by repeated reference to his law book. It was as if pointing to the text of the law would transform his suspect decision on the field into the unassailable act of a refereeing deity. It was painfully obvious to all of us that he was hiding behind the authority of the law book itself. Eventually, liquid intake necessitated a pit stop and the whistle-blower went to the bathroom.

What happened next was pure theater. The president of San Luis Obispo, Bo Kelly, seized the opportunity — he grabbed the ref's book from the table. Bo pronounced that the ref didn't know a thing about the game, and without his precious little law book to hide behind he'd be hopelessly lost. Showing good skills, Bo then produced a lighter and proceeded to set the law book on fire, to the cheers of both teams. Soon after, the referee emerged from the restroom to see what the commotion was all about. When he saw Bo holding his burning law book, the non-verbal message was self-evident — Bo was not at all impressed by the referee's incessant references to his law book.

Now please don't take this as an endorsement of book-burning generally, or law books in particular, or of being disrespectful to referees in any way. The lesson here is that a law book is nothing more than paper and ink. You get no authority whatsoever by simply carrying one around. The value of a law book is directly related to your approach to understanding the game and how you use it. Properly used, it's a good general guide, but you need to use your head to adapt the principles of the game to fit the particular situation you find yourself in.

You can quickly enhance your knowledge of the game by approaching the referee at the reception following a local match — most of them love the game every bit as much as the players do and enjoy talking about it. Also, referees are probably the most cooperative and friendly group to deal with in the rugby world, and are always eager to help people improve their knowledge of the laws of the game.

Approach referees in a friendly manner that reassures them you aren't going to start arguing the merits of a decision they just made. You'll soon find yourself immersed in the intrigue of what actually happened at the bottom of a ruck or why a certain transgressor was judged to be offside. You'll begin to understand the finer points of some laws that were once absolutely bewildering.

Another way to increase your level of understanding is to ask questions of your coach, who is often a good source of information about the laws. You may find that coaches are instant experts on referees, even though their views may be more derogatory than flattering. For all this, however, most coaches have a good basic knowledge of the law book — it's an essential requirement if they want their team to succeed. (See Chapter 18 for more information on coaches.)

Your coach should tell you during training sessions if you're doing something that would cause a referee to come down on you like a ton of bricks. If you repeat the offense in a match, your coach's behavior toward you is going to be less congenial, to say the least. Finding yourself banished to the reserve bench is a good indication that your knowledge of the laws is flimsy and you need to spend some quiet time with the law book. Just as a lack of knowledge of the laws can hurt your team immensely, an understanding of them will reap enormous benefits.

# Introducing the Match Officials

Running the game is a tough job that often attracts more criticism than praise. The referee is the main player in this drama, but he has help from other members of the refereeing fraternity who are there to make his job easier. Collectively, the referee, the touch judges, the substitution official, and the television match official (TMO) are known as the *match officials*. Should you aspire to become a referee or a touch judge, check out Chapter 20 for all the details.

## The referee: The one with the whistle

Whether you're a player or a spectator, the referee is the person to watch. The referee is the single most important person on the field during a game. The primary function of the referee is to manage the match and help create a spectacle for the fans to enjoy.

The referee is the official who has the ultimate power over what occurs in a rugby match. What he says, goes. He is the sole judge of fact and law during the match. The referee's position is probably the most demanding of all, requiring a broad depth of knowledge, a high level of fitness, and a very thick skin.

Players prefer referees who don't talk down to them. No one likes a dictator. The best referees understand what the players are doing and, whenever possible, try to let the game flow. Referees should be firmly in control without feeling the need to constantly assert their authority. This is a tough balance to strike for any referee. The ultimate accomplishment for a referee is when, at the end of the match, no one remembers who held the whistle.

Referees are passionate about the game and fervently believe they have the best job in the world. The top-level referee's job has been transformed by the advent of professionalism. Full-time referees are now needed to work the various competitions around the globe. In the past, police officers, school teachers, and business people volunteered their time as referees. Now there is a small but expanding group of professional referees who work matches all over the world, covering competitions from the Six Nations to the Tri Nations to the Super 14. (For a description of these tournaments, see Chapter 14.) Travel is often long-distance — Southern Hemisphere referees sometimes officiate at Northern Hemisphere matches, and vice versa. The reward is that they get to spend time in some of the most entertaining cities in the world — while getting paid well for doing something that they thoroughly enjoy.

The vast majority of referees are, and will always be, amateurs. Regardless of their status, however, the same duties and responsibilities are entrusted to them. Before the match they conduct a coin toss to determine which team will kick off and which end the other side will defend. They also do a pre-match inspection to ensure players are in compliance with the relevant laws on equipment and clothing.

It's worth stating again that during the match the referee is the sole judge of fact and law. His decisions are final, with no appeal to a higher authority available. The referee is additionally charged with keeping the official time and score, sending players off for serious offenses, and regulating the comings and goings of substitutes and replacements. In all these duties they're assisted by fellow refs in subordinate roles, depending upon the level of match being played. (The farther one travels down from the highest echelons, the less likely it is that a referee will have two other referees as touch judges.) A referee is allowed to consult with the other match officials, but the final decision in all matters is the whistle-blower's alone.

Your rugby-playing experience will be far better if you try to keep the referee happy — antagonizing the person with the whistle is not a good idea. Rugby players should always treat referees with respect and address them as "Sir" or "Madam." One of the ways that rugby maintains its reputation for sportsmanlike conduct is a zero-tolerance policy toward players and coaches at any level who are not civil in dealing with the referee. The badgering and browbeating of officials that occurs in other professional sports is totally unacceptable in rugby and is contrary to the spirit of the game.

To avoid being targeted by the referee, act as if you never intended to break the law, never question a ruling unless you're the team captain, and be courteous at all times.

## Touch judges: The ones with the flags

The two touch judges, one on each side of the field, play a very important role in a rugby match. As the name indicates, their primary responsibility is determining where a line-out has to be formed and which team throws the ball in to the line-out after it has gone into touch (we cover line-outs in Chapter 9).

The touch judges have to determine exactly where the ball crossed the touchline, which team was the last to touch it, and which team will throw the ball back in. They signal this by standing at the spot where the line-out is to be taken, raising a flag over their head, and pointing in the direction of the team that will throw it in.

A further duty is judging whether or not penalty and conversion kicks have been successful. To do this, the touch judges move to a spot behind each upright that will afford them the best view of the kick. If the kick goes over the crossbar and between the posts, they raise their flags to indicate that fact.

Touch judges also act as the referee's second and third pair of eyes. They advise the referee whenever they witness incidents of foul play that the referee didn't see. At the provincial and international levels, a touch judge is in radio contact with the referee and can alert him via a microphone built into his touch flag. In matches at the lower levels, a touch judge alerts the referee by holding the flag horizontally and pointing infield at a right angle to the touchline.

After you've watched a few games, you begin to realize that the touch judges are almost as important as the referee, and have to be as fit and alert as the one with the whistle.

## The substitution official: The one with the numbers

In the not-so-distant old days of rugby, it was rare for the 15 starting players of a match not to be the same players who finished it. In international matches a doctor used to have to certify that an injured player was no longer able to continue before he could be replaced. With the liberalization of the substitution law, which encourages coaches to make numerous changes as a strategic matter of course, the need arose for an extra official to supervise this activity.

The substitution official, sometimes called a reserve touch judge, handles the parade of players entering and exiting the pitch for trips to the blood bin, the sin bin, and the subbing and replacing of individuals from the reserve bench. For changes made by the coaching staff, this official will hold up two numbers, one for the player leaving the game and the other for the one joining it, letting spectators and the referee know exactly who is contesting the match at all times.

The duties don't stop there, though, because the substitution official has to be wary of teams trying to get around the various substitution laws through nefarious means. And the reason why this person has to be a qualified referee is that on rare occasions the match referee will suffer an injury and have to be replaced by one of the touch judges, necessitating the substitution official's move up the ladder to touch judge.

## *The TMO: The one with the video screen*

At most major rugby matches involving professionals, a referee is also required for a fourth important job, the television match official (TMO), or video referee. The TMO spends the game in a quiet room somewhere in the stadium perched in front of a television set. You may be thinking this sounds like quite a cozy little job, but keep in mind that the video referee has to be an actual referee because it requires someone with an intimate knowledge of the laws.

The video referee's role has expanded from when it was first introduced. Initially, only in-goal decisions could be considered and the referee had to ask specific questions of exactly what he wanted to be reviewed. The original purpose was basically to determine whether or not a try had been scored, as well as other in-goal issues, but that responsibility has evolved into helping the referee to identify players who have been involved in committing foul play.

### *Scoring a try*

When referees are uncertain whether a player has properly grounded the ball on or over the tryline, they make a hand signal that resembles a mime outlining a large imaginary box, to indicate a television screen. This means they've asked for the video referee to watch a replay of the incident and determine whether or not someone actually scored a try. At the same time, the referee contacts the video referee via a radio microphone hookup and explains what he wants the video referee to look for. Usually the video referee watches the play several times before informing the referee whether a try was scored. Occasionally, the replay won't definitively show the incident in question; in this case, the TMO will send it back to the referee without a recommendation. Either way, the final decision rests with the referee on the field.

### *Identifying foul play*

Beginning in 2003, the TMO was given the added burden of figuring out who was involved in an incident of foul play if the offender couldn't be singled out by the referee or the touch judges. The referee contacts the TMO and asks for help in unmasking the offender. In this case, the video referee can only look at the incident specified by the referee.

# *Recognizing the Referee's Signals*

If you're watching the match on television you have the advantage of being able to listen to the referee's calls, because they now wear microphones. Having the referees miked allows you to hear what they say to the players in the heat of battle; it also lets you eavesdrop on their conversations with touch judges and the TMO.

Many signals a referee makes are somewhat understandable because they mimic the infraction being called. Referees give signals to indicate what penalties have been given, all scoring plays, and whether a team has been awarded a free kick or advantage in play. The referee also signals when the clock is stopped. While the time left in the game is often shown on the scoreboard, remember that the referee is the final arbiter of time — what he says, goes.

Some signals are not so easily understood, though, and may take a little time to learn. But don't worry; the signaling system becomes very clear when you can identify each specific signal. The signals you'll see the referee make during a rugby match are shown in Figure 5-1.

**Figure 5-1:** The referee's signaling system.

Penalty kick

Free kick

Try and penalty try

Advantage

Scrum awarded

Forming a scrum

Throw-forward/ forward pass

Knock-on

Not immediately releasing ball in the tackle

Tackler not letting go of tackled player

Tackler or tackled player not rolling away

Entering tackle from wrong side

Unplayable ball at ruck or tackle

Diving to ground near tackle

Intentionally falling on a player

Intentionally bringing down a ruck or maul

Entering a ruck or a maul in front of the back foot and from the side

Unplayable ball in maul

Prop drawing down opponent

Prop pulling opponent

Wheeling scrum more than 90 degrees

Foot-up by front row player

Throw-in at scrum not straight

Failure to bind fully

Handling ball in ruck or scrum

Throw-in at line-out not straight

Closing gaps in line-out

Barging in line-out

Leaning on player in line-out

Pushing opponent in line-out

Off-side at scrum, ruck, or maul

Off-side at line-out

Obstruction in general play

High tackle (foul play)

Off-side option: penalty kick or scrum

Off-side under 10-meter law or not 10 meters at penalty and free kicks

Dissent (contesting referee's call)

Award of drop-out at the 22-meter line

Punching (foul play)

Physiotherapist needed

Stamping (foul play: inappropriate use of boot)

Ball held up in in-goal

Timekeeper to stop and start watch

Doctor needed

Bleeding wound

# Chapter 6

# Understanding the Fundamentals

● ● ● ● ● ● ● ● ● ● ● ● ● ● ● ● ● ● ● ● ● ● ● ● ● ● ● ● ● ● ● ● ● ● ● ● ● ● ● ● ● ● ● ● ● ● ● ●

## *In This Chapter*

▶ Knowing the aim of the game

▶ Moving the ball down the pitch

▶ Taking advantage of opposition mistakes

▶ Appreciating continuity at the tackle

▶ Taking advantage of the advantage law

▶ Understanding the all-important offside law

▶ Detailing foul play

● ● ● ● ● ● ● ● ● ● ● ● ● ● ● ● ● ● ● ● ● ● ● ● ● ● ● ● ● ● ● ● ● ● ● ● ● ● ● ● ● ● ● ● ● ● ● ●

*U*nderstanding the fundamentals of the game is the first step to becoming a full-fledged rugby enthusiast. Whether you're a player, spectator, parent, or coach, being familiar with the basic principles will make every rugby experience better and more fulfilling.

When you first watch rugby on TV or in person, it can appear confusing as 30 players run around the pitch in what appears to be semi-organized chaos. Their collective actions are mysteriously orchestrated by the whistle-blowing referee, who shouts indecipherable commands and periodically stops and starts play at seemingly random spots on the pitch. That's how we first saw rugby as well, attracted to the overall physicality of the sport but lacking even the most basic grasp of what was happening.

Our knowledge of the game developed from asking questions of more erudite fans along the sidelines and using the trial-and-error method on the playing field. Many light bulbs of awareness have gone off in our heads over the years as murky concepts suddenly became clear while watching and playing in countless matches. In this chapter, we discuss the object of the game, detail the skills that every rugby player needs, and clarify some of the most confusing rugby regulations, so you'll be able to bypass the initial confusion stage and move right into understanding the action.

# *The Object of the Game*

The game of rugby has one simple objective — to score more points than the opposition. This is an aim common to most ball sports, but where rugby differs is that the laws of the game prescribe that it be done by carrying, passing, kicking, and grounding the ball, and, most importantly, by observing fair play and doing it all with a sporting spirit.

Although individual positions have specific duties, all players are allowed to participate in offensive and defensive aspects of the game and thus must have a universal set of skills enabling them to do so.

Accumulating points in rugby can only be done by possessing the ball, either in scoring tries or kicking goals. This has led coaches and strategists down divergent paths with the same endpoint. Some focus on building excellent defensive teams that can withstand pressure and ultimately create enough turnovers and mistakes to produce opportunities to score points. Another school of thought stresses attacking prowess, placing a premium on creativity and speed.

Both approaches attempt to build squads that can capitalize on the concepts of interaction between offense and defense inherent in the laws of the game. The best teams are ones that master both disciplines and easily transition from one mode to the other. Too much emphasis on either one leads to a concentration of players without sufficient overall skills, exposing exploitable weaknesses.

## Running with the ball

Until I reached college, the only sport I played competitively was baseball. At Occidental College I decided to play football in my freshman year, and after one look at my bulky frame the coach declared that I was an offensive lineman. I didn't mind the physical contact involved but never really grasped the intricacies of the lineman's art needed to be successful. I felt I would have been better as a defensive player but the coaches deemed otherwise and I stayed at guard. Then in the off-season I discovered rugby. Suddenly, I was both an offensive and a defensive player. I was allowed to make tackles on ball-carriers of all sizes in addition to having a designated role in scrummaging and at line-outs. Best of all, I was encouraged to run with the ball and force others to tackle me. This opened up a whole new world of sporting enjoyment. I was actually playing an entire game instead of just fulfilling a narrow set of arcane duties. Once the athletic fullness of rugby came into my life, I never put on a helmet again.

# Running, Passing, and Kicking

Because the key to rugby is scoring points, the obvious requirement is to move the ball toward the opposition's half of the field to either ground the ball in their in-goal for a try or to get into range to successfully make a kick at goal. All the while, the defense will be attempting to stop this progress downfield. The three ways that teams change their position on the field are by running, passing, and kicking the ball.

## Running

Any of the 30 players on the pitch can run with the ball to their heart's content, provided they can maintain possession. Being a valued ball-runner entails never losing possession of the ball, either when tackled or by throwing errant passes. Unless you're superhuman, odds are pretty good that you're going to be tackled before you reach the tryline. To avoid being brought down, you can pass the ball backward to a teammate who is behind you.

## Passing

Requirement number one in passing the rugby ball is that all passes must go either backward or exactly horizontal, often called a *flat pass*. This standard is in relation to a team's own tryline, not the position of the player. If a player throws the ball and it travels parallel to the tryline then it's a legal pass. If its arc takes it anywhere behind that parallel line then it's also perfectly acceptable. (Illegal forward passes are discussed a little later in this section. A variety of passing styles are explained in Chapter 10.)

## Kicking

The third method of advancing the ball downfield is by kicking it. Every player is allowed to kick the ball, but most coaches want this chore to be handled by backs unless circumstances dictate otherwise. There are a number of different types of kicks, but they fall into three general categories: short, medium, and long. (We go over these kicks in greater detail and give them specific names in Chapter 10.)

---

# Creating space

By first running and then passing the ball at just the right time and place, you can draw the defenders to you, thereby *creating space* for your teammate to carry on with the charge. The ability to create space, or to entice the defenders in your immediate area to focus on you and therefore forget about your supporting teammates, is a critical skill that can make a good player into a great one. If you can draw the defenders slightly away from where the attack will come next and then time your pass perfectly, you'll have created space and unlocked the secret to winning rugby. The key here is that

you never want the player receiving the pass to be in a worse attacking position than you were. Passing the ball should be done to accomplish something. Simply passing because you're about to be tackled, without considering whether the receiver is in a position to advance the attack, will not help your team and may get your best buddy injured.

In rugby parlance, throwing a ball that forces your teammate into a defenseless position as he attempts to catch it, setting him up for a monstrous hit by the tackler, is called a *hospital pass*.

---

Short kicks, whether along the ground or in the air, are usually designed to be regathered by the kicker and then carried farther. These kicks make sense when the defensive line has come up fast and flat, cutting down the space and time available to run or pass the ball through them.

Medium kicks are mostly booted high in the air to test the catching abilities of the opposition under pressure as members of the kicker's team converge on them. If the chasers, or the fastest of the kicker's teammates, get there in time, they can contest the ball in the air.

Kicking also plays a crucial role in field position. Because it's harder to score points from your half of the field, you need a reliable kicker who can punt it long with good accuracy, to move play into your opponent's half of the pitch.

Long kicks are meant to gobble up large chunks of territory in one fell swoop. When a team is backed up behind its own 22-meter line these kicks are generally intended to go over the touchline so that play can be restarted with a line-out. At other times, long kicks are supposed to stay in the field of play and are followed up by marauding defenders to attack the ball-carrier before his teammates can retreat in time to help out.

# What Can Go Wrong?

If rugby just involved players running, passing, and kicking the ball up and down the pitch unopposed, it would be about as exciting as lawn bowling. What makes the sport a thrilling spectacle is that for every player attempting to run, pass, or kick, there is a corresponding player doing his darndest to prevent that from happening. When athletes collide in any competitive endeavor errors are bound to occur, especially if the goal of one team is to force the other into making mistakes. In rugby, these mistakes have specific names — and the two most common involve ball-handling.

## Knock-on

The most recognizable form of a knock-on looks very much like a fumble in football. A knock-on happens when a ball-carrier loses control of the ball for whatever reason and it goes forward (meaning toward the opponent's dead-ball line) and touches any other player or the ground before the player can regather the ball. If the ball goes flat or backward, that's not an infraction. The same is true if a player bobbles the ball in the air but is able to haul it back in before it touches the ground or any another player.

A knock-on is also called when the ball hits a player's arm or hand — whether they're trying to catch it or not — and bounces forward. The distance the ball travels forward is irrelevant; it can be a couple of centimeters or 9 meters, it's still a knock-on. Barely nudging the ball ahead with your hand while trying to pick it up is the same as having it ripped from your grasp in a tackle.

A ball that bounces off a player's head, chest, or shoulder is not a knock-on, provided that no hands or arms are involved. It's embarrassing to get hit in the face with the ball when it's passed to you — but it's a relief when the referee shouts, "Off the head, play on!"

 The one exception to the knock-on law is when a player is trying to block, or charge down a kick. The law is written to reward aggressive play, so if the ball hits the outstretched hand or arm of a player while he's attempting to block a kick it's not an infringement as long as the player doesn't try to catch it.

If play stops after a knock-on (see the advantage law section for when play stops and when it doesn't) the non-offending team gets to put the ball in at a scrum on the spot where it occurred. A knock-on then, in effect is usually a turnover by the team that had the ball.

---

## Mistakes — Intentional and otherwise

Rugby referees have to be some of the most perceptive beings on the planet, because they're called upon to determine intent as well as assign blame for mistakes on the field. A number of errors, when they occur in general play and there is no hint of purpose behind them, result in a scrum to the non-offending team. A knock-on is one such case. If, however, the referee thinks a player intentionally knocked a ball on in an attempt to spoil the offensive move to keep it from going quickly out wide, that is dealt with by awarding a penalty to the other side — giving them possession and a better tactical position than a scrum.

---

This is why coaches should always place an emphasis in training on practicing the basic handling skills. The better your team handles the ball, the less likely they are to knock it on during the game.

## Forward pass

Throwing the ball forward — meaning toward the opponent's dead-ball ine — is strictly prohibited. If you pass the ball and it travels forward as it leaves your hands, you've made a forward pass. From the safety of the sidelines a forward pass seems eminently avoidable. In the heat of battle, passing the ball forward is easier than it looks. Location on the pitch becomes jumbled and pressure from tacklers can be intense, causing wayward passes that are intended to follow the tenets of the law but somehow run afoul of it.

Once again there is an exception. If the ball is thrown backward and hits the ground and then bounces forward, it's not an infraction. The same exception applies if a pass is released backward and the wind catches it and takes it forward. You are responsible only for what you do with the ball, not what the ground or the elements cause it to do.

A good way to judge whether a pass is forward or not is to imagine a line running through the ball that is parallel to the goal lines at either end of the field. A pass that goes along that line or behind it is legal; a pass in front of it is illegal. (The same standard helps determine whether a ball has been knocked on.)

# The Tackle Law — Where Football Ends, Rugby Begins

When football emerged from the sport of rugby early in the 20th century, the biggest initial change was the concept of ending each play when the ball-carrier was tackled. In football, that's the signal for everyone to stop playing and head back to their respective huddles and spend the better part of the following minute getting ready for the next five seconds of action. In rugby, after the ball-carrier is tackled the game continues and gets even more interesting. What happens next may seem muddled and disorganized, but if you know what to look for it's actually well orchestrated and usually follows several different laws that govern the tackle situation, or what is known as the *breakdown.*

## The tackle situation and continuity

For years, rugby administrators at the International Rugby Board (IRB) have been fiddling around with the tackle laws in a bid to quicken the game. The admirable intention has been to speed up the process of making the ball available for further play. Concerned that matches were being slowed down by unsightly pile-ups of bodies fighting for the ball, the lawmakers have tried to simplify things. The result has been the assigning of responsibilities to both the tackler and the tackled player which, if unfulfilled, draw the referee's whistle and the awarding of a penalty. Even though the changes have been somewhat effective, this is still the most contentious area of the game.

The tackle law is written like this: "A tackle occurs when a ball-carrier, in a standing position, is simultaneously held by one or more opponents, and is brought to the ground, and/or the ball touches the ground. That player is known as the tackled player. Any opponents of the tackled player who go to ground are known as tacklers." The definition of "brought to ground" includes a player who is on one knee, sitting on the ground, or on top of another player.

## The tackled player

When players are tackled, they must immediately let go of the ball when their bodies hit the ground and their momentum stops so that play can continue. It's illegal to lie on the ground and keep tight hold of the ball. Tackled players must either pass the ball immediately or release it at once by placing it on the ground in any direction (ideally the ball should be placed backward, but that isn't always possible).

When the tackled player has released the ball he must attempt to roll away from the area — which in practice means that he can't lie on top of the ball, and can have no further involvement in play until he regains his feet. If the tackled player tries to play the ball in any way while still on the ground, he is liable to be penalized.

As a ball-carrier, your primary goal is to not lose possession of the ball for your team, whether you are on your feet or on the ground. Therefore, the best thing to do when being tackled is to manipulate your body position so that you fall with the tackler on the opposite side from where your team-mates are. That way, when you release the ball back, your team will have first crack at securing possession and the opponents will have to step over both the tackler and you to grab the ball. (We offer more tips for the tackled player in Chapter 7.)

## The tackler

When a player tackles an opponent and they both go to ground, the tackler must immediately release the tackled player. Then he must immediately get to his feet or move away from the tackled player and roll away from the ball. Exactly how far away the tackler must roll is not defined, but it's clear he must not interfere with play until he's back on his feet. If he makes the mistake of grabbing the ball while he's still on the ground, he attracts the whistle and the opposition is awarded a penalty.

If by the time he gets to his feet a ruck is already formed, he cannot then play the ball because he is now subject to the ruck law, which we discuss fully in Chapter 7. After a tackle, all other players must be on their feet when they play the ball. Players are on their feet if no other parts of their body are supported by the ground or by players on the ground.

## Tackling no-no's

In addition to the restrictions we've just described, the following rules also apply:

- A player cannot stop a tackled player from passing the ball.
- A player cannot stop a tackled player from releasing the ball, or from getting up and moving away from it.
- A player is not allowed to pull the ball from a tackled player before the tackled player has released it.
- A player may not fall on or over the tackled player.

What happens if the ball doesn't come out? Sometimes so many bodies are heaped together on the ground that neither the tackler or tackled player can move away no matter how hard the players try. If the ball becomes unplayable at a tackle the referee orders a scrum, with the put-in given to the team that was moving forward prior to the stoppage. If no team was moving forward, the scrum feed goes to the attacking team. Most tackles turn into rucks soon afterward — we cover how and why that occurs in Chapter 7.

# *The Advantage Law — When Play Stops and When It Continues*

When you watch a rugby match you'll notice that some of the things we describe in this chapter happen, yet play doesn't stop. Even those who are more familiar with the game may ask, "Why not?" The answer is because of the advantage law, which allows play to continue even after an infraction has been committed. The goal of the law is to keep play flowing by minimizing stoppages. The referees who tend to earn the highest accolades in the public's eyes — meaning they're the least complained about — are the ones who properly utilize this critical piece of judicial wisdom.

The advantage law is easy to understand if thought about in the right way. Simply put, when one team commits an infraction, the other team is afforded the opportunity to gain an advantage from the mistake. Instead of immediately blowing the whistle for every little blunder, the referee lets play continue, waiting to see if the non-offending team can profit from the miscue.

Let's say, for instance, that a player from the United States is running with the ball and is tackled hard by a player from Canada. When she hits the ground the ball spills forward from her hands. That's a classic knock-on. But instead of stopping play with a whistle blast, the referee calls out "Advantage Canada" (or more likely identifies the team by the color of jersey the players are wearing) and points an arm in their direction. Now the Canadian team knows they can try to make the best of the situation on attack. If they're successful and can capitalize on the error, the referee will call out "Advantage over" and the contest progresses without play being interrupted. If they're stopped or otherwise stymied in taking their opportunity, the referee will blow the whistle and bring the teams back to the spot of the infringement for a scrum, where the ball will be put in by the Canadian scrumhalf.

So what exactly does a team have to do to gain an advantage? Referees consider two criteria: territorial and tactical. To illustrate, we go back to our North American example.

To gain a territorial advantage, the Canadian team would have to advance the ball beyond where it was originally knocked on by the American player and end up gaining more territory than if the referee had ordered a scrum. They could accomplish this by running it downfield or kicking it and having it go out farther down the touchline. Territorial advantage gained must be clear and real — the possibility of gaining it is not enough to forestall a stoppage in play.

A tactical advantage can be gained by a team having the freedom to use the ball as they wish. In the same example, if the Canadian team decided to pass the ball out wide along the back line to give their winger some space to run, they might have gained a tactical advantage even if they didn't get past the point of the original infringement. Referees have to ask themselves, "Was the team able to make a conscious choice to employ a tactic that would have gained them an advantage?" Whether or not the option was successful is irrelevant.

Tactical advantage is harder for referees to judge than territorial because it involves more interpretation, whereas a territorial gain is easy to discern with the naked eye.

One of the oldest coaching sayings is directly related to advantage. Coaches from the international level down to the beginners should always encourage their charges to "play to the whistle." Newcomers to the game will often see an opponent make a mistake and immediately let up, assuming that the referee is going to blow the whistle. If you train your team members to continue playing at full speed, they'll have more chances to cash in on the opposition's errors. Besides, you never know if the referee will see every infraction.

The advantage law takes precedence over the rest of the laws because it's responsible for cutting down on the number of times the action is halted for inevitable infringements. Advantage can be played for all but five situations in a game of rugby; these instances are safety-oriented, and four of them deal with scrums.

A whistle must be blown at once with no consideration for advantage when:

- ✔ A player is lifted in the air on a scrum.
- ✔ The scrum collapses.
- ✔ The scrum is wheeled around more than 90 degrees.
- ✔ The ball comes straight out the other side of the tunnel from where the ball was put into the scrum by the scrumhalf.
- ✔ The ball, or a player carrying it, touches the referee.

Players with a good tactical head on their shoulders have figured out an interesting use of the advantage law that might help you score some extra points for your team. If you are within range of the goalposts and you hear the advantage call, try to make a drop goal. If it goes over the post, great, you've added three points to your team's score. If you miss, it's no big deal, because the referee will bring it back to the original spot of the infraction. When you're trying this, be sure you take the drop right away while the advantage is still on, otherwise you might waste a shot at goal that you could have gotten from the penalty kick.

# *Observing the Offside Law*

Without doubt, the most important rugby law involves what is offside and what is onside in general play. Like soccer, rugby is a sport that revolves around the offside law. The main difference is that in soccer, offside is really only a concern near the goals, whereas in rugby, offside is in operation from end to end and sideline to sideline.

Spectators and players alike are often totally bewildered by the offside law, but it really is quite simple, as we explain.

## *In general play*

A player is *offside* in general play if he is in front of a teammate who is carry-ing the ball, or in front of a teammate who last played the ball. If you are behind a ball-carrying teammate, you are *onside*.

Players who are offside are temporarily out of the game and should either stay where they are or get back onside. Figure 6-1 shows a team moving toward the opposition's tryline, with two players in the offside position.

To get back onside (and thus be able to take part in the game again), a player must retreat behind the ball. A player can return to being onside in one of four ways:

- ✔ The offside player runs behind the teammate who last kicked, touched, or carried the ball.
- ✔ A teammate carrying the ball runs in front of the offside player.
- ✔ A teammate who has kicked the ball forward runs in front of the offside player.
- ✔ A teammate runs past the offside player toward the opponent's tryline.

A player can also be put onside by a member of the opposition in three ways:

- ✔ An opponent carrying the ball runs 5 meters.
- ✔ An opponent kicks or passes the ball.
- ✔ An opponent intentionally touches the ball, but does not catch it.

**Teammates offside**

**Player with the ball**

**Team running this way**

**Figure 6-1:** Players who are offside are temporarily out of the game.

When an offside player cannot avoid being touched by the ball or by a teammate carrying it, the player is *accidentally offside*. If the player's team gets no benefit from this (meaning that no potential tacklers were blocked by the action), play continues. If the player's team does benefit because the offending player shielded the ball-carrier from a defender, a scrum is formed with the opposing team putting in the ball. The same applies when a ball-carrier hands the ball to a teammate who is in front of him. If it's accidental, it's remedied with a scrum to the opposition.

A good way to remember this law is to imagine you're the player with the ball. Everyone who is on your team and who is behind you is onside, and any teammate who is in front of you is offside. That should give you a better understanding of the most mysterious law of rugby.

### Being penalized for going offside

At some stage of the game, all players find themselves offside. However, it's important to remember that players are not penalized for being in an offside position unless they:

✔ Interfere with play

✔ Move forward toward the ball

✔ Fail to comply with the 10-meter law (we talk about this little beauty in the next section)

If the referee catches you offside — and you are offending — he awards the opposition a penalty (we discuss all the options after a penalty has been awarded at the end of this section). When a player knocks the ball on, a team-mate who happens to be in front of him can be penalized for playing the ball if he prevents an opponent from trying to play on.

Offside players must be careful that they're not caught *loitering*. This quaint rugby term refers to someone who is standing or retreating in an offside position and preventing the opposing team from playing the ball as they wish. Former South African whistle-blower Andre Watson — now the director of referees in his home country — popularized the term *lazy runner* to denote this individual. If you find yourself in this situation either fall back or get out of the way completely, or you'll attract the ire of the referee!

The offside law may sound rather tricky, but one simple solution applies if you are concerned about getting a penalty for being offside — get back behind your teammates before rejoining the fray.

### Crossing the 10-meter line

Players are penalized if they fail to comply with the 10-meter law. This law applies when a player kicks the ball ahead and a teammate is standing in an offside position in front of the kicker. The offside player is prohibited from moving toward the opposition or going within 10 meters of where the opponent is waiting to play the ball.

The offside player is considered to be illegally taking part in the game if he is in front of an imaginary line that runs the width of the field, which is 10 meters in front of the opponent waiting to play the ball, or from where the ball lands. The offside player must immediately retire behind the imaginary 10-meter line. If he doesn't, the referee penalizes him for being offside and intentionally obstructing an opponent by awarding the opposition a penalty.

Figure 6-2 shows a player who is inside the 10-meter line and who must move back behind it or be penalized.

The opposition player
receiving the ball

10 meters

Imaginary 10-meter line

Team running
this way

Teammate
who is offside
and who must
move back

The player kicking the ball

**Figure 6-2:**
Move back
or break the
10-meter
law.

While retiring, the offside player cannot be put onside by the opposing team. However, before the player has moved the full 10 meters, the player can be made legal by any onside teammate who runs in front of him. The key here is that he must be retreating when passed. If he is standing there waiting, he cannot be put onside.

## From set pieces

The offside laws are slightly different for the *set pieces* — which are scrums and line-outs. At a scrum, the offside line for every player except the scrumhalf runs through the hindmost foot of that player's team in the scrum. This is usually the number 8, so all of the back-line players have to stay behind this player's back foot. The offside line for scrumhalves is a line running through the ball, allowing them to follow the ball as it makes its way toward the back of the scrum. This law is in place to ensure the team that wins the ball has clear space to use it (we give more comprehensive details about the scrum in Chapter 8). The only players who ever really get called for being offside at the scrum are the scrumhalves, and even then very rarely. The IRB is considering changing this law to make the offside line 5 meters behind the last foot in the scrum.

At a line-out there are two separate offside lines parallel to the goal lines for each team. One offside line is for the players taking part in the line-out (the ones standing there waiting for the ball to be thrown in). Until the ball has been thrown in and has touched a player or the ground, this offside line runs down the middle of the two sets of forwards on a line from where the ball was thrown. After that, the offside line is wherever the ball is. Basically, this is to keep players from crossing over the initial line until the ball can be played. Players in the line-out are also prohibited from crossing the 15-meter mark infield before the ball is thrown in. If they do so, they're considered to have left the line-out and are thus offside and subject to penalty.

The other offside line applies to the players not taking part in the line-out, usually the backs waiting for the ball to be passed out to them. For the backs, the offside line is 10 meters behind where the ball is being thrown in from, or their goal line if that is nearer. Until the line-out is over the back-line players cannot advance beyond that line. If not closely watched by the referee, backs are naturally inclined to edge forward in anticipation of getting their hands on the ball or putting themselves in better position defensively to stop the expected attack.

## At tackles, rucks, and mauls

The offside laws for tackles, rucks, and mauls are similar to those highlighted above, with minor differences specific to the nature of each situation. After a tackle is made, if a tackler gets to his feet and plays the ball before a ruck has formed there is no offside line. Any other player attempting to pick up the ball must enter the area from a position on his side of the tackled player, no matter when he gets there. This forces other players to get back behind the tackle before playing the ball.

The sight of the ball on the ground must hit a certain circuit in some players' brains that turns them from thinking individuals to starving hyenas after a piece of meat, willing to risk anything to possess it. Not getting back behind the offside line before entering the tackle area will more often result in a negative outcome than in a successful poaching of the ball. The best thieves at the tackle situation are the ones who use their wits first and their quickness second.

A *ruck* is the term used when the ball is on the ground and at least two players from each team are in contact over it. After a ruck has been formed there are two offside lines. Each offside line runs through the rear foot of the player farthest back in the ruck, parallel with the goal line. A player may join the ruck alongside the last player — but not from the side, or he is liable to be penalized. If you are not part of the ruck you can't be in front of this line. (We provide more information about this in Chapter 7.)

Rucks are not neat, tidy things, so sometimes the temptation to help out in a hurry is greater than the discipline needed to join in at the proper place. Keep in mind that it doesn't help your team to win the ball only to have it given back by a penalty called against you.

It's virtually the same story for a *maul,* which happens when a player carrying the ball is held by one or more opponents: one or more of the ball-carrier's teammates then bind on the ball-carrier, and everyone involved is on their feet. Once again there are two offside lines parallel to the goal lines, one for each team. Players joining the maul have to do so from behind or alongside the hindmost foot of the player bringing up the rear of the maul. If you aren't joining the maul you have to stay behind this last player's foot. (Mauls are discussed in more detail in Chapter 7.) In most mauls there is usually an inviting place to slot into on the side, but you must resist the urge to do so.

Being offside at any of these phases of play is punishable by a penalty awarded to the non-offending team at the spot where the player was judged to be offside.

# Playing Foul

The laws are written with an eye toward proportional punishment, reflecting a widely held belief that the penalty should fit the crime. The foul play law has four parts — obstruction, unfair play, repeated infringements, and misconduct — with progressively stiffer sanctions meted out to wrongdoers.

## Obstruction

The first level of foul play is obstruction. When a player and an opponent are running for the ball, the players cannot charge or push each other. Other players cannot run in front of the player carrying the ball or block the tackler. This transgression is dealt with by calling a simple penalty. This is generally considered to be a heat-of-the-moment type offense.

# Unfair play

The second level of foul play is unfair play. These are intentional actions in direct opposition to the laws and result in a penalty and sometimes a warning that continuation of said behavior will be severely dealt with. A player cannot waste time by making the ball unavailable to an opposition player, throw the ball into touch or over the dead-ball line to slow the game down or prevent an attacking movement, or repeatedly commit the same penalty. If done subtly, the best players can get away with these callous infractions by hiding their intentions from the referee, but normally that works only once.

# Repeated infringements

The third level of foul play is repeated infringements, which are judged to be even more cynical and disruptive than unfair play. Rucks and the tackle area seem to breed this type of behavior. After a player or a team has committed several of the same infringements, drawing a penalty each time, they are cautioned. If the behavior persists, the player must be shown a yellow card.

A yellow card forces the player into the sin bin for ten minutes to think about his evil ways, forcing his teammates to soldier on with 14 men on the field. If he doesn't demonstrate he's learned his lesson upon returning to action, the next step is a red card, signifying total banishment for the remainder of the match.

# Misconduct

The fourth level of foul play is reserved for the most serious type of misconduct. A player cannot punch, strike, stamp, trample, kick, or trip an opponent. A player must not tackle an opponent above the shoulders, tackle an opponent who has jumped into the air to catch a high ball, or "late charge" someone who has kicked the ball. A *late charge* means to tackle or hit someone late, or well after the ball has left the area. Depending upon the severity of the misconduct, most often reflective of the referee's perception of malicious intent on the part of the offender, either a yellow or red card will be issued.

With the advent of television coverage at almost every major match, players guilty of misconduct are also subject to citing commissions that can issue suspensions and fines for an offense that the referee or his touch judges didn't see. Citing commissions usually consist of three officials who conduct a hearing with the offending player present to determine whether the player should be suspended for the offense. If the commission rules against him, the player may be suspended for further matches, depending upon the severity of the misconduct and his previous disciplinary record.

# Taking penalties

A multitude of actions on the rugby pitch can cause the referee to award a penalty. The primary result of being awarded a penalty is that your team gets possession of the ball and a choice of options on how to use it. The decision on what to do on the field rests with your captain, and the choice is governed by field position, how the match is progressing, time left, and the score.

The captain on a rugby team is responsible for making all the on-field decisions during the match, and must be a rugby-savvy individual with a command of the strategic nuances of the game.

# Kicking at goal

When your team is awarded a penalty kick, one of the options is to take a shot at scoring three points by attempting a penalty goal. To do this the captain or kicker informs the referee that the team wants to kick for goal. Once chosen, no other options are allowed. Unless a law states otherwise, the mark for a penalty is at the place of infringement. On a penalty-kick attempt, the opposing team must stand still with their hands by their sides from the time the kicker starts his approach until the ball is kicked. After receiving the tee from the sidelines, there's a one-minute time limit on taking the kick. When the ball is kicked it's live again and in play.

The decision to take a shot at goal is determined by a number of situational factors. The game score, time remaining, kicker's range, and the relative difficulty of scoring tries all figure large in the calculus of whether or not to kick for goal.

# Kicking for touch

Another option is to gain territory by kicking the ball downfield into touch. Normally a ball kicked into touch results in a line-out with the other team throwing the ball in, but on a penalty kick possession is retained by the kicking team. The key is to make sure the kick actually goes out of bounds. Most teams decide to do this if they're out of the range of their goal kicker or if they need to score more than three points.

## Choosing a scrum

A third choice for the non-offending team is to have a scrum formed at the place of the infringement with their put-in. This is a strategic decision that is usually made when there isn't enough time left to choose a line-out or when a team doubts their ability to get the ball to their jumpers. Also, an attacking scrum is a very difficult situation to defend against, even more so when the spot of the penalty is close to the defending side's goal line.

## Taking it quick

A *quick tap* occurs when the non-offending team immediately kicks the ball *through the mark* and continues play as soon as a penalty has been given by the referee. Through the mark means that the kicker must kick the ball a visible distance at or directly behind the spot where the penalty has been awarded. If the kicker is holding the ball, it must clearly leave his hands. If the ball is on the ground, it must clearly leave the mark.

Taking a *quick tap* can be an extremely effective weapon because the opposition's defense has little time to react and realign. However, this choice should be used judiciously, because when you take it quick, you're giving up a shot at three points, or a chance to gain territory.

A team also has the option of kicking through the mark and attempting to run the ball straight at the opponents or to use a designed play, particularly when they're close to the tryzone. This type of quick tap is referred to as a *tap and go*.

## Free kicks

A lesser degree of infraction, usually for technical violations rather than conduct, is called a *free kick*. The signal for a free kick also differs from a penalty, signified by a bent arm raised in the direction of the team that will get the ball (see the "Recognizing the Referee's Signals" section in Chapter 5 to see what this looks like). This gives the non-offending team possession but with far fewer benefits than a "straight-arm" penalty. A scrum is one choice available on a free kick, but kicking for goal is not. When kicking for touch from a free kick, possession is not retained at the ensuing line-out and ground is gained only if the kicker is behind his team's 22-meter line, making this an unattractive choice (the hows and whys of line-outs are covered in Chapter 9).

# Chapter 7

# Playing the Game

· · · · · · · · · · · · · · · · · · · · · · · · · · · · · · · · · · · · · · · · · · · · · · ·

## In This Chapter

▶ Starting and restarting the match

▶ Defining tackler and tacklee

▶ Understanding the breakdown

▶ Differentiating among the tackle, ruck, and maul

▶ Recognizing the ruck

▶ Manipulating the maul

· · · · · · · · · · · · · · · · · · · · · · · · · · · · · · · · · · · · · · · · · · · · · · ·

At the heart of rugby is the notion that in every situation there must be a fair contest for the ball. The laws of the game have changed over the years to promote this goal, and as a result the game has become faster and more technically demanding of all the players on the pitch.

The modern game is meant to be continuous and fast-moving with as few stoppages as possible. If players just ran around from end to end this could be easily accomplished, but the confrontational nature of the sport demands that one team try to stop the other from advancing whenever possible. This inevitably leads to contests for the ball that develop spontaneously after each tackle. Understanding what happens after a player has been tackled is at the core of developing a thorough knowledge for both fans and players.

The key to being a good rugby player is to understand the strictures governing each particular part of the game, and then have the skills to excel in those areas. The key to understanding the game as a fan, then, is to be able to recognize what is happening as a match progresses, and to understand why the referees make the decisions they do.

In this chapter, we start where the game begins, with kickoffs and restarts, then give further details on the seemingly complicated activity that accompanies a ball-carrier being brought to ground. That leads us to a comprehensive examination of the breakdown, followed by a closer look at the laws governing rucks and mauls. (These parts of the game may seem chaotic at first glance, but once they're explained you'll see how organized they really are.)

# Getting Started

Starting a match is a facet of the game that has undergone a significant change in the last few years. At one time, a place kick was used to start each half. At some point, somebody clever read the law and saw that it allowed for a tee (approved by the union sanctioning the match) to be used for this purpose. This led to a frenzy of plastic tee designs that ended up looking like traffic cones. The goal was to help get the ball as high in the air as possible to make securing it much easier for the kicking team. Sensibly, the International Rugby Board (IRB) stepped in and mandated that all kicking restarts would henceforth be *drop kicks,* which are kicks that are dropped from the hand and hit the ground before the kicker's foot comes into contact with the ball. (See Chapter 2 for an example of this type of kick.)

## Kickoffs to begin each half

A kickoff is the first opportunity for both teams to contest possession of the ball. Before the game there's a meeting of both captains and the referee where a coin toss is made and the winning skipper chooses either to kick off or defend an end. (If the captain decides to kick off at the start of the first half, the other team will do so at the start of the second half.) The choice of ends is especially important when the wind is a factor.

Kickoffs are taken from the center of the halfway line (check out Chapter 2 for details about the lines on a rugby pitch). Most pitches will have a half-meter dash line to mark this spot and referees will often direct wayward kickers back to that spot if they attempt to go astray. If the ball is kicked from in front of the halfway line, or too far from the center, the referee can order that it be taken again.

Every player on the kicker's team must be behind the ball until it's struck (Figure 7-1 shows the formation of the players in a kickoff). They're allowed to get a running start but their timing has to be right so that they don't inadvertently pass the ball before it's airborne. If they're judged to be in front of the kicker, a scrum is formed in the center of the field with the opposition getting the put-in. This is an inexcusable mistake that drives coaches nuts because it gives a great attacking opportunity to the other team.

The players on the receiving squad (the team that isn't kicking) must line up behind their own 10-meter line. The receiving team has a distinct advantage over the team kicking because the players are able to lift the locks (see Chapter 4 for more details about this playing position) up in the air to take the ball, while the kicking team has to rely on regular jumping. (Remember, the kicker's teammates have to charge down the field after the ball; the opposition has the ball coming to them.)

**Figure 7-1:**
Kickoff
formation.

The ball must reach the opponent's 10-meter line for the kick to be legal. Remember, it's not where the ball hits the ground that determines whether it has traveled the required 10 meters. (See Figure 7-1 for the alignment of the kicking and receiving teams.)

If the kick crosses the 10-meter line in the air and is then blown back across the line by a stiff breeze, it's play on! Even if the kick doesn't reach the 10-meter line you keep playing, because the receiving team can choose to play the ball and you need to be ready to tackle them. If the ball fails to reach the 10-meter line and is not played by the receiving team, the referee will give them the option of having another kickoff or a scrum at midfield.

Your goal as the kicker is to put enough air under the ball to let your team-mates charge downfield and secure it before the other team can do so. The temptation is to try to kick it exactly 10 meters, but this is unwise because if the ball doesn't go at least that far it's also a scrum to the receiving team.

A ball that is kicked off directly into touch, or out of bounds on the fly, gives the non-kicking team three options. They can have the ball kicked off again, take a line-out on the halfway line, or have a scrum at midfield (with their put-in). A kickoff that goes into the in-goal area and is immediately grounded also produces a choice of a re-kick or a scrum at center.

Unless your team is getting pummeled in the scrums, instruct the captain to always take the midfield scrum over another kickoff. The scrum is a vastly superior attacking opportunity for your side because the key back-row defenders are required to stay bound-in while scrummaging, which provides more space for your backs to operate in the midfield. (For all the details about scrums, see Chapter 8.)

## Restarts after scores and 22s

In addition to beginning each half, kickoffs are used to restart the game after either team has scored a try, penalty try, penalty goal, or dropped goal. A great feature of rugby is that when you score, you automatically get another chance to regain the ball because the non-scoring team kicks off to the one that added to their scoreboard total. The same regulations that control kick-offs also apply to restart kicks.

A 22-meter drop-out (a drop kick) is used to restart play after the ball is grounded in the in-goal area by the defending team if the attacking team caused it to go in there. This usually happens if a missed penalty kick is caught and grounded by the opposing team, or if the ball goes over the dead-ball line. Another way the ball can end up in the defending team's in-goal area is when an offensive player kicks ahead in general play and loses the race to touch it down.

A 22-meter drop-out can be taken anywhere behind the 22-meter line — and, as with a kickoff, everyone on the kicker's team has to be behind the ball. The defense has a little more leeway here and can attempt to block the kick as long as they don't actually cross the 22-meter line in doing so.

If you're the player taking the drop-out, you can prevent your teammates from being offside (in front of the ball) by doing two things before you kick it. First, look both ways to see if any of your teammates are in front of you. If they are, wave them back. When they're all behind the ball, signal that you're about to take the restart before you kick it.

Just like kickoffs, if the ball crosses the 22-meter line in the air and is then blown back, play continues. Similarly, if the ball doesn't reach the 22-meter line you still need to remain vigilant, as the receiving team can choose to play the ball even if it doesn't cross the line.

If the kicker gives the drop kick a bit too much juice and it goes directly into touch on the fly, the receiving team can either take another drop-out, or opt for a scrum midfield on the 22 or a line-out at the 22-meter line.

Nothing gets under the skin of your forward pack like overcooked restart kicks that go directly into touch, forcing them to defend a scrum from a disadvantageous position. So, if you've been entrusted with the kicking duties and want to keep on good terms with the big folks up front, be sure to keep your drop-outs within the field of play.

Another recent strategic development involves players drop kicking the ball a foot or so over the 22-meter line and regathering it immediately. This is perfectly legal because the law requires only that the ball cross the line — 1 inch or 50 yards are both acceptable.

# The Tackle Situation

Unlike football, where the contest comes to a screeching halt after every tackle, in rugby tackles are part of a continuing sequence of play. Without proper regulation what happens at the tackle situation can degenerate into constant stoppages and continual blowing of the referee's whistle. The laws have evolved to prevent this from taking place, and to turn the tackle situation into a transitional phase for the next positive use of the ball.

In rugby, a tackle is made when a ball-carrier is brought to ground and held there. (It's also considered a tackle when the ball touches the ground while the ball-carrier is being held, or when the player is being held and is lying on another player.) *Brought to ground* means no longer on your feet, which includes having one knee down. Simply put, if you're held and don't have both feet on the ground, you're tackled. Being knocked to the ground without a tackler holding on is not a tackle, and you're free to get up and run some more. But if you're held, a different set of laws takes over and you've got some serious responsibilities to take care of.

## The tackled player

The ball-carrier who is brought to ground is known as the tackled player. The first requirement of the tackled player is to immediately make the ball available. The tackled player can place the ball in any direction, but the best choice is to direct it toward supporting teammates and away from opponents. The key is to release the ball under control, so that your side has the best chance to recycle possession. If able to do so, a tackled player can also pass the ball at once. In practice this means that as soon as the ball-carrier comes to a stop on the ground it's time to release the ball.

The most important thing to remember is that once you've been tackled you can't hold onto the ball, especially if someone on his feet is trying to take it from you. The continuity theory in effect here is that if a player isn't on his feet he can't play the ball anymore, so he has to make it available for other players to use.

The error that most new players make in running with the ball is that they don't plan for being tackled. A good player avoids tackles whenever possible but prepares for their eventuality by positioning his body so that when he is brought down he has control over the outcome. This means securing the ball on the way down to stop it from being ripped away, using strength to go to ground with his body between the tackler and the ball, and placing the ball so his cohorts can maintain possession for the next phase of attack.

## The tackler

The tackler is also charged with making sure the ball is immediately available for other players. The tackler's first act after going to ground must be to let the tackled player go so the ball can be freed. A player cannot wrestle the ball-carrier for possession while they're both on the ground. Holding the ball-carrier tight on the ground will draw the referee's whistle just as quickly as not releasing the ball.

The second duty is to get away from the ball. Letting go and then using the body to cover it up or slow it down is both illegal and dangerous because it will draw unfriendly boots to the tackler's prone figure.

The tackler is also restricted from any contact with the ball until he is back on his feet. Getting back up is the best course of action, because it allows the tackler the chance to pick up the ball. Unlike subsequent players who enter the area, the tackler is free to play the ball from any position as long as he has regained his feet. This advantage usually only lasts for a short time, until players from both sides arrive and change the nature of what's happening.

Just because your feet are on the ground doesn't necessarily mean you're "on your feet" for the purpose of playing the ball after the tackle. If any part of your body is supported by someone on the ground, it's the same as if you were flat on your back — you're not allowed to play the ball.

Stealing the ball after the tackle is one of the most effective ways to create turnovers in general play. Coaches should teach all of their players, from full-back to the front row, how to quickly get back on their feet after making a tackle so they can legally contest for possession of the ball. Then they should demonstrate the low-body position they'll need to reach in with both hands and steal the ball off the ground. Make sure players understand that as others arrive and the ruck forms, they need to obey if the referee yells, "Ruck formed, no hands" (we cover the rucking rules later in this chapter).

## What happens next?

In a perfect world, there would never be any need to stop play at a tackle situation because tacklers would release tackled players immediately, the ball would come free, and play would continue. It isn't always that cut-and-dried on the pitch, however, and the laws outlining what happens next reflect that reality. The term *breakdown* is a catchall for the multitude of things that can happen from when the ball-carrier is brought down to when the ball is next played.

# Breaking Down the Breakdown

Whenever the ball is on the ground after a tackle it's a free ball and both teams have full rights to it. The events at the breakdown are the hardest to adjudicate because everything happens so fast and the referee's vision is routinely obscured by players flying in and bodies piling up on the turf. More penalties are called at the breakdown than in any other part of the game. The key to successful work at the breakdown is for players to be well coached, self-disciplined, and fully cognizant of the applicable laws.

When we first started playing rugby, the breakdown was a complete mystery. Not knowing the law made it impossible to distinguish between times when behavior was legal and when it was seriously wrong. The easiest way to improve your overall game is to learn the tackle, ruck, and maul laws. Knowledge is power. More energy is wasted at breakdowns by players who don't know what they're doing than in any other area of the game.

# Tackle, Ruck, or Maul?

Every rugby spectator, and we mean *every* rugby spectator, has at some stage become befuddled and bemused figuring out the difference between a tackle, ruck, or maul. Don't worry — you're not alone. We didn't pick this one up for at least five years!

A tackle is something that starts with two or more players on their feet, one of them carrying the ball, and ends up with them on the ground. As soon as a tackle happens, however, a new phase usually takes its place. This depends on what happens to the ball when it's released or passed. Tackles more often than not end up morphing into rucks as more players arrive at the breakdown.

The difference between a ruck and a maul is that in a ruck the ball is on the ground, while in a maul the ball is off the ground in the hands of a player. To put it simply: off the ground — maul; on the ground — ruck.

# Roughing It in the Rucks

A *ruck* is formed when two or more players, at least one from each side, are on their feet over the ball in physical contact with each other after a tackle has been made or when the ball is on the ground.

The player who has been tackled with the ball is allowed to place it on the ground, or push it toward his teammates. He must do this immediately after going to ground. The referee allows his momentum to come to a halt, then the ball must be released. The tackled player can usually get away with one good rollover but a second one is likely to be penalized. If the player hangs onto the ball too long, perhaps to allow his teammates time to catch up or to prevent a defender from poaching the ball, the referee blows his whistle and awards a penalty to the defending side.

The first players to arrive at a ruck have to bind to each other or the opposition, as shown in Figure 7-2. The players grab each other around the shoulders or waist, or whatever body part is handy, and then try to step over the ball. The players on both sides of the ruck can attempt to drive the opposition back and away from the loose ball, but under no circumstances can they play the ball with their hands.

Launching your body into a ruck like a Scud missile is illegal and dangerous. Good form and body position are more important than brute strength at ruck time. You need to stay low and balanced, keeping your shoulders above your hips and your head up as you go over the ball to secure possession. A well-placed, concentrated shove is vastly superior to the head-down charging rhino technique.

**Figure 7-2:**
Forming a
ruck.

When the ruck is formed, the prime aim is to remove the ball. Players can only use their feet to rake the ball back to a waiting teammate and are not allowed to touch the ball with their hands. Alternatively, the attacking group of players can drive forward, stepping over the ball and clearing defenders away from it, making the ball available for the waiting scrumhalf, who decides how the team attacks next.

Players should not make deliberate contact with an opponent who is on the ground unless a body part is blocking access to the ball. Kicking or raking an opponent who may have fallen is not tolerated, and can result in the referee sending the offender off. This is called *stamping* and is dealt with harshly. It is legal, however, to use your boot to clear away the part of the body that is directly covering the ball as long as a backward motion is used. The exception is if a player's head is slowing down the ball's path of egress.

The ball is won from the ruck when the attacking players successfully bind together, drive forward over the ball, and make it available for the halfback at the back of the ruck, who then distributes it. Good rucking means quickly providing the ball to the scrumhalf, which in turn allows the backs to attack before the defense can realign. If the opposition is denied time to realign before the next attacking wave, it's likely to have holes for your backs to exploit.

## Rucking rules

Attacking from the ruck can be highly effective and sometimes devastating, but it's also an area where countless infringements occur. The scope for foul play in a ruck is enormous and referees strictly enforce the rules. The whistle is blown if players who join a ruck:

- ✔ Come from an offside position. The offside line at a ruck is the hindmost foot of the last player in the ruck.
- ✔ Come into the ruck from the side. Even if you're onside you still must enter the ruck from behind the last player's foot.
- ✔ Loiter at the ruck. If you're not part of the ruck you must retire behind the offside line.
- ✔ Use their hands to mischievously get the ball back to their side.
- ✔ Use their legs to pick the ball up or prevent it from being played.

Players are not allowed to kick the ball back into a ruck, because once the ball comes out the back of a ruck it must leave that area. As the ball is coming out of a ruck, no player is allowed to fall on or over it.

One of the most common ruck infractions is when a defensive player gets his hands on the ball before the ruck is formed but can't quite rip it away. After the ruck is formed the referee will usually shout out, "It's a ruck, no hands" or something to that effect. It then takes a lot of discipline to let the ball go and avoid the whistle.

### Kick the ball, not the man

In rugby, the term *mountaineering* is used to describe the act of players unnecessarily attacking an opponent with their feet. It usually involves a situation where players stomp all over an opponent who has fallen and is lying near the ball.

## Ruck formed! No hands! — Listening to the ref

In 1999, New Zealand All Blacks flanker Josh Kronfeld was one of the world's best ball stealers. He could uncannily anticipate where the breakdown was about to occur and used his tremendous strength and commitment to consistently steal the ball off the deck before the ruck could form. His willingness to give up his body to poach the ball was awesome and, being a flanker myself, he was my personal hero. Whenever I played, I imagined I was Josh roaming the field, searching for a tackle so I could swoop in and steal the ball before anyone else could get there.

In my first game as "Josh," I repeatedly turned up at the tackle situation and reached in to grab the ball off the deck. To my surprise, the referee, who obviously didn't know I was Josh, blew his whistle and pinged me for hands in at the ruck. I foolishly protested that the ruck had not yet formed, and because I was clearly on my feet it

was totally legal for me (Josh) to steal the ball — but it was to no avail. A couple of phases later, despite my clear laws explanation to the contrary, I could hear the ref wrongly declaring "Ruck formed, no hands," followed by a loud whistle blast and a second penalty for hands in. Then a third, a fourth, a fifth, a sixth, and a seventh stoppage followed with the referee still wrong (in my book at least) about when hands can and can't be used. After the match, which we lost by three points thanks to my last error, my teammates read me the riot act for giving the match away.

The lesson here is that you need to play to the referee on the day and adjust your game to comply with his commands and overall management of the game. So, remember to listen to the referee at rucktime — and when you hear "Ruck formed, no hands" realize that means you, no matter who you think you are!

A player must strictly ruck for the ball and not ruck the man. If you're attempting to free the ball using a raking motion, where your boot is moving primarily backward as opposed to straight down, you may not get into trouble with the referee but you're still opening yourself to a possible penalty. If your boot is aimed at the ball and it unintentionally collides with a body lying near the ball, nowadays chances are you'll draw a whistle. If you strike an opponent with your boot and he's a long way from the ball, you'll find yourself in a lot of trouble and possibly be sent to the sin bin for ten minutes. Stamping directly down onto the legs, the body, or, worse, the head of an opponent who's lying helpless on the turf is unsportsmanlike.

Remember, there's no place in rugby for malicious acts, so keep your rucking technique within the spirit of the game. The ruck law generally has been interpreted differently by referees throughout the world, but there's a recent effort to bring all countries into line and stamp out the practice of over-vigorous rucking.

### Stay on your feet

Perhaps the most important law is that players joining or forming a ruck must have their heads and shoulders no lower than their hips — otherwise, it's dangerous. At rucktime the goal is to stay on your feet, and entering with your head down decreases your strength and may lead to serious injury.

Players in a ruck must be on their feet, and they must endeavor to stay on their feet. A player cannot deliberately:

- Fall or kneel in a ruck
- Collapse a ruck
- Jump on top of a ruck

Rucks can be unsteady and sometimes collapse, especially when players use the wrong technique causing them to lose their feet. For a ruck to be successful, players have to be well drilled, well coordinated, and disciplined — and know the laws.

## Directing the ruck

The most important player at the ruck is the scrumhalf, who directs proceedings by telling his forwards exactly where to go. The scrumhalf is usually the only person who can actually see where the ball is, how many opposing players are committed to the ruck, and where the defense is positioned. He can then decide if more of his forwards are required at the ruck, whether the ball should be released or retained, and exactly where his teammates need to concentrate their efforts to ensure they get the ball back.

After the ruck has been formed, the scrumhalf is basically the foreman, telling his forwards where to go, what to do, and whether they're being successful in getting the ball back to him. An experienced scrumhalf focuses the forward's energy and attention on the area where it's needed most.

## Working the pick-and-go

A successful attacking strategy from a ruck is the called the *pick-and-go*. In a pick-and-go move, the ball-carrier strategically places the ball some distance back from his prostrate body. Hot on his heels are several teammates, who step over the ball and quickly drive their opponents off it.

Another attacker, who now has a clear run to the ball, bends down, picks it up, and charges ahead until being tackled, setting up yet another ruck or another pick-and-go. This tactic, if done properly, can be carried out over and over, allowing a team to gain ground and keep the defense off-balance.

# Mastering the Maul

A *maul* is formed when a player who is carrying the ball and is on his or her feet is held by one or more opponents. In addition, at least one teammate must be attached to the player holding the ball. This phase of play is illustrated in Figure 7-3.

**Figure 7-3:**
Forming
a maul.

Mauls are mostly used as an attacking ploy from line-outs (see Chapter 9 for more details about line-outs). The coordination and cohesion at the line-out is perfect for forming a maul because the forwards involved are all right in the area and ready to bind and drive ahead.

The speed of a maul is not the most significant element. Slow, steady progress where everyone is in sync tends to produce better results than a bunch of forwards with their heads down going at full gallop. Mauls are occasionally created when a player carries the ball into a would-be tackler and then turns to face his supporting teammates in an effort to protect the ball and stop it being wrestled away by an opponent. Teammates can grab the ball-carrier between the waist and shoulders to protect him from the opposition and retain possession of the ball. The goal is to keep driving forward while moving the ball to the back of the maul for immediate use when the scrumhalf deems it's time to do so. This is the one time in rugby when it's legal to be playing while in front of the ball.

A central feature of any good maul is proper binding by all participants. The tighter you are with your teammates, the more force you can exert and the harder it is for the opposition to stop or split you apart. The other indispensable element is communication. Everyone should know where the ball is and where it's going to maximize its protection and sharpen the focus of the attacking platform.

## Mauling laws

To the spectator, mauls can look totally confusing, like an out-of-control amusement ride. On the pitch, though, a well-executed maul can ensure that one team totally controls the game. It requires an enormous amount of dedication and discipline, and a proper understanding of the laws.

An important part of the maul law is that players can only join a maul from an onside position. The mauling manual includes other basics such as the following:

- ✔ Players who are in a maul must endeavor to stay on their feet. Referees regard it to be dangerous play if anyone tries to collapse a maul or jumps on top of it. This is an obvious penalty. Unfortunately, the IRB is considering making collapsing legal in 2008 — let's hope they don't!

- ✔ Players are not allowed to remove an opponent from a maul. Dragging an offside player out of the maul is prohibited; remember, it's the referee's job to enforce the law.

- ✔ While in a maul the ball-carrier can go to ground, but must make the ball available immediately upon doing so. Players must respond accordingly when a maul goes to ground and it becomes a ruck.

The two main types of mauls are *driving mauls* and *rolling mauls,* which evolve after the maul has been formed.

### Attacking from a driving maul

When the attacking team tries to drive through the opposition, the tactic is called a *driving maul.* The ball is usually carried by a player in the second line of the maul to protect it from the opposition. The players in the front line of the maul stay relatively upright, with their teammates behind them, adopting a lower body position so they can get better leg drive and better leverage to push the maul forward. In effect, the maul becomes a driving wedge charging straight ahead, but the big difference is that the ball is being held by one of the players and is not on the ground.

What makes the driving maul so effective is that the defenders not involved in opposing the maul are required to constantly move backward to stay onside. Backpedaling defenders are much easier for your back line to beat. The key to taking full advantage of maul possession is to have your scrumhalf use the ball before the maul stops moving forward.

In the old days, mauls were allowed to stop and start repeatedly and seemed to go on forever. Then the IRB changed the law, mandating that when a maul stopped, the ball had to be used immediately or it was a turnover. This de-emphasized the use of the maul as an attacking strategy, much to the detriment of the game. Recognizing and remedying the unintended result, the IRB compromised and now allows a maul to stop once. The team in possession then has five seconds to start moving again or produce the ball.

This is a good change because mauling is an important component of a team's physical presence on the field. If your side can regularly drive forward using a controlled maul, your opponent will be physically taxed and mentally demoralized because it takes much more energy to stop a maul than it does to attack from one.

### Using a rolling maul

A *rolling maul* occurs when the attacking team transfers the ball into the hands of a player on one side of the maul where the opposition appears weakest or has the least number of players. His teammates roll around to that side, pushing the player with the ball forward in a fairly good imitation of a cyclone. This type of maul resembles a spinning top, with one player rolling onto another, enabling the maul to move forward as the ball is transferred from one player to the next.

When executed properly, a rolling maul is a powerful attacking weapon because it's so difficult to defend against (especially when the team in possession changes its direction, going from one side of the field to the other). Most of the time the opposition has its work cut out just trying to stop the rolling maul from advancing, and has no real chance of getting the ball back. Whoever is currently holding the ball watches for the moment when the opposition defense in front of him is in disarray. He then peels off and takes the ball into the open field once again.

## Directing the maul

As with rucks, the scrumhalf acts as the coordinator at mauls. He doesn't get directly involved in the maul but stands behind, right next to the action. The halfback looks for opportunities, decides where the opposition defense is weakest, urges his forwards on, and tells them where to go. He advises his teammates where they should join the maul, and indicates who needs support to ensure that the maul keeps moving in the desired direction.

### The motor home

I used to own a 1973 Dodge Brougham motor home. It was the old boxy style, 19 feet long and incredibly heavy. One summer in Cleveland it broke down in a no-parking zone and had to be pushed to safety up a slight grade or it was off to the impound yard. When I first tried to move the behemoth, I found it impossible to budge until I used the mauling position I had learned at rugby training. The idea was not to push it from up high but to get under the weight, into a body position where all the force possible could be directed into the bumper and then slowly inched forward, step by step. This technique, with hips lower than shoulders and a straight back, exactly duplicates the method for stopping the driving maul. I don't recommend pushing a motor home by yourself, but it's helpful to imagine that's what you're doing during mauling practice. The players I've coached over the years have probably grown tired of hearing this story, but I've yet to find a better real-life illustration of the unnatural act of stopping a maul.

## *Stopping the maul*

A good maul is difficult but not impossible to stop. When trying to stop a maul, the first thing to do is try to turn the ball-carrier or tear the ball away and gain possession for your team. (This is easier in mauls that occur spontaneously than in planned ones from line-outs.)

When the maul is near the sideline, the best option is to try to concentrate your opposing shove at an angle to force the attacking side out of bounds. It's also legal to burrow your way into the opposition's maul through the front as long as you remain on your feet and don't come from an offside position. This has to be attempted right away, though, because once the ball starts being funneled to the back it's impossible to get to.

If you can't get the ball, or drive the maul over the sideline, then you have to stop its forward progress. You can do this by hitting the leading edge of the maul with full force, at an angle lower than the opposition players who are driving at you. Be careful not to lose your feet and drag others down with you — that can cause the maul to collapse, which will result in a penalty and possibly a trip to the sin bin. A strong back and superb body position are required to stop a maul that already has momentum.

# Chapter 8

# The Art of Scrummaging

## In This Chapter

▶ Defining the scrum

▶ Identifying three rows of responsibilities

▶ Understanding the rules of engagement

▶ Keeping it legal at scrumtime

▶ Using the scrum as a strategic weapon

The scrum is rugby's signature element because it is unique in the world of sport. It's an easily identifiable part of the game, involving more than half the players on the field, two packs of eight battling for possession of the ball. Nothing comes close to the sheer power generated by eight players bound together as one with a singular purpose. Maximizing the combined force of all the forwards is the most technically challenging part of the game. It's also the most physically demanding, as the exertion required to compete in repeated scrums drains the life out of your body faster than any other aspect of play.

Because every game has numerous scrums to restart play after minor infringements, it's considered absolutely vital that a team be able to consistently win its own scrums. Scrums are often described as the engine room of rugby, delivering a team's prime power source. A team that's dominant in the scrum is usually well on its way to a win, because what happens in this area of the game affects so many other aspects of the match.

In this chapter, we demystify the scrum by providing an inside look at the heart of rugby's least understood phase, so you can compete safely and win the battle up front.

## Scrum Is Not Synonymous with Mayhem

If you watch other sports on television, you may hear the occasional commentator refer to a spontaneous pile of disorganized bodies on the ground as a scrum. Nothing can be further from the truth. The reality is that a scrum is a very well organized and synchronized activity where every player involved has a specific set of skills, roles, and responsibilities. For a scrum to be successful in restarting play, all players must remain on their feet. Scrummaging takes strength, technique, aggression, and courage — it certainly isn't a haphazard melee.

We cringe every time we hear or see uninformed announcers and sportswriters use this term inaccurately, because it reinforces negative stereotypes about the game and belittles one of rugby's most intriguing features. Scrummaging is an esoteric art form, practiced out of the limelight but thoroughly appreciated and respected by knowledgeable coaches, fans, and the other participants on the field.

Scrummaging is an intense, precise endeavor, where technique reigns supreme over brute strength. Your pack can boast eight incredible hulks, but if they can't work together in a coordinated fashion they'll be well and truly beaten by a side of average-sized players who have their act together.

BROWNIE SAYS

## My first time packing down

I first played rugby at Occidental College in 1987 under the guidance of Coach Michael Godfree. Like many coaches who were backs in their playing days, the scrum was somewhat of a mystery to Michael. He knew immediately that I was a prop, of course, but was somewhat vague on what I was supposed to do when it came time to scrum down. My total instruction in propping consisted of another player directing me to "get in there and push."

With one week of training under our belts (where we were mostly introduced to basic skills like passing and tackling) the many rookies on that year's Oxy squad faced off on a Saturday against Long Beach State, then a Southern California powerhouse. I played tighthead prop and came up against an Australian guy with a full beard who must have been about 30 years old. Every scrum was an adventure in survival. He lifted me in the air, bent me in half so

that I was kissing my knees, twisted me like a wet towel, and hit me so hard on every engagement that I'm sure I ended up several inches shorter. None of this would be legal now, but at the time it was considered the price to pay for being a rookie front-rower.

My day ended with a split cheek that required eight stitches — suffered in a tackle, not a scrum — and the next day I was sore in more places than I had ever been in my entire life, but I was also hooked on propping and still am to this day. It's the most directly confrontational position on the team and requires heart, strength, stamina, and a desire to not get individually beaten. Learning how to do it right is a long journey of experimentation and setbacks, but in the end the ability to confidently prop up a scrum is the most satisfying of rugby pleasures.

A scrum formation is like a battering ram: The front row (made up of three players) is reinforced with five more players strategically placed behind them in positions that best stabilize the formation and push the opposition backward. To make this configuration work, every player has to have proper alignment and balance, sufficient expertise to adapt to pressure and movement, and enough strength to withstand the force generated by eight individuals working as a unit to mercilessly smash them.

Becoming a good scrummaging team takes countless hours of repetitive drilling together as a unit. This can be done against either a scrum machine or an opposition pack. Training should be broken up into two types, each with different goals. The first is concentrated on correct binding, foot positioning, leg angles, balance, and spine alignment. All players are unique in the power they can generate from their body shape, so figuring out how to feel comfortable in the scrum while maintaining maximum effectiveness is the priority in these sessions. The second type of workout involves repetition in engaging hard, pushing as a pack, breaking up and running to a spot, and then reforming as quickly as possible to simulate the activity in a match. Undertaking this kind of physical conditioning is useless, though, if the proper techniques and muscle memory haven't been sufficiently developed.

# Sections of the Scrum

The basics of scrummaging include learning how to correctly bind together as the scrum is formed, using good body positioning prior to and after the engagement, winning the ball, and providing a solid platform for launching the attack (Figure 8-1 shows the formation of a scrum). The best way to explain the scrum is to go through the individual positions, describing how the players are arranged and what their responsibilities are.

## The front row

The formation of a scrum starts with the hooker (number 2), who is the central figure of the whole affair. After the referee marks the spot where the scrum will take place, the hooker moves there and raises his arms, enabling the two props (numbers 1 and 3) to bind onto the hooker. The props then slide their inside shoulders under, up, and through, so that they end up in front of the hooker's shoulders. The hooker then binds onto the props by gripping each of them by their rugby jersey, with his arms across their backs so that the three are closely bound together (see Figure 8-1 for how the front row binds).

**Figure 8-1:**
Binding together: The front row gets ready for a scrum.

The front row is where the scrum is usually won and lost. A bad front row cannot be saved by a good second row. A good second row, however, can make a good front row into world-beaters.

It's extremely important that the members of the front row are solidly bound together at the shoulders and hips, because the opposition's goal is to split them apart. The force exerted on the front row from the players behind them and the opposing scrum is enormous and any weakness in binding will be ruthlessly exposed and exploited. Practicing correct scrum formations should be part of your team's training routine. Strong scrums mean fewer injuries and more chances to beat the opposition.

When they're all linked up, the three front-row players bend their knees, sink their hips, and rock backward so that they're properly prepared to withstand the pressure when the second row and back row bind-in behind them. They also look directly into the eyes of the opposition's front-rowers in readiness for the battle ahead.

Playing in the front row requires specialized skills, so each player must be suitably trained for the position. For safety reasons, not just any reserve can come off the bench and slot in up front. Without proper instruction and experience, the front row can be a dangerous place. If you're learning to play prop it's best to be able to play on both the tight- and loose-head sides — because you never know when you may be called upon to do double-duty in a match.

The term *hooker* is not a pejorative one but instead refers to the action undertaken by this player when the ball is put into the scrum. He hooks it with his foot to be channeled to the back of the scrum for use by the scrumhalf or the number 8.

The props derive their names in the same fashion, because they "prop up" the hooker. The terms "loose-head" and "tight-head" refer to the placement of their heads when the scrum comes together. The loose-head is just that: loose on the outside. The tight-head has his noggin sandwiched in tight between the opposition loose-head and hooker.

## The second row

While the front row is getting ready, the two locks in the second row (numbers 4 and 5) place their inside arms around each other, gripping onto their jerseys at waist level. They bend forward and place one shoulder against the back of the hooker's upper leg just below the buttock and the other in the same spot on either the tight-head or loose-head prop, depending on which side of the scrum they're on. When the locks' shoulders are properly positioned, their heads should poke out between the props' and hooker's hips. Their heads should be slightly raised so they have full vision of the ball as it travels through the scrum.

The lock then thrusts his spare arm (the one that isn't holding on to his second-row colleague) between the prop's legs and grabs onto his waistband. This bind has changed over the years — the locks used to put their arms around the prop's hips. It was also common for both locks to go down on one knee before engaging, but this too is becoming a rarity at the highest levels.

Most international locks now get into position behind the front row without going down on one knee. As a lock, you can try this style by keeping both feet on the ground and bending deeply at the knees and the waist before you bind to the front row. The advantage of this technique is that as the scrum engages your feet are already planted and ready to lock out, and you don't have to reposition them after the engagement.

## The back row

After the second row is bound in, the two flankers (numbers 6 and 7) bind onto the second row. They reach across the backs of the locks with their inside arms and grab a handful of the locks' jerseys while using their inside shoulders to apply pressure to where the props' buttocks meet their hamstrings.

On an offensive scrum (where their team has the put-in), the two flankers are responsible for keeping the ball from escaping out the sides as it's being channeled back and for keeping the props in tight to the hooker. On a defensive scrum they're more involved in pushing forward and their angles at engagement change to reflect this.

In attack, the flankers need to always keep their eyes on the ball until the scrum is over so they can support the number 8 if he picks up the ball, the scrumhalf if he darts around the fringe, and the backs if they crash back toward the forwards. On defense, the breaks need to focus on where and when the ball is coming out of the scrum, so they're ready to immediately disengage from the scrum and be there to stop the ball-carrier if necessary.

The last piece of the back-row puzzle is the number 8. This player slots in at the back of the scrum, driving forward with both shoulders against the backsides of the two second-rowers. To help stabilize and hold the locks together, he binds his arms around the outside of their hips and puts his head between their bodies.

The number 8 has more to do at the end of the scrum than at the beginning. He must coordinate with his scrumhalf as to what their plan is for each ball he receives. If the scrum is moving forward the task is much easier, but if it's static or moving backward the difficulty level rises. Whether he is picking the ball up from the back and taking it on himself, passing to his scrumhalf, or giving his scrumhalf protection, he must be sure-handed and a quick decision maker. He is also charged with controlling the ball with his feet at the back to keep it from emerging too early or in an untidy fashion. This ability to manage the ball at the base of the scrum with his feet is a skill unique to the number 8 position.

## The ninth forward — The scrumhalf

Because the scrumhalf is responsible for much more than just putting in and removing the ball from scrums, and despite the fact that he's technically a back, forwards will sometimes pay the little guy a huge compliment by referring to him as the ninth forward.

The scrumhalf is crucial for effective attack and defense from scrums. This player is the direct link between what happens at the scrum and how the ball is delivered to the back line. If a scrum is barely holding off the opposition's push, the scrumhalf must adapt and be faster in distributing the ball. If the scrumhalf's team has the upper hand, the player can vary the attack and take advantage of opportunities off the edges of the scrum.

On defense, the scrumhalf first puts pressure on his opposite and the other number 8 to prevent them from easily clearing the ball. He's also called upon to make tackles when the offense targets his side of the scrum for attack.

Communication with the number 8 is vital to successfully transfer the ball from the back of the scrum to the back line. This transition from set play (scrums or line-outs) to general play depends upon how well in sync numbers 8 and 9 are in all situations.

# Engagement

By this stage, the eight forwards should be bound together into one powerful unit. Before a scrum can begin, the referee makes sure the scrumhalf has the ball and then begins a series of four calls.

1. **Crouch** commands the players in the front row to dip down so that their shoulders are slightly above hip level.

2. **Touch** makes the props reach out and touch their opposite on the shoulder to ensure the front rows are no more than an arm's length apart.

3. **Pause** lets the front-rowers get set and ready to come together.

4. **Engage** is an invitation rather than a command. The two teams charge into each other so that the heads of the front-rowers interlock with those of their opposite numbers (see Figure 8-2 for an example of this).

Next time you watch a match, listen carefully when the scrum engages and you'll hear bodies colliding and players grunting as they exert themselves to the limit. Sometimes, you'll also hear the pack calling out a cadence in unison to coordinate their shove.

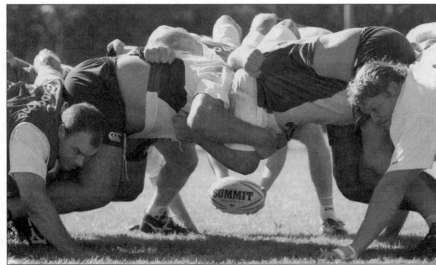

**Figure 8-2:**
The two packs engage to form a scrum.

Following the engagement, all 16 players in the scrum flex their legs forward and keep their backs straight.

The area on the ground that is formed between the two packs is called the *tunnel,* and is where the ball will be put in by the scrumhalf. If the scrum rotates, or moves off the mark too far and doesn't immediately stabilize, the referee will usually reset the scrum. Until the ball leaves the halfback's hands the scrum must be stationary, and neither team can push until the ball is inside the scrum.

## The put-in

Holding the ball in both hands, the scrumhalf prepares to throw it into the tunnel. When he is ready to begin, the hooker signals for the number 9 to deliver the put-in. When the scrumhalf gets the signal, he puts the ball in play. The throw-in must be done right away, and if the scrumhalf delays putting in the ball the defending side is awarded a free kick. The ball must be thrown in with a single forward movement, without any spin on it. Trying to trick the opposition with a fake put-in is strictly prohibited.

This is a case where what's written in the law book and what happens on the pitch is very different. The law says that the ball has to be put straight down the middle of the tunnel, but in practice this almost never happens. As long as the put-in is not too far on the side of the offensive team the referee will usually let play continue. This makes it very difficult for the defensive team to steal possession at scrumtime.

## The contest for possession

The scrum begins when the ball leaves the scrumhalf's hands. After the ball touches the ground in the tunnel, any front-rower may use either foot to win possession of the ball. What is not allowed is for any front-rower to have a foot in the tunnel before the ball is put in by the scrumhalf.

Hookers develop individualized styles of winning the ball, but the key is having a quick strike and soft touch on the ball so that you maintain good control of where it goes. Play around with different styles to see what feels the most comfortable. When you find a technique that works for you, practice to perfect it — you should find it easier to win the ball when your movements are deliberate, not spontaneous.

After the ball has been hooked, the ball is then channeled backward between the two second-rowers toward the number 8, who then holds it in the scrum with his feet until he or the scrumhalf decides to play it.

Whatever happens in the scrum, no one is allowed to touch the ball with their hands until the ball has been cleared. A scrum is over when the ball comes out in any direction (except out the tunnel), or when the number 8 unbinds from the scrum and picks up the ball.

# Laws at Scrumtime

The laws governing scrums are constantly being tinkered with in the interests of producing a fair contest for the ball and ensuring safety. First we'll give you some of the general restrictions, and then we'll move on to more specific rules.

When a scrum is called after an infringement, it's set wherever the infraction occurred (unless the infraction happened within 5 meters of the touchline or the tryline. In such cases, the scrum begins 5 meters in from those lines).

A full scrum has eight players from each side, but is legal with as few as five participants. There is no requirement for the opposition to reduce its numbers to match the other team when players have been sent off or because of injuries.

In cases where front-rowers are injured and there are no more suitable replacements, the referee will call for *uncontested scrums,* which means that the scrums come together gently and the team putting it in always wins the ball.

## Binding and releasing

Every player in the scrum is required to bind onto a teammate with at least one arm until it ends. When any player binds onto a teammate in a scrum, that player must use the whole arm from hand to shoulder to grasp the teammate's body. Placing only a hand on another player is not satisfactory binding. This prevents flankers from disengaging early from a scrum, enabling them to gain a defensive advantage.

Props are the only players who are permitted to grab an opponent. Loose-head props bind onto the opposing tight-head props by placing their left arms inside the right arms of the tight-heads and gripping the back or side of the tight-heads' jersey. The loose-head must not grip the chest, arm, sleeve, or collar of the opposition tight-head. Loose-heads must not exert any downward pressure. This is designed to keep the scrums from collapsing. (See the next section for more details about collapsing.)

Tight-head props bind onto the opposing loose-head props by placing their right arms outside the left upper arms of the opposing loose-heads. Using their right hands, tight-heads must grip the loose-heads' jerseys. They're also not allowed to grab anywhere else or force the scrum down. All other players in a scrum have to bind onto a lock's body with at least one arm. Everyone has to stay bound until the scrum is over.

## Collapsing

If a scrum collapses and goes to ground, the referee must blow the whistle immediately to ensure that players stop pushing. This is a safety precaution and is one of the few situations where advantage can't be played. (Chapter 6 explains when advantage *can* be played.)

There are a few rules that focus on preventing scrums from collapsing. Front-row players must not:

- ✔ Twist or lower their bodies
- ✔ Pull opponents, or do anything that is likely to collapse the scrum, either when the ball is being thrown in or afterward
- ✔ Fall or kneel in a scrum

There is a lot of leeway here between what is actually written in the law and what happens in most scrums. As long as it doesn't collapse and the ball comes out, most referees won't spend too much time scrutinizing everything that goes on in the front row. They will, however, strictly penalize any voluntary collapsing of the scrum because of the dangerous nature of this act.

You can't spend too much time working on your front-rowers' scrummaging technique. Regardless of the laws, opposing players will employ a variety of tactics that can result in a collapsed scrum. Your players need to know how to counter these moves and remain on their feet.

## Driving in and up

Front-row players are prohibited from lifting an opponent and can be penalized for doing so deliberately. Regardless of who's responsible, if a player in a scrum is lifted in the air or is forced upward out of the scrum the referee must blow the whistle immediately to stop players from pushing.

Lifting an opponent in the air during a scrum is now illegal. It has been banned by the International Rugby Board (IRB) because it can cause serious injury. Sometimes, though, players pop out of their own accord because they're under too much pressure. This move can also be penalized.

## Feeding

The scrumhalf is supposed to throw the ball straight down the middle of the tunnel between the two front rows but this almost never happens. On the infrequent occasion when a scrumhalf is penalized for this infraction it's called *feeding* and results in a free kick to the opposition.

Lax enforcement of the law against feeding has made stealing a put-in at the scrum a rarity. When you successfully hook the opposing team's throw in, that's called a *tight-head,* or *taking one against the head.*

The scrumhalf is also prohibited from *dummying,* or faking a pass, when the ball is ready to be removed from the scrum. If the scrumhalf reaches in and puts his hands on the ball to take it out, then emerges without it and fakes a pass, he can be both tackled and penalized.

# Strategic Scrummaging

In addition to securing possession, the scrum can be an outstanding attacking weapon. The primary goal of any pack is to at least be able to win your own scrum put-ins and provide a good platform for your backs to use the resulting possession. This is why most coaches will tolerate a prop that isn't the most effective player around the park if he is a good scrummager. Losing your own ball on scrums is a recipe for disaster on any team, and is certain to be ruthlessly exploited by the opposition.

The scrum can become a multi-faceted attacking platform in different positions and situations. The key to using the scrum effectively is having your pack players be well versed in a number of different techniques and options depending upon what you are trying to accomplish.

## Attacking from the scrum

What makes a scrum the ideal set piece to launch an attack from? First, the opposition's best defenders, their back-rowers, must remain bound to the scrum until it's over. This limits their range because it takes them longer to get into the open field. It also gives the offense the element of surprise because they can probe with either backs or forwards. Second, because the offensive back line of the team with the put-in is much closer to the point of attack on a scrum, the defense has less time to react to planned moves.

The best attacking position is a scrum in the middle of the field. This forces the opposition to split their backs because they don't know which side the thrust will come from. Ideally, your scrummagers will push the opposition backward during the scrum, which puts them into reverse and makes defending even more difficult. Any team worth its salt should be able to win almost every one of its own scrums throughout a match, which gives an air of confidence about starting the offense at scrumtime.

A scrum set near the sideline creates a natural attacking avenue down the *blindside,* or the short side, of the field. The reason why teams target the blindside is that it's less congested with defenders than the wide side of the field. Typically, the blindside is guarded by the weak-side wing, who's left all alone to stop the advance. Teams look to create a mismatch down the blindside, with a back-row forward charging at a wing. Nothing is more tantalizingly tasty to a back-rower than a lone wing isolated one-on-one between you and the promised land.

## Wheeling the scrum

Purposefully turning a scrum by a concerted effort of your pack is called *wheeling.* When the other team has the put-in, wheeling is a way of creating a turnover. If you can wheel the scrum past 90 degrees (so that the tunnel has passed beyond a position parallel to the touchline) it has to be reset and this time your team gets the put-in. (See Figure 8-3 for an example of wheeling the scrum.)

Situations also arise where a team would want to wheel its own scrum. When close to the goal line, wheeling causes one of the flankers to be rotated farther away from the point of attack. Remember, they have to stay bound until the scrum is over, and are thus at the mercy of the wheel.

Another time to use the wheeling technique is when you attack down the blindside. The main pack defender in this circumstance is normally the blindside flanker (who is closest to the short side of the field). If the flanker's shoulders are allowed to remain parallel to the tunnel of the scrum the player is in perfect position to stop a scrumhalf or the number 8 who charges down the short side. As the scrum wheels around, the player is forced to go with it, making the tackling angle more difficult.

Wheeling can be used to create turnovers at key times during a match. For example, if your opponent has the put-in on their 5-meter line (that is, near your tryline), turning the scrum past 90 degrees gets you the ball in an excellent attacking position with little risk involved. Late in the match when defending under your posts attempting to wheel their scrum is a risky choice, but if you have confidence your pack can work the wheel, you may get the ball and prevent the opposition from getting a try.

Screwing the scrum on your own put-in

The front row, side row and back row break off with the ball at toe

Ball held behind front row

Scrum beginning to be turned

Screwing the scrum on the opposition's put-in

Position of ball

Note the change of position of No. 8

**Figure 8-3:** Wheeling the scrum past 90 degrees.

If your scrum is getting repeatedly wheeled, you can counter by having your front row step sideways in unison against the direction of the wheel. The motion looks like a crab walking sideways, which is why it's called *crabbing*. Instead of the scrum continuing to rotate on its axis, crabbing causes the scrum to move sideways, stopping the wheel.

## Getting a shove on

If your team possesses the power and skill to win every one of your put-ins, the next step is to strive for physical domination of the opposing pack. This will help immeasurably in the execution of your goals in all other phases of play.

Initially your team should attempt to push the opposition off its ball at every opportunity in the scrum. Even if your players are unsuccessful at winning the opposition's ball, driving the other team backward is an important defensive tactic. Doing so forces the opposing scrumhalf and the number 8 to play the ball more quickly and under more pressure, often leading to rushed passes and mistakes in getting the ball to the flyhalf. It also causes their entire back line to edge backward while yours can be moving forward, thereby stifling the opponents' attack.

The same idea can be used as an offensive tactic. If your team can consistently shove the other team's scrum back it puts the opposition's defenders on the *back foot,* meaning they have to retreat to stay onside. This opens up more attacking options and demoralizes the opposition.

## Pushing it over the edge

If you have a scrum near your opponent's goal line you can attempt to score a *pushover try.* After the ball is hooked and channeled back under the number 8's feet, the scrum slowly advances toward the tryzone while the number 8 keeps the ball in, controlling it with his feet. When he thinks he can score, the number 8 picks it up and crashes over the line to ground the ball.

Scoring a pushover try is rare at the international level but much more common in club matches, where the scrums are more likely to be one-sided. There's nothing more uplifting than completing a pushover try — and nothing more demoralizing than being driven back into your own in-goal area.

In a physical sense, domination at scrumtime boosts your forwards and drains the other team's. This means less energy for them during rucks and mauls, further enhancing your conquering capabilities.

# Chapter 9

# Line-outs: Restarting from Touch

*In This Chapter*

▶ Identifying when a line-out occurs

▶ Identifying where a line-out occurs

▶ Identifying who gets the throw-in

▶ Getting information

▶ Playing roles in the line-out

▶ Understanding tactical options

▶ Knowing what's not allowed

▶ Quickly throwing in

*I*f you appreciate the aerial artistry of basketball, you'll love the line-out. It features the timing and technique of a jump ball with a twist unique to rugby — the jumpers are allowed to be lifted to even greater heights by their teammates. This results in a visual treat where players are hoisted high into the air and a competition for possession takes place a dozen feet off the ground.

Line-outs are the primary method of restarting play after the ball has gone over one of the touchlines (and therefore out of bounds). Line-outs always take place on a touchline and are instantly recognizable by the two parallel lines of players who face the sidelines waiting for the ball to be thrown in. (See Chapter 2 for full details about the touchlines.)

For most of rugby's history, line-outs were a confused jumble of bodies that usually ended up producing more stoppages than quickly usable balls. The introduction of legal lifting has made the line-out one of the more entertaining parts of the game, where true competition for possession flourishes. In a little more than a decade, the line-out has been transformed from an unsightly phase that favored one-dimensional players to a dynamic display of athleticism, strategy, and teamwork.

This chapter unlocks the secrets of this highly competitive part of the game. We give you a full description of the line-out, detail the variety of roles played by those involved, and explain the rules the players must follow. Plus, we provide insight into the tactics that make the line-out a thing of beauty, and finish up with an examination of prohibited behaviors.

# When Does a Line-out Occur?

The line-out is used to get play going again after the ball has gone over a sideline and into touch (out of bounds). It doesn't matter how or why the ball went over one of the sidelines; if it goes out of bounds, play is restarted with a line-out (we explain the one exception at the end of the chapter). Whether the ball is kicked out, carried out, driven out, or simply rolls unattended over either of the touchlines, a line-out is the prescribed way to re-ignite the action. That part is easy — where it gets more difficult is in determining when a ball actually has gone into touch, thus necessitating a stoppage in play.

So how can you tell if the ball is out of bounds? The touch judges are the arbiters of this question. If they deem the ball has gone into touch, they raise their flags to indicate this fact to the referee, who then blows the whistle.

Basically, the touch law states that any time the ball, or a player carrying it, comes into contact with the touchline or the ground beyond it, it's in touch. If the ball crosses the touchline in the air and is then blown back or caught by a player in the field of play, it's not in touch.

# Where Does a Line-out Take Place?

Line-outs always take place on a touchline. The exact location varies depending on factors such as where the ball went out of touch and how it got there.

In cases where a player is bundled into touch with the ball or an errant pass trickles over the line it's easy to figure out where the resulting line-out will ensue — it happens at the place where the ball crossed or came into contact with the line. The touch judge will then stand at that exact spot with a raised flag and not move to either side until the line-out is over.

It gets more complicated when the ball is kicked into touch by a player on either team. When the ball is kicked out, the spot for the line-out is determined by where the ball was kicked from and how it went out of play. (See Figure 9-1 for a diagram explaining touch and throw-in location.)

# Directly into touch

When the ball is kicked out of bounds and it doesn't touch the ground or another player on its way out, it has been kicked straight out or *directly into touch*. The location of the kicker determines where on the sideline the line-out will be held.

- ✔ If the player who kicked the ball out of bounds is on or behind his own 22-meter line, the line-out is formed where the ball went over the line (see Chapter 2 for an explanation of the 22-meter line). This is a strategically profitable kick because it gains territory.

- ✔ If the kicker is in front of his own 22-meter line when the ball goes directly into touch (kicked out *on the full*), the line-out is taken from where the player made the kick. This means the team doesn't gain any territory — and the kicker loses friends. (Tired and emotional forwards hate having to run back to where a player has kicked the ball out on the full.)

- ✔ If the player kicks the ball out of bounds on a penalty kick (to gain territory and set up an attacking line-out), it doesn't matter where the ball is kicked. The line-out takes place where the ball goes over the touchline.

- ✔ If the player kicks the ball directly into touch from a free kick, but is in front of his 22-meter line, the team does not gain any territory. The line-out is taken from where the player kicked the ball — so make sure you know the different signals for a penalty kick versus a free kick (see Chapter 5 for all the referee signals).

# Indirectly into touch

When the ball bounces infield or hits any part of a player before going out, it has been kicked *indirectly into touch*. When this happens it doesn't matter where the ball was kicked from, the line-out is taken at the point where the ball crossed the line.

If you have at least one foot either on or inside the 22-meter line, you're considered to be behind the 22-meter line. If you catch the ball outside your 22-meter line and then take it back behind the line before you kick it, you won't gain the territory. You can, however, pass the ball to a teammate who *is* behind the 22 and still gain ground from the kick. This is another potential change to the law that the International Rugby Board (IRB) is considering for 2008. Passing the ball back inside the 22-meter line may soon be the same as running it back there yourself, meaning no gain in territory.

On a penalty kick, where a player opts against kicking for goal and instead kicks for touch to gain yardage and set up an attacking line-out, it doesn't matter where the kicker is standing on the field. The line-out takes place where the ball went over the sideline. (See Figure 9-1 for examples of touch and the place for the throw-in.)

THROW-IN HERE

THROW-IN HERE

KICK TAKEN OUTSIDE 22

22 METER LINE

THROW-IN HERE

THROW-IN HERE

THROW-IN HERE

**Figure 9-1:**
Touch and
the place
for the
throw-in.

GOAL LINE

# Who Gets the Throw-in?

The law determining which team gets to throw the ball in at the line-out is straightforward. Whichever team last kicked, touched, or was in possession of the ball before it crossed the touchline loses possession. A member of the other team will get the honor of throwing the ball to the players in the line-out. (The team awarded the throw-in at a line-out has the advantage, because they know where the ball is going.)

It isn't always easy to tell which player was the last to have contact with the ball, so the touch judges are required to keep up with play and follow the progress of the ball as it makes its way up and down the pitch. When the ball goes into touch, one of the touch judges will signal by raising the flag and pointing with his free arm in the direction of the team that will throw the ball in at the resultant line-out.

The exception to this law is when a penalty has been awarded. In this case, the non-offending teams know that they will get the throw-in. (Remember, players can kick the ball directly into touch during a penalty kick and take the line-out where the ball leaves the playing area, gaining territory for their team.) This is especially common when a team is backed up in its own end and wants to advance the ball, or when it's near the opposition's tryline and needs to score more than three points. (See Chapter 2 to learn about the point system.)

When you carry or kick the ball into touch it amounts to a *turnover,* because the other team gets the throw-in. This enables tacklers to use the sideline as a 16th defender, by driving the ball-carrier into touch whenever the runner is near the sideline.

One of the most common errors for inexperienced ball-carriers is not being conscious of where they are in relation to the touchline. When coming into contact with a defender within 5 meters of touch, players should lower their body position and lean infield to prevent the defender from driving them out. This is easily practiced with a ball-carrier, a defender or two, and a sideline.

# Lining Up for a Line-out

In its simplified form, a line-out consists of two straight rows of designated players from each team who line up facing the sideline. The ball is thrown in between the two lines and the players attempt to secure it for their side to use. When the two groups get into position for a line-out it looks haphazard and casual, but the exact opposite is true. Every move and placement, from the initial location of each individual to the spacing between them and where they end up, is choreographed with attention to detail.

A line-out doesn't officially begin until the ball is thrown in, but the process starts as soon as the ball goes into touch. First, the line-out has to be correctly formed, then a decision on each team's strategic intent is internally taken. This is followed by the actual execution of the play and the distribution of the ball, all without running afoul of the law. A line-out is not over until the ball is passed or run out of the area between the 5- and 15-meter lines (except when a ruck or maul forms after the ball is thrown in; then the line-out isn't over until that phase has cleared the initial line of touch).

## Forming a line-out

A line-out is considered formed when at least two players from each team are lined up at the spot where the ball went into touch. The players from the competing teams face the touchline in two straight rows, with a space of 1 meter between them. Like in a scrum, this area is called the *tunnel* or *gap*. The middle of the tunnel should be at the spot where the ball went out, called the *line of touch*.

The line-out exists in a contained area. The front boundary is 5 meters from the touchline and is marked by the 5-meter line. The rear limit is designated by the 15-meter dash lines, giving each team a total of 10 meters to work with. Every player that is part of the line-out must stand between these two points. Two players who are exempt are the one throwing the ball in and the receiver, who stands behind his line of players. The defense is also allowed a receiver, plus a person to mark the thrower, usually the opposing hooker. He can stand between the sideline and the 5-meter line. (Figure 9-2 illustrates a typical line-out formation.)

The number of players taking part in the line-out is determined by the team that has the throw-in. The number varies depending on personnel and strategy. (In the 1999 World Cup, Ireland used a 14-man line-out against Argentina!) A standard line-out has seven players in the line and one player throwing the ball. A line-out formation with fewer than the standard eight forwards is referred to as a *short line-out*.

On offense, each team decides the best tactical way to win its line-out and can vary its numbers throughout the match. The opposing team can choose to have fewer players in the line-out, but it cannot have more. In 2008 the IRB may rescind this law and allow each team to put as many players as it wants in the line-out without fear of penalty.

On the offensive team, once a player is part of the formed line-out he cannot leave it. The defense has a little bit of leeway here. If it sends seven players to the line-out and the offense puts fewer in the line, a corresponding number of defenders can leave without being penalized, provided they do so in a reasonable amount of time.

## Calling the play

Just like a quarterback in football calling an audible at the line of scrimmage, a certain player (it varies from team to team and can be the hooker, the receiver, the captain, or anyone else in the line-out) is given the important task of making the calls. Timing and coordination are key aspects of success-ful line-out play, so it's absolutely vital that everyone involved knows exactly what the plan is on each throw-in.

Before every line-out, the attacking team decides who the ball will be thrown to and what they'll do after winning it. For example, a particular call may mean that the second jumper will receive the ball and then everyone is supposed to form a maul and drive forward. The line-out caller uses a code system to let everyone on his team know what is about to happen while preventing the opposition from knowing what they're up to.

At training under the coach's direction, the line-out players work on a system of codes for various plays. It may involve numbers or code names, but it has to be understood by everyone to avoid confusion. A throw can be short, long, looping, or bullet-like, depending on the signal or code words used. Some teams are even more sophisticated and have more than one player calling signals to confuse the opposition. Only they know which calls are real and which are decoys. Your code should be simple but flexible enough to accom-modate all of your line-out schemes, without requiring that your team be loaded with secret code breakers — you want to confuse the opposition, not your own players!

**Figure 9-2:**
Throwing in
at a line-out.

## Breaking the code

For the first several years of my rugby career, I played for Occidental College and the Oxy Olde Boys. Because there was significant interchange between the two teams we used the same line-out calls. A series of words and numbers would be shouted out by the hooker but it was the second digit of the second number that determined where the ball was going. Very simple and not too tough to grasp. As I played for other clubs I was exposed to more complex coding systems that I adapted to without too much trouble. Eventually, though, I ran into problems during my years playing in Latvia, especially in training with the national team. Their calls were a mix of Latvian and Russian numbers interspersed with slang. I never could keep them all straight, so ultimately the lock I was lifting, Wilmars Sokolovs, would wait until the calls were done and then he'd tell me in English where the ball was going! Problem solved, because he and I were usually the only English speakers on the pitch.

A few years later in Northern Ireland I ran into other issues while training with Ulster and playing for Portadown. The Ulster code was complex and involved using calls that began with the letters from three key words. For example, let's say the three words were "front," "middle," and "back." If the call began with one of the letters from the third word, the throw was going to the back (so if the call was "blue, yellow, green" the ball would be thrown to the back because the first letter of the call begins with the first letter of the third code word). Most of the time I'd get it right but occasionally I'd find myself lifting the wrong man or being in the incorrect spot. This perplexed me until a discussion with the other prop revealed that I had one of the three words slightly wrong because the player who explained the calls to me had a pretty thick accent, which I incorrectly thought I had figured out.

The Portadown club used countries, beers, and banks to signal where the ball was going, and after numerous training sessions I thought I had everything memorized. During the first match, though, I ran into trouble with a call I'd never heard and I guessed had to be a country. Scotia, however, turned out to be a bank. When I first started coaching the Oxy women's team I took the easy way out and had my players make dummy calls with the hooker indicating where the throw was actually going by holding the ball in either her left, right, or both hands. In subsequent years we developed a more complex system that worked even better.

## Throwing in the ball

The throw is usually made by the team's hooker, but anyone on the side can restart play if necessary. To be effective the hooker has to have the ability to vary his throws from quick hard ones at the front, to higher ones in the middle, and more lobbed ones to the back of the line. For a throw to be legal it has to travel at least 5 meters, straight down the middle of the tunnel. The thrower cannot step onto the field of play before releasing the ball. The referee will normally allow a throw that is slightly off center, but not a throw that blatantly favors the receiving team's side. The ball leaving the hooker's hands signals the official beginning of the line-out.

The player who throws the ball in must be consistent and precise in his delivery so he can hit his jumpers with regularity. Timing is of the essence to prevent the opposition from getting their hands on the ball. Mastering the technique of throwing in can be very difficult. The skill requires excellent hand–eye coordination and a good sense of spatial anticipation. The thrower needs to visualize the apex of the lifted player's hands as the target and throw to that spot before the jumper actually gets there. The beginner will miss the mark most of the time and provide the opposition with a chance to steal it. This can be extremely frustrating even for professional players, who go from hero to zero from one week to the next on the strength of their throwing accuracy.

Hookers need to practice throwing at every training session. They should start with both feet about half a meter behind the touchline, so they can step forward on their follow-through without stepping onto the field. Work on hitting all the spots where your jumpers will be using varying amounts of loft and zip to avoid defenders. The thrower needs to be in tune with each jumper's technique and preferences. If the wind is up at training, rejoice and take advantage of the inclement weather to have your hooker work on adjusting his throws to account for the force of the breeze.

Aspiring hookers can never get enough throws at training, and since it's unrealistic to recruit a pack of forwards to come over for a few hours while you play a one-sided game of catch with them (at least without a well-stocked cooler), the best thing to do is find a wall or set of goalposts to throw at. Make marks at different points on the target that approximate the varying maximum heights attainable by your jumpers and then alter your distance from them to simulate their different positions in the line. Then, throw until hitting them all becomes routine.

## Taking the throw

To help a jumper get as high as possible in the line-out, his teammates can lift him heavenward. The catch is that they're also responsible for bringing him safely back to earth.

The best result in a line-out is for the jumper to cleanly catch the ball. This isn't always possible, so the next best thing is to tap the ball back to your side in hopes that the receiver or another line-out player will be able to secure it. When they're up in the air, line-out jumpers can use either their inside arm or both arms, provided they're over the head, to grab or redirect the ball. When the ball is taken the jumper should turn his body on the way down, so that he's facing his teammates when his feet touch the ground. This allows the other forwards to bind-in around the jumper to protect the ball from the opposing pack and also provides a good mauling platform.

The opposition's jumpers try to figure out where the ball is likely to go and then try to launch themselves to the right place to win the ball. Defensive lifting is even more challenging, because the lifters never know where their jumpers will take off from. Contesting the line-out works best when you have instinctive leapers with excellent timing — plus a scouting report on the opposition's line-out tendencies!

# Starring Roles in a Line-out

The line-out requires an array of unique skills that must be performed with precision to successfully compete. Just like casting for a theater company, the line-out performers must be able to play various parts and be versatile enough to switch roles when the situation demands. The players involved in line-outs are almost always forwards, and they're usually required to fulfill multiple duties at various times during the match. (Review Chapter 4 for details about the positions of the players discussed in the following sections.)

## Jumpers and lifters

Before players were allowed to lift one another in the line-out, each player had a designated position that rarely varied. The advent of lifting led to more strategic line-outs, and now most teams will lift at least three different jumpers in various places up and down the line. To confuse the opposition they may also switch around the roles of players and use jumpers as lifters.

Winning squads used to be the ones with the tallest players who had the longest arms. Now the dominant teams are the ones with the most accurate throwers and best coordination between jumpers and lifters.

### Jumpers

Line-out jumpers are still usually the two locks and the tallest of the back-rowers. Whoever they are, they have got to possess balance in the air and good hands. Jumpers should have good footwork so they can quickly move into several different positions in the line. Part of their craft includes faking jumps to draw their opposite off the ground, and also not giving away their true intentions when they're going to get the ball.

The responsibilities of the lifters are as important as those of the line-out jumper. One lifter is positioned in front of the jumper and one behind him. They must work in tandem and be perfectly coordinated to ensure that the jumper reaches the top of his leap a split second before the ball gets there. Figure 9-3 shows a jumper being assisted as he reaches for the ball.

### Lifters

Lifters need to be strong and able to confidently lift some of the biggest players on the field. It's not easy to hoist a 240-pound man more than 6 feet in the air and then hold him there until he catches the ball!

Two similar techniques are used to lift a jumper, depending on whether you're in front of him or behind. When you're the front lifter, the key is to stay low and close to your jumper with your knees bent and your butt lowered. Support the jumper by gripping the thighs just above the knees so you can attain the maximum lift possible. The lifting power needs to come from your legs and not your arms or back. After the player jumps, extend your arms straight over your head and use your legs to push the jumper up even higher. When he reaches the zenith of his jump, your arms are locked out straight over your head. While the basic technique of lifting with your legs and extending your arms is the same for the back lifter, your contact point with the jumper is different. The back supporter should grasp the jumper's legs, just beneath the buttocks. The back lifter has the primary responsibility of providing the initial thrust to help get the jumper airborne.

**Figure 9-3:**
Getting a lift as the ball is thrown in.

## Keystone Kops in the line-out

Not all modern line-out developments have been good. Some coaches and players have become too fond of trying to outsmart each other by devising complex and elaborate line-out tactics — and sometimes they outsmart themselves. Wacky line-out maneuvers that have players running this way and that (some making dummy runs and others being used as decoys), can appear comical. In the end it looks like a totally out-of-control Keystone Kops routine where everything goes wrong and the opposition wins the line-out ball. There's nothing worse than running through a series of moves and then having the referee blow the whistle to penalize your side for delaying the throw. The best strategy is to keep unnecessary movement to a minimum, making it sharp and accurate with a definite purpose.

## The receiver

The receiver position has traditionally been filled by the scrumhalf. This makes sense because once the ball is won, he's the best person to distribute the ball to the waiting back line. Recently, though, teams have successfully expanded the role of the receiver by making him into another line-out jumper. From his position behind the players in the line-out, the receiver is allowed to enter the line before the throw-in.

Even if the receiver is not going to enter the line, he still has to be a player with great hands because he is invariably called upon to consolidate loose possession. When the receiver is a forward, teams will also use him to attack right away after a line-out or provide a critical shove to get the maul moving forward when the jumper comes down.

## Movement in the line-out

The concept of movement in the line-out is also a relatively new one that has flourished since the introduction of lifting. Movement of jumpers and lifters up and down the line is used to prevent the opposing jumpers from settling in one particular place to contest the throw-in. When a team's jumpers are on the move it's harder for the opposition to steal the throw because they don't know when the movement will end or where the ball is going.

A moving jumper can reach greater heights than a stationary one. It takes a lot of practice to coordinate a moving jumper, two lifters, and the throw-in to all converge on one spot at the same time, but when it's done right it looks effortless and is an incredibly graceful display of power and athleticism.

# Talking Tactics Down the Line

The line-out has become an elaborate action-adventure, with designated jumpers, special jumps, decoy moves, and more subterfuge than a James Bond movie. The basic aim, though, remains unchanged. Every team wants to set up a good platform to launch their attack. The key is to be able to execute different forms of incursions equally well, so as to keep the opposition off balance. When the jumper has his mitts on the ball, the options are limitless.

The element of surprise is one of the best weapons available to a team at a line-out. If the defenders are unclear about what form the assault will take, it's tougher to position themselves appropriately. Just when they get ready to counter one tactic you throw another one at them, thus increasing the overall effectiveness of both moves.

## Peeling off

One effective line-out play involves the jumper tapping the ball down to a moving (or *peeling*) forward. The peeling player has to stay within a meter of the line-out until receiving the ball, but can then cut upfield around the front or rear edge of the formation. The key here is to get past the line-out defenders quickly and thrust immediately into the back line. Timing is essential to pulling this move off, but because the peeling player is already moving and the defenders are static it can lead to clean breaks.

## Throwing to the front

Hitting a non-jumper at the front of the line is an option when your traditional jumpers are having trouble securing the ball. For this to work, the defenders must be concentrating on the jumpers, leaving the man at the front unguarded. The opposing hooker will generally be able to tackle this player as he goes down the blindside so the real benefit comes from the man who receives the ball being able to pass to his hooker, who is all alone with room to run.

One cheeky variation for throwing to the front of the line-out involves the front lifter getting in position to support the front jumper, but then just as the ball is thrown he turns around to face the hooker and receives the ball via a quick low throw. The key to pulling this off is having the player taking the ball position himself slightly infield, to make sure the ball travels at least 5 meters before he moves forward to take it.

## Setting up the maul

Line-outs are a particularly good time to initiate a driving maul (see Chapter 7 for details of the maul) because all the required players are in close proximity and the defense is preoccupied with stealing the throw-in. As soon as the ball is taken and the jumper is returned to earth, the other forwards bind in to form the maul and start pounding ahead with concerted effort. It's important to get the ball out of the jumper's hands and moved quickly back so that the opposition has no chance to take it away.

An effective variation on this tactic is to get the maul going (which sucks in defenders) and then immediately spin the ball wide. This gets the defense moving in the wrong direction and creates chances for your backs to break through. An extra benefit of successful mauling from the line-out is that teams will sometimes stop contesting the throw-in and concentrate exclusively on stopping the maul.

## Quick off the top

The standard method of distributing the ball from the line-out is to bring it down, consolidate it, and then have it ripped off the jumper and transferred to the scrumhalf. For a speedier way of getting the ball to the back line, the jumper can toss the ball directly to the scrumhalf as soon as the catch is made, saving valuable seconds. This requires a jumper with excellent balance in the air and a deft passing touch. If the jumper can't cleanly take the ball with two hands, the ball can also be redirected using one hand (either way, this move is called a *tap down*).

Every one of these tactical moves has a multitude of variations that can be adapted to your team's strengths. Don't try to pull off stunts that your players can't effectively perform. Get the basics right first and then experiment with adding more options.

# Things You Can't Do

More than any other area of the game, the line-out is all about being controlled in your behavior. The line-out law is the longest one in the book, detailing a laundry list of prohibited actions.

The primary focus is on the thrower's responsibilities. For a line-out to be legal the ball must be thrown straight down the tunnel, travel at least 5 meters, and the thrower can't step into the field before he releases the ball. The opposition cannot prevent the ball from going at least 5 meters.

Attention then shifts to the other players in the line-out and what they can't do. As a general rule they are not allowed to hold, push, grab, or in any way make contact with the opposition across the line of touch. It's okay to contest the ball, but you can't do so by taking out the other player in the air. When the jumper is in the air, leave him alone! The same goes for the other lifters; they have to be left alone until they bring their jumper down. Using an opponent to gain leverage for a leap is also on the banned list of techniques.

Other violations involve the offside lines at the line-out. Before the ball is thrown the offside line is the middle of the tunnel; afterward, it's the ball itself. A line-out is not over until the ball is passed or run out of the area between the 5- and 15-meter lines. When a ruck or maul forms after the ball is thrown in, the line-out isn't over until that phase has cleared the initial line of touch. For players not in the line-out, their offside line is 10 meters back from the line of touch and they can't advance until the line-out is over.

# Taking It Quick

At the beginning of this chapter, we said that there was one exception to using the line-out to get play going again after the ball goes out of bounds; it's called *taking it quick* (when a player opts to quickly throw the ball back into play instead of waiting for a line-out to form).

A quick throw can be used to restart play when the ball has gone into touch, but there are several restrictions governing this practice. A player on the team who will get to throw the ball in at the line-out can instead opt to throw it in quickly from anywhere behind the line of touch as long as the line-out hasn't already been formed. The thrower has to use the exact same ball that was previously in play and it can't have touched anyone on the sideline, including touch judges, ball boys, photographers, spectators, and so on.

The beauty of a quick throw is that it allows you to re-ignite the attack right away without letting everyone get realigned. Defenders often use the time after the ball has been kicked out to rest and regroup, making it a perfect time to launch an unexpected foray. (So, after a long clearing kick, the first concern of the chasers should be preventing a quick throw-in. This is easily accomplished by following the ball downfield and marking the player who picks it up.) The only danger of a quick throw-in is that you can't count on support from your teammates unless you advance the ball to where they are.

Taking it quick also has a unique aspect in that players can throw the ball in to themselves as long as it travels the required 5 meters. Quick tosses also have to be straight (but for some reason this is mostly overlooked by the majority of international referees and may be changed by the IRB in 2008).

Taking it quick can be a good decision when the kicking team has outkicked their coverage. This occurs either when the kicker really nails the ball and it carries beyond where the player's teammates can cover, or when the chasers fail to get downfield to play defense. Take it quick only if you have ample time and the right opportunity presents itself. Otherwise, since the majority of line-out balls are retained by the team with the throw-in, you're better off letting the forwards do their thing and take the moment to catch your breath.

# Chapter 10

# Individual Skills

● ● ● ● ● ● ● ● ● ● ● ● ● ● ● ● ● ● ● ● ● ● ● ● ● ● ● ● ● ● ● ● ● ● ● ● ● ● ● ●

## In This Chapter

▶ Evading the opposition

▶ Perfecting your passes

▶ Advancing your kicking skills

▶ Honing your tackling techniques

● ● ● ● ● ● ● ● ● ● ● ● ● ● ● ● ● ● ● ● ● ● ● ● ● ● ● ● ● ● ● ● ● ● ● ● ● ● ● ●

*I*n established rugby countries, learning the game starts at a very young age. The skills necessary to become a complete player are introduced and developed over time, building a solid foundation onto which tactical acumen can later be added. Coaches with a lifetime of experience guide youngsters through the essential steps to rugby proficiency as they grow and mature.

In North America we tend to pick up the game later in life, and coaches lack the deep reservoir of knowledge relied upon so heavily by nations where rugby is an imbedded part of the sporting culture.

Instruction in our part of the rugby universe runs the gamut from extraordinary to almost non-existent, and when it's offered ends up necessarily being more concentrated into a shorter time span and is more reliant upon trial and error while playing. As a result, sometimes even the best players who excel on superior athleticism tend to lack complete skill sets.

Rugby is a game where everyone must possess basic skills regardless of position. Players are expected to instantly switch from offense to defense and vice versa throughout a match. There's no place on a rugby team for one-dimensional players deficient in fundamental running, passing, kicking, or tackling skills.

In this chapter, we explain the basics of how to run, pass, kick, and tackle so you can understand the different techniques players use. We also provide plenty of tips so you can fill in any gaps in your game and perfect your rugby craft.

# Running Rampant

Running is an integral part of the sport, essential to playing both offense and defense. While there's certainly nothing wrong with speed, if you can't adapt your running style to handle and pass the ball properly you'll actually hurt your team more than help. Some of the best rugby players are not the fleetest of foot, but they fulfill their positional responsibilities by practicing good form.

When carrying the ball, you need to be constantly thinking of where the defenders are and what your supporting players are doing in relation to your movements. On top of all this, you need to always be mindful of your primary goal — not to lose possession of the ball.

Running in an upright position may work on the track, but try it in a rugby game and you'll get seriously thumped. The best running position for rugby is to lean forward for balance and effective weight distribution. The rugby running style enables you to adapt to whatever is going on around you. You need to be able to quickly react to the situation at hand, changing directions, accelerating, slowing down, and moving in all sorts of ways a lower body position facilitates. Lowering your center of gravity allows you to react more quickly on the fly.

Running at full pace with the ball will take a little practice before you feel entirely comfortable. When running in the open field, hold the ball in both hands in front of your body. This allows you to pass to either side of your body and keep the defense guessing. If you have to get ready to pass the ball, it's usually too late to do so.

When you can't avoid being tackled and there's no one to pass to, shift the ball into your outside arm and hold it tight against the side of your body. Tacklers will often target the ball in contact with the goal of dislodging it from your grasp, so you need to hang on to the ball to keep the bad guys from stealing it.

To preserve possession throughout the tackle situation, practice running into contact while carrying the ball under one arm, tucked or cradled between your arm and rib cage or armpit where it's protected from the opposition's defending players. Carry the ball in the arm farthest away from the defender and you can use the other arm to either fend off your opponent or push away from him when he attempts to tackle you. As you make contact, keep your body between the ball and the tackler. When you're brought to ground you have to release, but remember that you're entitled to place or immediately pass the ball, so don't relinquish it too early.

## Receiving a pass on the run

Receiving a pass is difficult at first because so many things are happening at the same time. Once the elements are broken down and methodically practiced with precision, your ball-handling errors will be dramatically reduced. The receiver should catch the ball while maintaining awareness of the defenders in order to choose the best option.

Whenever you're running in support of a ball-carrier, think about where space may be created and how you can exploit it if you get the pass. This is a very subtle and elusive skill that comes from game experience and watching world-class players. Because humans can only look in one direction at a time, your sense of the defensive team's presence and where the gaps are likely to be is primarily gathered through your peripheral vision.

Prior to receiving a pass, look at the passer and verbally communicate that you're ready for the ball to be delivered. Before the ball is passed, reach out with both hands with your palms facing the passer and your thumbs together to provide a target and get ready for the ball's impending arrival. As the ball nears, extend your arms to meet the ball and catch it with your fingers, while watching the ball into your hands. When a teammate passes to you, don't take your eyes off the ball until after you catch it. One of the most common mistakes is momentarily losing sight of the ball at the last second to sneak a peek at the defense. Changing your focus too soon may cause you to knock-on — and then get knocked silly — as you attempt to regather your fumble. (See Chapter 6 for full details about the knock-on.)

## Side-stepping the tackler

A *side-step* occurs when a ball-carrier heading in one direction suddenly changes course and heads off on a different path. This move is one of the easiest and most effective ways of getting past an opponent. A good time to use a side-step is when you're running with the ball and a defender lines you up for a one-on-one, open-field tackle.

To set up the side-step run directly at a would-be tackler, which will cause the player to slow down while preparing to make the tackle. Just before the collision, slow down a bit and tuck the ball under one arm for safety (see Figure 10-1a). If you want to side-step to your right, drop your body weight onto your bent left leg, planting the foot firmly on the ground. Drop your shoulder to your left, and then drive hard off your left leg and push away in a sideways direction to your right (see Figure 10-1b). (To add to the deception, before you push off toward the right, feint with your upper body to make your opponent think you're about to go left.) When you've side-stepped around your opponent, accelerate to full speed and continue your run. The key is to slightly reduce your pace before you make your move and to explode off the driving leg to create as much distance as possible between you and the defender.

Although the side-step may sound a bit like a fancy move from a '70s disco movie, it's a great skill in rugby because if it's done well the defender in front of you looks pretty foolish grabbing thin air as you cruise by.

## Curving into the swerve

If you have the pace and space to run around your marker, the swerve is the move for you. The *swerve* is similar to the side-step, involving the ball-carrier initially running directly at the defender and then curving away just before contact. The ball-carrier usually makes only a slight swerve of the body, and if done at high speed it can be very effective in getting past a defender.

To swerve to your right, first bob to the left with a slight turn of the shoulders as your right leg moves forward. Then take a long stride across the running line with your left leg and move your body away to the right as your right leg comes through. The key is to swerve as close as possible to the tackler to force him to commit, reducing the player's reaction time to adjust and make the play.

# Fending off forcibly

Occasionally, despite our svelte physiques and blistering pace, even your esteemed coauthors sometimes fail to completely evade all 15 defenders. When contact becomes inevitable you can use the tackler's momentum to your advantage by using your arm to push the tackler away, which is called *fending off*. This is a move common to both the rugby pitch and the football field.

To fend off, carry the ball in one arm, then just before the collision turn your body so that your free arm is facing the direction where the contact is coming from. As the defender attempts to make the tackle, thrust your free arm directly at the closest part of the defender's body, usually his head or shoulders (see Figure 10-2b). The ball-carrier pushes the tackler away and down to stop his momentum (see Figure 10-2c). This action gives the runner leverage and pushes him off the defender, so he can pick up speed and accelerate away before the would-be tackler has time to recover. (See Figure 10-2 for more detail about the tactics described here.)

**Figure 10-2:**
Fending off
a would-be
tackler.

## Going into a hit and spin

In the *hit-and-spin* move, the ball-carrier commits to contact and then bounces off and spins out of harm's way. Run at the tackler, get lower than your soon-to-be victim, and drive your shoulder hard into the player's upper body while keeping your feet under you. As you bump off the tackler, spin or roll away. The spin is made by quickly twisting, swiveling your hips, and turning your back on the tackler.

The more space you create with the initial bump-off, the easier it will be to spin away from your opponent. The key here is to keep your arms free so that the ball can be distributed if the tackler is able to hang on and stop your progress.

## Doing the goose step

The *goose step* occurs when the ball-carrier takes three or four quick steps, lifting his legs with his knees locked straight (as shown in Figure 10-3). If done quickly, it leaves the defense totally bamboozled and hopelessly off-balance. The goose step is a tricky, fairly advanced move that requires a very high level of athleticism to pull off.

Australian legend David Campese was the master of the goose step and left many otherwise solid defenders scratching their heads wondering, "Which way did he go?" If you think this move sounds easy, try it at full speed on the pitch.

### Notable running styles

The greatest single example of running rampant in recent memory was New Zealand's rugby colossus, Jonah Lomu, knocking over everyone in sight to score repeatedly in the 1995 World Cup. Lomu simply ran through, straight over, or around everyone and everything.

Players both past and present use guile and brilliant changes of pace and direction to make them extremely dangerous when they have the ball in hand. Because very few are blessed with Lomu's size, strength, and agility, the key to successfully running the ball is to use your head to beat the tackler. Smashing the tackler but losing control of the ball is a victory for the defense. You can't expect to make every defender miss, but if you're mindful of your body position in the tackle, are able to maintain possession, and provide recyclable ball for the next phase of attack, you've done your job as a ball-carrier.

**Figure 10-3:**
Goose-
stepping
your way
around the
opposition.

## Throwing the dummy

A *dummy* is simply a fake pass. By throwing a dummy, you lead your opponent to believe you're going to pass the ball to a teammate, but at the last minute (just as your opponent changes direction to follow the ball) you pull it back and continue running.

This move involves faking the pass with your eyes, arms, and body, while maintaining awareness to see if the defender bites on the misdirection. When the tackler takes the bait and commits toward the receiver, pull back the ball and cut upfield. If you don't do a good enough job of selling the dummy, get ready to be hit hard by the tackler.

# Passing with Panache

Passing the ball is one of the most elementary of rugby skills that should be the first one taught to all newcomers. The goal of passing is to provide a ball that is easily caught by a teammate who is in a better position to continue the attack.

When preparing to make a pass, hold the ball upright in both hands, with a hand on either side of the ball, fingers spread wide with the thumbs up to ensure control and balance. When you're ready to pass, swing the ball across your body in the opposite direction of the target (so, if the pass is going to the right, first swing the ball to the left side of your body). Then swing your arms and shoulders back toward the teammate you're passing to, and release the ball. The ball should leave your hands quickly and with a snap (see Figure 10-4).

Making a good pass means you involve your whole body and are well coordinated. Other factors that are critical to a good pass are the following:

✔ **Accuracy:** Accuracy is vital. When you throw the ball to your teammate, don't throw it directly to him, throw it just slightly in front of him so that he can run on to it and collect the ball at pace. It's much better for him to have to speed up to catch the ball than to have to slow down. A good pass travels on an upward arc that he can catch somewhere between his waist and his chest. If he has to bend over or leap to get the ball his stride will be broken and the defenders can more easily close on him.

For better accuracy and distance, increase the rotation on the ball by bending your arms and turning your wrists slightly as you release it. Your two pinky fingers should be the last digits in contact with the ball.

✔ **Velocity:** Speed is important. Throw the ball with some velocity to ensure it maintains its height and does not drop before reaching the player who is going to receive it. A pass that is headed downward is twice as hard to catch as one that is going up. When passing in tight spaces don't put too much mustard on that hot dog, or the receiver will struggle to control the ball.

✔ **Tactical awareness:** Pass only when your teammate is in a better position to continue the attack. Passing the ball to someone who is surrounded by defenders is not only pointless, it's dangerous. A good rule to think of is that you're responsible not only for your pass but also for the next one as well; don't pass the ball if the player you're passing to won't have the opportunity to pass it on — unless, of course, they're streaking down the sideline for a try.

## Bringing tactics into play

After you've learned how to pass, the next step is understanding when to do so. One of the most basic tactical skills is drawing the defender and then passing before you get tackled. *Drawing the defender* means getting the tackler to commit to you, which prevents him from covering other attackers.

**Figure 10-4:**
Passing the
oval ball.

If the player with the ball passes it too early, the defender may have enough time to change direction and chase down the receiver. To avoid this, lure the defender to commit by running at him. Then before you reach the defender, who is preparing for the tackle, you pass the ball to a teammate who is in a better position to continue the assault.

The ball can be passed much faster than players can run across the field. To demonstrate this principle, challenge your fastest player to run the width of the pitch in pursuit of the ball while it's being passed along the back line. If your team's passing skills are adequate, the ball will always beat the man. This is also known as *letting the ball do the work*.

## Spiral pass

A *spiral pass* is made when you put some spin on the ball, causing it to rotate as it moves through the air. The hand farthest away from the direction in which the ball is about to be thrown moves up over the ball as it's thrown, which makes the ball spin. (If the ball is being passed to the left, the right hand comes up over the ball, giving it a counter-clockwise top spin, as shown in Figure 10-5.) The advantage of a spiral pass is that it flies straighter and flatter because it's aerodynamically superior to a ball that doesn't have any spin.

**Figure 10-5:**
Spinning out with a spiral pass.

## Cut-out pass

When you pass the ball out along the line and deliberately skip the receiver next to you, it's called a *cut-out pass* (as shown in Figure 10-6). The pass travels right in front of the adjacent player, but instead of reaching out and taking the ball, he fakes grabbing it and lets it fly by to the next player in the line. The phrase *two-man cut-out* means that the ball-carrier has thrown the ball past the first two players next to him in the attacking line, sending it instead to the third man in the line.

For example, the flyhalf may pass the ball beyond the inside center and outside center, and straight to the wing (see Chapter 4 for an explanation of where each player lines up on the field). This is usually a predetermined move, but can be executed spontaneously if the passer sees the space outside.

If you're the player being cut out, do your best imitation of someone expecting to get the ball in order to deceive the opposition. The pantomime includes having your hands ready for a pass, running in your usual position in the back line, and sometimes includes breaking the silence with a loud "Now!" just as the passer releases it. The pass needs to be a fast spiral one because speed ensures that the cut-out is effective. The ball has to be thrown quickly and accurately so that the outer backs have the maximum amount of time to do something with it before the defense can react.

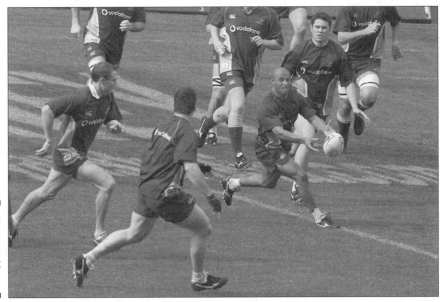

**Figure 10-6:**
Making a
two-man
cut-out
pass.

## Lob pass

A *lob pass* is a high, looping pass that goes just over the outstretched arms of the opposition. This type of pass is used when you're on attack and find yourself crowded by defenders who are running in the passing lanes between you and your support. The only way to pass in this situation is to lob the ball over the defender's heads to one of your teammates.

## Pop pass

A short floating pass in close quarters is called a *pop pass*. It's a versatile transfer where the pass is carefully weighted to allow the receiver to easily take the ball without breaking stride. The ball is passed using one or both hands. Start low and lift your arms and wrists to pop the ball up to the receiver. This should not be a bullet or flat pass, and should have a little loft under the ball so the receiver can catch it between his waist and shoulders.

If you find yourself caught in the tackle but your hands are still free, you can utilize a pop pass to deliver it to a teammate who's running close by in support. The goal is to make the pass as easy as possible to catch, as your receiver is likely to be charging through a tight gap and needs to focus on where the defenders are coming from, not on reaching for a wild pass. Scrumhalves often use the pop pass off the fringes of rucks and on tap penalty plays to transfer the ball.

## Dive pass

When you dive forward and pass the ball from underneath your body with a scooping motion, it's called a *dive pass*. This pass is mainly used by scrumhalves, usually at the back of the scrum, when they find themselves under pressure from the defense and need to get the ball away very quickly. Because you're diving away from pressure when it's made, the dive pass also creates a little distance between you and the nearest defender.

## Scrumhalf pass

The *scrumhalf pass* is the standard type used by the number 9 to distribute the ball. The essential elements for this pass are that the scrumhalf has his feet behind the ball and his weight initially over it. By staying on his feet and taking a step toward his target, the scrumhalf builds momentum without a time-consuming backswing. When executed properly, the ball goes straight to the target, quickly and with a nice trajectory, making it easy to catch.

The scrumhalf should be your team's best passer. He's responsible for passing it from set pieces and distributing it out of rucks and mauls.

Through practice, scrumhalves learn exactly how to get the ball to their closest teammates. The skill is acquired through hours of training, where the scrumhalf throws the ball to the flyhalf, centers, and wings without looking to see where they're positioned (rugby telepathy, if you like). Scrumhalves have to be the master of every type of pass because they're often forced to improvise when getting the ball out of tricky situations.

# Kicking Cleverly

Despite the fact that rugby emerged as a handling game from soccer, kicking still plays a central strategic and tactical role. Kicking in the oval game takes a variety of forms and is used primarily to gain territory, restart play, or score points. While all kicks are similar in that you launch the ball with your boot, they diverge greatly in technique depending on what you're trying to accomplish.

If you're just starting to coach youngsters or beginners, you can do your team no greater service than making sure every player has fairly good kicking skills. You can guarantee that sometime, somewhere in a game, every player is going to be called upon to kick the ball. Nothing is more pleasing than seeing a tight forward forced into a situation where his skillful footwork is suddenly called upon in a desperate circumstance and he delivers flawlessly. It may be the only time he ever puts boot to ball, but when it comes off it's a thing of beauty.

An adept kicker is an asset to any rugby team and, like every other basic skill, learning how to kick effectively requires heaps of practice.

# Spiral punt kick

The *spiral punt* is an all-purpose kick that is usually the first one you learn. The basic skill looks just like an NFL punter kicking it away on fourth down. The best method for punting the ball is to make it spin off your boot (shown in Figure 10-7). This corkscrewing action is extremely effective, because as the ball leaves your boot it goes the longest distance and is very accurate.

When you want to kick the ball deep into opposition territory with a *clearing kick* (a kick that clears the ball out of your end), the spiral punt is the best kick to use. It's also easy to learn. Here's a step-by-step approach to doing it right (see Figure 10-7 for more details):

- Hold the ball in both hands well out in front of your body, at an angle so it can spiral off your foot when kicked.
- Drop the ball at an angle of about 30 degrees toward the center of your body (see Figure 10-7a).
- Shift your weight onto your non-kicking foot, which should be aimed at the target, while drawing the kicking foot back (see Figure 10-7b).
- Swing your kicking foot straight through so that it strikes the ball along its long axis. Point the toe of your boot out as you make the kick.
- Adjust the flight of the ball by changing the angle of your foot and the point at which the ball is struck in its fall.
- Extend the arm on the opposite side of your body for balance.
- After the ball is dropped onto your foot your boot should move slightly across the ball, somewhat like a corner kick in soccer. Watch the ball move all the way onto your boot, and then follow through.

If the kick is done properly, the ball will spiral off your boot. The spiraling effect makes the ball go farther and straighter than the usual punt kick (which usually floats in the air with less distance gained). A right-footed kick will cause the ball to spin clockwise from left to right, and vice versa for a left-footed kick.

**Figure 10-7:**
Kicking a
spiral punt
for dis-
tance and
accuracy.

Just like a good golf swing, you don't want to kick the ball too hard. Through
trial and error you'll quickly discover just how much force you need to accurately propel the ball the full distance. When you have the right technique
and can regularly hit the ball's sweet spot, you'll be amazed at how far a
rugby ball can fly.

## Up and under

An *up and under,* or a *Garryowen,* is similar to the spiral punt but is modified
for a different purpose. The kicking technique is the same except that the ball
is held in the hands so the point and not the side of the ball is facing down.
On impact, your boot makes contact with the pointed end of the ball (see
Figure 10-8). The goal is to keep it in play and put it high enough to provide
hang time for your chasers to contest the ball as it returns to earth. The strategy behind an up and under is that it tests the nerve and concentration of the
recipient's fullback and forces the opposition's forwards to retreat.

**Figure 10-8:**
Testing the
opposition
with an up
and under.

When making an up and under you have to weight the kick so that the ball comes down just outside your opponent's 22-meter line. That way, the player trying to catch the ball has to deal with tacklers and pray for support from forward teammates. If the ball goes inside the 22-meter line the receiver can call for a *mark,* like a fair catch in football, which stops play and gives the opponent a chance to kick the ball away.

## Chip kick

A short punt kick that's calculated to go just over the head of an advancing defender is called a *chip kick.* The goal of a chip kick is to regather the ball in the open space immediately behind the opponent.

Taking a chip kick on the run is particularly difficult and requires a deft boot, but that's when the option usually presents itself and is hardest to defend against. Chip kicks work because the laws prohibit a defender from impeding any player who has just kicked the ball in his efforts to regain possession.

When chipped with just the right touch, the ball will often be caught by or bounce up for an attacking player to regather and continue the attack. Chip kicks are used when the defense is up flat with superior numbers, because after you kick the ball they've got to leave you alone.

## Grubber kick

A short punt kick that travels low across the ground is known as a *grubber kick*. The goal is to create top spin on the ball, causing it to quickly roll forward on the pitch, end over end (as shown in Figure 10-9). This is a good tactical kick when done properly, because the ball scoots along the ground and can bounce in any direction at any moment. Chasers have the advantage in gathering the ball because they're reading the bounce as they follow it and are less likely to be thrown off by an unpredictable hop.

To make a grubber kick, drop the ball and strike its back half just before it hits the turf so it skips low along the ground (see Figure 10-9a). This kick is an effective tactic when the opposing defensive players are coming up fast and you want to put the ball in behind them.

**Figure 10-9:**
Rolling out a grubber kick.

# Drop kick

Attempting a field goal during general play is called taking a *drop kick*. Slotting a drop goal is rare, but it gives your side another scoring option when you're near your opponent's goal line and can't break through to score a try.

To take a drop kick, move forward with the ball in both hands, plant your non-kicking foot, and draw back your striking leg as you drop the ball onto the ground. It should land on the pointed end and bounce straight back up a couple of inches. The place to drop the ball for a right-footer is about the width of your hips to the right of your planting left foot.

The object is to contact the ball with your boot a split second after it rebounds off the ground. Timing the kick and being able to control the dropping of the ball takes a very long time to perfect.

Over the past couple of seasons, before training started and while everyone else was getting their kit on, we developed a little fantasy game where we simulate the final drop goal from the Rugby World Cup 2011 . . . the Eagles are down by two, it's the last movement of the match, and the 40-something ageless wonder — out of nowhere! — gets the ball and squares up for the match-winner. He strikes the drop, the jam-packed Eden Park crowd holds its collective breath — and it's good! The Eagles win the Webb Ellis Cup! (We can dream, can't we?)

## 1 for 1 lifetime

In my junior year at Occidental College I became obsessed with the drop kick. It began with the Santa Barbara tournament the previous year where I heard that a drawn match would be decided by five players from each team taking drop kicks from the 22-meter line. Wanting to be ready to help my team if I was ever called upon in this unlikely situation I began practicing drop kicks before and after almost every training session for the next two seasons. Drop kicks are not easy and my success rate at first was pitifully low but eventually through trial and error I found the method that worked best for me. With a lot of practice I actually got pretty good at slotting the ball through the uprights (without any opposition, of course, and usually off a good patch of grass).

Late in my senior year, after blabbering endlessly to my coach and teammates about how I knew I could make a drop goal in a match, I finally got my chance. We were playing UC Riverside and as I was late arriving at a ruck (not an uncommon occurrence) our captain Dave Hodges, later skipper of the USA Eagles, told me to get ready to drop one so I took my place at first receiver. We won the ball, our scrumhalf passed it to me, I banged it through from about 30 meters out, and the referee blew the whistle and awarded us three points. To this day I've never attempted another in a game but still fantasize before and after training about winning a match with a long drop. If the situation ever arises, I'll be ready.

# Goal kicking

Goal kicking involves placing the ball on a kicking tee, making your approach to the ball, striking it, and following through. Contests between evenly matched teams are usually won by the side with the more accurate goal kicker. Having a reliable goal kicker in your team is a necessity, not a luxury. Goal kicking is a specialist skill, so usually only a few players can handle the responsibility. It's important to have more than one kicker so if the main guy is injured a suitable replacement is already on the field.

Virtually all kickers in the modern game use the round-the-corner style for kicking goals. The main elements are a measured approach (or *run-up*), planting the non-kicking foot, striking the ball, and following through. As shown in Figure 10-10, this requires the following step-by-step approach:

1. **Position the ball on the kicking tee.** The usual way to place the ball for a kick is to stand it on end, angled forward toward the goalposts you're aiming for.

2. **Walk back from the ball.** Take about four paces backward and then take two paces to the left, for right-footed kickers. (If you kick with your left foot, take two paces to the right.)

3. **Approach the ball in a slight arc, in a slow relaxed manner, with your eyes focused on the part of the ball you intend to impact.** Coming at the ball in a slight arc gives the required curl to the run as you approach the ball from the left (if you kick with your right foot). The curl to your run-up creates a slight right-to-left action on the ball when it's in the air, helping its trajectory and keeping it on line. The curl also improves the distance of the kick.

4. **Push your hips forward with the final stride, plant your non-kicking foot, and extend your arms for balance.** The last stride with your non-kicking foot must be the longest, with your planted foot ending up slightly behind and the width of your hips away from the ball. The plant foot should be aligned with the toes pointed at the goalposts.

5. **Swing through and kick the ball.** Your kicking foot should strike the ball on its end where the four seams come together. The top of your foot (near the big toe and instep) contacts the bottom of the ball, driving it forward and up. Your foot should be extended as you swing your leg through, pointed in the direction of the target. Your chest should be facing the target at impact.

Goal kickers can come from any position (see "The kick that won the game" sidebar for an example), so if you think you've got the knack for it, practice your goal kicking — you never know when you may be drafted into the role.

# The kick that won the game

Australian rugby seems to revolve around last-minute kicks. One of the most famous last-minute kicks occurred in 2000 when the Australian Wallabies met the New Zealand All Blacks in Wellington. Wallaby captain John Eales was given only a few seconds to compose himself before taking a kick that would determine where the Bledisloe Cup would end up. (The Bledisloe Cup is an annual trophy with great historical and emotional significance for the competing nations, Australia and New Zealand.)

Five minutes into extra time, New Zealand was leading 23–21 when All Black replacement prop Craig Dowd was penalized for an infringement at the breakdown. Eales assumed that the team's regular goal kicker, Stirling Mortlock, would take the shot, until he was informed that Mortlock had left the field a few minutes earlier

with severe cramps. So it was up to the skipper to select a replacement goal kicker. Having been the Wallabies' kicker in the past, he didn't hesitate to indicate to the referee that he would take the fateful kick himself.

Eales had the onerous responsibility of kicking a penalty goal about 25 meters out from the goalposts and 15 meters in from the sideline, in a swirling, fluky breeze, to determine the outcome of the match. A poor kick, and the Cup would be lost to New Zealand.

Rising to the occasion with ice water coursing his veins, Eales casually slotted the ball straight through the goalposts, prompting scenes of ecstasy among the Wallabies as they celebrated the tightest of victories over their fiercest rivals.

### Getting into goal-kicking form

Goal kicking requires hours and hours of practice to get right. So get a ball, go down to the local park, and experiment until you're comfortable with a goal kick that suits you. Concentrate on the ball until after the moment of impact by keeping your head down and your eyes on the ball. Always remember to follow through when kicking for goal. The follow-through ensures that the balance and coordination needed to put the ball through the goalposts is maintained.

If you carefully watch the world's leading goal kickers, you'll notice they each have their own particular style. From teeing-up the ball to approaching it, from striking the ball to following through, there's a myriad of techniques that work. The one thing leading goal scorers have in common is that each time they kick for goal they display the exact same routine and a relaxed kicking motion. So encourage your players to experiment and develop their own style to make kicking for goal routine.

**Figure 10-10:**
Goal-kicking
technique.

# Tackling Tough

In football, the object of tackling is simply to bring the runner to the turf by whatever means necessary, because that immediately stops play. In rugby, taking down the ball-carrier is only the first part of a sequential contest for possession that begins with the tackle itself.

Because the rugby tackler's job only starts with bringing the runner down, players must always be mindful of body position throughout contact to increase their team's chances of creating a turnover (stealing possession of the ball). This difference is particularly significant when trying to coach former football players, who tend to opt for the big hit instead of being focused on winning the ball.

For a beginner, the prospect of having to tackle someone is often daunting. Great emphasis should be placed on teaching newcomers how to tackle properly. *Tackle bags* (large, vinyl-covered bags filled with foam) are used to help players perfect their techniques without getting hurt and to ensure they get it right before they actually have to tackle in a match.

The key to teaching and learning how to tackle is to break down the activity into its basic elements and then work slowly to build a progression of drills that simulate the skill. Even though you'll start out on your knees, you need to walk before you can run when it comes to tackling training. When you have a solid understanding of the basics and confidence in yourself, tackling can become one of the more enjoyable parts of the game. Bear the following in mind:

> ✔ **The fear factor:** You can overcome the fear of injury. While it's natural to think that trying to stop a rampaging forward who is charging straight at you is going to inflict damage on your person, the reality is that you won't get hurt if you tackle correctly.
>
> ✔ **The focus factor:** To be a good tackler, you must possess the ability to block everything else out of your mind as you prepare to make the tackle. Tackling is a precise battle of mind over matter.

The real secret of tackling tough is to convince yourself that you can do it. When you overcome that hurdle, you'll discover it really doesn't matter what shape or size you are — you can effectively tackle any opponent and not get hurt.

When tackling, don't be cautious or half-hearted about it. Those who don't tackle with 100 percent commitment are the first to get hurt; those who trust their instincts become great tacklers and a vital asset to the team.

Developing a good tackling technique takes time, but it's not difficult. When you've acquired the skill, you can improve it at training sessions — even the best players regularly return to the tackle bags to keep their tackling techniques up to scratch. As with running, passing, and kicking, different types of tackles require different techniques.

## Front-on driving tackle

A *front-on driving tackle* is used when a ball-carrier is running directly at you. To make a front-on driving tackle correctly follow these steps:

1. **Assess the situation as your opponent approaches.** Figure out the best type of tackle for the situation and which shoulder you're going to use to hit the opponent, then convince yourself that you're going to be successful.

2. **Lean forward and use one of your shoulders to aim at the spot where you want to hit your opponent.** As you prepare to tackle, push forward with your shoulder, targeting the spot where you want to hit, as shown in Figure 10-11. You're not allowed to tackle above the line of the shoulders, and should aim between the hips and the knees.

3. **Use your legs to drive into your opponent.** It's important that you launch your tackle from a balanced, low position with both feet on the ground to generate as much power as possible when you drive your shoulder into your opponent. Good tackling begins with the lower body and is finished with the upper body.

4. **Keep your head aimed to the side of your opponent's body.** Your head position is very important. Your chin should be tucked in on your chest, which has the effect of hunching your shoulders, while your back should be straight. By choosing a shoulder to tackle with early on, and by placing your head to the side, you'll avoid flying knees and elbows that you would have taken if your head was in front. Never use your head as a weapon like in football.

5. **Drive into your opponent, grabbing him tightly around the waist.** Drive hard into the ball-carrier to push him backward and upward. Wrap your arms tightly around him and hold on (see Figure 10-11b). It's not crucial in rugby to smash the opponent; it's more important to make sure you bring him down, even if you get dragged a few meters.

6. **Try to get the ball from your opponent.** Keeping a strong hold on your opponent so he can't get out of the tackle, try to get some part of your hand, arm, or body on the ball, because that can help dislodge it from his grasp.

7. **Try to regain your feet and win the ball.** When you're both on the ground you must release the ball-carrier and immediately attempt to regain your feet and try to steal the ball before anyone on the other team arrives at the breakdown.

Start beginners off slowly by kneeling, standing, stepping, walking, jogging, and then finally running into tackle drills (see Chapter 18). This allows them to grasp the elements of the tackle slowly and builds their confidence.

**Figure 10-11:** Making a front-on driving tackle.

# Side-on tackle

When the ball-carrier is trying to run around you and turns slightly sideways, you'll want to use a *side-on* tackle. A *side-on tackle* is made when you aim your shoulder at the ball-carrier's hip, just below the waist, and place your head behind or alongside the player's inside buttock. After hitting the ball-carrier with your shoulder, put your arms around the player's thighs and squeeze tight. Keeping a strong grip on the thighs has the effect of dragging your opponent down.

When making a side-on tackle, never put your head across the body of the runner, as you're likely to catch a driving knee or thigh on your noggin. If you've played football you've been coached to put your head in front of the player, and you'll need to adapt your tackling technique for safety. Keep your head behind the ball-carrier and away from danger.

# Tackle from behind

Another variation of the driving tackle is the tackle from behind. When chasing the ball-carrier from behind, the tackler targets the area just above the knees, as shown in Figure 10-12. The tackler's arms encircle his opponent's thighs with a firm grip, which effectively traps his legs and drags him down.

**Figure 10-12:** Diving in to tackle from behind.

## Ball-and-all tackle

When the you tie up the ball and prevent the runner from passing in contact, it's called a *ball-and-all tackle*, or *smother tackle*. The advantage of this technique is that you slow down the runner's progress while hindering his ability to recycle the ball. The objective is to at least prevent the ball-carrier from quickly passing the ball to anyone else.

The technique can be made from the front chest-to-chest, from behind by wrapping your arms around the runner, or any other way you can pin the ball in the tackle. A successful ball-and-all tackle will prevent the ball from being passed by your opponent, so it can only be transferred to another player after you both go to ground and he releases it.

## Stationary tackle

The *stationary tackle* is similar to the ball-and-all tackle, but here the ball-carrier is running right at you while you're stationary. By preparing yourself for the front-on impact — and, when it comes, holding on tightly — you can topple your opponent forward and over your body using the ball-carrier's momentum.

Use the stationary tackle if you're a smaller player confronted by a large forward. If you hold on doggedly and vigorously, you can upset your opponent's balance.

## Ankle tap

Even if a ball-carrier has blown by you, you're still allowed to hit his feet with your hand in an attempt to trip him from behind in a last-ditch effort to bring him down.

An ankle tap takes perfect timing and an effective tap, but it does work. Usually the defender makes a diving attempt at the ball-carrier and tries to disrupt his stride by smacking one of his ankles inward, so that it collides with the other leg and trips the runner. When you ankle tap a player it's essential that you get right back to your feet and pursue him, because as soon as he regains his feet he can take off running again.

# Chapter 11

# Tactics and Teamwork

*In This Chapter*

▶ Formulating the plan

▶ Dealing with the elements

▶ Finalizing the plan

▶ Orchestrating the attack

▶ Organizing the defense

*I*n North America we have plenty of athletes; what we struggle to develop are instinctual rugby players. Even when the basic skills are mastered, we lack the key decision makers in critical positions that other countries produce in abundance. For example, the tactical awareness of a 15-year-old New Zealander is typically miles ahead of a 25-year-old North American, because we start playing the game so much later in life. This places an extraordinary burden on our coaches to open their players' eyes to the tactical possibilities available to them.

As a coach, you need to fully appreciate what your players can and can't do and then develop a style of play that best suits your strengths. Conducting a brutally honest appraisal of your side and a balanced evaluation of the opposition before each game will assist you in developing the most appropriate game plan for every match.

We're not going to promote a particular type of playing style in this chapter because we'd rather give you the information to make an informed decision based on what kind of talent you have at your disposal. In this chapter, we provide you with a framework for establishing a game plan, talk about adapting to the elements, detail how to put points on the board, and give you a structural way to defend against all comers.

# Creating a Game Plan

The most important element in any rugby team is that all of your players have a solid grounding in basic skills. Planning complicated moves and intricate defensive systems is useless if your charges can't pass, catch, and tackle. After the essentials are taken care of it's time to move on to strategic concerns. (See Chapter 10 for full details about running, passing, kicking, and tackling.)

The burden of choosing a particular strategy rests with the coach. Implementing a sophisticated game plan will only work if the time is taken to explain all aspects of it to the players so that they understand the concepts they'll be asked to carry out on the pitch.

The most important first step in attack and defense alike is to devise a good plan. Everyone in your team must understand the plan and know what is expected of them. Winning teams concentrate initially on working out the best method for overcoming the opposition, no matter what style they play. Whether they are simple or complex, plans have to involve the whole team because any weak link will be ruthlessly exploited by the opposition.

You also need to know which of your players are capable of adapting their game on the fly in case you need to alter the plan during a match. Your number 8, scrumhalf, and flyhalf should all be able to make in-game adjustments, so keep that in mind when selecting players for those key positions. A game plan doesn't have to be complex to work, so don't feel the need to script every play like a football coach. Keep it simple and stick to what the team does well.

## Understanding your team's strengths and weaknesses

The first step in assessing your team's strengths and weaknesses is to look at the size, speed, and fitness of the players. This can be done by testing on the pitch and in the weight room. Simple physical evaluations will give you a good idea of which players are your fastest, strongest, and most fit.

Your players' level of experience will also help in the decision-making process. Maturity and knowledge of the game are vital parts of a successful squad. When you've got a good handle on your players' physical abilities and match experience you're ready to select a team and start building a strategic foundation.

Just as every player possesses unique talents, each rugby team has a distinctive character that defines how it will play. To fully evaluate your side's strengths and weaknesses, break their performance down into its various elements. Assess the set pieces, rucking and mauling, how effectively they contest possession, and their overall competence in general play.

When you examine your side, look at both the positive and negative components of their play:

- ✔ Do you have a strong forward pack that usually wins their own scrums and provides good clean ball at the back, or are they being pushed around and barely getting the ball out?

- ✔ Are your forwards adept at rucking and mauling, or is the breakdown a source of frustration, turnovers, and penalties?

- ✔ Do you have reliable jumpers in your line-out that consistently win possession and occasionally steal the ball from the other team, or do your jumpers struggle to win their own throw-ins and concede the opposition's?

- ✔ Are your back-rowers getting to the tackle situation and making an impact there, or are they late, indecisive, and ineffective?

- ✔ Can your flyhalf and fullback read the game and make good tactical decisions, or do they lack the vision to make the correct choices under pressure?

- ✔ Do you have backs with the skills to move the ball quickly who utilize their pace to cross the gain line, or is every trip down the line a retreating exercise waiting for the next knock-on?

- ✔ Do your backs tackle well in the open field, or are they a line of matadors?

Your appraisal needs to be totally impartial. This is a time for clinical observation focused on what your players can and can't do. Put aside your preconceived notions to institute a style of play that takes advantage of their talent and minimizes their deficiencies.

## Winning the set pieces

The best way to guarantee that a team has every chance to beat an opponent is to have a solid forward pack, which means that the forwards must attempt to dominate in all areas of play. At the very least, these players must hold their own in scrums and line-outs, win the ball in tackle situations, and get the ball out to the back line.

If your team can't get or keep the ball in rugby, it's impossible to win. Forwards are responsible for winning possession of the ball a majority of the time, so it's logical to build the strongest pack from the best athletes available. A solid but unspectacular back line will perform exponentially better when they are working behind a dominant set of forwards. If the forwards are poor, however, a great back line will be wasted.

The primary focus of any pack is to be able to win their own scrums. This takes hard work, dedication to the task, and countless hours of training time. Shortchanging scrum practice is a recipe for disaster. Putting out a team of fantastic backs who never get the ball because their forwards are getting steamrolled is one of the most frustrating experiences in the game. To keep this from happening, scrummagers must feel confident they can win their own ball before moving on to other tasks. (See Chapter 8 for a rundown of requirements for a strong scrum.)

If you have a dominant tight five (two props, the hooker, and the two locks) that consistently drives the opposition off the ball, scrums will be attacking platforms for your side no matter which team has the put-in. On the other hand, if you're being beaten and pushed around up front, you need to adjust your game plan to minimize the damage.

After scrums, the line-out is the next most important set piece confrontation. Timing, teamwork, and accuracy of movement and throws are the key factors to winning the ball at the line-out. Even teams that lack height and gifted jumpers can be productive at the line-out as long as they work together as a unit. (See Chapter 9 for full details about line-outs.)

If you're winning your line-outs with regularity it opens up a whole host of attacking options. Start with the driving maul, transition to a rolling maul, and, when they make adjustments to stop it, try the peel into midfield or down the blindside. (See Chapter 7 for details of driving mauls, rolling mauls, and peeling.)

If you're consistently losing the line-outs on your team's throw-in, you've got a serious problem and need to change your approach. Try throwing deep beyond the 15-meter line, or to the front lifter to mix things up. Even if you lose these throws they aren't likely to make a clean steal. If you're not having any success contesting the opposition's throws, concede the throw-in and concentrate on stopping their mauls instead.

The most overlooked set pieces are kickoffs and restarts. A normal match usually has at least four or five opportunities for each team to secure possession in this way. Unfortunately, this is often worked on infrequently, if at all, by many lower-level teams. Being ready to contest kickoffs and restarts and having a definite plan for getting the ball and distributing it to the right players during these set pieces will markedly improve your team.

Well before each game, take your captain aside and discuss what options should be chosen in every situation. Do you prefer a scrum, a line-out, or a re-kick if the restart doesn't go 10 meters? When you have the choice, do you want to kick for touch to gain territory and restart play with a line-out, or elect to set a scrum to get things moving again? These decisions require a sense of how you expect to match up against the other team and will invariably need to be refined on the fly as the match unfolds. If your captain has the game plan down, making the right choices becomes much easier.

### Playing the ten-man game

The *ten-man game* refers to a strategy in which a team focuses play around the eight forwards, the scrumhalf, and the flyhalf. (The backs are usually neglected and hardly see the ball.) The object of the ten-man game is to keep the ball in tight among the pack and drive directly through the heart of the opponent's forwards.

Playing the ten-man game is a tactical decision to consider when the players on your team have a clear advantage over the competition up front but are comparatively weaker in the back line and out wide. This type of game requires a totally dominant pack, a scrumhalf who provides good service, and a flyhalf who kicks the ball accurately, efficiently, and deep. As for the rest of the backs, they are primarily selected for their defensive prowess and ability to prevent turnovers.

In the ten-man game the forwards usually keep the ball in hand, especially if they can gain territory by using driving mauls and quick rucking. If that doesn't work, the scrumhalf will pass the ball to the flyhalf, who will then kick the ball either toward the sideline to get a line-out, or in front of the forwards for them to chase and contest for possession.

The flyhalf kicks for the sideline, knowing that his team has enough good line-out jumpers to win the ball even if the opposition has the throw-in at the line-out. Inevitably, through turnovers and good defense, the team can get close to the opposition's tryline and score the points required for victory.

These tactics are not pretty — the ball is hardly sighted in open play, and watching a big bullocking forward bustle his way over the line from a few meters out isn't exactly a moment of aesthetic beauty. Nevertheless, playing the ten-man game often ensures victory under the right circumstances.

The ten-man game is not commonly used anymore at the international level, although South Africa still practices a version of it. The speed of the modern game and the importance of teams having fast, expressive backs make the ten-man game an anomaly at the highest level. The ten-man game, even though grounded in solid principles, isn't the most entertaining spectacle for the masses — but to those who fully appreciate the subtlety of the battle up front it's awe-inspiring stuff that can be every bit as riveting as a 100-point tryfest.

The teams that still play the ten-man game do so for important reasons. Teams with powerful packs and reliable line-outs and scrums find it a comfortable way to dominate possession and territory while wearing down the opposition.

Even though the ten-man game is out of favor at the highest levels, it's an effective strategy used by club teams all over the world and deserves inclusion into your array of tactical considerations.

### Running from everywhere

At the opposite end of the spectrum from the ten-man game is the concept of *running from everywhere,* which involves an all-out, attack-at-all-costs style. The goal of this stratagem is to run the ball to gain territory from every situation. Teams that are best suited to this tactic usually have very talented backs and may lack a dominant tight five.

The attempt to run from everywhere on the pitch has to be accompanied by mobile loosies (the two flankers and the number 8) who can support their backs wherever they're stopped by the opposition. The forwards must also be excellent ruckers and ready to run for the full 80 minutes.

In club rugby, you're likely to find that competing back lines can be severely mismatched based on speed, attacking acumen, experience, and combinational dynamics. This is the ideal time to unleash your backs, who can build their confidence by thrashing inferior opposition.

The most successful rugby teams are the ones that take elements from each of these two contrasting styles, striking a balance that allows them to best utilize the talent on offer. The most respected coaches are the ones who aren't married to a particular strategy and can guide their teams based on an evaluation of how their players can be most successful.

## Analyzing the opponent

In addition to having basic skills, a successful coach makes a point of assessing the opposition's strengths and weaknesses in advance and then works on devising a strategy to beat that team.

At the professional level coaches watch videotapes and prepare detailed scouting reports. At the club level you can at least get an idea of your next opponent's playing style by sending someone from your club out to watch the team play. If the person knows what to look for he or she can provide a wealth of information on strengths and weaknesses, general tendencies, and any outstanding players or unusual tactics.

### Exploiting weaknesses

The first order of business for taking down an opponent is to note any obvious chinks in their armor and take advantage of them. For example, you may notice that the opposition fullback or wings are nervous when the ball is kicked high into the air. If they've struggled with the high ball, test them repeatedly until either they perform successfully or you've gained lots of possession from their miscues. (The same goes for players who are hesitant in the tackle. Target them with strong runners and see if this can give you an advantage in attack.)

A fantastic area for exploitation is in the set pieces. If the other side is having trouble winning their scrums or producing good ball, have your team concentrate on the *eight-man push* (where all eight forwards use coordinated strength to drive the opposition back) and direct your scrumhalf to heighten his aggressiveness in pressuring his opposite.

Anywhere on the rugby pitch where you think your team can legally get the upper hand is a legitimate area to exploit, but be careful in doing so. It's more important that your team stick to the game plan than to try too many spontaneous tactics in the heat of battle. Of course, if your strategy calls for taking advantage of predetermined opposition inadequacies, by all means exploit away!

### Containing the stars

In any rugby competition certain players stand head and shoulders above everyone else by dint of their exceptional talent or skills. Even though rugby is a team game, it sometimes becomes necessary to put in place special measures to stop a certain rampaging opponent. Most of the time this means either denying that player the ball or applying additional pressure on him whenever he touches it.

It's not a good idea to rearrange your whole game plan to cope with the speed or power of one individual. What works best is to emphasize basics in tackling and review your defensive goals prior to the match. Containing the stars should always be done within the context of your established defensive pattern and definitely without resorting to cheap shots or illegal tactics.

Sometimes the best strategies for defeating star players are simple. If one of the opposition's jumpers is poaching all your throw-ins, try throwing the ball to a different spot in the line-out. Kicking the ball away from a particular player or cheating a little in spacing to reduce gaps for stars to run through can also be a simple but effective tactic. The best overall strategy is to minimize the impact by denying them opportunities to make big plays.

### Selecting horses for courses

*Selecting horses for courses* is an old-time rugby saying that means the players chosen for a certain match should be determined by the nature of that particular contest. If the opposition has a mammoth pack and you're worried about losing set piece ball, this is a good time to bulk up your own pack, even if it costs you some mobility. Similarly, if the opponent is loaded with pace in the back line you may want to choose quicker, more mobile players in your team to counteract their advantage.

The adage also applies to strategic concerns. When your team is forced to use a style of game it's not used to (either because of weather conditions or the strength of the opposition), certain players may be better suited for the revised game plan than your regular starters. For example, a flyhalf who specializes in kicking may be a more suitable selection than an attack-oriented flyhalf on a wet, windy day.

The emergence of impact players as substitutes has added another dimension to the "horses for courses" axiom. Some players are great at coming off the bench and making their presence felt but struggle if they have to play the full 80 minutes. Others can play solid rugby over the course of a match but are very ordinary when they come on as replacements. Recognizing these traits and filling your reserve bench with the appropriate performers is a coaching necessity.

# Weathering the Conditions

Rugby is a game meant to be played outside in all types of conditions. Gale force winds, sleeting rain, oppressive heat, or freezing temperatures usually won't keep a match from happening but will alter its character. In most cases the conditions on the pitch are the same for both sides. One team may have the wind in one half but the other gets it in the second stanza. Rain stopping and starting affects both teams equally, and humidity drains everyone's energy.

Depending on where your club is located, it may be normal to play in rainstorms or on excessively hot days. The difficulty emerges when you have to play in conditions that are completely foreign or that you're unprepared for. A good coach does everything possible to have his team ready to perform however the elements may intervene.

Altitude is one case where the home team does have a distinct advantage over the visitors. It takes the body at least a couple of weeks to fully adjust to changes in altitude, so unless a visiting side prepares for a fortnight in the opposition's backyard, they will feel the stress of reduced oxygen content sooner than their hosts.

# Adapting to inclement weather

Rain is the great equalizer in rugby because it makes the ball difficult to handle and slows everyone down when the ground gets waterlogged. When it's wet out, it's a good idea to keep the ball in hand as much as possible and avoid throwing it around like a giant oval-shaped bar of soap. This strategy calls for more mauling and working the pick-and-go (see Chapter 7 for more details), as opposed to passing incessantly (which is likely to produce a multitude of turnovers and scrums).

Many teams opt for a kicking-oriented, positional game when rain becomes a factor. If the weather dictates a radical change in tactics, it's better to put them into place right away, not after an attempt to use your regular style has failed.

A windy day calls for testing the opposition with the high ball, so be prepared for them to do the same thing to you. A strong breeze can also wreak havoc with line-out throws, so it's a good idea to stay away from long ones to the back that will end up being blown not straight or away from your jumpers.

# Playing the pitch

Rugby pitches in North America vary from plush carpets of immaculate green grass to concrete-like dirt interspersed with weeds. You have to be able to play on different surfaces from week to week depending on your league. Here are a few tips for being able to play on any pitch:

- Always arrive early and inspect the ground by walking around the pitch before the match begins. This includes looking for safety hazards and finding out if there are any noticeable slopes or abnormalities in the field of play or tryzones.

- Make sure your players always have a couple of different lengths of studs for their boots so they can swap them if necessary. On a very hard surface, wearing boots with long studs can be like running on an ice rink, but they provide better traction on a soft track.

- Figure out in advance where the sun and wind are headed so your captain can make an informed choice during the coin toss. If your defensive confidence is high, playing against the wind in the first half can provide a psychological boost to your team knowing that you'll have the advantage of the wind in the second half.

BROWNIE SAYS

## Adaptation

Growing up and going to college in Southern California shielded me from ever having to participate in sports during inclement weather (unless you count smog alerts). My first years of rugby were played in idyllic conditions, with heat being the only real climatic factor.

That all changed when I moved to Missoula, Montana, and began playing for the Maggots. Suddenly, I had to be able to adapt on a weekly basis. Late-summer snowstorms weren't uncommon, and a blizzard in October was considered normal. The idea of not playing just because a foot of snow was falling was anathema to the hardy denizens of the Montana Rugby Union, so the games went on as scheduled regardless of the conditions.

My atmospheric education continued in Riga, Latvia, where it seemed that only one match out of every ten wasn't played in the rain, and dirt was the surface of necessity until May 1. It was in Riga that I was also introduced to Winter 10's, played in subzero temperatures on a sheet of ice covered in snow for padding. Playing in these conditions I learned that you only get cold when you're standing around, so to avoid freezing to death you had to keep moving.

The biggest shock was when I went to play for Vail, Colorado, in 1999. I had heard about altitude affecting physical fitness, but since I was out of shape anyway I didn't think I'd be a victim. About a minute into my first match in Aspen I was gasping for breath and looking to the sideline for a replacement but there was none forthcoming. By the end of the summer I had acclimated and was warning the newcomers to the Colorado mountains.

Finally, back in Los Angeles after experiencing chilly climes all over the rugby universe, I now actually prefer playing in cold, rainy weather and reserve my complaining for when the mercury rises above 75 degrees. Adapting to unfamiliar conditions forced me to focus on basic skills and mental toughness to overcome challenging circumstances.

# Deciding on a Game Plan

Before the first match, a coach decides which style of play best suits the talents of his assembled charges. As the season unfolds and players begin to jell, injuries take their toll, and what works and what doesn't becomes obvious, the coach needs to adapt. He should employ a dynamic approach to preparing each week's game plan that takes into account the present state of his side and the opposition.

When trying to determine what type of play will lead your team to victory it may be useful to organize your thoughts by asking yourself a series of questions. Do you expect to win the contest for possession in the forwards? Are your backs superior to theirs? Where along the continuum, from playing the ten-man game to running from everywhere, takes best advantage of your team's comparative strengths? After you've settled upon an overall strategy that's calculated for your opponent, you then shift to specifics.

The initial area of concern is *first-phase possession*, which refers to a team gaining possession of the ball from set pieces (scrums, line-outs, restarts, and so on) instead of stealing possession from a ball-carrier from the opposing team. Do you expect to win the set pieces or will you struggle to get the ball from restarts? For example, if you think you'll have a clear advantage in the line-outs, you'll feel more comfortable kicking the ball for touch to keep your opponent pinned in their own end. On the other hand, if the other team is full of dominant line-out jumpers, your team would be better off with a plan that keeps the ball in play through several phases and avoids putting it out of bounds.

The next area to look at is how you match up at the breakdown. On attack, do you expect your loosies to get there first in support of your ball-carriers, or will they be beaten to the spot and have difficulty recycling the ball? If you have the upper hand in maintaining possession, you can implement a more expansive attacking style. If you think the enemy has better ball-ferreting skills, avoid the tackle situation by passing before contact and use kicks to advance the ball.

It's rarely a simple matter of saying we have better forwards or backs and therefore we should adopt one style or another. More often you'll identify areas where you expect to hold an advantage, others that will be even, and some where the opposition will be better. The best game plan utilizes these observations to accentuate your strengths and minimize your weaknesses.

Your game plan shouldn't be written in stone. You need to be able to adjust your strategy as the game unfolds. Watching and analyzing your opponents during a game is critical. The first 40 minutes of a match can give a quick-thinking coach plenty of material to rapidly digest and then make changes for the second half.

# Attacking Artistically

A successful attacking game plan relies on predetermined patterns and collective goals. Before a team goes into a game the players should have practiced a variety of attacking moves during training, with everyone clear on their roles and responsibilities.

Attack plans don't have to be overly innovative or elaborate, but they do have to be precisely executed and not easily read by the defense. When the defenders don't know what's going to happen next they're more likely to hesitate, which creates gaps for your side to exploit. Intricate moves that confuse your own side do more harm than good, so keep it simple at first.

## Launching an effective attack

Offensive attacks, where your team has the ball, can be initiated from set pieces, general play, or turnover ball. The starting point for every move is how the ball is presented before the attack begins. If the ball is made available from a controlled platform, it's called *quality possession.* When your attack begins with quality possession your back line's timing and coordination aren't disrupted, which increases their chances of success.

Quality possession at scrumtime means the ball is delivered cleanly, quickly, and accurately to the backs. Sloppy ball from a scrum that's moving backward is nearly impossible for a scrumhalf to use positively. Likewise, if you're struggling to win clean ball at the line-out, your scrumhalf will be under tremendous pressure distributing the ball. Because it's rare to score a try directly off first-phase possession, launching an effective attack more often depends on how efficiently you can reset your attacking pattern through multiple phases.

The most dangerous attacking opportunities come from turnover balls that are used quickly. Immediately after turnovers (when possession of the ball moves from one team to the other), the team that loses the ball will be ill-prepared to defend because the players will still be in an attacking formation. The key here is that the team with possession launches its attack before the opposition can assume a defensive posture. Rucks and mauls are the most common launching pads for attacking movements because they provide an excellent base for unleashing your back line. This is because defenders tend to get sucked into the fray at the breakdown, creating space and potential mismatches out wide.

If you can't run through or around the other team, you can integrate attacking with the boot into your game plan. You can kick into open space with the goal of regathering the ball, or boot it high to put pressure on the receiver.

## Breaking through

Breaching the opponent's line requires a targeted point of attack. If you can beat them out wide, use your speed. If they have a particularly weak tackler, run repeatedly right at him. If they're coming up hard and flat, use deception to draw them out of position. When you can't find a way through, kick it behind them to turn 'em around.

Successful attacking moves rely on correct alignment, running proper angles, and hitting the gain line at pace using a coordinated sequence of movements. Positioning your back line flat and close makes passing easier but provides less time and space to operate in. Placing them deeper and wider gives them more room to move, but allows defenders to cover multiple attackers and diminishes the space out wide.

Practice a new move over and over, first in slow motion and then gradually increasing the speed until everyone knows exactly where to be and what to do. Attacking artistically relies on good communication, with your playmaker calling the play and the rest of the team getting into position to run it.

You can usually tell when a set move is about to happen because the playmaker starts talking and gesticulating to his back line.

# Defending Devilishly

The ultimate goal of playing defense is to regain possession of the ball. The effectiveness of any defense is dependent on the structure used and the attitude of the players. The objective is to employ an aggressive, pressure-oriented scheme that focuses on stopping the offense and stealing the ball.

The most important defensive attribute is commitment. There's no place for half-hearted attempts to tackle in rugby, because the likely result is that you'll miss the runner and hurt yourself in the process.

## Coordinating the defense

The keys to team defense are communication, structure, and execution. Playing defense is a fluid activity where you need to constantly react to an ever-changing situation. Communication is vital, because as the attack changes you need to talk to each other to maintain your pattern. The defensive structure relies upon every player knowing where to cover, making good tackles, and understanding what everyone else is doing.

An effective defensive team plan requires working together as a unit, communicating well, and backing each other up when necessary. Walking and talking your team through their defensive system is every bit as important as hours and hours of tackling drills. Be sure your players understand the concepts behind what's expected of them.

## Blocking the advance: Defensive systems

Pressure, width, and depth are the three main principles of team defense. Pressure takes time and space away from the attacking team. Width prevents them from running around the outside of the defense. Depth provides additional levels of defenders who can step up and make tackles.

# The Crusaders

The Crusaders have won five Super 12 titles and one Super 14 title because they excel on defense. They have an enormous capacity to defend over long periods of time against multiple-phase attack without losing their defensive pattern. The Crusaders take great pride in their defense and it's the cornerstone of their entire game plan. They relish the opportunity to make a tackle, always trying to meet the runner behind the gain line and knock him back so that the ball can be turned over. At the fringes of rucks, you'll see Crusader players pointing and calling out to each other while getting ready to make the next tackle so everyone knows their role well before the ball comes out. As soon as the scrumhalf touches the ball they become an attacking force on defense, charging up the field to crush the infidels for daring to challenge the men from Christchurch. By sharing self-belief in their collective strength, the Crusaders prevent the attacking side from creating confusion and hesitation among the faithful defenders. They all know their mission and believe wholeheartedly in each other's desire to get the job done. Establishing trust is a fundamental part of developing the resolve necessary to maintain defensive solidarity and a critical element in creating a championship culture. Once that trust is established there's no limit to what your team will endure to achieve its collective goals.

Two basic approaches to applying defensive pressure, ensuring width, and maintaining depth are man-on-man and drift.

- ✔ **The man-on-man defense:** Defenders are responsible for tackling their opposites.

- ✔ **The drift defense:** Defenders drift sideways to cover the next attacker outside them.

### Man-on-man defense

In *man-on-man* defense, each tackler's assignment is to contain his opposite.

Figure 11-1 shows the defensive formation at a scrum, with the defenders *marking,* or matching up against, the attacking team (as shown by the arrows). For example, the defending flyhalf marks the attacking team's number 10. To cover the last player in the formation, the defending fullback moves toward the sideline to cover the attacking team's left wing.

### Drift defense

The *drift defense* involves the defenders all sliding outside in unison to take away the attacking team's ability to outflank them. It's often used after a line-out or a scrum and provides increased width and depth, but lacks the pressure element of the man-on-man defense.

Figure 11-2 illustrates a scrum with the defenders setting-up a drift defense. The normal progression is that the openside flanker takes the attacking flyhalf while the defending flyhalf pursues the inside center, followed by the inside center being responsible for the outside center, and so forth down the line. The defense drifts across field, cutting off any attempt to come back inside while forcing the ball-carriers toward the sidelines.

When executed properly, the drift defense accounts for an extra attacker being brought into the line. For example, if the extra attacker enters the line between the inside center and the outside center, that player would be tackled by the defending inside center.

**Figure 11-1:**
Ready to mount a man-on-man defense.

## Commitment and trust

The best defending sides all share a common trait — trust. Developing mutual trust among your players is essential when it comes to team defense. Confidence in your fellow defenders' ability and commitment to tackling builds the trust required to stay focused on your individual defensive responsibilities.

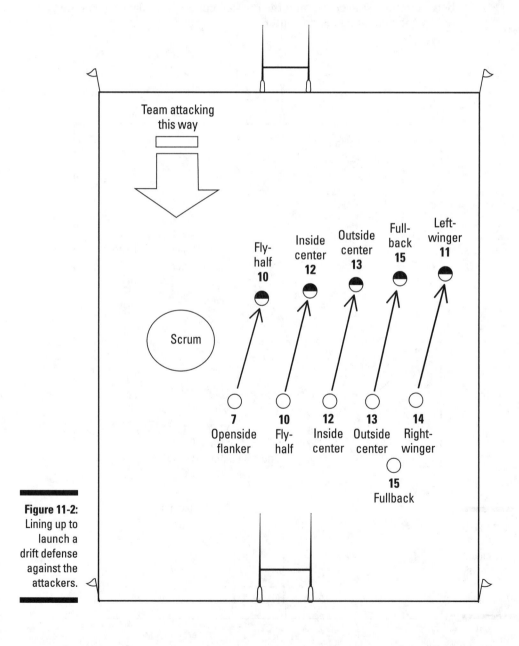

**Figure 11-2:**
Lining up to launch a drift defense against the attackers.

# Chapter 12

# Talented Training

*In This Chapter*

▶ Shaping up for action

▶ Winning with your wits

▶ Eating right for rugby

For most of its history rugby was largely an amateur sport where even at the highest levels players had to have a career outside the game to support themselves. Training was usually done after the end of the workday. That all changed with the advent of professionalism in 1995, when modern training regimens were introduced and the fitness required to excel in the game shot up accordingly. Rugby players at the international level are now the same as professional athletes in other contact sports, but the approaches to conditioning vary from country to country.

A typical rugby match involves miles of running interspersed with hundreds of bursts of energy when you encounter the enemy. To survive and pass this grueling test of cardiovascular and muscular endurance, you need to be strong and extremely fit. As the game has become less stop/start and more fluid in recent years, the fitness level required to keep pace has increased commensurately. This requires a more focused approach to physical preparation that develops both baseline conditioning and position-specific fitness.

In this chapter, we describe what you need to do to attain a basic level of fitness, how to mentally prepare for matches, and what to eat for peak performance.

# Getting Match Fit

Fitness is acquired in the hours spent running or working out on your own in the gym, not at training. For non-professionals, the limited amount of practice time necessitates a focus on skills and drills and leaves very little room for conditioning. All rugby players should be physically prepared for battle before the season begins instead of the old method of playing their way into shape. Nothing takes the place of hard work.

Before rashly starting any exercise program, think carefully about the physical demands made on you in a match. You need to build and maintain a level of fitness that ensures you have plenty of the following:

- **Stamina:** Because a match is played over 80 minutes, you need to develop both aerobic and anaerobic fitness. *Aerobic capacity* gives you the endurance needed to roam the pitch for the entire match. *Anaerobic capacity* provides energy for repetitive bursts of high exertion over the course of the game.

- **Strength and power:** Because you constantly encounter opposing forces who want to run over the top of you, you need to be strong enough to stop them and reply in kind. You also need muscular endurance to be as tough in the last minute of play as you are the first.

- **Flexibility:** When you have the ball in your hands, or are trying to take it away from the opposition in all phases of play, you need flexibility to be effective and avoid injury.

Even in the final minutes of the game, you should still be breathing easily. Sprawling face-down in the turf suffering from exhaustion or cramps does nothing to help your side and is not a good look.

Focus on exercises that target the parts of your body you want to strengthen, but be careful not to overdo it — we don't want legions of *Rugby For Dummies* readers turning up at their doctors' offices tomorrow with strains, sprains, and broken bones. Only do as much as you feel comfortable with and increase the intensity of your workout gradually. Fitness can't be acquired in a few days or even weeks so don't try to speed up the timetable — it will only lead to disappointment.

## Warming up and having a good stretch

Before every practice or fitness session, start with a well-planned warm-up. Establishing a routine that prepares the body for the higher level of exertion to follow is very important. Jogging a couple of laps, riding an exercise bike, jumping rope, or doing light calisthenics are all acceptable methods of breaking a sweat and warming up.

A good warm-up followed by a stretching routine minimizes the risk of injury. Improving your flexibility can help prevent ligament, joint, and muscle injuries on the big day. Devote at least 10 to 15 minutes to stretching before you start the more strenuous activities. All the stretches that are described in this chapter will help increase your flexibility and get you ready for action.

Perform stretching only if you're absolutely sure you can manage it. It's always a good idea to check with your coach and your doctor to determine whether a new program is right for you. This is especially important if you've been injured before or have any health problems.

## Stretching for performance

Stretching is an important part of any training program and should be performed with as much care and enthusiasm as the active part of any training session. The stretching program should be prepared before training starts and have goals and objectives already in place.

Obviously, different training regimens require the use of different muscle groups. The stretching that comes after training should be targeted toward those groups that have carried the biggest workload.

For example, if the session will feature sprint training, it needs to focus on stretching the hamstrings, calves, glutes, and hip flexors. If the workout involves upper-body weight training, you need to stretch the chest, back, and shoulders. Other areas still get stretched, but more emphasis should be placed on these target areas. Any stretching session should have goals and guidelines in place.

The goals should be:

- Preparing for training (dynamic stretching may be used)
- Maintaining flexibility (static)
- Increasing flexibility (developmental)
- Helping recover from injury (may include all of the above)

Stretching can have many benefits, including:

- Helping to reduce muscle tension
- Helping to clear metabolic waste (lactic acid) from muscles
- Increasing the length of and straightening muscle fibers
- Improving body awareness
- Increasing quality of muscle movement
- Helping with muscle firing patterns

All of these elements together increase the quality of recovery, thereby allowing players to train with a higher intensity and have less time in the rest/recovery phase (or on the physiotherapist's table with an injury). Many a promising player has had his or her career cut short because of an avoidable injury.

Dynamic stretching has become very popular before activity because it takes the muscles through a range of movement and stretches them in the same way they will be used during a game. It also helps establish firing patterns within the muscles' stretch reflex and proprioceptors (sensory receptors found in muscles that detect motion or position of the body or a limb by responding to stimuli arising within the organism) so the correct signals are being relayed at the appropriate time, thus preparing them to go from a slow jog to an explosive sprint without tearing.

### Dynamic stretch routine

Start your dynamic stretching routine with the usual jog, followed by some static stretching to slowly warm up and help with muscle lengthening. As you get warmed up, you can add in dynamic stretching. After you start stretching dynamically, don't go back to static stretching. Remember, static stretching slows the muscles down and dynamic stretching wakes them up.

Doing 6 to 10 repetitions of each of the following stretches is recommended, but on a cold day more may be necessary.

- ✔ Groin: walking, side-step, and standing
- ✔ Hamstrings and quads: walking and standing
- ✔ Waist and lower back: standing and bent at waist
- ✔ Back and hamstrings: ground and bent
- ✔ Waist and adductors: sitting
- ✔ Calves: standing and leaning forward
- ✔ Shoulders and upper back: standing

### Static stretching after training

Finish with a static stretch following your training session. Static stretching returns the muscles to the length they were when they started and is most effective when the stretching is focused on the muscles most heavily utilized in the session. Work for 5 to 15 minutes and hold the stretches for 15 to 30 seconds each.

A *stretching diary*, which keeps track of all your stretches, is very helpful in staying focused on the task at hand and keeping some form of order to your stretch routine.

## Developing a fitness program

To prepare yourself properly for rugby, you need a fitness program that develops speed, muscular strength, agility, and cardiovascular endurance. To improve your *cardiovascular endurance* — that is, to increase the fitness of your heart and lung system — you need a series of exercises that enhances the body's ability to take in oxygen and circulate it throughout the body to your muscles, which will be screaming for more O2. If you have plenty of stamina, you won't run out of gas or tire excessively while playing or training.

### Improving your stamina

When your heart is pumping fast and you're sweating bullets, whether you know it or not you're working on your stamina. One of the best ways to increase stamina is to run varying distances. A good combination is to do distance work and then finish with some sprinting (which we cover in the next section). For distance work, your ultimate goal is to be able to run nonstop for 6 miles (because this is roughly the ground you cover during an average match). To start off, try running around the pitch for about 20 minutes at a slow but steady rate and see how you feel.

If you're unaccustomed to running, increase the distance slowly. Stay within your comfort zone until you can hold a conversation or sing to yourself while jogging effortlessly. When you can do that, increase the distance in small increments. After you reach the 6-mile plateau, gradually increase your speed, lowering your total running time.

Don't do too much too early, otherwise you may cause muscle damage. Run well within your own limits and stop if you suddenly find yourself struggling. Your distance and speed will improve over time, but not overnight!

### Running at full tilt: Sprint training

Rugby involves periods of jogging mixed with flat-out sprinting. So, after you're comfortable jogging, you need to work on your speed by sprinting shorter distances. Try running at a brisker pace from one end of the field to the other, take a 30-second break, and then run back the other way followed by another break. Do this three or four times. You may struggle early on, but within days you will discover that the number of sprints you can make before collapsing in a heap rises remarkably.

Sprint training is an important element in building up speed. During a game, a player often has to accelerate from a standing start and hit top speed within a couple of seconds. To simulate this activity and improve your speed, your training schedule should include a series of sprints punctuated by prescribed rest periods, which is called *interval training*.

An effective sequence is to run ten 10-meter sprints with a 15-second rest between each one, move up to ten 20-meter sprints with a 30-second rest between them, followed by ten 30-meter sprints with 45 seconds of rest, finishing with ten 40-meter sprints with 60 seconds of rest between each.

As your cardiovascular fitness increases, you'll find that it progressively takes less time to recover during the resting intervals. Interval training mimics the type of exertion required in a match, so give it your full effort on every repetition — visualize yourself running toward the tryline for the game winner with an opponent hot on your heels.

Sprint training is demanding fitness work and should be done only after you've warmed up properly. If you begin your fitness program without stretching or warming up first you can cause some serious muscle injuries.

### Working on your agility

To improve your agility, construct an obstacle course with cones placed at intervals of 4 to 5 meters. With a rugby ball in your hands, weave through the markers and practice bounding off first your left foot and then your right foot, as if trying to get past a defender with the side-step or swerve (Chapter 10 gives full details about these moves). Begin slowly, but challenge yourself by trying to move quicker each time.

You can try this in your own backyard or at a neighborhood park. You'll not only improve your agility, you'll also keep the neighbors entertained. Watch out for small dogs yapping at your heels and local kids trying to figure out what on earth you're doing.

Another good drill is to run at speed through the same obstacle course, throwing the ball up and regathering it. Let the ball bounce occasionally, so you get accustomed to picking it up from the ground while on the run.

### Building up your strength

Increased competition among professionals has raised the physical demands of the sport. The lucky few who play for money have become reliant on lifting weights to improve their strength and power. Although weight-lifting is mandatory preparation for the advanced player it isn't essential for prepubescent youngsters, who can build up their strength by going down a different, perhaps safer path.

A heavy weight-lifting program can cause permanent damage to bones and muscles if the body is not yet ready to accept heavy weights. If you want to lift weights, ask your coach for advice about an appropriate, safe, and effective weight-lifting program.

Good old-fashioned push-ups and sit-ups are perfect for toning the body and increasing upper-body strength. If you begin slowly and gradually build up the number of repetitions your strength is sure to improve.

### Varying your routines

Variation is an important aspect of training. Change your regimen regularly and don't be afraid to attempt different ways to get fit. If you get bored while training you eventually won't bother, which won't do much to develop your conditioning. Training with a partner is also very effective, because you'll take turns motivating each other to get into the gym or out onto the track and push yourselves to achieve more than you may on your own.

Get adventurous: Invent your own drills that involve a rugby ball. The more times you have a ball in your hands, the more comfortable you'll become with it. Before long, the ball feels like a natural extension of your hands.

A simple, fun activity for two people is a kicking game. Start just outside the 22-meter lines on opposite sides of the pitch and try to kick the ball as far as you can over the other player's head. Then your partner has to kick it back to you from wherever it was caught. The goal is to gain ground and drive the other player back toward the tryline. If you're by yourself, kick and chase the ball up and down the field, trying out various styles of kicks and working on regathering. The constant kicking and running will improve your kicking accuracy, catching skills, and overall fitness.

Coaches should utilize a balanced approach to developing each player's individual and the team's collective fitness. Create a plan that addresses their particular and team deficiencies, monitors their progress, and adjusts as needed over the course of the season.

Because approaches often vary widely within a single country from international down to provincial and club levels, you'll find plenty of different schools of thought on virtually every aspect of getting match fit. The key is to welcome new ideas and make them your own.

# The Zen Theory of Rugby Fitness

Being match fit is crucial for peak performance over 80 minutes of gut-wrenching exertion. However, if you have the experience and mental powers required, no matter how unfit you are you can still make an impact over the entire match using the Zen Theory of Rugby Fitness. Under the theory, you conserve energy whenever possible and exert yourself only when it's absolutely vital, picking your spots carefully. The goal is to be the polar opposite of a rookie who chases the ball all over the field running aimlessly like a chicken with its head cut off. This can only be accomplished by wily veterans who draw upon all their vast reserves of rugby knowledge. The strategy necessitates an uncanny sense of anticipation as to where play is going.

If the ball is headed out wide and is likely to come back inside toward you, there's no point in running out there when you're already perfectly positioned to defend when the pill works its way back inside. As you roam the pitch, look for critical opportunities to inject yourself with a sudden burst of pace, a well-timed clean-out at a ruck, or a crucial tackle that will stop a promising movement cold just before it gets rolling.

The key to gaining enlightenment through the Zen Theory is concentration and mentally willing the ball to come back to where you are. You must remain totally focused on preserving what precious little gas you have left in that old rusted-out tank. You need to avoid at all costs the destructive effects of taking an unwarranted quick step, unless the circumstances dictate. The theory is definitely not for beginners, as they lack the rugby IQ to correctly pick their spots. In fact, the Zen Theory of Rugby Fitness isn't really appropriate for anyone other than gray-haired veterans like me, who occasionally turn out for master's games. But like most things in rugby, explaining the theory makes great conversation over a couple of cold beers at the reception.

# Psyching Up for a Stellar Performance

Although it's terrific to look good and be able to run effortlessly for 80 minutes, if you lack the right mentality your physical prowess won't translate into effective play. Getting mentally prepared doesn't mean spending days on a psychologist's couch or calling the psychic hot line to find out what the stars say about your team's chances in the match tomorrow.

Being mentally prepared means you're totally focused on the task at hand and can instantly sum up a situation and work out the best way to handle it on the fly. Rugby is often like a chess game revolving around intricate strategies with the best players responding instinctively to the variations as they unfold in front of them.

## The Zone

Former All Black Murray Mexted, who played in every International match for New Zealand from 1979 to 1986, had a unique way to mentally switch on prior to tests. In the changing room before each match, he would imagine reaching up with both arms to pull down a huge light switch that would put him into what he calls "The Zone." When the switch was thrown, he became totally focused on the task at hand, completely destroying his opposite and contributing in every way possible to an All Blacks victory. He cleared his mind of everything else so he could focus all his mental energy on the game.

Mental toughness separates the good from the great rugby players. While Murray's light switch method may not turn you on, you can develop your own technique to get mentally focused before each kickoff and stay that way throughout the match.

Before each game, take some quiet time and ask yourself these questions:

✔ What are my responsibilities in the game plan?

✔ What's likely to happen in the game?

✔ What do I want to accomplish and what am I expected to achieve?

✔ How can I best take advantage of any opportunities that present themselves?

Get motivated by visualizing yourself scoring the winning try, kicking the winning goal, or leading your team to a memorable victory. Most great players find this an effective way to build their confidence. If it works for them, it can work for you.

Good mental preparation means you're less likely to shy away when a big, intimidating second-rower runs straight at you. Fear is important so long as it doesn't hinder your performance. All players, at some stage of their playing careers, experience the fear of failure or the fear of injury. It's a natural emotion in a contact sport, but you can use it to your advantage by re-channelling the adrenaline flow into controlled aggression.

# Eating Your Way to Victory

Gone are the days when rugby players believed that loading up their breakfast plates with steak, eggs, and hash browns was the only way to win. A starvation diet that allows you only one celery stick a day is not the answer either. If you want to be a successful rugby player, common sense has to prevail — eating and drinking in moderation is the only way to go.

## Choosing a balanced diet

Nowadays most professional rugby teams have a dietician hovering somewhere in the shadows, someone who's counting calories and monitoring milkshakes all under the guise of recommending the optimal diet for rugby fitness. For the elite athlete, dietary modification is a proven method of marginally increasing performance.

For the club player, your diet should be dictated by your general level of fitness. Although no one single food is likely to make you a superstar, as a rugby player you have more energy requirements than the average Joe walking down the street. Common sense should lead you away from fast food and bingeing on too many pints of Ben & Jerry's.

Eat a balanced diet that includes proteins, carbohydrates, fats, and fiber, and foods that provide nutrients, vitamins, and minerals. This means taking in measured amounts of food from each of the four food groups. For peak performance, make 60 to 70 percent of your daily caloric intake come from carbohydrates, along with 15 percent protein and 15 percent from fats.

Clearly, the best thing a rugby player in training can drink is not the amber fluid — it's water. Dehydration causes fatigue more than any other dietary factor. Contrary to the prevailing wisdom contained in the Oxy Olde Boys training manual, beer does not, in fact, help you take on water to play the game. So drink plenty of water all week long to replace the water you've lost during training. Two hours before kickoff is too late to guzzle a gallon of water to prevent dehydration.

## Taking in fuel

Never eat too close to game time. Consume your pre-game meal about four hours before kickoff, allowing enough time for food to settle in your stomach. The most effective pre-game fuel is high in carbohydrates, low in fat, and low in protein. Loading up on a couple of double cheeseburgers and a giant bag of fries is definitely not recommended before you play. Instead, opt for a bowl of meatless pasta with lots of vegetables and tomato sauce.

At all costs, avoid eating on the way to a game or just before kickoff. Nothing is guaranteed to make a player more sluggish than running on a full stomach.

After you finish punishing your body at training you need fuel to recover, so it's a good idea to eat within an hour following practice. Milk and yogurt are very good for recovery purposes because they contain about 50 percent carbohydrates and 50 percent proteins. And if your club assembles for a post-practice chat, it certainly won't hurt to drink a pint of water before each pint of ale.

## Choosing your supplements carefully

Professional players who use supplements to maximize performance do so under the guidance of dieticians and doctors. In these circumstances, supplements can have a safe and beneficial impact on your play.

If you're a club player and are considering taking supplements, schedule a doctor's appointment and discuss whether they're safe and appropriate for you. Eating right, training smart, and getting plenty of rest are the tried-and-tested ways to improve performance. Don't be tricked into thinking that supplements can provide a shortcut to success.

One line of products to avoid are so-called energy drinks. If they contain heaps of caffeine and other stimulants, they aren't appropriate for use because they lead to an elevated heart rate and dehydration.

# Part III

# Welcome to the Oval Planet

Several injuries resulted from this year's running with the bulls event in Pamplona, Spain, involving a European rugby team. The bulls remain in stable condition, while the team members expressed their concern from a local cafe.

# In this part . . .

This part of the book explores the various rugby competitions around the globe. We start our tour of planet rugby with a look at the Rugby World Cup, the sport's crowning jewel, where we offer up all you need to know about the quadrennial tournament, including its history and format, plus some of the most memorable moments dating back to 1987.

Then we explain how the game is controlled worldwide and take you on a tour of the world's annual international tournaments, including the Six Nations and the Tri Nations Series. The interprovincial scene is next, with a glance at the Super 14, Heineken Cup, and Magners League. We conclude our international sojourn with a peek at the leading domestic leagues in New Zealand, South Africa, and Europe.

Closer to home, we discuss the North American international picture and then focus on the heart and soul of the game, the local club. We finish with a survey of the collegiate, high school, and youth rugby scene.

# Chapter 13

# The World Cup

- - - - - - - - - - - - - - - - - - - - - - - - - - - - - - - - - - - - - - - - - - - -

## In This Chapter

▶ Polishing the William Webb Ellis Cup

▶ Charting the World Cup from beginnings to behemoth

▶ Qualifying for the tourney

▶ Looking at the North American experience

▶ Learning from experience: Small countries tackling rugby giants

▶ Reviewing some great World Cup moments

▶ Checking out other cups on offer

- - - - - - - - - - - - - - - - - - - - - - - - - - - - - - - - - - - - - - - - - - - -

For most of its history, rugby has been an insular game. Development and expansion of the sport was seen as despoiling its traditions and uniqueness. With the exception of a few poorly attended inclusions in various Olympic games, until 1987 determining a world champion was always an unofficial bit of guesswork, open to interpretation and argument. That all changed in the mid-1980s when the International Rugby Board (IRB) was dragged kicking and screaming into the modern era.

In this chapter we give you an overview of what the Rugby World Cup has become in just 20-odd years, explain how it came about, provide qualification details, and look at some other components of the World Cup system.

## The Crown Jewel of Rugby

The Rugby World Cup is the pinnacle of achievement for players and coaches around the oval planet. Every four years, touring fans converge on the tournament to display their national pride and revel in historical rivalries, while attending a multitude of social events and enjoying plenty of rugby camaraderie. The pool matches are like the NCAA Basketball Tournament, where long shots get a chance to topple the favorites and pretenders emerge as contenders. The knockout stages culminate with the Cup final, producing a Super Bowl–like atmosphere with the world's collective focus on one single match. In fact, only the Soccer World Cup and the Olympics command a larger worldwide television audience!

From the first hastily organized 16-team tournament in Australia and New Zealand in 1987, the Rugby World Cup has grown into to a quadrennial spectacle that's watched by more than three billion people around the globe. Staging the tournament has become an immense undertaking that involves the resources of an entire nation or region, worldwide corporate sponsorship, and an army of volunteers and paid administrators.

The prize awarded to the winner of the Rugby World Cup is the William Webb Ellis Cup, named after the legendary founder of the game. Lifting the cup in triumph has become the primary goal of the world's leading rugby-playing nations, more important than any other rivalry or competition. For years prior to each edition, national unions and their coaches focus on developing players and strategies to bring "Bill," as the trophy has come to be known, back to their shores.

In its current format, which is determined individually during the bidding process to host the next event, the World Cup brings together 20 teams that have qualified either by their performance in the previous Cup or through regional elimination. The participants are seeded according to world ranking and placed in four pools of five teams. Every pool member plays each other and the top two teams advance to the quarterfinals. The eventual finals victor gets the title of World Champion for the next four years.

# The Origins and History of the Rugby World Cup

The World Cup was born out of a desire by the Southern Hemisphere nations to increase the visibility of the game around the world. From its beginnings, rugby was mostly amateur and all aspects of commercialization were tightly controlled by each national union and the IRB. The more tradition-bound members from the Northern Hemisphere feared that commercialization would lead to the encroachment of professionalism — which is indeed what happened, albeit a few years later.

In the early 1980s Australia and New Zealand both proposed the idea of holding a World Cup, and by 1985, after much study and committee work, they were finally able to force a vote on the issue in the IRB Executive Committee. With backing from France, which had always been inclined toward moving the game into the professional ranks, and a late decision by South Africa to support the idea, the measure passed and the world's third great sporting competition came into being.

## 1987 World Cup — Australia and New Zealand

The first World Cup in 1987 involved 16 invited teams and was held in Australia and New Zealand. The tournament was a moderate commercial success but achieved much more in the area of exposure, with more than half a million fans attending matches and some 300 million supporters following the game on television.

France, Australia, Wales, and New Zealand made the semifinals, giving the tournament an even north–south distribution. The New Zealand All Blacks were the eventual champs, winning at home in Auckland's Eden Park over the French Tricolors 29–9. Direct competition in a tournament format showed that the Southern Hemisphere teams had surpassed their northern rivals.

## 1991 World Cup — Great Britain, Ireland, and France

The 1991 Rugby World Cup took place in Great Britain, Ireland, and France and was again a 16-team affair, but this time the IRB implemented a qualification process whereby 8 sides had qualified through a regional formula to join the 8 quarterfinalists from 1987. The surprise of the tournament involved eventual champions Australia upsetting the defending titleholders New Zealand in the semifinals. Australia went on to beat England 12–6 at Twickenham in the final. The World Cup audience also grew substantially, with more than one million in-stadium attendees and nearly two billion watching over the airwaves.

## 1995 World Cup — South Africa

In 1995 the World Cup moved to South Africa, whose Springboks competed for the first time. President Nelson Mandela opened the tournament wearing a Springbok jersey, long a symbol of the apartheid era, and appealed for the Rainbow Nation to come together through sport. The tournament was a smashing success from the opening match to the tense final, when in a near fairy-tale ending the Boks beat the All Blacks 15–12 in extra time on a Joel Stransky drop goal.

Their victory at Ellis Park in Johannesburg was the third consecutive triumph of a Southern Hemisphere team. It also marked the end of the amateur era in rugby. With the sport's governing body no longer able to stem the tide of professionalism, the IRB had been forced to acquiesce and allow the game to become a marketable commodity, with paid players and commercial opportunities galore.

The worldwide television audience shocked even the most biased rugby optimists, with more than 3.1 billion viewers around the oval planet tuning in. Rugby had arrived as a worldwide television product just as professionalism was about to take hold.

## 1999 World Cup — Wales, England, Scotland, Ireland, and France

The 1999 tourney moved once again back to Britain, France, and Ireland, with Wales taking the lead role as hosts. The finals tournament was expanded from 16 to 20 teams, and for the first time included quarterfinal playoffs.

The semifinals were thrilling affairs with South Africa and Australia going into overtime and France shocking the world by knocking off a heavily favored All Blacks side in one of the most exciting Rugby World Cup games ever played. The Wallabies then comprehensively defeated the French 35–12 in the final, becoming the first country to win the Rugby World Cup twice. The 1999 tournament broke all previous records for attendance, TV audience, and revenue.

## 2003 World Cup — Australia

The 2003 Rugby World Cup was originally scheduled to be co-hosted by Australia and New Zealand, but after a commercial dispute over advertising in stadiums Australia ended up staging the entire tournament alone. Building on the success of the 2000 Olympic games in Sydney, the Australian Rugby Union set a new standard for hosting excellence.

The tournament returned to a four-pool format where the top two nations advanced to the quarterfinals. Australians of all backgrounds embraced the tourney and set new attendance marks while showing their true colors in a unprecedented display of international sporting camaraderie.

The final pitted the pre-tournament favorite England against the host Wallabies. In the most riveting World Cup final to date, Jonny Wilkinson booted England to victory at the end of extra time, becoming the first Northern Hemisphere team to hoist the William Webb Ellis Cup overhead. It was a fairy-tale ending for the Men in White and a fitting conclusion to the best World Cup ever.

## 2007 World Cup — France, Wales, and Scotland

After a particularly contentious host-nation bidding process that pitted old rivals England and France as the two finalists, the 2007 Rugby World Cup was ultimately awarded to France. In a political move to gain the support of the Welsh and Scottish Rugby Unions, four World Cup fixtures were awarded to Wales and two to Scotland, with the remaining 42 matches scheduled for play in France.

The 2007 Finals Tournament will be played under the 4-pool, 20-team format, with each pool producing 2 teams for the quarterfinals. The United States is pitted against England, South Africa, Samoa, and Tonga in Pool A. Canada is faced with Australia, Wales, Fiji, and Japan as their Pool B opponents. Pool C features New Zealand, Scotland, Italy, Romania, and World Cup debutantes Portugal. The "pool of death" pits Ireland, Argentina, Georgia, Namibia, and hosts France in Pool D. The 2007 Rugby World Cup kicks off September 7 from St. Denis at Stade de France, where the Tricolors will host Argentina, and concludes at the same ground with the World Cup Final on October 20.

In just 20 years, the World Cup has evolved from an idea that met stiff resistance to a colossus on the world's sporting stage. In the process, the game itself was changed from an exclusive, clubby activity to a professional game with a worldwide audience. Such is the power of creating an international competition that determines ultimate bragging rights for an entire sport.

# Qualification and Finals Tournaments

Originally, the World Cup was by invite only. In 1991, the IRB instituted a qualification structure, which enabled teams from all over the globe to aspire to compete on the rugby world's premier stage. The first eight slots in the tournament are reserved for the champion, runner-up, beaten semifinalists, and the losing quarterfinalists.

BROWNIE SAYS

## How I earned a cap for Latvia

The first qualifying match for the 1999 Rugby World Cup was in September of 1996 between Latvia and Norway in Riga. Because it was the kickoff match of a tournament that would eventually culminate in a world champion being crowned in Cardiff, the fixture drew journalists from the rugby capitals of Europe and the post-match function was a lively affair. I lived right across the street from the University Stadium and Uldis Bautris, my club coach for Rigas Miesnieks, was also in charge of the national team squad, so naturally I attended the game and the following festivities. After chatting with various Norwegian team members it became apparent that very few of them were actually Norwegian. Most were expatriates from rugby-playing nations living and working in Oslo, who gained eligibility for Norway on residency grounds.

That night, at the suggestion of Latvian lock Wilmars Sokolovs, the notion was born that I could become the first foreigner to play for Latvia.

What transpired over the next seven months was a personal odyssey involving a never-before-seen devotion to fitness, twice-weekly training sessions in the snow and rain on dirt pitches, bewildering eligibility paperwork for the Latvian sports ministry, a stint at hooker in both a possibles-versus-probables match and a friendly against Lithuania, and, finally, selection to the Latvian team. Listening to the national anthem with my teammates before we crushed Bulgaria 89–0 in a World Cup qualifier was the proudest moment of my life. Unfortunately, our hopes of progressing out of our pool to the next level were dashed by Croatia the following week.

The World Cup is such a powerful motivating force that even to have been involved at all will always be the highlight of my rugby career. I believe that one day Latvia will make it to the World Cup, and when they do I'll be in the stands cheering rabidly for my adopted nation.

RUGBY JARGON

Qualifying is a two-year-long process of more than 100 matches that involves almost every member of the IRB. Ten places go to qualifiers from Africa (1), the Americas (3), Asia (1), Europe (3), and Oceania (2). The last two berths are determined by use of the *repechage* system, or runner-up's last chance, where near-qualifiers are given the chance of sneaking in by knocking each other off in a home-and-away series.

Qualifying begins with the lowest-ranked nations playing in a regionalized pool system to weed out the least deserving sides and minimize travel costs. Winning a pool allows that country to advance to the next level, where they face stiffer competition from more established international teams.

In 2007 the qualifying unions were Namibia, from Africa; Argentina, Canada, and the United States, from the Americas; Japan, from Asia; Italy, Romania, and Georgia, from Europe; and Fiji and Samoa, from Oceania. Tonga and Portugal were able to sneak in the back door of the qualification process through the repechage.

# North Americans in the World Cup

North American teams have been a part of every Rugby World Cup since its inception in 1987, with Canada competing in all five tournaments and the United States missing out just once. And while they haven't exactly been powerhouse performers, they have had their moments at the pinnacle of the sport.

## Fighting Eagles

Since the U.S.'s back-to-back Olympic triumphs 80 years ago, the Eagles have struggled to field a competitive international side. After winning their opener against Japan in 1987, the U.S. was shut out in 1991, and failed to qualify for the World Cup in 1995. In 1999, the Eagles lost a heartbreaker to Romania and went three and out for the second time. The Eagles barely made the 2003 finals, coming in the back door via the repechage tournament.

The United States was placed in Pool B alongside France, Fiji, Japan, and Scotland. They charged out of the gate against Fiji but a missed conversion denied them their second Rugby World Cup win in 16 years. Against Scotland, the Eagles were brought back down to earth; they rebounded with a win over Japan, before losing heavily to France.

The Eagles will have a chance to get another World Cup win in 2007 when they square off against Tonga in Montpelier and Samoa in St. Etienne. Less likely is the possibility of upsetting England or South Africa in their other two pool matches.

## Competing Canadians

Canada has been competitive in all five Rugby World Cups. The Canadians have won 6 and lost 11 finals matches, including wins over Tonga, Fiji, Romania, and Namibia. Their best showing was in 1991, when they advanced to the quarterfinals where they lost by a very respectable 13–29 score against New Zealand.

In 2003, Rugby Canada was placed in Pool D with New Zealand, Wales, Italy, and Tonga, comprising the most evenly matched group in the tournament. Going into the tournament the Canadians had hopes of again making the quarterfinals, but lost first to Wales, were crushed by New Zealand, and played Italy tough in a losing effort, but salvaged some pride with a convincing victory over Tonga.

Canada has a real chance of doing some damage in pool B at Rugby World Cup 2007. Beating Australia or Wales is probably out of the question, but they will definitely be favored when they take on Fiji in Cardiff and Japan in Bordeaux.

# Mammoths and Minnows

For countries that have very little chance of ever hoisting the Webb Ellis trophy (refer to "The Crown Jewel of Rugby" for more), the tournament is an opportunity to measure themselves against the best in the world. Winning a match or even just playing well against a major power is a source of intense pride and a reason for commendation.

Rugby is a sport where there's no such thing as letting up on an overmatched opponent. The way you show respect for the other side is to continue to play as hard as possible against them, no matter how large the lead. This "no let up for 80 minutes" ethos results in some awfully lopsided scorelines. Even so, a 100-point loss is not a source of embarrassment in the rugby community, but instead a measuring stick of how much needs to be done to become more competitive. So, although some of the results may be a bit lopsided, the over-all effect is to lift the game of the up-and-coming nations by exposing them to a higher level of play.

The upside of the relative disparity between nations occurs when a country is able to move up the international pecking order. In 1999, Argentina beat Ireland in a quarterfinal playoff match, an unlikely victory that lifted rugby's profile within a soccer-mad country and has since led to steady improvement for the Pumas. Although they failed to make the quarterfinals again in 2003, since then the Pumas have continued to improve and are now ranked sixth in the world. Again they are a dark-horse candidate to overcome the Irish and make it to the knockout stage of the tournament.

In 2003 Georgia made it to its first World Cup by beating rival Russia in Tbilisi in front of a crowd estimated at over 80,000. Making it to Australia was a dream come true for the mostly amateur Lelos, and even though they were serious underdogs in every match, they played their hearts out all four times they took the pitch. They opened the tourney with a heavy loss to England, got crushed by Samoa, played a little better against South Africa, and were at least in the match versus Uruguay. Four years on from that appearance, Georgia has qualified for France in 2007 and will be looking to secure their first-ever win when they meet Namibia in pool play on September 26.

# Great World Cup Moments

Some World Cup matches become part of history because of the moment in time when they took place, and others for the pure drama of the battle joined. Over the 185 finals matches played from 1987 to 2003, there have been several contests that rise above the rest.

## Australia versus England — 2003 final

The 2003 Rugby World Cup final pitted host Australia against the pre-tournament favorites, England. The home nation against the former colony, the best of the north against the best of the Southern Hemisphere, this match had a story line longer than the queues waiting to catch a train after the match at Homebush station. The stadium was half full of English and half full of Aussie supporters, as white and gold jerseys dominated the jampacked venue. The match started well for the home side when Lote Tuqiri hauled in a cross-field bomb by Stephen Larkham and the Wallabies took a five-point lead.

England kept their composure as Jonny Wilkinson converted three shots at goal to put England in front 9–5. Then, just before halftime, Wilko put Jason Robinson into the clear down the right sideline and England went into the changing rooms with a well-deserved 14–5 halftime lead.

The second half settled into a contest of wills: The Wallabies scratched their way back into the match with two penalty goals, but England still led 14–11 as fulltime approached. On the Wallabies' final possession in injury time, a penalty gave Elton Flatley his chance to level the scores and force extra time. With ice water coursing through his veins and the rugby world holding its breath, he calmly slotted the goal and the fulltime whistle was blown, leaving the world's two best teams even at 14–all.

In extra time, the teams continued the pattern. England took the lead on a penalty, and then Australia leveled the scores with 30 seconds left in the second of the two ten-minute periods. With just seconds remaining and the commentators speculating about a third ten-minute sudden death period, England's scrumhalf Matt Dawson somehow broke through the Wallaby defense and got close enough to the line for Jonny Wilkinson to line up a final drop goal attempt. Everyone in the stadium knew what was coming: Jonny stroked the drop and history was made when the ball sailed through the uprights and England became the first Northern Hemisphere nation to ever win the World Cup. All hail Sir Clive Woodward and England!

## South Africa versus New Zealand — 1995 final

The most incredible moment happened after the 1995 World Cup final when New Zealand faced an inspired South Africa. With the score tied at the end of regulation the match went into extra time, and was eventually won 15–12 on a drop goal by South Africa. Without at all minimizing the monumental effort put in by the players on the pitch, what we'll never forget took place at the trophy presentation.

At a time when South Africa was struggling to reunite a nation divided by generations of apartheid, the sight of Nelson Mandela up on the podium in a Springbok jersey, pumping his fists in the air, as Bok Captain Francois Pienaar lifted the Webb Ellis Cup was truly inspirational. It was a moment when sport transcended politics and a divided nation took a brief respite from the enormous task of nation-building to celebrate as one.

## Australia versus South Africa — 1999 Semifinal #1

The 1999 semifinals both stand out because of what happened on the field of play. In the first semi, South Africa faced Australia after drop kicking England out of the quarterfinals. The game went into extra time and was won by a drop goal from the Wallabies' Stephen Larkham. The game had all the elements of a classic, smash-mouth encounter, punctuated by patches of enterprising play throughout a seesaw affair that sapped the collective energy from the capacity crowd at Twickenham. After the match, supporters from both sides were so exhausted and emotionally drained from the twists and turns of the match that you couldn't tell which team had won. Everyone in attendance knew they had witnessed something special that would be remembered for years to come and were gracious in victory and defeat.

After the drama of the first semifinal, we all chatted over a few beers and came to the well-reasoned conclusion that Sunday's semifinal couldn't possibly match the drama and excitement of the Wallabies' win over the Springboks. The next day, in observing the procession from Twickenham station to the stadium, the All Black fans were relaxed and cocky in contemplating the destruction to come, while the French supporters looked to be on a death march, with heads down and nary a smile among them.

## Walking Twickenham

Every now and then, being a rugby TV producer has its perks. After being sequestered by my boss to the windowless edit bay in the basement of Fox Sports World for the round-robin stages of the 1999 Rugby World Cup, my boss approved a classic junket as a reward for my dedication. Being a licensed broadcaster, Fox received a few semifinals and finals tickets as part of the deal. When the top brass passed on them, I played the advantage and asked whether I might be released from my underground dungeon to pop over to London for the semis and then immediately return to L.A. before we taped our studio show.

My "job" was to make sure the pay-per-view signal was all sorted out so the folks back home in the U.S. and Canada could watch live. With a few minutes to spare before kickoff, inspiration struck. It occurred to me that Brown and I had been issued all-access media passes and that we were entitled to walk out onto the hallowed Twickenham turf if we so desired. So, just before the teams took the field, we marched out of the tunnel and past an array of security guards stationed to keep out the riffraff.

Before we knew it, we were walking the perimeter of the pitch, being careful not to step on the field and stopping periodically to feign a purpose for our perambulation, by pointing up at some imaginary friends that were seated among the 50,000-plus who anxiously awaited the impending kickoff. The atmosphere at pitch level was totally and completely awesome. Before we finished our walk around, Brown ran into a photographer he knew from Latvia who asked what possible business we might have walking out on the field before such a huge match. We explained that we had to perform a safety check of the ground just to make sure everything was ready for the match to proceed! Finding everything in order, we marched back up the tunnel and took up our positions in the TV truck. Of course, after our pre-game blessing ritual set the stage, the French team shocked the world with an awesome display of attacking rugby that left the heavily favored All Blacks in tatters. I still get chills thinking about the feeling of looking up at that crowd and the spectacle that followed.

## *New Zealand versus France — 1999 Semifinal #2*

The game that followed gets our vote as the most exciting World Cup match ever played. At a time when a beef row had elevated tensions in the Anglo–French relationship, a curious thing happened within the mostly British crowd when the French began their second-half comeback. The crowd suddenly realized that the French had a chance after all, and virtually every non–New Zealander in the stands started pulling for the French to win. The Tricolors, displaying all their Gallic flair, scored 26 unanswered points playing vintage champagne rugby that left the Kiwis dazed and confused. By the end of the match, a Stade de France crowd couldn't have cheered any louder for Les Blues. Their 43–31 victory proved the old adage that any team can win on the day, and on October 31, 1999, that day belonged to the French.

# Other Cups on the World Stage

As the popularity of the Rugby World Cup grew from very modest beginnings, the IRB slowly realized that nothing fired the imagination like the possibility of being crowned a world champion. In subsequent years they sanctioned competitions that provided the opportunity for sevens devotees, women, and age-grade players to earn that coveted title.

## Sevens World Cup

The sevens game — so named because it's played with only seven on each team and characterized by lots of scoring (see Chapter 15 for more info on the abbreviated version of the sport) — has long been a fixture on the international scene, but the first IRB Sevens World Cup wasn't played until 1993 in Edinburgh. The participants play for the Melrose Cup, named after the city in Scotland where the seven-a-side game developed in the 1880s. In the inaugural final, England defeated Australia 21–17.

The second Sevens World Cup moved to Hong Kong, the venue responsible for popularizing the game and bringing it international attention. It delivered a multitude of exciting games and plenty of local color. Fiji, led by their legendary sevens magician Waisale Serevi, defeated South Africa in the final 24–21.

The Sevens World Cup, following the pattern of almost all sevens events, features consolation brackets. The USA Eagles made an impressive showing, beating a very capable Japanese side 40–28 in the Bowl Final to take home some hardware.

In 2001, the third edition of the Sevens World Cup moved across the Pacific to Mar Del Plata, Argentina. Sevens is a unique game that allows smaller nations to become competitive at a much faster rate than is possible in the 15-a-side game. Qualifying tournaments for the event were held all over the globe and a total of 91 countries took part. New Zealand totally dominated the tournament, scoring 251 points while giving up only 40 points over 8 matches, including their 31–12 victory over Australia to win the Melrose Cup.

Fiji captured their second Sevens World Cup crown in Hong Kong in 2005. With the old master Waisale Serevi once again calling the shots and scoring a try in the Final, the fabulous Fijians defeated the defending champions from New Zealand 29–19 to re-establish their dominance of the seven-a-side game.

# Women's Rugby World Cup

The Women's Rugby World Cup was not sanctioned as an official IRB championship until 1998, but the first competition took place in Wales in 1991. Twelve countries participated and the surprise winner was the United States, beating England 19–6 in the final to become the first modern-day U.S. rugby team to be crowned World Champions! (See Figure 13-1).

**Figure 13-1:** USA Women team photo after winning World Cup 1991.

After the first one it was decided to alter the timing so that the event wouldn't be held in the same year as the men's World Cup. Thus, the next tourney was scheduled for 1994 in Holland. Various problems in the lead-up prevented the IRB from giving its approval to the competition in the Netherlands, and as a result most national unions pulled funding from their squads. An alternative tournament was organized in Scotland, and it was attended by 12 sides. The U.S. faced England again in the final. This time, however, England knocked them off their perch as World Champions, winning 38–23 in an exciting affair. With scant support from their national union, the Eagle women soared high on the strength of their individual ability and team spirit.

In 1998 the IRB made it official and 16 teams competed in Amsterdam. The Canadian women reached their first World Cup semifinal but lost 46–6 to the United States. The Black Ferns from New Zealand rampaged through the tournament and ended up easily winning the final 46–12 over the Eagles.

Barcelona, Spain, was the site for the Women's Rugby World Cup in 2002. England and New Zealand met in the final and the Black Ferns won their second consecutive title 19–9, firmly establishing themselves as the dominant force in the women's game. New Zealand and England have clearly created a gap between themselves and the rest of the world as a direct result of their unions' vision and investment in developing the women's game.

The 2006 Women's Rugby World Cup was the first IRB World Cup event contested in North America; Rugby Canada hosted the tournament. But despite the new continent, the Black Ferns of New Zealand solidified their position at the top of the world pecking order completing the three-peat of women's World Cup titles with a 25–17 victory over England. The Canadian women lost heavily to New Zealand in pool play and then crushed Spain 79–0 and Kazakhstan 45–5 to qualily for the semifinals. In the knockout stage, they lost to England 20–14 in the semifinal, and then 17–8 to France to finish in fourth place overall.

The USA Eagles went down to England 18–0 and then beat Ireland 24–11 and Australia 10–6 in pool play, but narrowly missed qualifying for the semifinals on points differential. They went on to beat Australia once again 29–12 in the knockout stage, and then shut out Scotland 24–0 to finish in fifth place overall. The Eagles finished a very respectable 4–1, having lost only to beaten finalists England.

# The Under-21 Rugby World Cup

The Under-21 Rugby World Cup grew out of the SANZAR/UAR Under-21 tournament that began in 1995 involving Argentina, Australia, New Zealand, and South Africa, and steadily added other countries in following years. The cup exposes promising youngsters to a high level of international competition, and numerous alumni of the annual event are among today's brightest stars.

The inaugural IRB Under-21 World Cup was held in South Africa in 2002. The Baby Boks continued a South African tradition of winning World Cups on home soil with a 24–21 victory over Australia in the final.

In 2003, the Under-21 World Cup was staged in England. The second edition saw New Zealand and Australia play to a thrilling 37–all draw in pool play, only to meet again in the final, where the young Kiwis prevailed over the mini-marsupials 21–10.

France hosted the 2006 Under-21 World Cup, and reinforced the old maxim that home field advantage matters when they beat the defending champions from South Africa 24–13 in front of 13,000 partisan fans in Clermont-Ferrand.

# *The Under-19 World Championships*

The IRB created an annual Under-19 World Championship competition in 2005. South Africa defeated New Zealand to win the inaugural title 20–15 at the ABSA Stadium in Durban. In 2006 the tournament moved to Dubai, where Australia turned back the Kiwis once again, winning 17–13 to claim Under-19 worldwide bragging rights. The 2007 edition moved to Northern Ireland and was won by New Zealand, who dismantled South Africa by a score of 31–7. Canada finished second in Division B and the United States took third.

In the span of just 20 years, the IRB has created four distinct World Cup competitions giving men, women, sevens specialists, and future stars their own championship to aspire to, where they can test themselves against the best in the world. The challenge for the IRB is to raise the standard of play of the lower-level nations, which will inevitably lead to rugby becoming a truly global game.

# Chapter 14

# The International Calendar

*In This Chapter*

▶ Making sense of how the game is organized

▶ Governing the oval universe

▶ Rounding up the interprovincial action

*R*ugby fans around the world enjoy a plethora of international and provincial competitions that run year-round. For more than 130 years, until the first Rugby World Cup in 1987, international test matches served as the highest level of the game. Over that period, leagues gradually developed on a regional basis.

In 1996 the rugby calendar changed forever when the three leading Southern Hemisphere powers, South Africa, New Zealand, and Australia, joined together and created the Tri Nations Series and the Super 12 (since 2006 the Super 14). This established an annual schedule of international matches for each nation and included an interprovincial competition where the leading regional sides from the big three would play a full season of matches leading to a winner. The 1995–96 season also saw the Six Nations unions launch the European Cup, the north's version of the Super 12.

Despite these international developments, the heart and soul of rugby is the game that is still played at the domestic provincial level. All of the leading rugby nations have their own leagues where future stars are cultivated amid deep-running local passions. In this chapter, we give you a tour of rugby's annual calendar, looking first at the international order, then dropping down to the interprovincial scene, and finishing off with a dab of local provincial color.

# How the Game Is Organized

As an entirely amateur sport for most of its history, rugby was controlled by volunteer administrators in individual countries. Each rugby-playing country had its own organizational structure and was responsible for internal decisions regarding finances, eligibility, competitions, and development. Interaction between different nations was managed on a union-to-union basis. In the last quarter of the 20th century, however, the growth of the game led to the strengthening of an existing but limited governing body, the International Rugby Board (IRB).

## Rugby's rulers — The IRB

The IRB was founded in 1886, but it didn't attain its all-powerful status until nearly a century later. Headquartered in Dublin, the IRB is the world-governing and law-making body for the game of rugby union. The day-to-day business of the board is conducted by a professional staff of more than 40 people. The IRB has 95 member unions, 20 associates, and 6 regional associations.

The Executive Council, made up of representatives from the eight foundation unions, meets twice a year. The eight foundation unions — Scotland, Ireland, Wales, England, Australia, New Zealand, South Africa, and France — each have two seats. Argentina, Canada, Italy, and Japan each have one seat on the council, as does FIRA–AER (the International Amateur Rugby Federation–European Rugby Association). The full membership meets every two years at the association's general meeting; regional meetings are held at regular intervals.

The IRB is now responsible for setting the international test schedule; developing the game worldwide; running the World Cup through a subsidiary organization, Rugby World Cup Limited; and generally acting as overlord to the sport.

A number of tournaments are under IRB control, including the Women's Rugby World Cup, Rugby World Cup Sevens, IRB Sevens World Series, Under-21 World Cup, and the Under-19 World Championship. The principal money-making IRB property, however, is the Rugby World Cup, which is held every four years.

## National unions

The first national union was formed in England in 1871 and called, appropriately enough, the Rugby Football Union (RFU). The union came about in response to the need for order and uniformity in the rapidly expanding game. Before the standardization of rules created by the RFU, matches varied significantly in rules and length, depending upon where they were played.

A national union is usually a large, professional organization that has a multitude of responsibilities. The union's composition and role depends on the size of the rugby-playing population and the popularity of the game in a particular country.

In a country like New Zealand, for example, the New Zealand Rugby Union (NZRU) negotiates with sponsors, staffs and runs the various national teams, hires coaches, and contracts professional players for their services. The staff at the NZRU are full-time employees engaged in developing and promoting New Zealand rugby in all its forms, from youth to international competitions.

In a small country like Latvia, with only seven rugby clubs, it's a much different story. The national officials are usually either volunteers or they're paid a small stipend for their work. The responsibilities are often the same as in a large union, but the scale is much smaller.

The United States Rugby Football Union (USA Rugby) and Rugby Canada are somewhere in between New Zealand and Latvia. They both have paid professionals running the organizations, but they also rely heavily on volunteers from both countries to ensure the smooth functioning of the game in all its aspects.

## Provincial unions

In countries like South Africa, where rugby is entrenched in the nation's sporting landscape, provincial unions are powerful champions of their regional interests. In addition to training referees and coaches, running youth programs and academies, and selecting and funding teams for competition in national events, provincial unions have a say in how the game is run at the national level. North American equivalents are the regional or provincial unions like the Pacific Coast Rugby Football Union and the British Columbia Rugby Union.

## Local unions

Local unions are concerned with administering the game within a certain geographical area. In the U.S. these are called local area unions, and in Canada they're referred to as sub-unions. These unions are staffed by volunteers and are responsible for scheduling matches, providing referees, organizing playoffs, and resolving disputes between clubs.

# The Powers That Be

The first international, or *test match,* was played between England and Scotland in 1871. A test match is a game where caps are awarded by the respective national unions to signify that the players are representing their country. In the early days, caps were made of wool with fancy embroidery and served as a keepsake for those who were lucky enough to earn one. In the modern game, with a few notable exceptions among the smaller amateur unions, this practice of actually awarding a cap has fallen by the wayside, and the term "cap" simply means that the player has appeared on the pitch in a full international match for his country.

In the 1880s, England and Scotland were joined by Wales and Ireland, and the International Championship began. These four home unions were joined by France in 1910 to form the Five Nations. Although France was thrown out of the competition from 1931 to 1939, the Five Nations served as the world's first and most prominent annual international competition from the early 1900s to 1999, when it expanded to include Italy and become the Six Nations.

While Europe focused on the Five (and then Six) Nations, the southern powerhouses of Australia, New Zealand, and South Africa had to be content with organizing periodic tours, as they lacked an annual international set of fixtures. Although New Zealand's first recorded test match was against Australia in 1893, it took the southern giants more than 100 years to organize their own yearly international competition.

## Where tradition is king — The Six Nations

The Six Nations is the world's oldest rugby tournament, possessing a rich and colorful history that tracks the regional rivalries and the tumultuous times that Northern Europe has endured over the past 125 years. Over that period, England and Scotland have played 124 tests, each one a microcosm of the unique political and social circumstances prevailing at the time.

Over the course of 12 decades two historically distinct terms, the Triple Crown and the Grand Slam, have developed in the Six Nations. To take the *Triple Crown,* which was first contested only among the four original "home unions" of England, Scotland, Wales, and Ireland, you had to win all three games against those teams. The *Grand Slam* was added into the mix after the French joined. To win the Grand Slam, you must make a clean sweep and defeat every other country. England has won the most Grand Slams and Triple Crowns.

From February to April of each year, the Six Nations occupies the attention of rugby fans around the world. Each nation plays all five of the other teams and the winner is determined by a scoring system that takes into account wins, draws, and points differential for tie-breaking purposes. The fans bring with them all the attendant historical regional rivalries that have colored the Anglo–French, Anglo–Welsh, and Anglo–Irish relationships (plus all the other national permutations) over several generations. The Welsh team can lose all their other games, but if they beat England that makes their entire campaign a success. Such is the nature of the rivalries in the Six Nations.

## South versus North — The SANZAR home tests

When the Southern Hemisphere unions of South Africa, New Zealand, and Australia joined forces to create SANZAR (SA, NZ, AR) in 1996, professionalism was ushered in with the force of a cosmic Big Bang. Suddenly, the three juggernauts were charged with producing a series of annual rugby events to satisfy the requirements of a mammoth $550-million US television contract.

One part of that commitment included SANZAR's agreement to regularly host touring sides in-bound from Europe, the Pacific Islands, and Argentina each June. The IRB sets the fixtures on a rotating basis where England, Ireland, Wales, Scotland, France, Italy, Argentina, Samoa, Fiji, and Tonga make tours to the SANZAR countries. For example, in 2007 England played two matches in South Africa, France two in New Zealand, and Wales two in Australia. The IRB schedules the games so all of the teams play each other on a rotating basis and the smaller unions get a chance to periodically measure themselves against the best.

## The battle of the Big Three — The Tri Nations

The Tri Nations Series delivers some of the world's most exciting and tense rugby action every year. The Series features New Zealand, South Africa, and Australia (the three countries that won the first four Rugby World Cups) in a home-and-away extravaganza that produces six huge tests a year. Each nation hosts two games and plays one on the road in the other two countries. In 2006 the series was expanded to include nine tests but in 2007 it returned to its traditional format. Since its inception in 1996, the Tri Nations Series has produced some of the finest international matches ever played — including the 2000 Australia–versus–New Zealand encounter, which is regarded by many as the best test match of all time.

# The greatest test ever

In 2000, Australia and New Zealand played before a world-record 109,874 fans at Stadium Australia in Sydney in what has since come to be regarded as the best test ever played. The World Champion Wallabies had won ten straight tests and boasted the world's most skilled back line, the best scrumhalf combination on the planet in George Gregan and Stephen Larkham, and arguably Australia's best-ever captain in John Eales. The All Blacks went into the match with the burden of sky-high expectations that plague every Kiwi side, plus a boatload of talent, including the most feared attacker in the game, a 6'5", 265-pound monster named Jonah Lomu. The Tongan Torpedo had wreaked havoc at the 1995 World Cup running over and through everything that got in his path, and after a bout with a rare kidney illness the big man was again primed for action.

The game started magically for New Zealand, with three converted tries and a penalty in the first eight minutes. The Wallabies had barely even touched the ball; it was a dream start for the All Blacks and a nightmare for the Wallabies. Being down 24 to zip, the Aussies could easily have given up, but in his typically icy cool fashion, John Eales summoned his troops under the posts and instructed them to stick to the game plan and told them they were capable of getting back into the match if they just didn't panic. From the ensuing kickoff, the Wallabies controlled the ball and Stephen Larkham broke the line to find Stirling Mortlock, who dotted down for the try. By halftime the Wallabies had scored 24 unanswered points of their own and it was 24–24 at the interval.

The second half was a seesaw affair in which the reserve hooker, Jeremy Paul, scored a try with two minutes left and put the Australians up 35–34. The Australian crowd went crazy, as they thought the match was surely won! Then, three minutes into injury time, the All Blacks worked the ball out to Jonah Lomu and the big fella rounded the corner to score the match winner.

The final score was 39–35 as New Zealand clinched victory at the death in a breathless match that produced ten tries over 80-plus minutes of heart-stopping action. It was an extraordinary match for the ages that we've watched about a dozen times since and will never forget.

Like the Six Nations, the Tri Nations is a natural outgrowth of the traditional rugby rivalries that exist among these three rugby-mad behemoths. New Zealand and South Africa's rivalry on the pitch is well established in each nation's collective consciousness, going back to South Africa's first tour of New Zealand in 1921. Since their first meeting in Dunedin, the All Blacks and Springboks have battled each other with a fierce intensity that is rarely matched in any sport. New Zealand holds a very narrow lead in the all-time series, which serves as a testament to how evenly matched these nations have been throughout the years on the pitch.

Since the inaugural campaign in 1996 New Zealand has dominated the Tri Nations Series, winning 7 of 11 titles, with Australia and South Africa having won twice each.

The *Bledisloe Cup,* which is awarded to the winner of the annual test series between New Zealand and Australia, is the most coveted piece of hardware on offer between these two antipodean nations. The cup is named for the governor general of New Zealand who donated it in 1931. Under the current Tri Nations Series format, the two All Blacks–versus–Wallabies games double as Tri Nations and Bledisloe Cup encounters. The importance of the Bledisloe Cup to Kiwis was emphatically demonstrated at Eden Park in 2003 when the crowd politely clapped as Captain Rueben Thorne lifted the Tri Nations Cup — then roared with approval when he hoisted the Bledisloe Cup for the first time in more than five years. Since that night in Auckland, New Zealand has yet to relinquish the trophy. The Cup is by far the biggest prize in any sport within the trans-tasman rivalry.

## North versus south — The Fall tests

In October and November of each year, the Southern Hemisphere teams head north to face the European powers. Similar to the SANZAR tests in June, these matches afford an opportunity to see how the best of the north shape up against the south. Australia, New Zealand, and South Africa, plus occasionally Argentina, and the Pacific Island nations of Fiji, Samoa, and Tonga, make the journey to play against some combination of England, Scotland, Wales, Ireland, Italy, and France. The in-bound sides generally play two or three European nations over a three- to four-week tour.

## The British & Irish Lions

The British & Irish Lions are an all-star team composed of the best national team players from England, Scotland, Wales, and Ireland. The Lions assemble every four years and have a long and storied tradition dating back to 1888, when the first representative side from Great Britain made a mammoth five-month tour of New Zealand and Australia, playing an incredible 35 matches. Since that first tour, the Lions (or a derivative side from the U.K.) have played 575 matches around the world.

One of the main features of a Lions tour is that they make a point of playing numerous games against the smaller provincial or club sides in the country they visit. This brings world-class rugby out to the people around the country and gives local players the chance to get a game against some of the world's best rugby players.

A Lions tour is a huge party for legions of British & Irish fans who take leave from work for a month-long rugby celebration that, in many cases, takes about four years to recover from.

The Lions have been hugely successful both on the field and more recently as a commercial enterprise. They have dominated the Wallabies winning 15 and losing only 5 games; trail the Springboks with 21 losses, 16 wins, and 6 draws; and have struggled against the All Blacks winning just 6 while losing 29, with 3 ties. The Lions teams of 1955 and 1974 earned series victories in South Africa, the 1971 side won their only test series in New Zealand, and the 2001 Lions were the first to lose a series in Australia after four successive triumphs down under.

The Lions' 2005 Tour of New Zealand was beset by problems before the team even left the Northern Hemisphere. In a warm-up match prior to departure they drew with Argentina at Millennium Stadium in Cardiff. Coach Clive Woodward's record-breaking squad of 44 players and 26 staff members endured huge criticism in the press at home. As soon as they played their first match in New Zealand the injuries began, with the number 8 Lawrence Dallaglio breaking his ankle against Bay of Plenty. Things got worse when the Lions lost to a fired-up NZ Maori side in Hamilton. The problems continued just a couple of minutes into the first test in Christchurch, when captain Brian O'Driscoll suffered a dislocated shoulder, thus ending his campaign. The rest of the tour was filled with accusations of dirty play and poor sportsmanship as the Lions were soundly thumped by the All Blacks in all three tests. The next British & Irish Lions tour is scheduled for 2009, to South Africa.

# The Barbarian Football Club

The Barbarian Football Club was created in England in 1890 to foster goodwill and fellowship among rugby players around the world. The Barbarians' (also known as the Baa-Baas) creed is "Rugby Football is a game for gentlemen in all classes, but for no bad sportsman in any class." The club is unique in that they are a touring-only side that doesn't have a home field, clubhouse, or membership fees. Players are selected by invitation only and the Barbarians' list of rugby luminaries is loaded with legendary names.

When the Australians toured the U.K. in 1948, the Barbarians played them in a fundraiser to finance the Wallabies' desire to play a match against Canada on their way home. Since that watershed moment, the Baa-Baas have been a regular fixture at the tail end of U.K. tours, promoting a wide-open style of attacking rugby designed to entertain without the pressure of having to win. As a result, the scorelines are normally well above test averages and provide value for money to the paying customers, whose hard-earned money goes to a variety of charitable causes.

The most famous Barbarians victory is the 1973 win over New Zealand. In that match the rugby world's all-time greatest scrumhalf, Wales's Gareth Edwards, scored "The Try" — regarded by many as the best try ever scored. The Baa-Baas went on to win 23–11 before a hysterical Cardiff Arms Park crowd. In typical Barbarians camaraderie, the moment of the match came after the fulltime blast when the teams gathered at midfield and joined together to sing "Now Is the Hour" and "Auld Lang Syne." At least nine Barbarian clubs have formed around the world to emulate the unique ethos of the original club, including the New Zealand, French, South African, and South American Barbarians.

## The World Sevens Series

The IRB's Sevens World Series was launched in 1999 and serves as the annual international competition for the seven-a-side game. While several events had long been a fixture on the annual sevens calendar, including the oval planet's weeklong party each March in Hong Kong, the advent of the Series instituted a points system to crown a Sevens World Series Champion. Series points are tallied over the course of the year to determine a winner.

The IRB Sevens World Series consists of eight individual tournaments. In 2006–07 the schedule included stops in Dubai, South Africa, New Zealand, the United States, Hong Kong, Australia, England, and Scotland. New Zealand has been the dominant team in the official series, winning the first six titles before Fiji finally broke through in 2006, a year after they won the Rugby World Cup Sevens. (For more details about the Sevens World Cup, refer to Chapter 13.)

Since 2004 the United States has hosted a stop in the series. For the first three years the venue was the Home Depot Center in Carson, California, but in 2007 it switched to PETCO Park in San Diego.

# Interprovincial and Provincial Rugby

Positioned just below test rugby in the global rugby pecking order, inter-provincial competition pits the best teams against others within their regions. For example, the Tri Nations countries of Australia, New Zealand, and South Africa also compete at the interprovincial level in the Super 14. Likewise, the Six Nations members compete interprovincially in the Heineken Cup. While international, or test, rugby drove the development of the amateur game over its first 125 years, since the dawn of professionalism in 1996 the Super 14 and the Heineken Cup have had an enormous impact on the way the game is played around the world.

The next level is national provincial action, where traditional rivalries abound among the New Zealand, South African, and Irish provincial sides. The heart of rugby will always reside at the provincial level, where local rivals compete within a rich tapestry of historical encounters.

## The sensational Super 14

The Super 14 annually delivers the world's most exciting rugby action. The competition was established in 1996 with 12 sides, and in 2006 it expanded to 14 franchises. Five teams hail from New Zealand, five from South Africa, and four from Australia. The Kiwi sides are the Blues, Chiefs, Crusaders, Highlanders, and Hurricanes. The Aussie teams are the ACT Brumbies, Reds, Waratahs, and the Western Force. The Bulls, Cats, Sharks, Stormers, and Cheetahs are the South African representatives.

The Super 14 season runs from mid-February to late May each year and features 14 weeks of regular season play, followed by the semifinals and the final. In all, there are 93 Super 14 games every year. The sheer number of games and the length of the season make the Super 14 a fan-friendly tournament, as enthusiasts can follow their teams' progress through the course of a long and difficult season. The relative parity among the teams also makes the Super 14 an exciting competition to follow because the race for semifinal berths always comes down to the final regular season weekend.

New Zealand teams have won 9 of the 12 titles since 1996. The Blues won the first two, and again in 2003; the Crusaders have won six times; and the Brumbies in 2001 and 2004. In 2007 the Bulls became the first South African team to win the Super 14, with a victory over the Sharks. The Super 14 is the breeding ground for the Southern Hemisphere's stars of tomorrow, as the season directly precedes the selection of the SANZAR countries' national teams for the June tests and Tri Nations.

## The Heineken Cup overfloweth

The Heineken Cup is Europe's version of interprovincial competition. The tournament was launched in the fall of 1995 by the then Five Nations committee to provide a new level of cross-border play.

Twelve teams competed in the inaugural season, with Toulouse lifting the European Cup for the first time. In 1996–97 the league expanded to 20 teams in four pools of five, and after 46 matches the French were singing in the streets of Cardiff, when Brive were crowned Heineken Cup Champions in front of 41,664 at Cardiff Arms Park.

In the 1997–98 season, the format was changed again with pool matches being played both home and away, and the addition of three quarterfinal playoffs, bringing the total number of games to 70. In the final, England's storied Bath club lifted the Heineken Cup after overcoming the defending champs 19–18. Our Man of the Match was none other than USA Eagle Number 8 Dan Lyle, who created Bath's only try of the match.

The politics-driven absence of the English sides in the 1998–99 season prevented Bath from defending their title, opening the door for Ireland's Ulster to defeat Colomiers 21–6 for the first Irish victory on the European interprovincial scene.

In the 1999–2000 season, perennial bridesmaids Northampton pipped Munster by a single point to earn the Saints' first major cup title in the club's long and tortured history of coming up second best in a variety of competitions. The Leicester Tigers pounced on the Cup in 2000–01 and became the first team to defend its title when they repeated the feat in 2001–02. The 2002–03 season saw Toulouse join Leicester as the only teams to hoist the Heineken Cup twice.

In 2003–04 Toulouse made it to the final again but were defeated at Twickenham by a gutsy London Wasps side. The 2004–05 championship game was an all-French affair, with Toulouse notching their third title by beating Stade Francais at Murrayfield. The 2005–06 final was played at Millennium Stadium and featured Munster versus Biarritz. The Munstermen won a close contest by the score of 23–19. The 2006–07 title match was the first to pit two English squads, and was won by the Wasps — who beat Leicester in front of a record-setting crowd at Twickenham.

## *The Celtic scene*

With the success of the Guinness Premiership making a British league impossible, the Celtic nations of Ireland, Scotland, and Wales launched the Celtic League in 2001 to raise the standard of their domestic competitions and to provide additional income. In 2006–07 the competition got a new sponsor and is now known as the Magners League. Currently there are 11 Celtic League teams: four from the Welsh regions, four Irish provinces, and three Scottish franchises (although Borders is expected to fold before 2008).

The first-ever Celtic League fixture was held on August 17, 2001. Over the course of the inaugural campaign Irish sides earned three of the four semifinal berths. The final was staged at Lansdowne Road in Dublin, with Leinster defeating Munster for the hardware. In 2002–03, Munster erased the memory of the previous final, with a comprehensive 37–12 victory over Welsh side Neath.

## The Ranfurly Shield

The Ranfurly Shield is the most coveted piece of domestic hardware in New Zealand sports. It's contested on a challenge basis, with the holders usually defending the Log of Wood at selected home matches. The trophy was presented to Auckland in 1902 by the Governor General of New Zealand, the fifth Earl of Ranfurly. Since then, the Ranfurly Shield has dominated the thoughts of all New Zealand rugby players and inspired the dreams of countless Kiwi youngsters, imagining themselves making the critical play to win the Shield. One of the things that makes it so special is that even the smallest provinces periodically get a shot at lifting the Shield. When Marlborough upset Canterbury in 1973, the entire town broke into a delirious celebration that will always be remembered as the high point for local pride.

For the challenger's fans, Shield week is a glorious time of eternal hope where numerous receptions and prefatory events focus on the upcoming encounter and culminate with a mandatory road trip to the holder's venue for the game. For the holders, each defense comes complete with a defense song and a full complement of hospitality and shield fervor. For the few players who get the chance to play for the Shield, it's the highlight of their careers and they leave everything on the pitch in pursuit of their place in New Zealand's rugby folklore.

In 2006–07 the Magners League did not have a playoff system and the top finisher and champion was Ospreys from Wales. In all likelihood the Magners League will return to a playoff format in 2007–08.

The proliferation of interprovincial competitions like the Super 14, the Heineken Cup, and the Magners League all serve to create an intermediate step in the professional era from provincial to national team play. It's no surprise, then, that the likes of Australia, New Zealand, South Africa, England, France, Ireland, Wales, Scotland, and Italy have all consistently improved since these competitions were created. The challenge facing the Americas is to develop its own framework of provincial and interprovincial leagues to stop losing ground.

## The Air New Zealand Cup

The Air New Zealand Cup came into being in 2006, replacing the National Provincial Championship. New Zealand is divided into 26 provincial unions that all field representative teams. Although the format has evolved somewhat since the National Provincial Championship (NPC) was established in 1976, the current setup has 14 teams in the top flight, broken up into two divisions. The remaining 12 teams compete in the Heartland Championship.

The Air New Zealand Cup features a rich wealth of talent throughout the 14 first-division teams. With the recent expansion of the competition, teams that used to be in the lower echelon are now getting a chance to play their larger neighbors, giving fans in all areas the opportunity to see the best rugby players New Zealand has to offer. Many of the provinces play a unique style of rugby that developed through adaptation to particular local conditions and coaching styles. Even though the All Blacks' availability to participate in the Air New Zealand Cup is limited, it's still loaded with outstanding performers — a testament to the incredible depth of the talent pool in the Land of the Long White Cloud!

## The South African ABSA Currie Cup

Even though rugby-mad South Africans think it's delicious, the Currie Cup is not in fact a hot Asian dish served over rice, but rather South Africa's premier domestic rugby competition. The Holy Grail of South African rugby is named after Sir Donald Currie, who first presented the cup in 1891 to Griqualand West. The inaugural Currie Cup Tournament was held in Kimberly in 1892. In subsequent years, the trophy was awarded periodically using various tournament- and log-style formats. In 1939 the first Currie Cup final was played at Newlands in Cape Town, and after Transvaal beat Western Province the trophy was on offer only occasionally until the return of the annual finals system in 1946.

The Currie Cup format is currently broken into an eight-team Premier Division and six-team First Division. The top four sides from the Premier Division meet in semifinals and then a final to determine a Currie Cup champion. The top finisher in the First Division has a shot at promotion to the top group if it can beat the lowest finisher in a home-and-home series.

Western Province has dominated the Currie Cup, winning 32 times, while the Blue Bulls have taken top honors 22 times. Together, the two teams account for 54 of the 67 times the Currie Cup has been officially awarded.

## The English domestic scene

Until recently, the English domestic game was contested through knockout play for various cups. Under this model, teams from all divisions would compete in a single elimination tournament leading to an annual English Cup Champion. The establishment of an English League is a recent invention since the launch of the Courage Leagues. With multiple changes in corporate backing, the Courage League became the Allied Dunbar Premiership in the 1997–98 season, the Zurich Premiership in 2000–01, and the Guinness Premiership in 2006.

The process of playing a league season with points tables leading to a playoff and a champion is now an integral part of the English club game. The Guinness Premiership, more than any other domestic league on the planet, contains a huge contingent of foreign players from New Zealand, South Africa, Australia, Ireland, Wales, Scotland, France, and other leading rugby nations. Leicester has historically dominated the competition, winning eight titles since 1987.

## The Top 14

The Top 14 is France's premier domestic competition and has been in existence in various formats since 1892. The annual round-robin tournament is run by the Ligue Nationale de Rugby. The season runs from August until June and features relegation for the two lowest finishers and promotion for the two highest from Professional Division Two. The champion is determined by a semifinal and final playoff featuring the top four teams on the ladder after 26 rounds of action.

This competition is hugely popular in France and regularly attracts enormous crowds, with the last six finals drawing nearly 80,000 people each. Over the years Stade Toulousain and Stade Français have won the most championships, the former garnering 16 titles and the latter 13. Biarritz Olympique won in both 2004@05 and 2005–06 but in 2006–07 Stade Francais returned to the top of the ladder by triumphing over Clermont Auvergne in Paris.

# Chapter 15

# North American Rugby

*In This Chapter*

▶ Following rugby in the U.S.A.

▶ Getting into the game in the Great White North

▶ Exploring North American international tournaments

*U*nbeknown to all but the most die-hard fans, rugby in North America has a long and storied history. From hazy beginnings at the collegiate level, the United States managed to win two Olympic gold medals in the 1920s before the game all but vanished from the American sporting consciousness. In Canada, the game developed mostly on both coasts and was able to sustain a continuous if low-key presence for the entire 20th century.

In this chapter we give you an overview of the somewhat nebulous history of rugby in North America, including the formation of the two national governing bodies, detail the significant accomplishments of both American and Canadian representative teams on the world stage, and look at their current involvement in two key international tournaments.

## Checking Out Rugby in the United States

Knowledgeable rugby commentators from around the globe often remark that the United States is a sleeping giant. The theory is postulated that as soon as the U.S. is properly exposed to the game, a vast supply of superior athletes will take the world by storm. Unfortunately, this school of thought totally misses the mark on two key points. The first assumption is that superior athleticism will make Americans world-beaters. This ignores the critical role that learning the game from a young age serves in developing players with rugby vision. Knowledge of the game and finely honed skills are more significant than physical attributes in separating the good from the great players. If the NFL Pro Bowl team lined up against the All Blacks, even with a solid year of rugby-specific coaching the NFLers would get a massive lesson in tactics, and would struggle to compete at all.

The second misperception is the notion that American expertise in the business of sports will be able to transform shortcomings on the field with a magic bullet of slick marketing and boatloads of cash. This is false for two reasons:

- ✔ The U.S. sporting marketplace is incredibly crowded with well-established sports all competing for a finite pool of television time and sponsorship dollars. This is further complicated by the emergence of made-for-TV sports like the X-Games, which are created and backed by the networks themselves.

- ✔ Rugby is viewed by most Americans as a foreign game and therefore ignored by mainstream media companies and sports marketers. Americans are notoriously parochial and inward-looking when it comes to sports.

The reality is that the United States is not a sleeping giant, it's a comatose one. The good news is that new leadership at the top of the game finally has the country poised to get off life support and back on the right track to catch up with the rest of the world.

## Origins and Olympic gold

In this age of all-encompassing media coverage of sports it's easy to forget that in earlier times games were played largely for fun. Many different kinds of ball sports emerged and flourished on a regional basis throughout the United States without benefit of central governing bodies to codify every rule and legitimize each individual competition. Rugby was one such game that was played in various forms across the country. The origin of the game of rugby in England was deliberately obscured by those who wanted to promote it as an exclusive endeavor. In America, the beginnings are murky because rugby's roots are intertwined with those of American football — and for a while they were one game before splitting into completely separate sports.

It is generally agreed that the first rugby match in the United States of which a written record exists occurred in May 1874 when Harvard University played host to Montreal's McGill University. This contest led to attempts at determining a definite set of rules and inspired collegians in various parts of the country to take up the game. For the next 30 years, rugby was the primary form of football competition in the United States. If you could go back in time to watch, however, the game would bear little resemblance to rugby union as we know it today.

The catalyst that split the game into rugby and American football was the attention of President Theodore Roosevelt. Following an outcry over numerous deaths and injuries caused by the then violent nature of the game, reform was demanded and Roosevelt led the charge to modify the more extreme parts of the sport. The end result was that most of the leading colleges latched on to the reconstituted game, which eventually became gridiron, while in certain areas, notably the West Coast, rugby continued to be the dominant version of the sport.

In the years before World War I, teams like the All Blacks and the Waratahs, the precursor to the Wallabies, toured from Los Angeles to Vancouver on their way to Britain. Thus, it was no surprise that when the U.S. Olympic committee authorized a team to compete at the 1920 Games in Antwerp almost all of the players were from Northern and Southern California. The rugby competition at the Seventh Olympiad was really just a match between the United States and France, which the Americans won 8–0 to earn the gold medal.

The 1924 Games in Paris were far more dramatic but still featured only the United States, France, and Romania. After the Americans and the French both dispatched the Romanians, who were awarded the bronze medal, the two sides met in front of a 50,000-strong, heavily partisan crowd at Colombes Stadium. The Frenchmen in the stands had come to see their countrymen win a gold medal — and when the match swung decisively in the visitors' favor, the audience took on the characteristics of a mob. A 17–3 triumph by the Americans only inflamed the assembled spectators (see Figure 15-1 for a look at the victors).

The poor behavior in the stands of that 1924 match is sometimes pointed to as one of the reasons why rugby was never again contested in the Olympic games. Any momentum for the sport gained by winning two consecutive gold medals quickly ebbed when subsequent Olympiads failed to include rugby in their program of events.

# Formation and reformation of USA Rugby

In response to the need for a centralized national structure, the United States of America Rugby Football Union (USARFU, later renamed USA Rugby) was formed in 1975 to serve as the game's governing body. The formation of the national union was essential to coordinate test matches with the International Rugby Board (IRB) and its member unions. The Eagles' first test under the USARFU banner was played against Australia on January 31, 1976, in Anaheim, California.

**Figure 15-1:**
1924 USA
Olympic
Gold Medal
Team.

Although the Eagles lost 24–12 in their inaugural flight, they played the Wallabies close and had landed quite respectably on the world stage. Later that summer, a bicentennial-inspired group of Eagles pushed the then Five Nations runners-up France to the limit, scoring two fabulous tries before finally being vanquished 33–14. The early Eagles sides were renowned for their fearless and aggressive American football–style tackling technique. What they lacked in skills they made up for in commitment. From 1976 to early 2007, the Eagles played 140 tests, winning about 30 percent of them. Although they've yet to beat a founding IRB country (England, Ireland, Wales, Scotland, France, New Zealand, Australia, or South Africa), over the years they've defeated Canada, Fiji, Samoa, Tonga, and Japan.

After 30 years of amateur administration by well-meaning but essentially unqualified personnel, in June 2006 the USA Rugby Board of Directors voted to make itself redundant. (Patrick knows, because he was one of the board members who raised a hand in that historic vote.) The 27-member constituent board was unwieldy and incapable of leading the union into the future. So, after a comprehensive review of the governing structure by Atlantic Sports Management and Training, a new governance model was proposed for USA Rugby. The new board was reduced from 27 to 9 members. The makeup of the board of directors was truly revolutionary — 6 independent directors, 2 international athlete representatives, and only 1 member appointed by the USA Rugby membership. The committee men were all relegated to participate in the newly created USA Rugby Congress, which serves to bridge the gap between the membership at the grassroots level and the executive staff and new board of directors. The real power in USA Rugby was given to a new board that would be dominated by independent directors.

With the improved governance model in place, an impressive new board was recruited — with Kevin Roberts, the flamboyant, rugby-loving global CEO of Saatchi & Saatchi Worldwide, selected as the new Chairman of USA Rugby (see Figure 15-2, and check out the sidebar "How I persuaded Kevin Roberts to be chairman"). The new board's first order of business was finding a new chief executive, and after a worldwide search Nigel Melville was hired as both the CEO and president of Rugby Operations for USA Rugby.

The upshot? After a tumultuous two years of transformation, USA Rugby has a new and dynamic board in support of a new chief executive with actual rugby credentials. The National Office is located in Boulder, Colorado, and oversees the 7 Territorial Unions and 37 Local Area Unions that compete for regional and national championships.

**Figure 15-2:**
The new face of USA Rugby, Chairman Kevin Roberts.

GUTHRIE SAYS

## How I persuaded Kevin Roberts to be chairman

When I first stepped up to the responsibility of becoming part of the solution to fix USA Rugby, it was born out of my belief that the wrong people were running the organization. I naively thought that if we could just get rid of all the dead wood and bring in some top sports managers, the pathway to success would open up before us in just a few years. As I matured in my rugby knowledge it became clear that nothing short of a revolution would be significant enough to shake off the vestiges of the old regime and set USA Rugby on a course to long-term success.

In the background of all the political moves related to gaining approval for the various governance changes (which we talk about in "Formation and reformation of USA Rugby"), Frank Merrill led the search committee to recruit the new board. If we were unsuccessful in attracting top managers to populate the new board, nothing good would come from the momentous changes that were underway. What we needed was to identify and recruit our own Jack Welch to shape up the new rugby back office — someone who understood how to win in business and who had vision, leadership qualities, and an unquestionable track record and passion for our beloved game.

So, naturally, I called Kevin Roberts. He expressed his reluctance to be drawn into an organization that had a less-than-stellar record; I spent the better part of an hour explaining the union's political history and why it was the perfect time for someone of his stature to give USA Rugby a helping hand. At the conclusion of our call, and even though it was not yet a done deal, my gut was telling me that Kevin was up for the challenge of taking the union to new heights. Kevin ultimately accepted our invitation to lead the new board and was elected Chairman of USA Rugby at the first meeting. With a true visionary, rugby man, and marketing genius at the helm, only time will tell how high and how fast USA Rugby climbs in the rugby world's pecking order. So when the USA Eagles win the World Cup in 2015 I'll toast the boys with an extra measure of satisfaction — along with 26 other courageous former board members — knowing that I played a small part in the transformation from rugby backwater to rugby powerhouse.

## *Soaring with the Eagles*

The Eagles represent the United States around the world in international play. USA Rugby fields nine national teams — Men's and Women's Fifteens and Sevens, the Under-23 Women's, the Collegiate All-Americans, Under-19 Boys and Girls, and the newly formed Boys' Under-17 team. Being chosen to play for one of the U.S.'s representative sides is an honor bestowed upon only a select few players each year.

## The Dallen Stanford story

Dallen Stanford was born in Cape Town, South Africa, and like many of his countrymen he developed a passion for rugby at a young age and dreamed of one day pulling on the iconic green jersey of his nation. He attended Rondebosch Boys High School, studied at the Cape Technikon, and played rugby at the University of Cape Town (UCT). Along the way he played with and against numerous current and former Springboks like Hanyani Shimange, Gcobani Bobo, Brent Russell, and Schalk Burger, as well as England and Australia internationals Stuart Abbott and Daniel Vickerman. In 2000 he captained UCT to an unbeaten season and earned a certain amount of notoriety as a writer of sport and party stories on the Internet. This was all a fairly typical path for a young Capetonian with good rugby skills and athleticism, but "Paki" — the nickname he earned while detailing the sporting and social exploits of his compatriots on the Web — was about to embark on a much different journey.

Excluded from higher rugby opportunities in South Africa because of his size — not because he once tackled Springbok coach Nic Mallett at a formal function — Paki visited California on vacation in 2003 and was introduced to a fellow Rondebosch alum named James Walker who just happened to be the coach of the Oxy Tigers Rugby Football Club. After a stellar summer playing sevens for the Tigers, Paki obtained a visa to return for the Tigers' 2004–05 fifteens season. During that campaign he met his future wife Verity at the Springbok Bar in Los Angeles and they were married in November 2005, which made him eligible for selection to the US national team. In 2006 the Tigers qualified for the USA Sevens national championships and, based on his performance there, Paki was selected to represent Southern California at the ITTs, which they won. The next step was a momentous one as Paki was chosen to represent the USA in the IRB Sevens Series (see Chapter 13 for more info on this worldwide tournament). He played in all the Eagles games in 2007 in Wellington, San Diego, and Hong Kong. Although the outcome was significantly different from the one he envisioned as a boy in South Africa, Dallen Stanford's dream of playing international rugby came true in the land of opportunity, proving once again that the oval planet is truly a wondrous place.

**PLAYER TIP**

The aspiring male or female player can become an Eagle by following one of a variety of pathways. Those fortunate enough to get started early can compete to make the Under-17s, Under-19s, Under-23s, or Collegiate All-American sides. For the club side player, being chosen for your union's representative team can provide exposure to the national coaching staff at the annual National All-Star Championships. For the senior men, starring for one of the 18 USA Rugby Super League teams can provide a fast track to the national team. Players who soar high enough on the international stage in the Eagle jersey may earn professional rugby contracts overseas. Several of the current Eagles are fully professional players who ply their trade in the U.K. and elsewhere in Europe.

## Eagles atop the world: Women's rugby

Unlike men's international rugby, which started 132 years ago when England first played Scotland, women's tests are a relatively new phenomenon. Because the United States was one of the first nations to play women's rugby, it has been able to compete at the highest level right from the beginning, without having to play catch-up like the men.

The United States women's national team program was very successful right from the outset. Since their first match in 1987 against Canada, the American women have amassed an impressive 39–21 record, winning 65 percent of their tests. The Eagles won the first unofficial Women's Rugby World Cup in 1991 over a heavily favored England 19–6. The Eagles continued to be one of the world's top teams throughout the 1990s, making the Women's World Cup Final in both 1994 and 1998. Suffering from internal strife going into the 2002 event, they were eliminated at the quarterfinal stage. In 2006, the Eagles went 4–1 at the IRB Women's Rugby World Cup in Edmonton. Losing only to the beaten finalists from England, the Eagles defeated Ireland, Australia twice, and finished their campaign by shutting out Scotland 24–0 to finish in fifth place in the WRWC rankings (see Figure 15-3).

The Eagles' early success was a result of an increased emphasis on women's sport within the United States and a reluctance of the established rugby powers to get behind the women's game. Women's sporting participation in the U.S. grew dramatically in the 1980s, and with the unique allure of rugby's full-contact action and special camaraderie the game spread quickly across the country on collegiate campuses. This occurred during a time when women's rugby was largely ignored by rugby unions around the world. And so in the early days of women's international rugby, the U.S. had a larger pool of gifted athletes to draw upon and was thus able to compete quite well at the highest level.

**Figure 15-3:**
USA
National
Women's
Team at
WRWC
2006.

## Sevens

With only seven players per team playing on the same size pitch as a fifteens match, sevens rugby offers a spectacle of nonstop action where speed, skills, and athleticism rule the day. In contrast to the limited accomplishments of the United States in the 15-a-side game, the Eagles have had some minor successes in sevens rugby. The Eagles have competed well at the Hong Kong Sevens, winning the Bowl Final in 1997 and occasionally making the Plate semifinals. The 2007 Eagles Sevens team performed well at the USA Sevens, winning the Shield Trophy for the second time on home soil and going on to post an impressive 3–2 record at the Hong Kong Sevens, where they narrowly lost 19–22 in the Plate Semifinal to the eventual champions from Wales.

The Eagles compete in the IRB's Sevens World Series each year, where the best men's teams in the world battle it out for the championship. Fiji and New Zealand have dominated the Series from its inception. The USA Sevens kicked off in February 2003 at the Home Depot Center, marking the first time the United States ever hosted an official IRB-sanctioned international sevens tournament. In 2007, the USA Sevens moved to beautiful PETCO Park in downtown San Diego. With the stadium nestled in the heart of the city and just two blocks from the Historic Gaslamp Quarter, the USA Sevens has truly found a perfect new home for the tournament to flourish over the next few years. Add to that a worldwide TV audience and 16 national teams converging annually in California, and it's easy to see that the USA Sevens will only continue to boost rugby's profile within North America.

# Investigating Rugby in Canada

Rugby in Canada dates back to the 1860s when it was initially played by army and navy personnel in British Columbia and Nova Scotia. The first recorded match was played in Montreal among the members of an artillery unit in 1864.

The early desire for standardized play, always a crucial moment in any burgeoning game, was met by Toronto's Trinity College, which published a set of rules for rugby that same year. In 1868 the Montreal Football Club was formed, making it Canada's first official rugby organization. These identifiable firsts point to a growing interest in the sport in diverse parts of the country.

Over the next two decades, as more and more clubs sprouted across the width of the nation, an administrative structure also developed, beginning with the establishment of the British Columbia Rugby Union in 1889, and followed by the formation of the Maritime Provinces Rugby Union in 1890 and the Manitoba Rugby Football Union in 1892.

Rugby's development in Canada was slowed considerably by both world wars, but since 1945 it has spread to every province. Rugby is now a permanent fixture on the Canadian sporting landscape.

# The birth of Rugby Canada

The first incarnation of a national governing body for the sport took place in 1929 with the creation of the Rugby Union of Canada. The organization functioned for the next ten years before going into hibernation for the duration of World War II and beyond. Following the war, most administrative issues were dealt with on a provincial level until the re-formation of the national group in 1965. During the 1960s Canada played test matches only sporadically, so there wasn't actually a mountain of responsibility placed on the volunteer administrators.

In 1974 the body that is now known as Rugby Canada was incorporated and took over the day-to-day running of the sport at the national level. This was sufficient until the first Rugby World Cup in 1987. The desire to compete in the tournament prompted Canada to become a member of the IRB. (For more details on the IRB, refer to Chapter 5. For more details on the Rugby World Cup, refer to Chapter 13.) Since that momentous decision, Rugby Canada has placed a high priority on regular participation at the international level in men's, women's, under-19s, under-21s, and sevens rugby.

The Canadians played their first recognized international in 1932 against Japan, but it wasn't until the 1970s that they began to play tests on a regular basis. Canada has always been known as a tough team that can't be intimidated on the pitch. Occasionally over the last 15 years the national team has competed successfully with the top teams in the world.

In the 1991 World Cup, Canada opened the tournament by beating Fiji and Romania before losing a close contest to France. The two wins, however, were good enough to advance to the quarterfinals for the first time. On a quagmire of a pitch in Lille, France, Canada hung tough against the All Blacks but came up short, losing 13–29.

In 1993 Canada shocked Wales 26–24 at the Arms Park in Cardiff, and in 1994 they beat France 18–16 in Nepean. In 2000 Canada continued the tradition of battling strongly against quality opposition by drawing a match 27–27 with Ireland in Markham, Ontario. Their most recent triumph over a Six Nations side came in 2002 when the touring Scots were upended 26–23 in Vancouver after flyhalf Jared Barker kicked 16 points. In 2005, the 13th-ranked Canadians upended the 8th-ranked Pumas from Argentina 22–15 at Calgary Rugby Park.

Since the game went professional in 1995, Canada has contributed numerous players to the top leagues in Great Britain and France. Unfortunately, this has prevented the members of the national team from training together in a cohesive fashion before big tournaments and has led to some disappointing results. Canada had high hopes of making its second quarterfinal appearance going into the 2003 World Cup, but was able to win only one match against Tonga and failed to move on to the knockout stage.

## Canadian women on the rise

Women's rugby in Canada began in the late 1970s in various parts of the country, but there was no organized interprovincial competition until 1983. Four years later the women's national team played its inaugural match in Victoria, British Columbia, against the United States.

Canada has competed in all five Women's World Cups beginning in 1991. In the first tournament in Wales, Canada lost to New Zealand in the opener but drew with the hosts to end up 0–1–1. In Scotland, for the 1994 event, the team lost in the quarterfinals to England, beat Japan in the Shield semifinal, and fell 5–11 to the Scottish women in the final for an eighth-place finish.

The 1998 World Cup in Amsterdam was the first to be officially sanctioned by the IRB, and the Canadian women benefited from increased support from Rugby Canada. The national side reached their first World Cup semifinal in the Netherlands but lost 46–6 to the United States.

In 2002, Barcelona was the site for the fourth Women's World Cup and once again the Canadians were solid contenders. An opening-round 57–0 destruction of Ireland was followed by another shutout, this time 11–0 over Scotland. That victory propelled Canada into the semifinals to face England, where they were thumped 53–10.

Rugby Canada hosted the 2006 IRB Women's Rugby World Cup in Edmonton, Alberta, making it the first-ever IRB-sanctioned World Cup event to be staged in North America. The Canadian women lost heavily to the eventual champions from New Zealand 66–7 in pool play, but still managed to qualify for the Cup Semifinals on points differential after beating Spain and Kazakhstan by a combined scoreline of 124–5. England then defeated the Canadian women 20–14 in the Cup Semifinal, and France beat the locals 17–8 in the third-place match. Canadian Heather Moyse was the leading tryscorer in the tournament, with seven.

## Canadian National Women's League

A central plank in Rugby Canada's Long-Term Development Strategy is the evolution of the women's club game. To foster the development of women's clubs across the country, Rugby Canada partnered with the provincial unions to create the National Women's League (NWL) in 2007. Similar to the concept underpinning the formation of the Rugby Canada Super League (RCSL — which we discuss in Chapter 16), the NWL was formed to provide more high-quality games for women's club players, coaches, and referees as part of the overall high performance plan for women's rugby in Canada.

The NWL comprises nine representative teams — one from each of the nine Canadian provinces. The side are divided into two divisions: East and West. The West includes British Columbia, Alberta, Saskatchewan, and Manitoba. The East features teams from Ontario, Quebec, Newfoundland, New Brunswick, and Nova Scotia. Each team plays all the others in its division in pool play from May to August, with the divisional winners meeting to determine the annual National Women's League Champion.

Rugby Canada is keen to see the NWL structure of provincial representative play expanded down to the lower-age grades as part of their national elite player development plan in future years.

## Sevens

The Canadian Sevens team has performed very well in the seven-a-side game. They have regularly collected hardware in the World Sevens Series, and in 2004 they won two Bowl trophies in Dubai, UAE, and George, South Africa, and were beaten finalists in the Plate division in Los Angeles. Some of Canada's stars of the future can be seen on their sevens team today.

# Going Global: North American Internationals

One key to improving performance on the international scene is to regularly play matches against quality opposition. In the last decade there have been a variety of attempts to provide Canada and the United States with the opportunity to play in annual tournaments that will serve to raise their level of competitiveness. The Barclays Churchill Cup and the North America 4 are two of the most important.

# Barclays Churchill Cup

The Barclays Churchill Cup (BCC) is a cooperative alliance among the Rugby Football Union (England), USA Rugby, and Rugby Canada. In 2007, the BCC featured six teams including the USA Eagles, Rugby Canada's National Team, England Saxons, Ireland A, Scotland A, and the New Zealand Maori. The format included two groups of three teams that played each other to determine the finalists for the Cup, Plate, and Consolation Finals.

The New Zealand Maori defeated Scotland A in the 2006 Cup Final at Commonwealth Stadium in Edmonton 52–17. In the Plate Final Ireland A nipped the England Saxons 30–27 at the death in an exciting match, and Canada took the Consolation Final beating the USA 33–18 in the local derby to avoid the wooden spoon.

The 2007 BCC was set entirely in England and the Saxons, and New Zealand Maori proved to be the class sides of the competition, easily advancing to the Cup Final, which was surprisingly won by the Saxons. The USA and Canada met in the fifth-place playoff match with Canada taking the honors by a score of 51—3 at Edgeley Park.

# North America 4

The North America 4 (NA4) was launched in 2006. Thanks to a considerable financial investment from the IRB, the NA4 serves as the penultimate level of men's elite player development in North America, just below the National Team programs of both unions. The NA4 was created to narrow the considerable gap that exists between the amateur club game and international play and that has effectively stunted the pace of development and consistency of performance by the North American National Teams. The new cross-border competition currently pits two representative sides each from Canada and the United States in 12 matches played over three rounds in both countries. The two Canadian sides are Canada West and Canada East; the American teams are the USA Hawks and the USA Falcons. In the inaugural season, Canada West were the 2006 NA4 Champions.

In 2007 the standards of play rose considerably, confirming the basic theory that all the players, coaches, referees, administrators, and others involved in the NA4 would benefit greatly from staging this new level of representative play across North America. In the future, the plan is to expand the NA4 and use it as the launching pad to introduce professional rugby in the Americas.

# Chapter 16

# Amateur Rugby in North America

●  ●  ●  ●  ●  ●  ●  ●  ●  ●  ●  ●  ●  ●  ●  ●  ●  ●  ●  ●  ●  ●  ●  ●  ●  ●  ●  ●  ●  ●  ●  ●  ●  ●  ●  ●  ●  ●

### In This Chapter
▶ Checking out club rugby throughout the U.S.A.
▶ Getting acquainted with the Canadian club scene

●  ●  ●  ●  ●  ●  ●  ●  ●  ●  ●  ●  ●  ●  ●  ●  ●  ●  ●  ●  ●  ●  ●  ●  ●  ●  ●  ●  ●  ●  ●  ●  ●  ●  ●  ●  ●  ●

The rugby club is the heart and soul of the North American game. It's where new players are introduced to the sport, where lessons are learned, and where rugby's unique camaraderie and love for the game are nurtured. In contrast to the professional game around the world, the North American club scene still embodies the amateur ethos of the game. The local club is the place where anyone can show up and become part of the action. Inclusiveness distinguishes rugby clubs from most other sporting activities. No matter where you come from or when you arrive at a rugby club function, you'll immediately be welcomed into the family as the bonds of the game supersede race, religion, sexual preference, politics, and any of life's myriad trivialities that may otherwise divide us.

North American rugby clubs are all amateur and organized in a series of tiers. At the top of the heap are the Rugby Canada Super League and the USA Rugby Super League. The club structure is further divided into several divisions, which serve to offer meaningful championships for teams of varying size, gender, and skill levels. In this chapter, we focus on the backbone of the North American game: the clubs.

## Clubbing with the Yanks

Club rugby in the United States is played solely for the love of the game. The players compete for the joy of the contest, the administrators organize club activities on a volunteer basis, and everyone involved shares the common kinship of commitment to the rugby lifestyle. This participant-based focus, where the main goal is to make sure that next week's game comes off, has resulted in rugby developing very quietly across North America over the past 135 years. More than 68,000 registered players in the United States play for nearly 2,100 clubs, from Alaska to Arkansas and New York to California.

# Maggotfest

I can proudly say that I'm a Maggot and have been since 1994. No, I'm not a terrible person, I just happen to belong to one of the finest rugby clubs in the world, the Missoula All-Maggots. The Maggots are by charter dedicated to playing hard rugby and having fun, and to that end they have hosted a unique festival on the last weekend of April or the first weekend in May every year since 1977.

The Maggotfest gathers 28 men's and 8 women's sides from throughout the U.S. and Canada for what can only be described as a celebration of the ideals of the sport and a spur to the inclinations of those who choose to play it. The party kicks off on Thursday afternoon, when a specially selected "hosted team" arrives early and plays an opening match against the home side at Maggot Park. A raucous party soon follows and eventually spills into downtown Missoula. Early the next morning both teams board the Maggot Bus for a long ride into Idaho for a white-water rafting trip down the Lochsa River. Survivors who make it back to town are treated to the Friday-night arrival bash at a local watering hole, where the other 34 teams make their first appearance and begin vying for the weekend's honors.

In a normal rugby tournament, wins and losses are the measure of success. At the Maggotfest, overall team spirit on and off the pitch is the most highly revered quality. A good showing on Friday night can put a team in the running for the most coveted of awards, that of "Most Honoured Side." The rugby gets going and the beer starts flowing at 9:00 on Saturday morning. Fixtures are determined with an eye toward producing interesting matchups between sides with similar skill levels and tendencies.

After a long first day of competitive rugby, the Fest really hits its stride with the Saturday-night party. Held in a llama barn at the Western Montana Fairgrounds, it's part Mardi Gras, part Halloween, and all rugby camaraderie extraordinaire. Teams dress thematically or not at all, and a thousand people infused with the rugby spirit dance to the band, drink beer, throw beer, and generally have a smashingly good time. Sunday features one more match for each club and the awards ceremony. An award is bestowed for "Best Play on the Pitch," but it is wholly secondary to the "Most Honoured Side".

The real winner at Maggotfest is the community of rugby devotees who live for the one weekend a year when the game and lifestyle they love and cherish are celebrated with wholehearted devotion.

The development of the game in the United States has been largely driven by initiatives at the club level. Prior to the formation of USA Rugby in 1976, pockets of rugby activity existed on the East and West coasts and a few spots in between. The leading clubs played a critical role in spreading the word about the sport and providing a means for rugby people to enjoy their chosen game.

Ever since the birth of USA Rugby, there has been a very palpable tension between the clubs and the national office. The clubs have viewed the national administration as posers and control freaks working largely for their own personal profit, while the clubs rightfully have seen themselves as the embodiment of the true ethos of the game. Hopefully with a new administrative structure in place (refer to Chapter 15), this tension will disappear altogether in coming years.

Traditionally, the United States club model includes an administration consisting of a club president, vice president, secretary, and treasurer, as well as various crucial appointees. The club officers are usually current or former players whose age and leadership skills have cursed them into taking on an organizational role. The *fixtures chair* is responsible for making sure the pitch is ready, and the *social chair* has the all-important job of looking after the third half, the mandatory reception following each home game. Add to that a coach and a slew of willing players, and *voilà* — you've got a rugby club.

# The USA Rugby Super League

The USA Rugby Super League represents the top tier of club rugby in the United States. The league was launched in 1997 to address the need of the country's top clubs for a higher level of competition week in and week out. Before the Super League was created, the top teams would only play one or two regional rivals of similar standard before the national playoffs each year. The concept behind the Super League was to create a competition where the best teams in the country would play against evenly matched opposition throughout the season, and then compete for the national championship.

## How I became president of the Oxy Olde Boys

After my triumphant return to Los Angeles following a short, ill-advised stint in Boston in 1992, I was keen to get fully stuck back into rugby with the Oxy Olde Boys RFC. Although a relatively new convert to the game, I enthusiastically welcomed and relished the physical challenge and camaraderie that my newfound game provided. Because I was a young lawyer and not afraid to speak my mind about how things should be run at the club, it was suggested that I consider running for president at the upcoming annual elections. Unfortunately, the elections were being held while I was in the heat of a major trial, which prevented my personal attendance. So to make my case for the office, I offered the following statement of my platform to be read aloud to the membership by proxy: "If elected as your President, I promise to faithfully uphold the social tradition of the Oxy Olde Boys, providing two kegs at all receptions and I will make sure that our bar tab at the Big-O is always paid on time. Yours in Rugby, Guthrie." By all accounts, the assembled electors rose to their feet and I was thrust into office by acclamation. The lesson here is that becoming a rugby administrator is not particularly difficult (and sometimes happens even if you're not there). The tricky part is making sure that you do your mates proud once you've taken on the responsibility.

Like most good things in that era of USA Rugby, the Super League was started by a group of leading club visionaries who, being unable to persuade the national office to address their need for better regular competition, took matters into their own hands and created the league over the objections of USA Rugby. With leadership from former USA Rugby President Bob Watkins and Keith Engelbrecht of the Dallas Harlequins, the Super League clubs joined together in 1996 and signed up Harp Lager to sponsor their first two seasons of play. The benefits of the league were immediately apparent to all — with the best teams being matched against opponents of similar ability every week the scorelines were much closer and the standard of play was raised for all involved.

After four successful years of operation outside of USA Rugby's control, the Super League was finally sanctioned in 2001 by the national governing body as the top-level rugby competition in the United States. The nation's top 18 teams are now divided into the Red, White, and Blue Conferences, with six squads each. The Super League delivers the best club rugby on offer and is strategically positioned in 13 major markets (see www.usarugbysuperleague.com for more on the Super League).

Although some limited exceptions exist, most Super League players are unpaid for their services. Most often, if a player is being paid, it usually involves a foreign player who was recruited from overseas to bolster the local talent. Even those being paid are only semi-professionals at best as the money is barely enough to live on, with most needing a real job to supplement their income from rugby.

The 2006 RSL Final pitted old Southern California rivals Belmont Shore and Old Mission Beach Athletic Club (OMBAC) at Shaw Stadium in Santa Clara. In a thrilling ending to a spectacular championship game, OMBAC (see Figure 16-1) scored a go-ahead try in injury time after trailing the entire match to win their first Rugby Super League championship 36–33 over previously unbeaten Belmont Shore.

**Figure 16-1:**
Old Mission
Beach
Athletic
Club, 2006
USA Rugby
Super
League
Champions.

# USA Club Championships

Whether playing for a local social club or one the few established national powers, there's a championship for American clubs to aspire to win. The USA club structure is multi-tiered, with men's Division I, II, and III all playing off to crown a national champion. The women's club structure includes Division I and II playing to determine annual champions. There are also National championships for Sevens rugby in nearly all the divisions for men and women. Regardless of division, competing for and winning a USA National Club Championship is a highlight of any American player's career.

The road to becoming a National Champion isn't easy. First, clubs have to advance out of their local area union competitions, which are basically the teams within their leagues. The next level is to qualify for one of the territorial berths that each of the seven territories have for their respective divisions. Depending on the past year's performance, two or three openings per territory are available in the divisional playoffs.

After a club secures its ticket to the big dance, the journey becomes much more arduous, as team members scramble to get time off from work and to cobble together the money needed for airline tickets and hotel expenses. USA Rugby provides the structure, but the clubs are responsible for all the costs. From regional tournaments a quartet of winning teams advance from the round of 16 to the final 4. The final four teams play off over a long weekend, with the winning team having to play two matches in 72 hours. Despite these challenges, the joy of being a National Champion, like the New York Rugby Club (see Figure 16-2), is something that remains dear forever as the accomplishment grows in stature every time the story is retold.

**Figure 16-2:**
New York Rugby Club, USA Rugby Women's Club Division 1 Champs 2006.

### Finding the right club to join

The key to finding the right club is to first figure out what kind of rugby experience you want to have. If you're a newbie and don't know what to expect, then you're probably better off hooking up with a second- or third-division club. They'll be familiar with taking aboard new players and you'll have a better chance of getting playing time sooner at those levels. If you've played a bit of footy already and are looking to improve your skills, focus on first-division clubs, paying special attention to how the coaching staff interacts with the players at training. Rugby is unique as a team sport in that you're immediately welcome at virtually any club in the world when you say you're a rugby player. Even so, before you join a club, it is absolutely imperative that you go to a training session to meet their players, coaches, and supporters before deciding if they're right for you. After you go through a practice session and then get a chance to chat with the team after training over a beverage, you'll be ready to make the call.

# Considering the Canadian Club Scene

There are more than 450 rugby clubs in Canada, serving 30,000 registered players throughout the entire country — from British Columbia to Newfoundland. The clubs are governed by the ten provincial unions and play in a variety of championship leagues and formats. The three largest unions — British Columbia, Alberta, and Ontario — also have sub-unions that run the sport on a regional basis. Each provincial union is responsible for selecting its own representatives for competition in the Rugby Canada National Championships.

Like rugby countries the world over, Canada's clubs range from huge organizations fielding numerous teams at different levels to small ones that put out only two men's teams each weekend.

As can be expected, players from provinces where rugby is less ingrained in the sporting environment were often overlooked when it came time for national selection and honors. To help even the playing field and provide for nationwide exposure and competition for all, Rugby Canada and its member unions helped to found the Rugby Canada Super League in 1998.

## The Rugby Canada Super League

The Rugby Canada Super League (RCSL) represents the highest level of club competition within Canada. Formed in 1998, the RCSL was created to improve the overall level of play by providing the top club sides with a greater number of high-quality games each season. By playing against teams that were more evenly matched at the higher end of the national club spectrum, RCSL members were able to collectively and individually improve their standard of play. Since the introduction of the North America 4, the RCSL clubs have become the main sources of talent for the Canada West and Canada East representative sides.

Prior to the formation of the Super League, Canadian selectors, the men who choose the players for the national team, had few opportunities to see all of the talent on offer across the nation. As a result, individuals from less prominent provinces had a harder time making the national team than those from rugby hotbeds like British Columbia and Ontario. Now the best players in the participating provinces have the chance to showcase their wares on a weekly basis against other top teams.

Because of the vast travel distances between the clubs across the country, the 12 RCSL teams are divided into two geographical divisions — the Western and Eastern Conferences. The Eastern Conference has seven teams, which currently include the New Brunswick Black Spruce, Newfoundland Rock, Niagara Thunder, Nova Scotia Kelts, Ottawa Harlequins, Quebec Caribou, and Toronto Xtreme. The Western Conference comprises the Calgary Mavericks, Edmonton Gold, Saskatchewan Prairie Fire, Vancouver Island Crimson Tide, and Vancouver Wave. Each team plays all the others in their division once and the conference winners play in the annual RCSL Championship match.

Of the nine previous RCSL champions, the Vancouver Island Crimson Tide have won four titles, the Fraser Valley Venom have won twice, the Calgary Mavericks once, and the Newfoundland Rock have emerged victorious in 2005 and 2006.

As the competition grows in stature through increased visibility, making it onto one of the Super League teams becomes a necessary first step in earning a spot on the men's national team.

## Canadian National Championships

Rugby Canada holds national championships in five categories:

- ✔ Senior Women
- ✔ Under-19 women
- ✔ Under-18 men
- ✔ Under-17 women
- ✔ Under-16 men

In 2006, a consolidated National Championship Festival was staged in Winnipeg, Manitoba, with more than 1,000 participants who saw Ontario sweep the women's slate, winning the Gold Medal for Senior women, Under-19 women (see Figure 16-3), and Under-17 divisions, while British Columbia took the top honors for Under-18 and Under-16 men.

**Figure 16-3:** Ontario U19 Women, the 2006 National Champions.

Combining the championships into one festival setting served to make the event into a major happening on the Canadian sporting landscape. In addition to family members and enthusiastic rugby spectators, the festival drew national selectors, executive board members from participating unions, and staff from Rugby Canada. The future stars of Canadian rugby had a chance to strut their stuff in front of the very people they wanted to impress and work closely with in the future.

# Chapter 17

# Collegiate, High School, and Youth Rugby in North America

- - - - - - - - - - - - - - - - - - - - - - - - - - - - - - - - - - - - - - - - - - - -

## In This Chapter

▶ Knowing and loving the most popular club sport on U.S. college campuses

▶ Sizing up the growth of high school and youth rugby in the U.S.A.

▶ Looking at Canadian interuniversity rugby

▶ Starting them young in Canada with high school and youth rugby

- - - - - - - - - - - - - - - - - - - - - - - - - - - - - - - - - - - - - - - - - - - -

College campuses were the first home of organized rugby competitions in North America. From the first game in 1874, through rugby's dark years at the end of World War I, to the early 1960s, the collegiate game was the only consistent presence keeping rugby's torch lit in the United States. Even today, for the vast majority of North American participants, playing in college is their first exposure to the game and remains the primary developmental arena for local clubs to stock their teams.

Recently, however, the sport has enjoyed unprecedented growth in high school and youth programs across the United States and Canada. In this chapter, we focus on the three areas that are the future of the North American game: collegiate, high school, and youth rugby.

## Playing the American Collegiate Game

On May 5, 1874, Harvard University hosted Montreal's McGill University in the first recorded match of rugby played on U.S. soil. Over the next 30 years, the game evolved through the process of rules codification and modification. These changes culminated in the 1906 legalization of the forward pass, the final deviation that forever divided rugby from American football. By 1906, most colleges across the country had switched from playing rugby to playing American football.

Bucking the national trend, the West Coast held firm and the University of California at Berkeley and Stanford University actually dropped American football in 1906, setting the stage for later Olympic glory. (Refer to Chapter 15 for more details.)

In 1910, an All-Star team comprising primarily Cal and Stanford players toured Australia and New Zealand under the banner of the American Universities team. Rugby had become the contact game of choice out West and regularly drew up to 20,000 fans for the annual showdown between Cal and Stanford. In 1912, 1913, and 1914, the New South Wales Waratahs, New Zealand All Blacks, and an All-Britain side toured the West Coast to play the All-Americans.

By the end of World War I, however, American football took center stage on collegiate campuses throughout the country and rugby suffered through a period of stagnation that would last until its revival in the mid-1960s.

Today, rugby is the most popular club sport on U.S. college campuses. With 370 men's teams and 280 women's programs competing in 2007, collegiate rugby is once again flourishing on campuses across the United States. USA Rugby awards four national collegiate titles for men and women in Divisions I and II. Like the club playoff structure, each territory produces a predetermined number of teams to compete in regional playoffs, leading to a national final four tournament to crown the annual USA Rugby National Collegiate Champions.

Most people's initial impression of collegiate rugby is of a bunch of rowdy, beer-swilling frat boys getting naked and having a good old time. And while that reputation isn't entirely unearned, USA Rugby is working hard to turn it around by offering heaps of best-practices advice for the administrators and coaches of collegiate programs who are determined to lift the standard of play and rehabilitate collegiate rugby's image on campuses nationwide (see www.usarugby.org for more information).

Meanwhile, the NCAA has placed women's rugby on its list of emerging sports, and with *Title IX* fairness concerns at work (Title IX requires that there be relative parity in the number of men and women who participate in NCAA-sanctioned sports), we may see the NCAA install women's rugby as an intercollegiate sport under its control. If the NCAA opts to include women's rugby, the result would be a substantial increase in coaching and administrative support for the women's game on campus.

On the paddock in 2007, the University of California at Berkeley won their 23rd Men's Division I National Collegiate Championship when they defeated BYU 37–7. Penn State University (see Figure 17-1) took the women's DI title, denying Stanford the three-peat at home in a thrilling encounter that saw PSU come out on top 22–21.

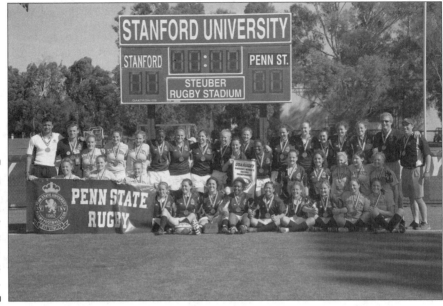

**Figure 17-1:**
Penn State
University,
USA Rugby
Women's
Collegiate
Champs
2007.

# Starting Young: High School and Youth Rugby in the U.S.A.

The bad news for the rest of the rugby world is that more Americans than ever before are playing rugby, which means it's only a matter of time until the U.S.A. becomes competitive at the highest level. The good news for all those fans from rugby powerhouse nations around the world who are shaking in their boots right about now is that USA Rugby still needs at least another 10 to 15 years to translate this growth into substantial success on the international stage.

In the nine-year span from 1999 through 2007, every important sector within USA Rugby has experienced growth ranging from steady to spectacular. The most significant trend has been the fact that for the first time in the history of the organization, the single largest segment within USA Rugby is now players under 18 years old — the result of unprecedented expansion in the high school and youth segments.

The positive growth trends in participation present a double-edged sword to USA Rugby. How can the national governing body best utilize its very limited financial and other resources to serve a growing constituency? And how should those resources be allocated and prioritized going forward? We believe the key to making the United States truly competitive around the world is to nurture an ever-increasing crop of younger players in order to produce individuals who have the instincts to compete with those who have been playing barefoot since they were five years old.

## High school championships

The rapid growth of high school rugby is one of the least well known but nevertheless biggest success stories in the advancement of the oval game in the United States. In the eight years from 1999 to 2007, the number of high school programs across the country more than doubled, from 226 to 555. If these high school students stick with the game through college and then join the top clubs over the next several years, USA Rugby's representative sides will improve by having a larger pool of more experienced talent to choose from.

USA Rugby introduced the national high school championship tournament in 1985. The tournament now involves the top eight nationally ranked high school teams, which play for the USA Rugby National High School Championship.

---

### Rugby can thrive anywhere

A rural farming and ranching community of just 200 with a total high school enrollment of about 110 students and more than 30 miles from the nearest city of any decent size, Simms, Montana, seems an unlikely place for a rugby team. And yet the Simms Tigers High School Rugby Club is flourishing against the odds.

The club was started by local teachers Steve Lundgren and Randy Thompson in 2004 and immediately had to confront obstacles such as low numbers, school board and athletic department skepticism, raising participation money in an economically disadvantaged area, and isolation from other rugby-playing high schools. Eventually — through recruitment of non-traditional athletes, education about the sport, good old-fashioned hard work, and general enthusiasm — those problems were overcome. Now the club is a source of pride in the community and has even spawned similar programs in other Montana cities.

Simms' success has been a group effort. When Lundgren was called up to active duty with the Army in 2006, assistant coach Russ Bloom stepped in to fill the void. Helped by local former Maggot players Bill Dahlgren, Logan Sayler, and Tom Duff (see Chapter 16 for information about Maggotfest), Bloom has managed to put the Simms Tigers on the map. They now log lots of hours on the bus and play matches all over the West, including annual participation in the prestigious Starship Tournament in Vulcan, Alberta. And in May 2007 they hosted the first Montana high school Rugby Fest — to honor their former coach, Lt. Col. Lundgren, on his return from Iraq.

If you're thinking of starting up a rugby club but are daunted by the barriers involved, think of the challenges faced by the Simms Tigers. Then get out there and do it!

In terms of national high school titles, Highland High School from Utah has set the standard, winning 17 national championships including the 2007 crown with a convincing 24–8 victory over Jesuit of Sacramento.

# Youth rugby

Developing youth rugby is the biggest long-term challenge for the sport in the United States. From 1999 to 2007, the number of youth rugby teams in the U.S. has quietly leapt from 240 to 625. (Check out Figure 17-2 to see youth rugby in action.)

### Understanding youth rugby's growth

Despite youth rugby's rapid growth, it's also the least understood segment of the sport. The recent substantial gains in numbers are the result of three trends:

- ✔ More and more players are now reaching the age where they are no longer actively playing the game and have young children who are looking for a sport to compete in.

- ✔ Rugby's visibility on television (and the Internet) has grown over the past dozen years, giving rugby parents a chance to sit down on the couch and show their children the game they learned to love in college.

- ✔ Youth rugby has been integrated into existing state competitions. All around the country, new youth programs are being created as the students' demand for the game increases.

**Figure 17-2:**
Youth rugby.

# Youth development

In the United States, the median age that players begin participating in rugby is 19 years old. By the time most Americans have figured out the nuances of the game, they're approaching 30 and beyond their athletic prime.

As more and more local rugby leagues pop up across the country, USA Rugby has targeted youth development as a key area for growth. With support from the International Rugby Board (IRB), USA Rugby has implemented a Youth & High School Strategic Plan. The strategy involves utilization of local youth leaders. The youth leaders are located in nearly every state nationwide and are trained to provide expertise, materials, and other support needed to launch, maintain, and nurture new youth teams. The program contains physical education curriculum lessons, a youth development guide, a coaching text called *Play the Game*, plus videos and other helpful aids. In addition, the plan targets an increased reliance on the state-based development model — where youth rugby is promoted through inclusion in statewide youth sports programs.

To learn more about youth development, visit www.usarugby.org and click on Youth & High School.

USA Rugby's Youth Program and local youth leaders are no doubt providing an important service in helping to create new teams, but it's very important to realize it's really a groundswell of demand from kids and parents that's driving the increased number of youth teams.

# Women's rugby on the rise

Women's rugby is the fastest-growing segment of the game in the United States. From 1993 to 2007 women's rugby more than doubled in size on U.S. campuses, growing from 125 to 280 teams. This unprecedented increase has led directly to a dramatic surge in the number of women's club teams, which saw a 38 percent increase from 88 to 120 clubs over the same period of time.

Rugby attracts women because it's one of the few full-contact sports where they play by the same rules as the men and can be as physical as they choose. We've coached men and women collegians for a few years now, and while the men are all about bash and crash, the women actually listen at training and are much more technically sound in the basics of the game. Moreover, for most women, playing their first rugby match is like a baptism of fire — they've never experienced anything remotely close to the physicality of the game, and after they've made it through that first test they're hooked on rugby for good.

Rugby is the perfect sport for an ever-increasing number of confident women who are no longer content with the relative safety of, say, softball when they can choose to compete in a game where they're able to physically test themselves to the limit.

### Introducing non-contact youth rugby

For children too young for full-contact rugby, non-contact or touch rugby is used as an introductory tool. This version of the game eliminates tackling and other contact, minimizing parents' safety concerns. The result has been a smashing success, thanks to the efforts of visionaries like Pat Walsh and Mike Sagehorn, who have dedicated much of their free time over the past several years to create thriving non-contact youth leagues in the Washington, D.C./Virginia and Northern California areas.

The main advantage of non-contact rugby is that all players still get to run with the ball and play both offense and defense, but because there's no tackling, rucking, or mauling the collisions are replaced with a two-handed tag of the ball-carrier. The non-contact game is ideal for boys and girls from 6 to 10 years old. After their bodies are ready for the stress of the tackle game, they can move on to playing rugby with a local youth side.

# Canadian Collegiate Championships

No formal national collegiate championship exists in men's rugby in Canada. Individual provincial unions hold their own competitions to determine their divisional winners. This is partially because greater emphasis is placed on the under-21 national championships, but it also results from the multi-tiered nature of Canadian clubs, which feature many age-grade teams.

The women's collegiate rugby national championship is played under the auspices of Canadian Interuniversity Sport (CIS). The CIS is the national governing body for 19 different sports at the university level, including track and field, basketball, and hockey. In women's rugby, 35 teams compete in the Canada West, Ontario, Quebec, and Atlantic divisions for six playoff spots.

The 2006 qualifiers were the University of Guelph Gryphons, the St. Francis Xavier University X-Women, the University of Waterloo Warriors, the Lethbridge Pronghorns, the Université Laval Rouge et Or, and the University of Western Ontario Mustangs. At the 2006 CIS Championships, the St. Francis Xavier X-Women defeated the Guelph Gryphons 10–5 to win the CIS Gold Medal match and hoist the Monilex Trophy.

# High School and Youth Rugby in Canada

In the most competitive rugby-playing nations around the world, by the time kids reach high school age they're already steeped in rugby skills and culture because they've been playing and watching since they were very young. In a place like Canada, where rugby is well down the national sporting ladder, many players have their first introduction to the game at the high school level, although youth rugby is growing in popularity.

## High school rugby

Rugby at the secondary level in Canadian schools is organized and run by high school athletic associations in each province, with assistance from the provincial unions. Every province has its own organizational structures to fit its specific needs.

According to Rugby Canada, there are approximately 450 boys' and girls' high school programs in the greater Toronto area alone, with an estimated 300 more in British Columbia. Although high school players aren't required to register directly with the national office, approximately 12,000 boys and girls play at the high school level across Canada. Throughout the country, high school rugby is a valuable introductory component of the sport — its continued growth is essential to the long-term health of Rugby Canada.

## Youth rugby

Youth rugby (or mini rugby, as we call it) is a catchall term that includes players between the ages 5 and 15. In Canada, the development of young players is handled mostly through individual clubs as part of an overall provincial strategy.

The advantages of starting players from as young an age as possible are borne out by the success of rugby-playing nations where mini rugby is taken as the natural order of things. The sooner players begin to amass the basic skills of passing, running, and kicking, the easier it is to develop critical thinking and strategic skills at the high school level.

Mini rugby players start without boots, and because the game is initially non-contact they don't engage in tackling. An appropriately sized ball is also used, the better to be passed by smaller hands. The fundamentals are introduced in a non-threatening environment where the emphasis is on having fun and learning sportsmanship, rather than serious competition. Girls and boys play on the same team, usually until about age 10. Like the sport at the highest level, mini rugby is great for all kids because, regardless of size or development, there's a place for everyone in the team. (Refer to Chapter 2 for details on player positions and characteristics.)

The goal of mini rugby is to acclimate kids to the essentials of the sport and then slowly introduce the finer points of the game. Along the way they grasp the beginnings of teamwork, physical fitness, and social skills. A rugby club with a mini rugby program is by definition a family-friendly place.

# Part IV
# Coaching and Refereeing

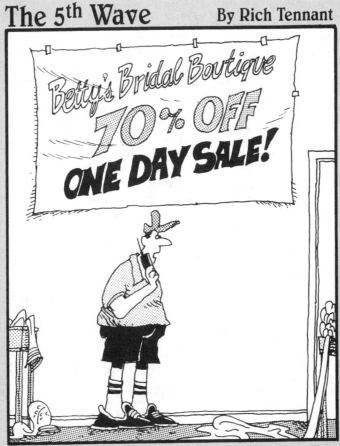

The 5th Wave          By Rich Tennant

"I've got a ruck in aisle 5. I'm going to call a scrum unless I see that veil pretty soon."

# In this part . . .

This part addresses the two areas key to developing the game in North America: coaching and refereeing. We start with the basic requirements needed to become a rugby coach. Next, we examine the false assumptions about injuries in rugby and discuss how coaches can make the game safer for their charges, and follow it up with the steps coaches need to take to become certified in the United States and Canada.

To round off this part, we concentrate on refereeing. We start with a discussion of what it takes to become a referee and then explain the certification process on both sides of the border.

# Chapter 18

# Coaching

## In This Chapter

▶ Appreciating the qualities of a good coach

▶ Ensuring your team's safety

▶ Being everything to everyone on the team

▶ Making the coaching decision

▶ Finding yourself a supporting role

Coaching isn't really a profession — rather, it's an obsession, attracting some of the strongest individuals in the game. In North America, because only a handful of lucky ones actually make a decent living from the job your motivation to coach has to come from reasons other than financial gain.

The hard work that coaching requires is rewarded by the warm feeling of being an integral part of a team. You get an enormous amount of satisfaction when your team achieves greatness, or when a player you've nurtured is selected for a representative side and goes on to be successful. Numerous people rely on you and look to you for guidance. Their success is your success.

The effectiveness of the coach is paramount, because good players without a good coach make a mediocre team. Although rugby players often get all the kudos for strong performances, much of the credit should really go to the coach.

In this chapter, we explain the abilities and talents required of a coach. Should you decide that the hot seat is just a little too hot for you, you can choose from a range of other jobs that give vital support to the team.

# Grand Obsession: The Making of a Good Coach

Picture the scene: It's the end of the tournament, the winning captain stands there clutching the trophy with a smile as wide as the Grand Canyon, and an interviewer pushes through the crowd and shoves a microphone under his nose, asking him to explain just how his team managed to do it. The inevitable response is, "I'd just like to thank our coach for getting us to where we are today." Cue to rapturous applause, hugs, and kisses all 'round.

Although natural talent and a strong work ethic will take you a long way, to make it to the very top in any sport you need the trained eye, dedication, and cajoling of a coach. Someone who cares enough about you to coax, nag, bully, and pester the very best out of you. Someone who's there to monitor your progress at that 5 a.m. training run or to demand you do another 30 minutes on the tackle bag when all you want to do is have a shower and go home. Although sometimes you love to hate them, coaches can make all the difference between being good and being great.

It's usually pretty easy to figure out who the coach is at a rugby game — the person trotting along the sideline, gesticulating at the players on the pitch and shouting advice. He or she is invariably the most emotionally involved person at the ground.

A coach has three main areas of responsibility. A coach must

- ✔ Improve a team's skill level
- ✔ Improve the fitness, strength, and power of a team
- ✔ Motivate players so that the team reaches its potential

## Improving skill levels

A coach should do everything possible to ensure the skill levels of all players improve as the season progresses. Obviously, skill levels vary from individual to individual, so you need to adjust your training program to make allowances for these variations. Your main aim, though, is to improve the overall skill level of the team as a unit.

To improve your team's skills, implement a challenging and mixed training schedule that maintains the interest of all the players. For example, you can mix it up by incorporating both skill drills and weight training into the regimen. See Chapter 12 for some ideas on how to do this.

## Getting your team fighting fit

A good team is a fit team, so it's important that you incorporate fitness routines into your schedule in order to build up stamina. (See Chapter 12 for details on how to devise the best exercise program for your team.)

For your team to succeed, you need to develop a good, simple, and effective training program. When you have your training program, stick to it.

## Motivating your team

Motivating players depends largely on trust — and trust comes through openness and honesty. When you have to drop a player, don't make up feeble excuses or blame your decision on someone or something else. Players will quickly find out if you're bending the truth, so always be honest and upfront.

The members of any team will talk to each other and look after each other's interests, both on and off the pitch. If you lose the trust of your players, your future with the team is limited because the players won't be motivated to listen to your advice or instruction. But if you earn the trust of your players they'll do anything for you.

Motivation also involves saying the right words at the right time. You don't have to memorize the speeches of Winston Churchill; being positive during training and in the dressing room gets your players in the right frame of mind to get on the pitch and defeat the competition.

Never underestimate the importance of encouragement. As long as it's not overdone, praise can cure many ills. Guide your players and give them direction and purpose. Whatever support you give them will be returned to you on the rugby pitch. The art is to keep things simple without insulting the intelligence of your players.

A smart coach has to be prepared to mix the message up a bit to avoid the problem of players getting sick and tired of just one person ranting at them. Calling in experts from other fields, or other authoritative voices, will often inspire weary players.

# Coaching Safety

Safety is a principal concern to everyone involved in rugby. It resonates throughout the laws of the game and directly affects coaches and players. There are two very good reasons for this preoccupation with safety.

First, rugby is a team game where players repeatedly assemble into set formations. Scrums and line-outs require careful coordination and specific binding of several players to accomplish a collective goal. The combined force of several working together as one is much greater than a single player, and the laws of the game reflect this. Coaches are responsible for understanding, explaining, and enforcing the rules of the game.

Second, rugby is a full-contact sport where players must repeatedly tackle each other. A typical international match may have 150 tackles over 80 minutes of play. Being able to make tackles over and over again without injuring oneself is essential to playing the game. As such, defenders must develop proper tackling techniques and ball-carriers have to learn how to engage the tackler in contact and fall correctly. As the coach, it's your job to ensure that your players learn the correct techniques so they can safely play the game.

## Keeping your players safe

The most important factor in preventing rugby injuries is coaching. Injuries often occur when new players are thrust into situations they're not prepared to handle. For example, coaches must avoid placing beginners in the front row of a scrum without first making certain they're ready for that particular position. A good coach needs to withstand the temptation to allow new players to participate in matches until they're sufficiently trained in all the skills required in a live game.

For North American coaches, special attention should be paid to teaching your players how to safely tackle in rugby. You can be sure that many of your players will arrive with bad habits learned from playing gridiron. These bad habits are very difficult to overcome, which is why rugby coaches should review safe tackling in training on a regular basis.

Former footballers will be keen to mix it up but are likely to approach the point of contact with their heads in dangerous positions. They will have been taught to use their helmets as a weapon and to get their heads across the face of the ball-carrier when making contact. This exposes the head, neck, and spine to serious injury. In rugby, the tackler is instructed to place his or her head alongside either hip of the ball-carrier to avoid frontal collision with the head and neck. The shoulder is used as the main point of contact.

Another factor in preventing injuries is conditioning. Rugby is a demanding aerobic and anaerobic activity that requires short bursts of energy over long periods of sustained exertion. Football players are not rugby fit, and without getting their one-minute rest breaks after every five seconds of action they falter quickly under the strain of continuous play. When players get fatigued the first thing to suffer is mental concentration, which makes them more prone to fall inappropriately or enter contact situations with poor technique and get injured.

As a coach, your responsibility is to ensure that all your players are sufficiently experienced at their particular position, have a solid command of how to safely manage contact, and are in good physical condition before they take the pitch.

## False assumptions and the truth about injuries in rugby

Parents often shy away from rugby at the thought of subjecting their children to the rigors of "football without pads." To understand the fundamental difference between rugby and football, a crucial distinction must be drawn here — rugby is a contact sport, whereas football is a collision sport.

### False security

Something curious happens when a player suits up in the protective armour worn by football players. With a helmet, shoulder pads, and hip, leg, knee, and other assorted pads covering nearly every inch of football players' bodies, a false sense of invulnerability results and is only heightened by gridiron coaches encouraging youngsters to throw their bodies around with reckless abandon. This is further reinforced by the football tackling technique, which places a premium on either stopping the ball-carrier cold in his tracks or driving him backward. All the padding and the emphasis placed on impacting the runner head-on combine to produce football collisions that are extremely forceful, violent, and unpredictable.

In rugby, players don't have a false sense of security brought on by being encased in body armor. Moreover, and especially at the youth level, safety in contact is a central teaching concern. Not having 10-pound crash helmets to hide within, rugby players are *not* taught to "put their head in there and smash the ball-carrier" like in football, but rather are specifically warned to keep their heads out of harm's way in the tackle situation.

### Learning how to tackle

The point of contact for the tackle in rugby is lower than in football, with the knees to thighs as the target, so the ball-carrier's head and shoulders are avoided by the tackler on impact. The goal of the tackle in rugby is also significantly different. In stark contrast to the football objective of not surrendering even an inch lest the offense make a first down, in rugby tacklers are taught to opt instead for the sure tackle rather than the big collision.

Also, new players are carefully introduced to tackling, starting first on their knees and then progressing to walking, jogging, and finally running only after they've demonstrated proper technique and are comfortable enough to advance to the next stage.

In football, all 22 players can hit each other at any time and from almost any direction, which encourages players to make huge "blindside hits" where the victim never sees it coming before getting absolutely smashed. In rugby, unless you're carrying the ball, about to receive it, or directly involved in contesting possession, players on the opposing team are prohibited from hitting you. This means that in rugby you have a much better sense of when and where the contact is coming from.

Knowing when you're at risk usually allows you to brace before impact and then fall in a manner so as to absorb the kinetic energy through the thick muscles of the back, buttocks, legs, or hips (as opposed to bouncing off the turf, as happens when you're taken by surprise). For these reasons, contact in rugby is much more controlled, predictable, and safe than in football.

# Tackling a Tough Job

The coach has the onerous task of successfully putting together the most bewildering of jigsaw puzzles. He or she has to mold 15 very different, often diverse, and sometimes uncooperative individuals into one perfectly interlocking unit.

The coach has to be an adviser, mentor, psychologist, teacher, diplomat, comrade, leader in arms, master of subterfuge, butcher, baker, and candlestick-maker. If you aspire to be a coach, you need to have:

✓ **A superior understanding of the game:** Coaching is best learned from practical experience, because players soon figure you out if you don't know what you're talking about. It also helps if you're a former player, though you don't have to have reached superstar level! Many of the best rugby coaches were mediocre players who during their playing days developed a good grasp of the game, especially the laws, tactics, and strategies required to win matches.

✔ **A genuine love of the game:** You need to love the game and be fascinated by all its subtleties. Like your players, you must constantly be learning because you'll never find yourself knowing everything about the sport. Rugby is a game that is continually evolving and throwing up quandaries that confound even the most brilliant of rugby minds.

✔ **A democratic approach:** As a coach you need to be firm without being a dictator and have the ability to get along with and get the best out of a diverse array of characters. Many coaches fall into the trap of taking all the praise after a victory, and blaming everyone but themselves for a loss. Good coaches don't go on about how their team won because the players followed instructions, or lost because they didn't.

Coaching can't be learned entirely from textbooks. Coaching is a mind game, a skill, and an art. You need initiative, creativity, intuition, and a vast amount of personal get-up-and-go. When you encounter 20 different problems at once you'll soon discover whether or not coaching is for you.

Bob Dwyer, who coached Australia's national team in the '80s and '90s, described what is required to be a successful coach. According to Dwyer, a winning coach requires not the intellect of a nuclear physicist, but experience, common sense, imagination, and a very, very good memory. As far as Dwyer is concerned, if coaching is approached in the right vein, it's "an honorable profession."

If you want to become the coach of a winning team, the simplest approach is the best. Taking Bob Dwyer's criteria one by one, a successful coach has:

✔ **Experience:** to know what to do when under pressure.

✔ **Common sense:** to stay levelheaded and calm no matter what the circumstances.

✔ **Imagination:** to come up with innovative moves and tactics.

✔ **An excellent memory:** to remember the weaknesses and strengths of the opposition so that tactics and strategies to exploit and counter them can be devised.

No one criterion is more important than the others. The key is finding the right balance that suits your individual style of coaching.

---

## The art of communication

One day at training, Welsh coach John Dawes told his players that if the blindside flanker was to break quickly from the scrum, the halfback would shout a code word beginning with the letter "P." If the openside flanker was to break early, the code word would begin with the letter "S." A scrum was set. Suddenly halfback Gareth Edwards screamed: "Psychology!"

Neither flanker moved.

---

# Deciding Whether Coaching Is for You

You won't really know if you have the capabilities to be a coach until you try it. You'll know you have the right temperament for the job when you find yourself on a muddy pitch on a Saturday morning teaching a bunch of children, juniors, young men, or young women — and enjoying it.

Deciding whether coaching is for you requires a bit of self-assessment. The first thing to consider is whether or not you enjoy being around other people — this is a vital characteristic of a rugby coach. In addition, you must:

- Relate well and get along with just about everyone
- Know how to communicate with the many people relying on you to provide them with the right information
- Be even-tempered and able to handle the pressures of being in charge of up to 20 children (or adults who act like children)

Also ask yourself these questions: Do you love rugby? Do you like offering advice and helping other people? Are you prepared to work hard? Do you excel when under pressure? If the answer to all these is "yes," then give coaching a go.

After you've been involved in a few games you'll know whether coaching suits you — and whether you suit coaching. If you can successfully get the message across to teams that are difficult to organize and motivate, you just may have the coaching touch! (See Chapter 19 for information that will help you get into the coaching game and details about the different coaching opportunities that are available.)

# You're Not Alone: Support Staff

A coach may sometimes feel like a rock, solitary and endlessly battered by the elements. At the bottom rung you find yourself doing all the jobs necessary to make a team run, but as you progress more help is available.

At higher levels a strong network of support staff surrounds the head coach in order to spread the stress and responsibilities more evenly and to help the team reach its full potential. Such support occurs not just in the professional ranks but at the top amateur clubs that are well organized and well funded.

For those who don't want the full-blown responsibility of being head coach, numerous other jobs are available that can be perfect for you. A support role can be just as important to the running of a rugby team as that of the head coach.

At the lower levels of the game, support staff are relatively few and no one gets paid. You usually find a head coach and maybe an assistant coach and a volunteer trainer. At the higher echelons of rugby, however, teams from the representative level and up are usually professional in their approach and the support staff can involve a cast of many.

## Coaching: Assistant coach

Most teams from club level upward have at least one assistant to the head coach. At a typical training session, teams eventually break up into two groups: forwards and backs. As one person cannot oversee both, more pairs of eyes and hands are needed.

The best teams usually have a three-man coaching structure, comprising a head coach, a forwards coach, and a backs coach. The forwards coach is usually a specialist at scrums, line-outs, rucks, and mauls. The backs coach has particular expertise in back-line strategies and moves and understands the requirements of all the positions from 9 to 15 (see Chapter 2 for details about all player positions). The three coaches work closely together and are usually responsible for selecting the team.

Someone who has played forward does not necessarily make a good forwards coach, nor does a former back automatically make the best backs coach. Sometimes an outsider's perspective is refreshing and more thorough because it comes from someone who has had to learn the intricacies of the position from the ground up without benefit of direct playing experience.

## Coaching: Defense coach

In recent years, professional teams and international sides have employed coaches who have focused on improving the defensive strategies of the team. Often, these coaches are former *rugby league* players who, because of the tight defensive structure of their game, are able to pass along important tips on tactics that stop opponents. (Rugby league is a rugby derivative played with 13 men, popular only in Australia and northern England.)

## Managing the team

Because the coach is primarily focused on the squad's performance on the field, an effective team manager is needed to make sure that everything runs smoothly off the pitch.

The duties of a team manager normally include ensuring that:

- Training venues have been reserved and are ready for use
- Players know exactly where they have to be and at what time
- Transport for the team and support staff is organized
- The team has the right playing and training equipment such as rugby balls, tackle bags, and kicking tees

In addition, team managers need to have all the information that's relevant to their team on match day, including directions to the pitch, kickoff times, where the team will change, and who the match officials are.

The team manager has to attend to the needs of the coach and the players, which means becoming mother, father, nurse, and everyone's best friend. The role also encompasses that of psychotherapist, as the team manager's shoulder is the one players usually cry on when they have been dropped from the team or feel as though they have failed.

The team manager's job is probably the most demanding one within the organization because it requires an abundance of common sense, a tough hide, a willingness to work, and the ability to solve problems logically. While the job can be a thankless one, many consider it to be very rewarding.

# Training the team

At lower levels, a team probably won't have a trainer. At the representative level, however, teams often have their own fitness gurus.

The trainer puts the players through their drills during training and makes certain that when they're off the field they're involved in appropriate weight, exercise, and nutritional programs.

# Massaging the players: The physiotherapist

For professional organizations, the physiotherapist works closely with the team doctor and trainer to ensure that injured players receive the right course of treatment. A rugby team's physiotherapist specializes in sports science, injury management, and treatment, and is an important member of the support staff.

When a player is injured on the field, the physiotherapist runs out onto the pitch with the doctor to treat him or her. Between them, they quickly assess the seriousness of the injury and decide whether or not the player should come off the field.

The physiotherapist may also pre-tape players on match day and at training sessions. This involves using bandages, braces, and tape to prevent new injuries from occurring or previous ones from reoccurring.

# Calling on the team doctor

At the professional level the team doctor is a paid position, while at club level the doctor is usually a volunteer. In addition to working with the physiotherapist to assess injuries sustained during a match, the team doctor helps players recover from those injuries. The team doctor diagnoses injuries on the field and tracks the progress of the injured players while they recover. The coach relies on the team doctor to advise when an injured player has recovered and is available for selection.

In accordance with the blood bin rule, the team doctor is usually found doing quick stitch-up work on injured players during matches so they can get back into the game as quickly as possible.

# Chapter 19

# Coaching Certification and Advancement

*In This Chapter*

▶ Getting certified to coach in the U.S.A.

▶ Getting certified to coach in Canada

▶ Pursuing advanced overseas options

▶ Finding the right level for you

*A*fter you make the fateful decision to become a rugby coach, a whole new world of agony and ecstasy awaits. Before you grab your clipboard and start barking orders at your new charges, you need to get properly certified as a coach. USA Rugby and Rugby Canada have similar but slightly different accreditation programs to assist both new and experienced coaches.

In this chapter, we describe the coaching certification process, discuss international resources to continue your training, and focus on issues presented by the various levels of the game.

## Coaching Accreditation in the U.S.

USA Rugby's Coach Development Program (CDP) has recently undergone a massive overhaul. Input from the International Rugby Board, Rugby Football Union, Positive Coaching Alliance (PCA), and the National Center for Sports Safety (NCSS) has produced a more comprehensive system for training coaches than the one that was in place before 2005.

Under the new program, all coaches in the U.S.A. certified under the Coach Accreditation Program have to renew their certificates before August 2008. After that date, everyone who coaches rugby in the U.S. will be on the same page.

# Looking at the Coach Development Program

The new Coach Development Program (CDP) mixes study on the Internet with participatory conferences that give coaches the opportunity to tailor their development to the level of the players they're going to be coaching. Coaches first read information and are tested on it in an online environment — then they're checked at the workshops to see if they've fully grasped the material presented to them.

Currently, USA Rugby offers two different workshops:

- ✔ **Introducing Rugby:** This course enables coaches to present the game to total newcomers to the sport. Extra stress is placed on learning the basics before moving on to the more complicated aspects of rugby.

- ✔ **Developing Rugby Skills:** This course concerns itself more with how to run training sessions, how to teach strategy, and how to formulate drills that give players the skills required to perform in the most rigorous of competitive arenas.

   If you aspire to coach a first-division club, a Super League side, or a representative team, then this is the course for you.

Two more workshops — Non-Contact Rugby and Orientation to Coaching Rugby — are being tried around the country by USA Rugby and will be available soon.

# Getting certified

To gain certification a coach has to be a current member of USA Rugby, register for the Coaches' Portal online — the site is filled with coaching and educational info — do the online modules for his desired coaching level, complete the "Foundations of Rugby Coaching" and the PCA's "Double-Goal Coach" programs, and pass the NCSS exam. The final step is to go to a workshop (see the previous section for more about workshops). Workshops are held around the country, and if you pre-register 15 days in advance cost $145 for a full weekend of instruction.

If you pass all the tests and successfully demonstrate your understanding at a workshop, you get a three-year USA Rugby Coach Certificate. You can then get a three-year extension by attending other seminars, workshops, and forums sponsored by USA Rugby.

For more detailed info on all of USA Rugby's coaching programs and a schedule of workshops in your area, go to www.usarugby.org and click on Coaches.

# Coach Training in Canada

Rugby Canada has a well-established and successful coach education program that's been in existence for more than 30 years. The National Coaching Certification Program (NCCP) consists of a partnership among Rugby Canada, the Coaching Association of Canada, and the Government of Canada through more than 60 provincial and territorial National Sport Federations.

The NCCP offers four coaching courses based on the different levels of the game:

- **Community Coach:** This course provides a basic introduction to the principles of play for non-contact rugby, and is designed for new coaches and parents of youth under 12.

- **Introductory Coach:** This course is for high school, university, and club-level coaches. Full contact is introduced and the concepts of tactical and technical improvements are brought into focus. This course is for coaches responsible for novice- to intermediate-level players.

- **Developmental Coaching:** This course emphasizes positional play and specialized technical and tactical skills. This level is designed to help develop representative team and top club coaches.

- **High-Performance Coaching:** This course was created to serve Super League coaches and provide coaching talent for the Canadian National Teams. At this stage, positional play, tactical awareness, and technical skills for the national team level are featured.

Go to www.rugbycanada.ca for more information and to register for the next coaching course in your neighborhood.

# The International Rugby Academy

The International Rugby Academy (IRANZ) is based in Wellington, New Zealand, and offers a variety of coaching courses. IRANZ was founded by former All Black the number 8 Murray Mexted, former All Black coach Laurie Mains, and legendary All Black hooker Sean Fitzpatrick. The list of course instructors is chock-full of former stars and rugby luminaries unmatched anywhere in the world.

For club-side coaches, the Practical Coaching Course is an outstanding way to discover how the leading coaches in the oval world are preparing their teams. With an all-star staff of former All Blacks, Wallabies, and esteemed experts from other sports, the Practical Coaching Course is well worth the time and money required to attend the program. (We know this firsthand, as we were the first Americans ever to be certified by IRANZ!)

For coaches who aspire to a professional career in coaching, there are three options:

✔ Advanced Coaches' Course

✔ Coach Development Course

✔ High-Performance Coaches' Course

All three are considered the gold standard among coaching academies around the world. These courses are held in conjunction with IRANZ's Elite Players course at the Adidas Institute of Sport in Palmerston North, so the coaches can work with some of the world's leading talent in a practical setting. With a host of coaching greats like David Nucifora, Nick Mallett, Eddie Jones, and Jim Telfer providing instruction, these three courses are the place to go for those seeking the best training available. See www.internationalrugbyacademy.com for more information on dates and custom courses.

# Coaching Hatchlings to Eagles

Before the professional era in rugby began in the mid-1990s, almost all coaches from mini rugby to national teams were volunteers or lightly compensated individuals who served because they loved the game. In those days, nearly every coach began his or her progression up the coaching ladder by working with kids. By the time superior coaches had reached the top level, they had years of experience in dealing with all age groups and situations, cementing their knowledge of the sport in the process.

Sadly, this is no longer the case in many parts of the world, and coaching has become a big-money occupation. The desire for wins and publicity at the highest levels has attracted recently retired international stars to take the reins of professional clubs without the benefit of ever having coached before, while seasoned veterans of the coaching game look for work.

One place where that is not true is in North America. Only a very few coaches make a living running rugby teams, meaning the rest of the multitudes are still in it because they have a passion for the game. However, because rugby is a sport played mostly by collegians and adults in the United States and Canada, relatively few coaches have experience coaching at all levels and can appreciate the distinct demands of each rung on the rugby ladder.

## Nurturing the youth

An area of phenomenal growth in North American rugby is the exploding number of children who are being exposed to the game. Unfortunately, more kids want to play than qualified coaches are available to handle them. Coaching youth players (aged 5–15) takes a tremendous amount of patience — not to mention a good rapport with nervous parents.

The key element to coaching youngsters of all ages is to always emphasize the fun aspects of the sport. When introducing the game, never put pressure to win on your juvenile charges. Rather, make the primary message you deliver be the inherent value of competition for its own sake. Instead of striving for victories, encourage players to enjoy themselves while obtaining the skills necessary to play the game at higher levels.

## Having an oval ball in high school

The secondary school setting is rapidly becoming an important entry point for young rugby enthusiasts — which means the high school coach has to focus on bringing newcomers up to speed more quickly than does the youth coach, but without neglecting to instill a healthy respect for the sport itself in a competitive environment. Tackling, passing, and ball-handling drills should be supplemented with lectures on sportsmanship and the overall ethos of the game.

Getting the basics right at this stage is still far more important than wins and losses. No competitive person likes to lose, but learning how to do so is every bit as important for teenagers as is winning with good grace. It always has to be highlighted that rugby is not a sport that tolerates trash-talking, showboating, or disrespectful behavior of any kind toward opponents, officials, spectators, or teammates.

The most beneficial concept that high schoolers can take away from rugby is the value of teamwork. By its very nature, rugby is a game that requires trust, communication, cohesion, and shared desire to achieve results. Learning how to work with others and how to be selfless while putting the team first is an invaluable lesson for future success in academics, business, and life in general.

## Corralling collegians

The collegiate arena is by far the most difficult milieu in which to coach because of the intensity of the participants involved. Most collegians are new to the sport and many are attracted not just by the game but by the social atmosphere that surrounds it on many campuses. Rugby at this level is often seen as an outlet for athletes who are no longer playing other organized sports, or as a chance to vent pent-up aggression. Channeling this energy in a positive direction is the duty of all college coaches.

## Godfree's last season

When I initially started playing rugby at Occidental College, Michael Godfree was my first coach. Godfree had numerous ties to the college and was a long-serving volunteer, selflessly donating his time to mentor the somewhat wayward individuals that made up the Oxy Blackshirts team. The veterans on the team at the time informed me that after more than a decade of coaching, 1987 was to be Godfree's last year at the helm because of business and family commitments. Yet, when the next season rolled around, there he was, running practice and distributing sage advice.

It wasn't until at least a dozen years later when I became the coach of the women's rugby team at Occidental that I fully realized the amount of time and effort that Godfree had put into coaching us all those years. I also came to understand that if he hadn't done so, the club would certainly have ceased to exist — it wasn't as if there was a long line of eager applicants for the job. When I started coaching the options were basically me or no one, and I'm sure that's the case at many institutions all across North America. If USA Rugby wants to sustain and capitalize on the recent growth in collegiate rugby, one of its top priorities has to be the recruitment and training of suitable individuals to coach teams throughout the United States.

As for Godfree, he finally did retire in 2006 — after 31 seasons!

As the game grows in North America, more and more collegiate programs are moving away from the traditional free-wheeling, hard-partying setup to a more structured and better-funded model. Coaches at places where this is the case have a distinct advantage over their colleagues at institutions where the sport is less organized.

Beyond simple instruction in technique and discipline, a critical component of coaching collegians is to impart the necessary information about the game's history, traditions, and worldwide camaraderie. Seeing themselves as part of a bigger picture when they take up the game breeds attention to issues like fairness and situation-specific sociability. A coach shouldn't try to temper the boisterousness and natural experimentation of these burgeoning adults, but rather help them to examine what sorts of behavior are appropriate in the rugby context on and off the pitch.

## *Catering to the clubs*

The requirements for successful club coaches differ depending upon the division in which their teams play.

At lower levels, the coach must be a total club person, dealing with all the elements that affect the entire group. Recruiting players, fundraising, and various other managerial tasks can be a large part of this coach's job description. The ability to teach the basics is also necessary, because new players are the lifeblood of the future. Striking a balance at training between preparing a team to win and developing new talent from scratch is the toughest challenge for a coach at this level. Winning in the present is important, but continuously building and solidifying the entire club, including families and supporters, is the key to any coach's long-term success.

At the upper levels, coaches function more like their professional counterparts, concerned mainly with strategic decision-making, training programs, and the upcoming weekend's opponent. A coach in this situation is usually a veteran of the sport who has taken on the challenge of guiding a squad of rugby-enthused individuals with a strong desire to perform and win. Coaches at this level can focus directly on the players because they usually have a support staff to take care of the day-to-day running of the club.

# Chapter 20

# Managing the Game —
# The Referee

. . . . . . . . . . . . . . . . . . . . . . . . . . . . . . . . . . . . . . . . . . . . .

*In This Chapter*

▶ Reviewing the duties of the whistle-blower

▶ Joining a society in the U.S.A.

▶ Becoming an adjudicator in Canada

. . . . . . . . . . . . . . . . . . . . . . . . . . . . . . . . . . . . . . . . . . . . .

*T*he most important person at any rugby match is the referee — without the services of this crucial official the game cannot be played. Despite being the whipping boys for the media at the international level, and the victim of ill-informed derision from sideline hecklers on local pitches, referees are almost always unbiased adjudicators and conscientious guardians of the sport they love.

In this chapter we look at what it takes to be a referee, the responsibilities for those of us who decide to join this honorable society, how to begin refereeing, and how to climb your way up the appointment ladder in North America.

## The Responsibility of the Whistle

According to the laws of the game, the referee is the sole judge of fact and law during a rugby match. To properly discharge that awesome portfolio of absolute authority, a referee must be able to fulfill the requirements in five areas of responsibility:

- ✔ Knowledge
- ✔ Consistency
- ✔ Communication
- ✔ Temperament
- ✔ Fitness

# Knowledge

Referees must know the laws of the game. Now, that doesn't mean they have to memorize the entire law book before ever taking up the whistle, but something more than a passing familiarity with the dictates of the lawmakers is essential when starting out. Knowledge of the most frequently enforced laws and all the potential choices when things go wrong promotes trust in the referee among the players being controlled.

A referee should strive to know more than any player who is subject to his or her decisions for the simple reason that it bolsters confidence in calling the game. Knowledge is indeed power. If referees are uncertain about the law, it makes them hesitant in blowing the whistle (and nothing is worse than an indecisive referee). The process of becoming a referee, which we get to later in this chapter, provides for constant learning and evaluation. All good referees take quiet pride in their knowledge of the law and don't feel the need to lord it over their less-informed rugby brethren.

# Consistency

Although it would be ideal if every referee called a match in exactly the same way, inevitably different styles and slightly varying interpretations develop around the world. At the international level, the International Rugby Board (IRB) strives to minimize these deviations as much as possible by careful assessment of all test match whistle-blowers. At the other end of the spectrum, local referees have less supervision and training and are thus more likely to vary in their performance from week to week. The goal for any individual referee is to work toward personal consistency.

By consistency, we mean calling the game in the same fashion from start to finish. A penalty for not releasing the ball in the tackle has to be the same for both teams in all situations, whether it is in the first or 80th minute. Nothing is more frustrating for players than to perform an action at one point in the game and have it be legal, then to be called for a penalty for the same action later on in the match. Consistency breeds respect, because even if a player disagrees with a call, if it is always called that way he can adapt his game to reflect the referee's interpretation.

# Communication

Until very recently, the only sound that came out of a referee during a match was the high-pitched blast of the whistle. An occasional chat with a touch judge or a serious offender was basically the extent of their conversational output. In the modern game, however, the referee is expected to manage the game by being a consummate communicator.

In professional and test rugby almost all referees are wired for sound. Listening in on their chatter for 80 minutes is like hearing a condensed version of what a preschool worker must sound like when talking to young children. The referee constantly identifies phases of play, admonishes potential wrongdoers, gives warnings, and signifies that everything is okay when players follow his commands. For example, a common refrain may be, "Ruck formed, no hands, leave it alone 7, that's fine, play on." By communicating what they see happening and calling this out to the players, fewer infractions are likely to be committed and thus fewer stoppages in play occur, which is better for the game. Because players are now coached to actively listen to the ref's directives, smart players are avoiding penalties, which keeps the game flowing.

The referee also has the responsibility of being a teacher for less experienced teams at the lower levels. New players are often more aggressive than they are rugby-smart, and it's always better for a referee to help these players learn than it is for the other team to show them the consequences of their actions in nonverbal ways; this is especially important at the high school and collegiate levels. Players can learn more in one match with a good referee than in a dozen training sessions. No matter how many times a particular concept is taught at practice by a coach, when a referee provides real-time direction during live competition of what players should and shouldn't be doing, understanding is greatly accelerated.

## Temperament

Not everyone is cut out for refereeing. A referee must be intelligent, tolerant, calm under pressure, approachable, and have a genuine love for the game. These qualities are needed to maintain a positive relationship with the players without pretending they're your best friends or, alternatively, treating them like naughty schoolchildren. Belligerence and arrogance are the two least-becoming qualities on referees — those who have these characteristics in abundance give the rest of their colleagues a bad name.

Referees must always remember their role is to be fair and impartial, to let the players decide the outcome, and to call the game as they see it without resorting to bias based on reputation or previous misconduct. As a player, it's horrible to see a certain referee turn up a match and think, "This ref hates us." What you want them to feel is, "This ref's fair." By making decisions dispassionately and without personal animosity, a referee builds a reputation for fairness that goes a long way when trying to control 30 agitated rugby players.

The highest compliment that can be paid to any referee is to go unnoticed at the end of a match. The best referees are stewards of the game who don't try to impose themselves or their beliefs on a particular contest.

## Fitness

Referees can satisfy all four of the previous criteria, but if they can't keep up with play enough to see what's going on, it won't do them any good. If they're able to run for 80 minutes without tiring, they're more likely to maintain mental sharpness throughout the entire match.

As most refs are former players, they have an initial sense of what it takes to run for an hour and a half with very few chances to rest. What they don't realize, at least until they take charge of their first few matches, is how much extra running referees do because they are constantly chasing the ball. As a forward or a back there are few moments in a match where you continually chase after the ball, but that's exactly what a referee has to do the whole time.

# Becoming a Ref in the States

A simple fact in the United States is that there are more rugby matches every week than there are qualified referees. The result is that rugby as a whole suffers because it's usually the younger players (who are most in need of quality refereeing) that are neglected. Fortunately, though, the upside of this chronic shortage is that anyone who thinks they may want to take up the responsibility of the whistle has ample opportunity to give it a go. If you've ever thought you can do better than the person out there calling the game, our advice is to get started studying your law book and buy yourself a whistle.

## Getting started

Before you head out onto the pitch for the first time as a whistle-blower, it helps to have watched a fair bit of rugby on TV and in person so that you can at the very least be familiar with how to position yourself at set pieces and breakdowns. The next step is to volunteer to referee a second side game or a scrimmage for your club or a team in your area (very few offers to referee are ever turned down; we think the last one was in 1982). You'll be assigned second side matches, which give players who didn't make it into the first team a chance to play, so that a more experienced referee can watch and help explain any questions afterward.

Another option is to first attend a refereeing clinic. These are put on by local referees' societies and are a good introduction to the basics of how to manage a match. The introductory-level referee course "Introducing Officiating" is designed for anyone who wants to ref but hasn't had any formal training and hasn't already been around the game for a long time as a player or coach. To find a referee organization in your area, put "rugby referees" and your location into any online search engine.

The first designation you receive is Associate Referee, which is your title until you get some experience and demonstrate a working knowledge of the laws of the game. The next step is to take a Level 1 Referee course. This workshop is for Introducing Officiating graduates or for new referees who know the game well enough to be considered appropriately knowledgeable to start directly at this level.

After you're evaluated a few times by higher-ranking referees you're assigned to the entry-level C panel at the rank of C-3. This begins a process of evaluation and hopefully progression up the refereeing ladder, from the C, to the B, and all the way up to the A panel.

## Moving up

As you gain experience and are assessed you can be moved up from C-3 all the way to C-1. To reach the C-1 designation you have to take a Level 2 Referee course. This workshop is good preparation for referees who want to control important local matches or maybe even more.

The higher you rise the more likely you are to receive assignments to referee in top matches, usually among the highest divisional teams in your area. If your performance, desire, and fitness warrant the move, you'll eventually be elevated to the B panel.

The progression through the B panel is much more rigorous than the C panel. You'll be required to travel and referee outside your home area and you have to receive above-grade evaluations from a national evaluator.

To reach B-1 or above, you'll have to take the Level 3 Referee course. This highly sophisticated certification involves studying the theories underpinning the laws and is designed for referees who aspire to rise to the top of the craft.

## Reaching the top

If you have the skills, knowledge, on- and off-field demeanor, *and* you're in good enough physical shape, you'll receive appointments to referee national-level games and show your stuff to the top decision makers. If they like what they see, you may be moved up to the National, or A Panel, and then be eligible to receive test match appointments.

Very few referees ever gain this distinction and the ones who do seem born for the job. It's crucial to remember, though, that refereeing at any level is a rewarding experience and provides immeasurable service to the game. To get started refereeing in the U.S. or to find courses in your area, go to www.usarugby.org and click on Referees.

# Picking Up the Whistle Up North

Taking up the honorable profession in Canada is similar to doing so in the United States, with the main differences being terminology and organizational structure. All ten provincial unions are responsible for developing their own referees and every effort is made to provide consistency in evaluation.

GUTHRIE SAYS

## Who's the ref?

On a classic junket to the Rugby World Cup 1999 semifinals with Brown, I ran into Welsh international referee Derek Bevan in the media accreditation area before the first semifinal. We had interviewed him in 1998 in Wales as part of our build-up to the 1999 tournament, and I was impressed by his graciousness and wanted to let him know we really appreciated his taking the time to work with us. He recognized me, and after exchanging pleasantries — oblivious to the fact that he was in charge of the impending match — I asked him which team he was picking to win the first semi.

In typical Welsh fashion, without so much as uttering a word, he smiled almost imperceptibly, and just then the IRB referee liaison thrust himself between us and directly declared, "Of course, *ahem*," clearing his throat, and continuing, "it would be inappropriate for the match referee to make any comment whatsoever on the outcome of the match." Having realized my gaffe, I immediately retreated from the engagement nodding apologetically, knowing that further exchange of words would only cause greater harm and embarrassment.

Flash forward to one week later at the World Cup Final in Cardiff. I was walking through the stands before the game and noticed Mr. Bevan in the stands holding court, telling a rather animated story to a fellow ref. Just then, Derek looked right at me, pointed, and said, "and that's the guy!" Both refs laughed heartily, as I forced an embarrassed smile and waved back, acknowledging my identification as the subject of the story. Ever since then, I've made it a point to check all the referee assignments, which is a good idea if you want to avoid the joke being on you!

Referees in Canada are designated as "Introductory" until they receive their first evaluation, when they are moved up to C-3. This follows the same international structure that is also employed by the Americans, all the way up to the A, or Canada, Panel. Advancement is by individual assessment, and referees also have the opportunity to enhance their skills at Level 1, 2, and 3 clinics conducted at varying intervals across the country.

One area where Rugby Canada differs from its southern neighbors is in its aggressive push to recruit new referees. Referees have tended to come from the ranks of retired players who take up the whistle to stay involved in the game when their playing days are over. Referees' societies throughout Canada are now encouraging virtually any young player who shows the slightest inclination toward refereeing to consider making a career switch at an earlier age, potentially making it to the international level with a whistle in their mouth rather than in their ear.

# Part V

# Following the Game: The Informed Fan

POLAR LEAGUE RUGBY FANS ARE PARTICULARLY APPRECIATIVE OF A GOOD JUMPER IN A LINEOUT.

©RICHTENNANT

# In this part . . .

After you know the basics and where you fit into the rugby food chain, you probably want to know where you can get more rugby information, what media outlets can improve your knowledge of the game, and how to get the most enjoyment out of watching it being played.

In this part we detail the various options for watching the game on television and the Internet and suggest which channels and Web sites to visit if you want to catch all the action from around the world. We also take a look at the media personalities involved in bringing the game to the viewing public and explore some of the jargon unique to the game.

Then it's off to the match itself, where you discover how to find a contest to watch and how to find your place in the crowd. We finish with a survey of all the best sources of rugby information in magazines, books, and Web sites.

# Chapter 21

# Get Your Game — Rugby on TV

## In This Chapter

▶ Recalling the origins of rugby on TV

▶ Watching televised rugby in the U.S.A.

▶ Enjoying rugby matches on the tube in Canada

▶ Speaking the same language as the announcers

*R*ugby television programming can be difficult to find. But don't worry, because we've got all the details on where and when you can watch on five different TV channels across Canada and the U.S.A. In this chapter, we survey access to rugby programming in North America so you'll know where to go to get your weekly dose of the game they play in heaven.

## The History of Rugby on TV in North America

In the dark ages prior to 1995, rugby was a very closely held secret in North America. Unless you played the game in college or lived in one of the few pockets of rugby activity around the country, chances are you wouldn't have the slightest clue about the game. If you had heard of rugby at all, it was most likely in a negative context having to do with college kids gone wild or as an indecipherable foreign game. In effect, rugby didn't really exist — because it almost never appeared in mainstream print media, and it wasn't regularly covered on television. Of course, there were a few rugby snippets on ABC's Wide World of Sports in the early 1970s, and ESPN provided limited coverage of the 1987 Rugby World Cup and the Hong Kong Sevens, but other than those isolated instances if you wanted to watch rugby on TV the lack of access left you crying in your beer.

If you wanted to watch a live match, your only option was to go to an English pub that carried closed-circuit viewing of the Five Nations. Other than those ten matches per year, there was simply no way to watch rugby from the comfort of your own living room. Rugby enthusiasts were forced to have their overseas friends make recordings, ship them to North America, and then get them converted from PAL (European format) to NTSC (North American format). In total, it might have cost you $75 US just to watch a match that was two weeks old by the time it arrived.

That all changed in February 1995 with the launch of *Championship Rugby*, North America's first and only weekly rugby program, which delivered the best rugby from around the world. In 1998, *Championship Rugby* became part of the Fox Sports family of properties and continued as the voice of rugby for more than 500 two-hour programs until its final episode in December 2003, when it was replaced by *The Rugby Club*. *The Rugby Club* program ran throughout 2004, and when Fox Sports World was re-branded as the Fox Soccer Channel in February 2005, rugby was dropped entirely from the new channel lineup under the soccer-only format.

Since becoming televised in North America, rugby has grown by leaps and bounds. This is because the game itself is compelling entertainment. North Americans have a natural inclination to enjoy and appreciate many of the basic elements of the sport. Running with the ball, making big hits, and scoring tries are actions easily translated by North Americans raised on football. They love the physical contact and appreciate the fitness of today's players. Television has been the vehicle, but the reality is that the game has sold itself to North Americans. USA Rugby's membership has more than tripled from 21,000 to 68,000 registered players since rugby has been shown on TV.

# Rugby on Television in the U.S.A.

Sadly, you can't get regular delivery of rugby programming on a national network that is generally available in the United States. Two channels, however, distribute at least some rugby on TV in the United States:

✔ **Setanta Sports on DirecTV:** The service is primarily focused on European soccer but does telecast live rugby (so long as it doesn't conflict with a soccer match). The channel is not part of the basic DirecTV package, so you'll need to pay for DirecTV each month and then add another fee on top of that to subscribe to their Setanta Sports service a la carte.

Setanta focuses on international soccer, but covers the Six Nations, selected matches from SANZAR, and some European competitions on a delayed basis. Although Setanta Sports offers a solid lineup of rugby competitions, less than one percent of the U.S. population can actually see the channel.

✔ **Versus:** Formerly known as the Outdoor Life Network (OLN), Versus started covering rugby in 2007. Versus is part of basic cable for most Americans and is available in more than 71 million homes. It telecast the 2006–07 IRB Sevens World Series, including three hours of coverage from the 2007 Steinlager USA Sevens from PETCO Park in San Diego. Versus also plans to show selected Rugby World Cup 2007 matches.

# Rugby on Television in Canada

Like in the U.S., rugby on television in Canada is a relatively new product. Beginning with the 1999 Rugby World Cup, Canadian rugby fans have been able to watch weekly rugby programming. Two national cable networks and a few regional cable companies offer rugby programming in Canada on a regular basis:

✔ **The Score:** A cable network that is available nationwide as part of most Canadians' basic cable packages, The Score produced the world feed of all the matches for the 2006 IRB Women's Rugby World Cup plus all the Canadian-based matches in the 2006 Churchill Cup. The Score telecasts the IRB's weekly magazine program, *Total Rugby,* on Sunday mornings. It also produces a daily 30-minute program called *Sportsworld* that contains regular features on Canadian National Team players and Rugby Canada Super League events. The Score also airs some of the IRB Sevens World Series events in two-hour programs that focus on the Canadian team.

✔ **TV 5:** Part of the basic cable package for most Canadians, TV 5 delivers programming in French. It covers all France's games in the Six Nations live, plus periodic coverage of the French domestic competition, the Top 14. TV 5 also airs a weekly magazine program featuring French domestic club highlights on Sunday mornings.

Because many of the Canadian professionals are playing for French clubs, the weekly highlights on TV 5 allow Canadian fans to follow their National team players who are plying their trade abroad.

✔ **Local cable:** Several of the local Canadian cable companies are involved in supporting the game at the grass-roots level. In the Toronto area, Rogers–York Region produces and airs 14 games each year from the Marshall Premiership, which is the top men's league in Ontario. The coverage runs from May to November. Other regional cable companies produce and distribute local rugby events on an ad hoc basis each year.

## Rugby on the Internet — on your TV!

The availability of rugby programming took a quantum leap forward in 2005 with the launch of MediaZone Rugby (www.mediazone.com).This online service was revolutionary because for the first time ever, rugby fans worldwide could get access to all the games being played on any given weekend. Media-Zone Rugby offers both live and downloadable matches through broadband Internet connections directly to any Windows-enabled PC. And with a simple PC-to-TV converter device, you can watch more than 250 live matches on your TV each year. Now admittedly we're biased because we both work for the company, but on a personal level as rugby fans it's fantastic to be able to pick and choose which matches we want to watch without being dictated to by some uniformed network programmer.

MediaZoneRugby shows all the televised matches from the Super 14, June Tours, Tri Nations, Currie Cup, and Air New Zealand Cup. MZR also offers rugby TV shows from New Zealand (Friday Night Football, Test Match Fever, Try Time, Re:Union) and South Africa (Boots & All). And if you don't have time to watch every contest, they provide a full array of weekly previews and highlights, plus the best tries and most interesting plays of the week. For more about MediaZone Rugby, check out Chapter 22.

# Speaking the Language

Rugby has its own unique language. All the major rugby-playing nations of the world have developed their own lexicon of rugby terminology that is used by fans and the media alike (without a domestic rugby vocabulary of our own, we revel in this cornucopia of linguistic diversity). Because 99 percent of televised rugby originates outside North America, before you can understand and fully enjoy foreign play-by-play, you need a short course in the lingo that's used to describe the game and its traditions.

## Rugby's TV jargon glossary

The particular dialect of rugby-speak depends on the country of origin and the commentators who are calling the game. And while this list is by no means intended to be exhaustive in its scope, here's a sampling of a few rugby terms and phrases you may hear and what they really mean in plain English:

- ✓ **"They're going to keep it in tight":** The team in question is going to play a conservative game plan and try to keep the ball in the forwards to maintain possession.

✔ **"It's getting a bit niggly out there":** Some of the players are beginning to lose their discipline and are stamping, punching, or otherwise communicating their unhappiness with each other.

✔ **"He's having trouble finding touch":** The player kicking the ball is having difficulty with his accuracy and the ball is not going out of bounds where he wants it to.

✔ **"He launches a huge Garryowen!":** The kicker has punted a high ball in the middle of field for his chasers to pursue and hopefully re-gather.

✔ **"Monstered in the tackle":** The ball-carrier is flattened by the tackler and loses control of how the ball is presented for the next wave of attack.

✔ **"They're really working hard in the engine room":** A team's locks are putting in a mighty effort.

✔ **"That's a bit one-eyed":** Someone is able to see things only from a single perspective.

## Marvelous Mextedisms

Former All Black number 8 Murray Mexted is a well-respected commentator for Sky Television in New Zealand who has a penchant for spontaneously delivering some of the most interesting lines you'll ever hear (see Figure 21-1 for a look at Mexted). Here's a sampling of things that Murray has actually said on television:

✔ "You don't like to see hookers going down on players like that."

✔ "He's looking for some meaningful penetration into the back line."

✔ "Spencer's running across field calling out, 'Come inside me, come inside me.'"

✔ "I can tell you it's a magnificent sensation when the gap opens up like that and you just burst right through."

✔ "I don't like this new law, because your first instinct when you see a man on the ground is to go down on him."

✔ "Darryl Gibson has been quite magnificent coming inside Andrew Mehrtens, and I'm looking forward to seeing more of the same today."

✔ "There's nothing that a tight forward likes more than a loosie right up his backside."

✔ "Everybody knows that I have been pumping Martin Leslie for a couple of seasons now."

Thanks, Murray — enough said.

**Figure 21-1:**
Murray
Mexted.

## *The best of the commentators*

Having had the distinct pleasure of watching and then rewatching every single rugby match that's been on television over the past 13 years, we naturally have our own list of the best rugby commentators:

- ✔ **Grant Nisbett (Sky, New Zealand):** Nisbo is the world's best play-by-play man. He's cool and impartial under pressure, is technically sound in laws knowledge, and communicates a genuine love for the game. A real class act and consummate professional behind the mic.

- ✔ **Miles Harrison (British Sky Broadcasting):** Miles is the best of Northern Hemisphere, but tends toward hyperbole at times. Best when paired with Stuart Barnes.

- ✔ **Greg Clark (Fox, Australia):** Clarkie is smooth as silk at calling all the action and has a solid command of the finer points of the game. He's the best of the Aussies by a wide margin.

- ✔ **Murray Mexted (Sky, New Zealand):** Enough said already about Mex. But seriously, besides the flowery language, Murray's technical knowledge is outstanding and he actually uses the replays to explain what just happened.

✔ **Tony Johnson (Sky, New Zealand):** He communicates the excitement of the match without being partial and is extremely well prepared. He gets the hard names right and possesses a wealth of knowledge about the game.

✔ **Ken Laban (Sky, New Zealand):** Ken has developed a unique approach to play-by-play where he actually describes what the players are trying to do while on attack and in defense, plus he gets all the tough names right and blends his extensive knowledge from league and union.

✔ **Gordon Bray (Channel 7, Australia):** Bray may be overly dramatic at times, but he makes a point of explaining the laws during his call.

✔ **Andy Capostagno (SuperSport, South Africa):** Andy is the most balanced of the South African commentators and delivers the call with a relaxed, friendly demeanor and soothing voice.

✔ **Joel Stransky (SuperSport, South Africa):** The 1995 Springbok RWC hero is finally coming into his own as an in-studio analyst, but still has a way to go on his color commentary.

✔ **Stu Wilson (Sky, New Zealand):** One of the most outspoken and opinionated color men on TV, he gets it right more often than not.

✔ **Phil Kearns (Fox, Australia):** Phil is not afraid to speak his mind and has plenty of opinions to share. He's a no-nonsense type who relishes the battle up front but tends to be a bit one-eyed if the Wallabies or Waratahs are involved.

✔ **Hugh Bladen (SuperSport, South Africa):** A true icon in the Republic, Bladen's been around since tries were only worth three points, and has an encyclopedic memory of South African rugby gathered from calling virtually every Springbok test over the past 40 years.

# Chapter 22

# Spectating and Staying in Touch with Rugby News

*In This Chapter*

▶ Finding yourself in the stands

▶ Doing the right thing by your fellow spectators

▶ Globe-trotting with your national side

▶ Accessing the media to learn more

**S**pectating at a rugby match can range from standing on the sideline cheering on your local club side to sitting way up at the back of a stadium, rooting your national side to victory. Regardless of the setting, rugby crowds are some of the best behaved and most pleasant in all of sport.

In this chapter, we give you advice on how to get the most from your visit to a rugby match and become the model rugby spectator. For those of you who really want to get into the spirit of things, we offer some tongue-in-cheek tips on how to impress those around you with your incredible rugby knowledge. We also provide a vast array of resources to bring you up to speed with rugby happenings in the U.S., Canada, and around the world.

## Finding a Match to Watch

Congratulations — you're about to take the plunge and actually attend a rugby match. Rugby is one of the most user-friendly sports, generally attracting an intelligent, passionate crowd who believe that watching rugby at any level is a wonderful treat.

If you're interested in attending a club match but don't know if there's a team in your area, a little online searching can fill the void. For the United States, go to www.usarugby.org, and in Canada go to www.rugbycanada.ca to find a club near you.

Another option is to use any of the major search engines to find a local club. Type "local rugby unions in _____," filling in the blank with your state, province, or geographic region. You'll end up with a long list of choices to at least give you a starting point to track down a club. Most union sites will have links to their clubs, or contact details for a responsible party who can supply further information. Most club sites will provide roughly the same team-specific details.

To find out when and where international and representative matches will be played in Canada and the U.S., check out the above-mentioned Web sites for dates, venues, and how to purchase tickets.

# Blending In with the Crowd

Whether you're going to watch a full-blown test match or a local Division II encounter, the spectator areas at rugby games are safe and suitable places for a family outing. Even at 80,000-seat stadiums in rugby hotbeds the atmosphere in the crowd is still relatively restrained and positive.

In this section, we give you guidance on how to behave so as not to upset other spectators. We also give advice on the right kind of clothes to wear to maximize your comfort.

## Following rugby etiquette

Rugby definitely has an unwritten code of conduct for its fans. Remember, players, supporters, and everyone involved with the game are rightly proud of the fact that rugby retains its civilized nature even in the age of professionalism. So that you know what's acceptable and what's not at a rugby match, we've put together a few words of wisdom that may save you from embarrassment:

✔ **Don't be afraid to ask questions:** If you're a novice fan, feel free to query your neighbor about things you don't understand that are happening in the match. Most rugby fans love nothing better than to help out newcomers with the intricacies of the game because it allows them to show off their superior level of expertise. If you feel like making comments of your own, you should at least sound well-informed. You don't need to spout Shakespeare; initially, your immortal lines can include phrases like, "Excellent tackle" and "Great take in the line-out." The section on how to sound like an expert later in this chapter can also give you some ideas for comments that sound deep and meaningful.

✔ **Criticize, but don't denigrate, the referee:** It's okay to take issue with the referee's decisions — but it's not acceptable to make him or her the target of verbal abuse. Demonstrating regard for the referee shows you're a spectator who understands the traditions that make rugby the noble game it is. In other sports referees are called all sorts of horrible names, but in rugby the referee is a figure of respect, which is why the players always address the person in charge as "Sir" or "Ma'am."

✔ **Show respect for the opposition:** The good rugby fan applauds the opposition when they do something impressive. Friendly, civilized behavior makes the occasion more enjoyable — even if your team is losing.

✔ **Maintain decorum:** When an opposition player is about to take a shot at goal, be silent. Don't imitate the idiots who try to distract the goal kicker. Such antics are frowned upon — most rugby spectators believe rugby is an intellectual pursuit to be treated as a thinker's game, not as an opportunity for hooligans to misbehave.

✔ **Check the allegiances of those around you very carefully:** If you're among fans of the same team, you can get away with a lot more than if you're among supporters of the other team. If you find yourself surrounded by people supporting the opposition, be more circumspect in your comments.

✔ **Buy someone a beer (where available):** If you go off to buy a beer, ask the person next to you if he or she wants one. This will instantly make you a friend. Having friends around you at a rugby match gives you a nice feeling of solidarity and the opportunity to exchange views on the game.

## Dressing for the occasion

A good choice at any rugby match is rugby-related gear like jerseys or hats, either purchased from online retailers or obtained from your local club. This allows you to declare your rooting proclivities without saying a word. Some fans believe that the height of fashion is to deck themselves out in clothes that scream out their rugby allegiances (see Figure 22-1).

The best clothes to wear to a rugby match combine a bit of fashion with a lot of function. You need to be wearing something that can protect you from whatever type of weather a rugby afternoon or evening can bring. Rugby in many parts of the United States and Canada is a spring-and-fall sport, so you often have to confront chilly or wet weather. Dressing appropriately for the weather conditions usually means more clothes rather than fewer. Don't forget that, as a spectator, taking off layers of clothes if you get too warm is easier than trying to get warm when you haven't got anything else to put on. If in doubt about the weather, at the very least take a waterproof jacket.

**Figure 22-1:**
Showing
their true
colors,
rugby fans
cheer their
team on.

# Spectating across North America

The best place to watch a game is near the halfway line, because a spot here gives you a good view of the whole field. For test matches, the seats at the halfway line are the most expensive. Another good place that affords a fine view of the action is near the 22-meter lines.

At the club level you can generally follow the ball up and down the sidelines (taking care to stay back far enough to let the touch judge have unfettered access), so you're always in position to see what's going on in every situation.

## Going to watch a test match

A *test match* occurs when the top representative teams of two national unions meet in a game sanctioned by the International Rugby Board (IRB). This is the elite level of competition — playing for one's country is a rugby player's highest honor. Various teams around the world may have adopted nicknames like the All Blacks and the Wallabies, but make no mistake — when they meet it's New Zealand versus Australia, direct country-to-country combat.

A test match, or *full international,* is marked by the playing of both national anthems prior to kickoff and the presence of a neutral-country referee. Every player who sees action in a test is awarded a *cap* for his efforts. Many teams around the world mark the occasion of a player's first appearance for his country by actually giving him a ceremonial cap, as was done in years past.

Test matches can be part of a larger competition like World Cup qualifying, the Pan-American tournament, or as part of a tour by the visiting side. In one-off tests sides meet on an irregular basis as determined by the IRB. This is usually done to bolster the lesser teams by having them play rugby power-houses from around the globe.

Tests in North America are still generally played in smaller stadiums, but in rugby-mad countries they can be held in mammoth venues. The all-time record for a test was set in Sydney in 2000, when an Australia–versus–New Zealand Tri Nations clash drew 109,874! Whether a test is attended by that number or several hundred die-hards, the atmosphere is special because the teams are playing first and foremost for national pride.

## The club experience

If you're geographically challenged and unable to make it to a test in North America, don't fret. There's probably plenty of other rugby being played somewhere near you. The beauty of watching matches at the local level is that crowds are rare and you can follow the game in its purest form.

### Getting a close-up view of the action at club level

A great way to learn the game and enjoy rugby in its essence is to attend a local club game. In most divisions it's free, but at the semi-professional level of Super League in the States and Canada a reasonable entrance fee is usually charged. Standing close to the action you get a better appreciation of the intensity and physicality of the game. This is the ideal way to learn the referee's signals and discover what the different players actually do, what is required for each position, and how players react to different tactics. Overall, being close to the sideline helps you get a good feel for the game.

### Enjoying the camaraderie of local clubs

At a club match everyone is there because they love rugby or someone playing it. This is where you find the really passionate rugby supporters who follow their club through thick and thin. Clubs rely on good community spirit and volunteers for their very existence. Quite apart from the outcome of the game, a successful match day means everyone has enjoyed themselves in a welcoming environment.

The atmosphere at club games is generally amiable, and you quickly feel at home. Faster than you can say "kick for touch," someone is usually selling raffle tickets to help make money for the club. Pitch in and buy a ticket or two — in your own small way you may be helping develop a club champion who can eventually end up representing the United States or Canada on the world stage.

Spectators are almost always welcome at the post-match function, where the two teams and their supporters get together to share a beer or three and talk about the game. This is when you can sense the genuine bonds that develop in this sport.

## Sounding like a rugby expert

You really need only a few phrases to sound like a rugby genius. After the first scrum, turn to your neighbor and say, "That tight-head will have to watch himself, because he's pushing in at an illegal angle." We guarantee you that the person next to you will turn, look at you as if you're a sage old hand, and nod his or her head. You'll get this reaction even if what you say is not happening, because no one can really tell if the tight-head prop is pushing into the scrum at the wrong angle — it's such a fine line of judgment. (We discuss scrums in detail in Chapter 8.)

Another crucial phrase to remember is, "They're offside." No matter which team you're following, or whether the opposition is offside or not, every person in the crowd *believes* the opposition is offside, and just loves telling the referee about it. If you say "They're offside" at various well-timed moments of the game, you're sure to get knowing nods from those around you. (See Chapter 6 for an explanation of the offside law.)

All kidding aside, if you're in doubt about the kind of reception your comments may attract, just applaud when everyone else applauds and you'll be safe.

## Touring Overseas

Touring to far-distant places is a great rugby tradition. Due to the strong international flavor of the game, any club, no matter what level, is usually able to find plenty of overseas clubs willing to offer a match. So if someone in your club is up to the task, a fascinating itinerary can be organized, enabling players to discover the delights of playing and watching the game in some of the most unexpected rugby pockets of the world.

A tour can be organized around a major event like the Rugby World Cup or a British and Irish Lions tour, or undertaken for no reason other than that everyone wants to get out of the country and play some rugby. When and where you go is a decision for individual clubs, but certain elements are common to successful touring.

Cost is number one, because unless at least 20 players can go it makes for a lonely and body-battering tour. Itinerary is also crucial. Trying to squeeze too much into a couple of weeks of travel is more taxing than relaxing. Finding the right clubs to play is another necessary component. This can be achieved by being honest about your club's capabilities and skill level. It's no fun to be beaten by huge margins in every tour match because you're playing teams way above your level.

For players and fans, rugby tours are the ultimate way of letting their hair down and getting to know each other. Living with your teammates and fellow club members for a couple of weeks in the close quarters of buses and hotel rooms is an ideal way to build spirit and cohesiveness. Of course, one maxim that always has to be followed is that *What goes on tour, stays on tour* — meaning that particularly funny, embarrassing, or debauched moments are for consumption only by the tourists themselves and not casual listeners back home.

# Learning More about the Game

After you watch some rugby either at club or test level, or anywhere in between, you'll probably want to find out more about this fascinating sport. Although very little coverage is available in most North American newspapers and on broadcast television, a multitude of other resources can help you fill in your knowledge gaps about the game played with the oval ball.

## North American magazines

The best way to get a feel for rugby in North America is to pick up the two magazines that cover the sport in their respective countries. These are all-purpose magazines designed to keep fans informed on events and all facets of the game within their nation.

Don't hesitate to read these rugby magazines — there's something for everyone. The more you read, the more fluent you'll become in the special language of rugby.

# Rugby books

Rugby books generally fall into three categories: autobiographical or biographical, instructional, and events-related/historical nonfiction. Rather than providing an endless list of titles, I'll give you my favorite titles from each of these classifications.

### Autobiography: *Boots 'n All* by Andy Haden

This remains my personal favorite because it was the first book I read about rugby after starting to play. Haden is a legendary All Blacks lock with a huge appreciation for the game and a healthy appetite for challenging the established order. It was published in 1983 so it's hard to find and is a bit dated, but still a pleasure to read.

### Instructional: *Thinking Rugby* by Ken Hodge and Alex McKenzie

Rugby is a thinking game, and this book takes that idea to another level. This was the first book to examine in a clinical way the steps necessary to becoming a better rugby player through Psychological Skills Training. Coauthor Ken Hodge is also a fellow All-Maggot! (See Chapter 16 for a description of Maggotfest.)

### Nonfiction/historical: *The Rugby War* by Peter FitzSimons

This book tells the inside story of the battle for the soul of rugby when it first went professional in 1995. The author is a former Wallaby who knows all the key players in the saga and presents it in a very readable fashion. The book was updated and re-released in a new edition in 2003.

### Nonfiction: *Provincial Giants* by Paul Neazor

If you're a fan of New Zealand rugby then you've got to read this book, which closely examines one year's team from each of New Zealand's 27 provinces — not necessarily the best side ever but, as the author says, "Rather than claiming paramount position for these 27 teams, it is claimed that they achieved such a high level of performance that they are worthy to stand up to even the most searching examination of their caliber." Very entertaining throughout.

## National Rugby Post

If you want to know what's going on in Canadian rugby, the *National Rugby Post* is a must-read. Canada's rugby magazine is published in Edmonton on a bimonthly basis. It covers all aspects of the game in Canada, including international competition and provincial news. Inside every issue you'll find player profiles, match reports and schedules, Super League news and provincial standings, commentary and opinion, plus feature articles on a wide variety of rugby topics and events.

Amid the informative and entertaining writing are advertisements for everything from rugby gear to far-flung tournaments. To find out how to obtain a copy, e-mail publisher Davie Graham at `mcscrum@telus.net` and he'll get you set up.

### Rugby magazine

*Rugby* magazine provides complete coverage of U.S. and international rugby, plus numerous departments geared to improving the level of U.S. play. During a 12-month cycle, *Rugby* posts detailed reports on all of the U.S. National Championships, plus the results of all matches played by the various U.S. National Teams. *Rugby* also covers the local and territorial union championships, plus many of the 250 independent tournaments that take place in the U.S. each year.

A signature feature is the inclusion of "transferable information" pieces: in-depth interviews with members of the U.S. rugby community who have found innovative ways to fund fields and clubhouses, conduct successful youth programs, make inroads with school administrators, and more. *Rugby* also profiles members of the rugby community who distinguish themselves in various ways outside of the game. Included among the departments in each issue are profiles of male and female players, referee and coach profiles, referee's corner, coach's corner, masters rugby, nutrition, and domestic and international calendars. *Rugby*'s International Round-Up provides a digest of all significant matches and developments around the world. For more information visit www.rugbymag.com.

## Rugby matches on the Web

If you want to watch every rugby match, whenever and wherever you want, Rugby Channel on MediaZone.com is a godsend. Launched in June 2005, Rugby Channel delivers more than 250 live games each year. Rugby Channel covers the Heineken Cup, Super 14, June Tours, Tri Nations, Currie Cup, and Air New Zealand Cup, plus selected North American events. Games are available live and archived for on-demand streaming and download access. The service requires a broadband Internet connection and can be seen on your computer screen or television. Rugby Channel features forums, previews, highlights, rugby TV shows from around the world, and more.

## Rugby news in cyberspace

Rugby is blessed with some excellent Web sites, so it isn't hard for the addict to get his or her daily fix of information, the latest news, or in-depth detail on any aspect of the game. Most of the leading sites also have excellent archive sections, where you can easily access background information on a wide variety of rugby-relevant subjects. Some Web sites focus on the game in a particular country, while others present broader coverage reflecting rugby's status as a global game.

As Internet and television rugby producers we rely on several of these Web sites to stay up-to-date on everything that's going on in the competitions.

### Planet Rugby

Planet Rugby (www.planet-rugby.com) is the world's leading rugby Web site. We use this site every single day. Based in the United Kingdom, it gives in-depth coverage on what is going on in the Northern Hemisphere and around the world. Planet Rugby also has a string of international correspondents who report on what's going on in their part of the world. It's a good balance of news, analysis, and opinions.

### Rugby Heaven

Rugby Heaven (www.rugbyheaven.smh.com.au) is the leading Australian rugby Web site. The site relies on the resources of the *Sydney Morning Herald,* the *Daily Telegraph* in London, *Australian Associated Press,* and various other news agencies, enabling Rugby Heaven to provide the latest news from around the globe.

Rugby Heaven boasts numerous interesting sections, such as World Cup, Six Nations, Tri Nations, Super 14, Provincial, and Off the Field. The site also has online competitions, chat rooms, polls, and many interactive services. It's a good starting spot to find out what's going on in the game.

### Scrum

Scrum (www.scrum.com) is another U.K.-based Web site. It covers the international game but is particularly strong in the areas of Six Nations, Heineken Cup, Magners League, and Guinness Premiership information. Scrum also features podcasts, news feeds, and an E-zine.

### Stuff

Stuff (www.stuff.co.nz) is a useful Web site if you're looking for information about rugby in New Zealand. The sports section of this all-Kiwi site will tell you what's going on in rugby all over New Zealand. Articles from newspapers throughout New Zealand appear alongside original commentary from various luminaries.

### SuperSport Zone

If you want to follow the game in South Africa, SuperSport Zone (www.superrugby.co.za) is the recommended site. It provides plenty of news and commentary on the Currie Cup, Vodacom Cup, and all other domestic issues in the republic. The site also follows the Springboks religiously.

### Telecom Virtual Rugby

If you want to test your rugby prognostication ability, this site offers the best online pick-em game in cyberspace. Go to `www.telecomvirtualrugby.co.nz` to register and see how you do against more than 150,000 other players in the Super 14 and Air New Zealand Cup.

### Yahoo Xtra NZ

This site (`http://yahooxtra.net.nz/rugby`) recently consolidated and features stories, video and audio clips, readers' polls, and photo galleries. As the name suggests, it focuses on New Zealand and the various domestic and international competitions they're involved in.

## North American focus

Two excellent sites highlight all the rugby action in Canada and the United States. Both are run by individuals who live and breathe the sport, which is obvious in the depth of their coverage.

### Canadian Rugby News

A cornucopia of Canadian rugby information, CRN (`www.canadianrugbynews.com`) was created by rugby lover Doug Crosse and covers all aspects of the game in Canada. Whether you're interested in the Rugby Canada Super League, provincial, international, over-40, university, age-grade, or women's rugby, CRN has all the available news from north of the border.

### American Rugby News

ARN (`www.americanrugbynews.com`) is the one stop in cyberspace to find out everything that's going on in American rugby. Brian Lowe keeps you informed about the Super League, Division I competition, the Eagles, collegiate rugby, women's rugby, and U-19 action. He also hosts weekly podcasts with a variety of entertaining guests.

## IRB and union Web sites

A good starting point to find out about the game of rugby is the Web site for the worldwide governing body of the sport, the International Rugby Board (`www.irb.com`). This site gives information on every national union in the world and features sections on all IRB-sponsored competitions, as well as a complete version of the laws of the game and other relevant material. You can also find useful tidbits on refereeing, coaching, and training, or you can look at the current world rankings.

The IRB also hosts an official Web site for Rugby World Cup 2007 at www.rugbyworldcup.com, where you can find all the info you need to follow the rugby world's quadrennial showcase before, during, and after the tournament in your choice of English, Spanish, or French. If you want to watch the 2007 Rugby World Cup online, go to www.rwcplus.com for video-on-demand of all 48 matches. Many individual unions have Web sites that comprehensively cover the game in their country. You can find these either on the IRB site or by typing the name of the country, followed by the word "rugby," into any search engine. The best of the bunch is put up by New Zealand.

### The New Zealand Rugby Union Web site

As one would expect from the official site of the organization in charge of the country's unofficial religion, the New Zealand Rugby Union (NZRU) site (www.allblacks.com) cleverly caters to the passionate rugby fan who's interested in the goings-on in the Land of the Long White Cloud.

The site also offers the latest breaking news, details of upcoming games and results, and extensive information about the New Zealand team. You'll find information about the union's leading players and what's happening at all levels of New Zealand rugby.

### The United States and Canadian Rugby Union Web sites

USA Rugby's official site (www.usarugby.org) contains a wealth of information on the USA National Teams, plus the various annual National Championships, news, and membership data. This site has been recently updated, giving it a sharper look and making it much easier to use.

Rugby Canada's site (www.rugbycanada.ca) offers a full array of information on the game, from youth development programs to the Super League and everything Canadian in between. If it's happening in Canadian rugby, you can find it on this site.

# Part VI
# The Part of Tens

The 5th Wave                    By Rich Tennant

PAINTING THE DEAD BALL LINE ON A RUGBY FIELD

© RICHTENNANT

# In this part . . .

*E*very *For Dummies* book includes a Part of Tens, chapters that each contain ten or so interesting pieces of information.

In this part, we offer our list of the ten best North American rugby players as a ploy to get the debate flowing. Next, we list and justify our ten best moments, with five from around the world and five from the American and Canadian experience. We conclude with a look at some of the more peculiar facts about rugby, a game that is played by some of the world's most colorful people and where anything can, and often does, happen.

# Chapter 23

# The Ten Greatest North American Players

### In This Chapter

▶ Getting to know the best men and women to play for the U.S.

▶ Celebrating the best Canadian rugby players

▶ Giving an honorable mention to some players who just missed the list

*I*n this chapter we profile the ten greatest players ever to pull on a USA or Canada national team jersey — the very best to have ever graced our North American fields with their rugby genius.

Compiling a list of the ten best American and Canadian rugby players of all time was no easy task considering how many outstanding men and women have played the game in North America. In making our selections we considered not only their individual accomplishments, but more importantly how their particular talents helped their teams to succeed. As with any top ten list, some very qualified candidates didn't make the cut. To recognize their accomplishments, we've added an honorable mention section.

## Gareth Rees

Gareth Rees (see Figure 23-1) is the highest-profile North American rugby player of all time. He made his debut against the United States in 1986. In an international career that spanned 13 years he earned 55 caps for Canada. He was the only player to appear in each of the first four World Cups from 1987 to 1999. Rees retired following the 1999 Rugby World Cup as Canada's all-time leading scorer, amassing a career total of 487 points. He played for several leading professional clubs in Europe including Castres (France), Wasps and Harlequins (England), and Newport (Wales).

With outstanding vision and an excellent tactical and goal-kicking boot, Rees stands head and shoulders above all other North American flyhalves. In May 2002 he became the Chief Executive Officer of Rugby Canada and reinstated national team coach David Clark before stepping down on the eve of the 2003 Rugby World Cup.

**Figure 23-1:**
Gareth
Rees.

## Dan Lyle

Dan Lyle is the best rugby player ever to put on an Eagles jersey. He was a talented tight end who played college football at the Virginia Military Institute. Like so many Americans who switch from football to rugby, Lyle was introduced to the sport in his 20s, yet still managed to assimilate the finer points of the game using intelligence and hard work. He debuted for the USA Eagles in 1994 against Ireland, then went on to play professionally in England for Bath and Leicester. He became one of Europe's finer players, setting up the only try in Bath's 1997 European Cup triumph. Dan earned 45 caps (24 as captain) before retiring following the 2003 Rugby World Cup — on the heels of a towering performance where he earned our praise as the outstanding number 8 of the tournament.

At 6'5" and 250 pounds, Lyle's solidly built frame was impressive, but his greatest assets were his intelligence and tremendous athleticism. A number 8 with power, speed, and good distribution skills, Lyle was also an imposing defender. Perhaps his greatest skill was claiming restarts and line-outs, where he was one of the world's best players at contesting possession in the air (see Figure 23-2).

**Figure 23-2:**
Dan Lyle
soars for a
line-out.

# Al Charron

Al Charron is an ironman who appeared 72 times for Canada since his debut against Argentina in 1990. A tall and rangy back-row forward, Charron played flanker, the number 8, or lock with equal skill. He was invited to play with the Barbarians RFC five times and was named to a World XV in 1999. Following Rees's lead, Charron's participation in the 2003 Rugby World Cup earned him the distinction of having appeared in four World Cups. He captained Canada 22 times during his career and was a fixture for many years on the Canadian Sevens Team.

## Dave Hodges

Only the second American to earn 50 caps, former USA Eagles Captain Dave Hodges is just the kind of player you want leading your team into battle. At 6'4" and 235 pounds, Hodges was a fierce defender who led by example, putting his body on the line every time he took the field. He was a versatile forward possessing a full complement of back-row and locking skills. He played professionally in Wales for Llanelli and Bridgend and was named Llanelli's 2001–02 Player of the Year.

A 1989 All-American linebacker at Occidental College, Hodges played professional football in Europe for the Hamburg Blue Devils in 1993–94 before dedicating himself full-time to rugby. Like Lyle, Hodges's intelligence and tremendous work ethic enabled him to smoothly adjust from football to rugby without missing a beat.

## Mike James

Mike James is one of Canada's all-time great forwards. The big lock has played 51 times for his country in the second row. Standing almost two meters (6'5.6") tall, James has been a line-out force throughout his career. James retired in 2007 from professional club rugby in France after a seven-year stint with Stade Français. Prior to moving to Paris, James played for Perpignan. He made such an impact in the Top 14 and the Heineken Cup that he has been named three times to play with the French Barbarians. The British Columbia native has been counted on to provide the Canadian national team with an extra bit of experience and aggression since he made his debut against the U.S.A. in 1994.

## Brian Vizard

The Vizman debuted for the Eagles against Japan in 1986 and went on to earn 22 caps for the United States, captaining the team eight times. An imposing figure at 6'6" and 230 pounds, Vizard played the number 8 in the days before lifting in the line-out, when having a tough line-out enforcer was absolutely critical. Foolhardy would-be tacklers encountered an Edward Scissorhands–like fury of razor-sharp elbows and relentlessly churning knees. He made numerous appearances for the Eagles Sevens side in Hong Kong and elsewhere around the world. Viz played the majority of his club rugby for the Old Mission Beach Athletic Club, leading them to six USA Rugby National Club

Championships along the way. From what we can gather from tall tales, artifacts, and fossil remains, Viz was the kind of player everyone wanted on their team but dreaded playing against — a big, strong, determined, aggressive, and angry man who wanted to win more than anyone else on the pitch.

# Patty Jervey

A top-class player with more than 23 years of experience, Eagle Patty Jervey (see Figure 23-3) competed in five World Cups and retired after the 2006 WRWC as the USA's all-time leader by a country mile in women's caps (37), points (178), and tries (38). A tenacious defender and powerful attacker, seven of her USA tries were worth four points!

# Jen Crawford

Jen Crawford is the finest female player that North America has ever produced. The former all-time leading Eagles tryscorer, Crawford captained the Eagles to the final of the 1998 Women's World Cup while earning a record 20th cap. Still deeply involved in the club game, she led the Berkeley All-Blues to nine consecutive USA Rugby National Women's Club Championships as both a player and an assistant coach.

Crawford had an instinctive feel for the game and a deadly ability to set up defenders and either sell the dummy or blow straight through them. She was a devastating finisher when the goal line was in sight and led representative sides to national titles in fifteens and sevens.

# Gillian Florence

A powerful and aggressive flanker who's amassed 44 caps representing her country — the most ever by a Canadian woman — Florence earned the game MVP in her test debut at the 1994 World Cup. A devastating tackler and hard runner with the ball in hand, she was a key performer on the fourth-place Canadian team at the 1998 Women's Rugby World Cup. Florence was selected to the 2003 All-World Team. She's a graduate of McGill University and was named one of their top 20 athletes of all time.

**Figure 23-3:**
Patty Jervey
prepares to
make a
tackle.

# Heather Moyse

Heather Moyse made her Canadian Women's National Team debut in 2004, and since then has consistently shown she's one of the best fullbacks in the game. She was Canada's only member of the All-World team at the 2006 World Cup, and was the leading tryscorer in the tournament with seven. Moyse has been named to the All-Canadian CIS team three times, twice as an undergraduate at the University of Waterloo and once as a graduate at the University of Toronto. She is also a Canadian Olympian, having represented her country in the two-person bobsleigh event, where she placed fourth at the 2006 Games in Turin.

# Honorable Mentions

Whenever you construct a list like the one above, you're forced to leave off some worthy candidates. To properly acknowledge their achievements, we've come up with a list of notables who deserve recognition.

Outstanding male players from the Eagles who deserve mention include:

- ✔ **Vaea Anitoni:** A speedy wing, Anitoni is the Eagles' all-time leading tryscorer in 46 tests.
- ✔ **Mike Hercus:** Since making his debut for the USA in 2002, Hercus has become the Eagles' all-time leading scorer with 361 points.

- ✔ **Luke Gross:** At 6'10", Gross was a monster in the line-out and when he retired from international play was the most capped American with 62 appearances for the Eagles.

- ✔ **Fred Paoli:** Perhaps the U.S.'s best all-time prop, Paoli was a no-nonsense captain and natural team leader who earned 20 caps.

- ✔ **Dennis Jablonski:** A standout fullback in defense and attack (and the first in a long line of Eagles from Occidental College), Jabbo was also the first American ever named to a World XV representative team.

For the U.S. women, this quintet stands out:

- ✔ **Ellie Karvoski:** Ellie Karvoski has played in two World Cups for the USA and in 2006 was named to the All-World team. She scored a hat-trick of tries in the USA's win over Australia. A gifted athlete — she has also represented the United States in field hockey — she is also one of the country's most talented back-line players. An outstanding scorer from her wing position, Karvoski has been named the MVP at the ITTs in both sevens and fifteens.

- ✔ **Kathy Flores:** A slightly undersized the number 8, Flores was an integral part of the 1991 and 1994 Eagles World Cup champion and runner-up teams. Kathy now coaches the USA Rugby Women's National Team and was named the IRB's Female Personality of the Year in 2003.

- ✔ **Candi Orsini:** This gifted and ageless center combined speed, agility, and power to wreak havoc from the midfield. Another veteran of the U.S.'s 1991, 1994, and 1998 Rugby Women's World Cup squads, Candi now serves as an assistant coach with the national team.

- ✔ **Phaedra Knight:** The only American woman named to the 2003 World XV, the athletic prop combines size, power, and quickness, plus good technique up front. Her contribution is huge in attack and on defense.

- ✔ **Dianne Schnapp:** She was a stalwart flanker for both the Eagles and the Berkeley All-Blues. One of the best players ever at the breakdown, Schnapp was tough as nails in contact situations.

On the Canadian men's ledger, the following players are worthy of an honorable mention:

- ✔ **Dan Baugh:** Although his career was cut short by injuries, the 30-times-capped and very athletic Baugh played some very tough rugby for Canada and Cardiff.

- ✔ **Winston Stanley:** A fantastic finisher, Stanley earned 66 caps for Canada and was part of the 2001 treble-winning Leicester Tigers. Stanley also played on Canada's 1997 and 2007 World Cup Sevens sides.

- **Dave Lougheed:** This rangy and deceptively fast winger was a veteran of three World Cups and one of Canada's best-ever finishers.

- **Bob Ross:** Upon his retirement in 2003 Ross was the world's longest serving international. He made his debut in 1989 against Ireland, earned 54 caps, and was Canada's second all-time leading scorer.

- **Rod Snow:** A versatile prop, Snow was a rock of consistency with 57 caps and was named to a World XV in 1999. He had a long professional career before returning home to help his hometown Newfoundland Rock win the Rugby Canada Super League Championship in 2005.

The Canadian women who deserve to be singled out include:

- **Sommer Christie:** Christie played for Canada in the 2002 and 2006 World Cups and was part of the first-ever World University Sevens Championship team.

- **Julie Foster:** Still playing at the age of 38, Foster has earned 39 caps playing at both wing and center.

- **Josée Lacasse:** Previously the most-capped Canadian woman, Lacasse retired after the 2002 Women's Rugby World Cup — her third WRWC — having earned 29 caps at prop.

# Chapter 24

# The Ten Best Rugby Moments

*In This Chapter*

▶ Defining the top five moments in world rugby

▶ Choosing the top five moments in North American rugby

*R*ugby fans are particularly passionate about the history of their game and love nothing more than to discuss fantastic moments from the past over a cold beverage. Good-natured debate about the greatest game, best try, and most awesome team is a staple activity in clubhouses around the globe.

In this chapter, we provide our picks of the five greatest moments in the history of the game from around the oval planet and then put forth our selections for the top five moments in the game for North American teams.

## Top Five Around the World

In the more than 125 years since the first test match was played between England and Scotland in 1871, rugby has delivered hundreds of great games marked by dramatic finishes and featuring monumental team and individual performances. The process of paring this mountain of history into just five games demonstrated to us yet again why rugby is such an amazing sport. Here's our list of the five best games of all time:

### The greatest test ever

On July 15, 2000, Australia hosted New Zealand at Olympic Stadium in Sydney in what we believe was the single best test ever played. The setting befit the occasion, as a world-record rugby crowd of 109,874 filled the stadium to watch the defending World Champion Wallabies face the New Zealand All Blacks with the Bledisloe Cup on the line in the opening match of the Tri

Nations. The match started with a flurry as Tana Umaga scored an intercept try off an ill-advised pass by Chris Latham. From the ensuing kickoff, the Kiwis controlled the ball and Jonah Lomu got into the action, by putting Pita Alatini in the clear after a break down the touchline. Fullback Christian Cullen was next on the scoresheet, stunning the Aussie crowd with a burst through the Wallaby defense for the third try. Then, after an Andrew Mehrtens penalty, with just nine minutes gone, the scoreline read Australia 0, New Zealand, 24. With 70 minutes left to be played, it was shaping up to be the worst beating that the All Blacks had ever inflicted on the Wallabies.

Wallaby Captain John Eales summoned his troops and told them to keep their cool and stay focused on the game plan — the key thing was not to panic. From the next restart, Stephen Larkham broke the line and put Stirling Mortlock into the clear with a perfectly weighted pass. The huge crowd let out a collective sigh of relief as they all wondered . . . "Can the boys come all the way back?" Over the next 25 minutes the World Champions did exactly that to level the scores at 24–all at the half.

The Aussies took the lead 27–24 with a penalty in the 58th minute, but the All Blacks answered with a try by Justin Marshall to reclaim the lead 29–27. After the conversion and a Mehrtens penalty the Kiwis led 34–27. Stirling Mortlock then added a penalty and the lead was down to 34–30 with only a few minutes remaining. In the 78th minute, Wallaby hooker Jeremy Paul drove over the tryline in the corner and raised his arms in triumph as the all-time record crowd went absolutely nuts, celebrating yet another amazing comeback by their beloved boys — who had moved ahead of their biggest rivals 35–34.

All that remained was to run out the clock. Trailing by one point, the All Blacks had to score on their last possession. After several phases of slowly advancing the ball, reserve scrumhalf Byron Kelleher moved the ball wide to Taine Randell, who drew two defenders and passed over the top to Jonah Lomu. The big man rumbled around the corner, beating Larkham's last-ditch tackle attempt to score the match-winning try!

We've seen the match at least 15 times and it still gives us chills to watch the finish. If you ever want to explain to someone who's unfamiliar with rugby what the game's all about and you're lucky enough to have it on tape, show them this match — they'll be a believer in no time.

# The 2003 World Cup final

The 2003 Rugby World Cup final pitted host Australia against the pre-tournament favorites, England. The home nation against the former colony, the best of the north against the best of the Southern Hemisphere, this match had a story line that was longer than the queues waiting to catch a train after the match at Homebush station. The stadium was half full of English and half full of Aussie supporters, as white and gold jerseys dominated the jam-packed venue. The match started well for the home side when Lote Tuqiri hauled in a cross-field bomb by Stephen Larkham and the Wallabies took a five-point lead.

England kept their composure as Jonny Wilkinson converted three shots at goal to put England in front 9–5. Then just before halftime, Wilko put Jason Robinson into the clear down the right sideline and England went into the changing rooms with a well deserved 14–5 halftime lead.

The second half settled into a contest of wills: The Wallabies scratched their way back into the match with two penalty goals, but England still led 14–11 as fulltime approached. On the Wallabies' final possession in injury time, a penalty gave Elton Flatley his chance to level the scores and force extra time. With ice water coursing through his veins and the rugby world holding its breath, he calmly slotted the goal and the fulltime whistle was blown, leaving the world's two best teams even at 14–all.

In extra time, the teams continued the pattern. England took the lead on a penalty, and then Australia leveled the scores with 30 seconds left in the second of the two ten-minute periods. With just seconds remaining and the commentators speculating about a third ten-minute sudden death period, England's scrumhalf Matt Dawson somehow broke through the Wallaby defense and got close enough to the line for Jonny Wilkinson to line up a final drop goal attempt. Everyone in the stadium knew what was coming: Jonny stroked the drop and history was made when the ball sailed through the uprights and England became the first Northern Hemisphere nation to ever win the World Cup. All hail Sir Clive Woodward and England!

## Barbarians versus New Zealand 1973

Before July 15, 2000, when the subject of greatest games came up the 1973 contest between the Barbarians RFC and the New Zealand All Blacks topped the list. The game matched a Barbarians team chock-full of Welsh legends, including the incomparable Gareth Edwards, JPR Williams, Phil Bennett, and John Dawes, plus Irish icons Willie John McBride, Mike Gibson, and Fergus Slattery, and other notables from Scotland and England. The All Blacks featured the uncompromising Ian Kirkpatrick, Alex Wyllie, Sid Going, and Brian Williams, who had just shut out England 9–0 and now faced the star-studded Barbarians to finish up their tour.

After the opening kickoff the teams traded deep kicks, jockeying for field position until the All Blacks' Brian Williams launched a high kick deep behind the Welsh 22-meter line. Instead of taking the sensible option and kicking for the safety of touch, Phil Bennett counter attacked, beginning an 80-meter movement that would be forever etched in the memories of rugby fans around the world.

Bennett picked up the ball around his own 10-meter line, and made three successive sidesteps to elude Alister Scown, J.A. Hurst, and Ian Kirkpatrick. Bennett then passed on to JPR Williams, who nearly had his head ripped off but still managed to offload to John Pullin. Pullin transferred the ball to John Dawes, who sold a dummy, covered more ground, and passed inside to Tom David as he crossed the halfway line. David made a one-handed pass inside to Derek Quinnell, who moved the ball on with another one-handed pass inside. Just then, Gareth Edwards blasted from nowhere to join the line at precisely the right angle and pace to round the corner, evaded Joe Karam's covering tackle, and covered the final 20 meters to dive headfirst into the left-hand corner of the river Tafft end to score what is now known as "The Try." The capacity Cardiff Arms Park crowd erupted into a delirious state of rapture and the Barbarians went on to defeat the mighty All Blacks 23–11.

If you ever get lucky enough to hear Gareth Edwards describe "The Try" in person, you'll see his eyes light up as he relives every step of the movement from more than 30 years ago like it was yesterday, despite the fact that it's the 25,000th time he's told the story. Some things really do improve with age.

## The Bulls win the Super 14

Until 2007 first the Super 12 and then the Super 14 were dominated by sides from New Zealand and Australia. In the early years of the competition the South African squads occasionally made the postseason but were never able to hoist the trophy. Beginning play as the Bulls franchise in 1998, the former Northern Transvaal were far and away the worst team in the tournament for many years. Their turnaround began in 2004 when they finished sixth, followed by semifinal appearances in 2005 and 2006. In 2007 they started slowly, had a fantastic tour of Australia, and gained significant momentum when they returned to their fortress, Loftus Versfeld in Pretoria. Going into the last match of the season they knew that they had to outscore the Reds by 72 points in order to host a playoff match. So what did they do? They scored 13 tries and won 92–3!

The Bulls semifinal against the six-time and defending champion Crusaders wasn't the prettiest rugby match of all time, but their 27–12 victory earned the desired result — a spot in the final the following week against the Sharks in Durban. The Sharks had topped the Super 14 table and had beaten the Bulls in their meeting back in Week One so everyone in the Republic knew that this would be a walkover.

The match was played in somewhat windy conditions and the Bulls were definitely the second-best team for the first 78 minutes. The Sharks looked like they'd wrapped up the title late in the contest when Albert van den Berg crashed over from a ruck near the goal line and gave his team a 19–13 lead. Young winger Francois Steyn missed a tough conversion and the Bulls had one last chance to win with less than two minutes to play. The Sharks twice got possession and kicked it back to the Bulls during the final sequence. The Bulls then held on to it and made ground for phase after phase until finally winger Bryan Habana got around and through the Sharks defense and flew over for the try! Flyhalf Derick Hougaard — the competition's top goal kicker in 2007 — calmly stepped up and slotted the kick to give the Bulls an improbable 20–19 win and their first Super 14 title!

## 1995 World Cup final

The 1995 Rugby World Cup was staged in South Africa and marked the return of the mighty Springboks to the international order after years of isolation because of their government's apartheid policies. The tournament started with a bang for the hosts, when they beat the defending Champion Wallabies in the opening match. The Boks eventually faced a heavily favored New Zealand side in the final.

The 1995 World Cup final was not the most exhilarating exhibition of tryscoring rugby ever played — neither team was able to touch down over the more than 100 minutes of play. However, the contest's dramatic ending made up for this: With time running out in the second extra time period, Springbok flyhalf Joel Stransky drop kicked a monster goal that sailed high through the uprights to set the 62,000 spectators into a frenzy of delight.

South Africa had indeed returned to claim the top spot on the world stage, and when Nelson Mandela joined Francois Pienaar on the podium for the trophy presentation and pumped his fists in the air to celebrate the Boks victory, sport had transcended politics; the Rainbow Nation rejoiced in harmony as one.

# Top Five North American Moments

Although the United States and Canadian Men's National Teams have yet to win the Rugby World Cup, that doesn't mean North American rugby teams have failed to impress around the world. In fact, if you look back in time, both the American and Canadian men's and women's teams have had their fair share of moments over the years.

## Women's Rugby World Cup final 1991

The first Women's Rugby World Cup was staged in Cardiff, Wales, in 1991, as the United States, France, the former Soviet Union, Wales, Japan, Sweden, Canada, the Netherlands, Italy, and New Zealand battled it out for the inaugural unofficial women's world championship. The United States beat the Netherlands and the former Soviet Union to qualify for the semifinals, where they faced the New Zealand Black Ferns. The Eagles defeated the New Zealanders and qualified to meet England in the final. The Eagles soared over the Arms Park and defeated England 19–6, much to the delight of the Welsh crowd and the U.S. supporters. Women's rugby had finally arrived as a real sport, and the Eagles were perched on top of the world.

## Canada versus France 1994

In June 1994 Canada played host to France in a test match played in Nepean. The highly rated French brought over their first team, which included the likes of Philippe Sella, Emile N'Tamack, Philippe Saint-Andre, Abdelatif Benazzi, and Laurent Cabannes. The upstart Canadians were quietly confident after having defeated Wales at the Arms Park the previous November (read on).

Even though the French scored the only try of the match, flyhalf Gareth Rees carried the Canucks on his back with six penalty goals, and the locals came out the winners, 18–16 to take their biggest scalp of all time.

## U.S. Olympians versus France (1920 and 1924)

In 1920 in Antwerp, and again four years later in 1924 in Paris, the United States defeated France in the Olympic Gold Medal rugby match. The U.S. team was composed primarily of players from Stanford University and the University of California at Berkeley. In 1924 the Americans beat Romania to advance to face France in the Gold Medal game.

The match was the first gold medal contest of the games and a partisan French crowd expected their countrymen to dispose of the Americans with ease. To the shock of the 17,000-plus in attendance at Stade Colomiers, the United States defense totally frustrated the Tricolors attack, and when it was all over the upstart Americans were victorious 17–3 to take the Gold. Because rugby was dropped following the 1924 Games, the United States are still technically the two-time defending Olympic Gold Medal champions.

## Wales versus Canada 1993

On November 10, 1993, the Canadian team posted their first-ever win over an International Rugby Board (IRB) founding nation when they defeated Wales at the venerable Cardiff Arms Park. The final score was Wales 24–26 Canada, but what made the victory even sweeter was the fact that Canada scored two tries and managed to keep the Welsh from scoring a try, with all of the Dragons' points coming from the boot of Neil Jenkins. Canadian Captain Ian Stewart and future skipper Al Charron both scored five-pointers while Gareth Rees was perfect with his kicks, converting both tries and slotting four penalties of his own.

## Canada versus Argentina 2005

The most recent high point for the Canadian Men's team occurred at Calgary Rugby Park in 2005 when they beat Argentina 22–15. At the time Argentina was ranked 8th in the world, while Canada was in 13th position. To put the victory in perspective, the previous time the two nations had met was in 2003 and the Pumas had won 62–22 in Buenos Aires.

In this encounter Canada took a 9–0 lead into halftime through Argentine indiscipline and fullback Derek Daypuck's accurate boot. The Canadians dominated the line-outs on the day and held their own against the Pumas' renowned scrum. What really won them the match, though, was outstanding defense and hard tackling near their own line as they repeatedly kept the Pumas from scoring. Leading 15–0 with 25 minutes to play, Canada finally allowed Argentina to kick their first penalty. That blot on the scoreline was erased 15 minutes later by number 10 Ryan Smith, who capitalized on a gap in the Pumas defense to score Canada's first try. Daypuck converted, and the lead was 22–3. The Pumas never gave up and scored a couple of late tries to make the scoreboard look respectable in the end, but this was a convincing and comprehensive triumph over a side threatening to break into rugby's elite nations.

# Chapter 25

# Ten Peculiar Facts about Rugby

*In This Chapter*

▶ Meeting some little-known rugby names

▶ Making it to the top in rugby

▶ Landing in some strange places

▶ Scoring in interesting ways

▶ Getting into trouble: Players and officials

▶ Witnessing touring incidents and accidents

"To play rugby union, you need three things: A good pass, a good tackle and a good excuse." Though we wish we were the ones to coin that phrase, we have to hand the credit to that ubiquitous person, Anonymous.

This chapter is a good excuse for us to tell you about some of the strange, odd, even bizarre things that happen in the world of rugby. If you're a collector of rugby trivia, you're in for a treat.

## Rugby Attracts Some Surprising People

Rugby players come in many political stripes. Just take a look at the names of some of the famous (and in at least one case, infamous) men who once wore rugby jerseys before rugby jerseys became fashion statements:

✔ **Che Guevara:** Best known as a failed exporter of revolution and as a guerrilla leader, Ernesto "Che" Guevara was also a passionate rugby player. Che was a medical student at the University of Buenos Aires in Argentina when he developed a love of the game. An enthusiastic half-back, Guevara played several seasons of club rugby before being distracted by a belief that he had to change the world.

✔ **Idi Amin:** Before becoming the president of Uganda and an infamous despot, the all-imposing Idi Amin was not only a keen heavyweight boxer but also a better-than-average rugby forward, playing the occasional representative match. Amin was educated in Britain. They didn't know it at the time, but when the British Lions squad touring Africa in 1955 prepared to take on East Africa, they almost played the man who became one of the most despised dictators of the 20th century. He didn't take the field against the British Lions; rather, he remained on the reserves bench. In 1964, the British Dominion Office described Amin as ". . . a splendid type and a good rugby player . . . he is virtually bone from the neck up and needs things explained in words of one letter."

✔ **Bill Clinton:** Yes, it's true. Bill Clinton actually played the 15-man game. His rugby career was fleeting, but he was a keen participant. After completing college in 1968, Clinton won a Rhodes Scholarship which allowed him to study at Oxford University in England. Clinton, a big believer in doing what the locals do, was soon lured into trying his luck on the Oxford rugby fields. He didn't make much of an impression but he did run around in several low-grade games.

✔ **George W. Bush:** The presidential successor to Bill Clinton went one better than the sax-playing leader. In 1968, George Dubya, allegedly a wild man at college, played in the Yale First XV. *Sports Illustrated* even has pictures to prove it!

# Unlikely Lads Can Make It to the Top

As a clear reminder that in rugby you should never give up, we offer the stories of three players who came out of nowhere to achieve great things:

✔ **Which cocky player?** After the main England trial for the test team against the first Springboks tour in 1906, it seemed a certainty that Liverpool and Lancashire representative Noel Slocock, a forward, would be selected. Slocock was a formidable line-out jumper, something desperately required against the touring South Africans. Although the national selectors put Slocock's name on the test list, an administrative bungle led to the name of Arnold Alcock appearing on the list instead. Alcock was a little-known medical student who had played in a hospital cup team. Somehow, Alcock played for England and managed to help his country to a 3–all draw.

✔ **Whose autograph?** One man who did all he could to get noticed was England international winger Carston Catcheside. After his first international game, Catcheside made certain that the people who mattered knew who he was. He wrote his name all over the bald head of one of the selectors!

✔ **Deserves a Merrick increase?** One player who wasn't expected to get there, but did anyway, was Australian test scrumhalf Steve Merrick, who emerged from the small New South Wales country town of Singleton to play in the two-test series against New Zealand in 1995. When rugby turned professional later that same year, the salaries that could be earned turned the heads of a number of Australian players. Merrick was different: He didn't want to be a well-paid, high-profile sportsman. He simply didn't want to move from peaceful Singleton to be part of the Sydney rat race — so he turned his back on lucrative player contracts and the chance of holding both the New South Wales and Australian scrumhalf positions.

# Siblings Like to Battle It Out Together

Rugby seems to run in the blood of some families. Brothers frequently wind up playing side by side — usually on the same team. The following list names some of the firsts in sibling players:

✔ The first brothers to appear together in a rugby international were John and Francis Luscombe, who played for England in 1871.

✔ The first instance of three brothers in a test match occurred in 1875 when Scotland's N. J., A. B., and J. F. Finlay played in a scoreless draw against England.

✔ The first time that brothers appeared on both test teams was in 1885 when George and Richard Maitland played for Scotland and Bob and Arthur Gould appeared for Wales.

✔ Stewart and Jim Boyce became the first twins to play in a test when they played for Australia against New Zealand in 1964.

✔ Gordon Brown of Scotland was the first brother to replace a brother when he replaced his injured brother Peter in a match against Wales in 1970.

✔ When twins Jane and Emma Mitchell lined up opposite each other in Bermuda in 2002, the pair earned the distinction of playing against each other for different countries. Emma played for England and Jane for the United States.

# Players Injure Themselves in Bizarre Ways

Much as we would like you to believe otherwise, it is a sad fact of life that, yes, players do sometimes get injured while playing rugby. Some of the better-known accidents are better known because of the utter embarrassment of the players concerned.

- **Blinded by the sun:** In 1969, French flanker Jean-Pierre Salut could not contain his excitement as he prepared to face Scotland at the great Parisian stadium, Stade Colombes. To calm himself down, he decided to be the last player to run onto the field. To get to the ground from the dressing rooms, the players had to run down a very long corridor and negotiate several flights of stairs before emerging into the sunlight. Everything was going really well — until Salut tripped on the final step and broke his ankle.

- **Maneuvering around the media:** Northern Transvaal center Pieter Nel missed the 1990 Currie Cup final when he injured his ankle running onto the Loftus Versfeld pitch in Pretoria. Nel tried to get around a photographer with a side step then slipped on some dung left behind by a bull (which happened to be the local mascot!).

- **Kneecapped in midair:** In 1997, after struggling with a string of injuries, Scottish halfback Andy Nicol was delighted he had returned to full fitness and was able to lead his country on its tour of South Africa. He was happily sleeping away on the flight to Johannesburg when an errant drink cart smashed into his knee. Nicol was sidelined for several weeks.

# Rugby Players Hate to Cancel Games

Some rugby players are so passionate about the sport that nothing (and we mean nothing) gets in the way of a match.

- **Portsmouth Victoria versus Southampton Trojans:** Numerous matches have been interrupted by stray dogs running onto the pitch, but only one dog has ever been used to score a try. In an 1890s game between Portsmouth Victoria and Southampton Trojans, a ball kicked into the Trojans' in-goal area rebounded off a dog. One of the Portsmouth players gathered the ball and claimed a try. Although the Trojans protested, the try stood. The Rugby Football Union ruled that the decision was correct, because dogs were not classified as spectators. If the ball had bounced off a spectator, it would not have been allowed.

✔ **Williams versus Randall:** In 1909, two Welsh families decided to play each other in a sevens game, with £100 in prize money to the winners. Seven brothers of the Williams clan from Pembrokeshire met seven from the Randall clan of Llanelli on neutral ground at Carmarthen. Several thousand spectators crowded the ground to watch the match degenerate into a wrestling bout. While the match hardly resembled a rugby game, the Williams boys still won the money.

✔ **East Midlands versus Barbarians:** Former England halfback Adrian Stoop refereed the 1921 East Midlands versus Barbarians match. Somehow he managed to blow the final whistle 14 minutes early. After complaints and protests, the players and referee had to get out of their baths and finish the match.

✔ **All Blacks versus Tahiti 15:** When international teams play, the after-match function is usually held, well, *after* the match. Not so when the All Blacks decided to play a friendly game against a Tahitian 15. The Tahitians decided to have their function *before* kickoff. They offered the New Zealanders a sumptuous feast including copious amounts of wine and champagne. The tactic backfired when the Tahitian team decided to join in and have a few drinks, too. They ran onto the field somewhat worse for wear and suffering from extremely blurred vision. The All Blacks won by more than 70 points.

# Rugby Is Played in Extreme Weather and in Strange Locations

Since the game was developed in England in the 19th century (see Chapter 1 for more details), rugby has turned up in some rather unexpected places. Equally unexpected are the settings of some rugby playing fields and the extraordinary range of climate and weather in which the game is played.

✔ **Antarctica:** Rugby is truly a global game that's played on all seven continents! In 2001, the United States and New Zealand research teams faced off on a snow-covered pitch over ancient sea ice in Antarctica. The Kiwis from the Scott Base defeated the Yanks from McMurdo Sound station 9–3.

✔ **Bahrain:** Some countries, such as Bahrain, play rugby on the desert sand, often in the highest temperatures imaginable.

✔ **England:** Teams touring England have often discovered the delights of playing in the fog. The 1978 Australian Schoolboys team, playing the England Under-19s at Twickenham, could not see more than a meter in front of them. The fog was so thick the spectators couldn't see a thing — so they were allowed to stand on the sidelines and near the dead ball lines in the hope that they might be able to follow the game.

- **Indonesia:** One of the main rugby grounds in Indonesia is found deep in a jungle, while another is almost at the summit of a mountain, near a tea plantation.

- **Jordan:** Few grounds can beat the Amman Rugby Club, whose players play on the floor of the Dead Sea. The pitch, whose surface is soft sand, lies 385 meters below sea level.

- **Russia:** Some of the coldest rugby venues are in Russia. In 1978, Krasnoyarsk played Polyechnika Alma when the temperature was minus 23 degrees Celsius. No one even contemplated calling the game off — the team from Krasnoyarsk had traveled 2,000 kilometers in order to play. To overcome the chill, the players wore stocking masks, gloves, and several layers of tracksuits.

- **Western Samoa:** Rugby legend has it that when Western Samoa began playing tests, their home ground had a large coconut tree growing on the halfway line. Sounds unbelievable, but then again, Samoans have always prided themselves on their relaxed style.

# Players Score in Unorthodox Ways

The aim of rugby is to score more points than the opposition. No surprises there. However, over the years, some rather unorthodox methods of scoring have been observed on the field. (You can read about the regular scoring system in Chapter 2.)

- **The unlikeliest try:** During a game in Builth Wells in Wales about a century ago, the visiting fullback kicked the ball into some tree branches that were overhanging the pitch. Surprise, surprise — the ball got stuck. While officials went off to find another ball and the players had a rest on the pitch, the ball suddenly fell from the tree. A quick-thinking player grabbed the ball and scored under the posts. The opposition naturally complained but the referee awarded the try because, under local rules, the ball had not gone out of play.

- **The fastest try in test history:** This is an honor claimed by Scotland's New Zealand import, John Leslie. Leslie scored with only nine seconds gone on the clock in the test against Wales at Murrayfield in 1999.

- **The only jointly awarded test try:** Welsh players Howie Jones and Harry Peacock shared credit for scoring in a test match against Ireland in 1930. The referee was unable to work out which player grounded the ball, so the only joint try in an international game was awarded.

✔ **The accidental try:** In the late 1950s, George Nepia, probably recognized as New Zealand's greatest fullback, was well into retirement but continued to play in social matches. In one of these games, the ball hit him perfectly in the chest. Noticing a gap straight in front of him, he sprinted for the line and grounded the ball right under the posts. Only one problem — he was the referee.

## Sometimes Officials Make Unofficial Calls

A *send-off* occurs when a player commits a serious violation and is ordered by the referee to leave the field for the rest of the game. Sometimes even the officials are not safe from the wrath of other officials. For example, at a Plymouth club game in England in 1967, the referee ordered his own touch judge sent off after he was involved in a melee with players and spectators.

Even the most serious rules can be taken too seriously. For example, the strangest send-off wasn't actually meant to be a send-off. In 1988, former Irish test front-rower Gerry McLoughlin was playing for Welsh club-side Gilfach Goch when he was involved in a brawl. According to Irish and Welsh lore, when referee Roy Rees had sorted the fight out, he looked at McLoughlin and told him, as a general warning, "Push off and let's get on with the game."

When a scrum was set about 15 minutes later, Rees discovered that the local club was missing their tight-head prop — Big Gerry. McLoughlin had misinterpreted what Rees said and thought "push off" meant he'd been sent from the field. By the time Gerry was told of his error, he was in his street clothes. Gilfach Goch had to make do with 14 men for the rest of the game. Somehow, Gilfach won.

## Rugby Blunders into Multicultural Minefields

When a player is sent off, he or she usually has to appear before a judiciary committee, which is a rather formal occasion. Unfortunately, formal occasions have a habit of being undermined by human folly, especially in cross-cultural exchanges, and sometimes result in embarrassment all around.

One of the more entertaining judiciary committee incidents occurred while Malcolm McPhee was chairman of the Sydney Rugby Union Judiciary Committee. As Neil Marks wrote in his book *Tales from the Locker Room* (Ironbark Press), McPhee and his committee had to interview two players, both recruited from overseas, who had been cited by referees. One was a large Samoan second-rower from the Drummoyne club in Sydney and the other an even larger Fijian second-rower from the Sydney club of Hornsby.

The Hornsby player was the first to arrive, wearing a Fijian lap-lap and sandals. Accompanying him was his wife, a very large woman dressed identically to her husband. The player introduced himself as Charlie Levula from Hornsby.

"How do you do, Charlie," the chairman replied, politely shaking the big forward's hand. McPhee then noticed Levula's wife standing in the background. Thrusting out his hand, he said, "And you must be from Drummoyne!"

Rugby may need to introduce a new law — for sending judiciary officials to the sin bin when they make social blunders.

# If It's Going to Happen, It'll Happen on Tour

Strange as it may seem, some of the most memorable things that happen on a rugby tour do not occur on the pitch. Touring teams often like to play with the minds of local journalists. When the Fijian team toured Britain in 1970, a young scribe asked one of their huge forwards how they celebrated after matches. "The winners eat the losers," was the reply. The scribe thought he was serious and included it in his report.

✔ **Nobody meets the queen:** The highlight of several Wallaby tours to the United Kingdom has been the chance to meet Queen Elizabeth at Buckingham Palace. Not surprisingly, these meetings have had their hiccups. In 1984, Australian team manager "Chilla" Wilson forgot the name of winger Ross Hanley as he was about to introduce him to the queen. Similarly, in 1988, Wallaby manager Andy Conway struggled to maintain his composure when ACT center Paul Cornish met the queen — the queen turned to Conway and asked, ever so nicely, "Doesn't this player have a name?"

✔ **A right royal salute:** During the 1984 visit, another royal incident occurred when Queensland back-rower Chris Roche decided to perch himself on an antique hall table. Within a few seconds, the table, unused to heavy weights like Roche, crashed to the floor. As Roche looked for somewhere to hide, Prince Philip turned around and casually said, "Don't worry. There are plenty more of them in the storeroom."

✔ **War stops play:** Unfortunately, not everything that happens on tour is amusing — tragedy strikes everywhere. During their 1939 tour, the Wallabies arrived in the United Kingdom just before World War II was declared. The tour was immediately abandoned. After spending several days filling sandbags to protect their hotel in Torquay, the players returned home without a game being played. But they still endured a hazardous trip, with their boat forced to zigzag to throw off submarine attacks.

# Appendix A

# U.S. and Canada Tests

## United States Test Record

| Date | Match | Score | Location |
|------|-------|-------|----------|
| 18 May 2007 | versus England Saxons | 3 – 51 | Manchester, England |
| 07 Oct 2006 | versus Uruguay | 33 – 7 | Palo Alto, U.S. |
| 30 Sep 2006 | versus Uruguay | 42 – 13 | Montevideo, Uruguay |
| 12 Aug 2006 | versus Canada | 7 – 56 | St. John's, Canada |
| 01 Jul 2006 | versus Barbados | 91 – 0 | Palo Alto, U.S. |
| 17 Jun 2006 | versus Canada | 18 – 33 | Edmonton, Canada |
| 07 Jun 2006 | versus NZ Maori | 6 – 74 | Santa Clara, U.S. |
| 03 Jun 2006 | versus Ireland A | 13 – 28 | Santa Clara, U.S. |
| 25 Jun 2005 | versus Canada | 20 – 19 | Edmonton, Canada |
| 19 Jun 2005 | versus Argentina A | 30 – 34 | Edmonton, Canada |
| 06 Jun 2005 | versus Wales | 3 – 77 | Hartford, U.S. |
| 29 May 2005 | versus Romania | 28 – 22 | Tokyo, Japan |
| 25 May 2005 | versus Canada | 26 – 30 | Tokyo, Japan |
| 27 Nov 2004 | versus Italy | 25 – 43 | Biella, Italy |
| 20 Nov 2004 | versus Ireland | 6 – 55 | Dublin, Ireland |
| 03 Jul 2004 | versus France | 31 – 39 | Hartford, U.S. |
| 19 Jun 2004 | versus Canada | 29 – 32 | Edmonton, Canada |
| 13 Jun 2004 | versus NZ Maori | 31 – 69 | Calgary, Canada |
| 31 May 2004 | versus Russia | 41 – 11 | Tokyo, Japan |
| 27 May 2004 | versus Canada | 20 – 23 | Tokyo, Japan |
| 31 Oct 2003 | versus France | 14 – 41 | Wollongong, Australia |
| 27 Oct 2003 | versus Japan | 39 – 26 | Gosford, Australia |

*(continued)*

## United States Test Record *(continued)*

| Date | Match | Score | Location |
|------|-------|-------|----------|
| 20 Oct 2003 | versus Scotland | 15 – 39 | Brisbane, Australia |
| 15 Oct 2003 | versus Fiji | 18 – 19 | Brisbane, Australia |
| 30 Aug 2003 | versus Uruguay | 31 – 17 | Buenos Aires, Argentina |
| 27 Aug 2003 | versus Canada | 35 – 20 | Buenos Aires, Argentina |
| 23 Aug 2003 | ersus Argentina | 8 – 42 | Buenos Aires, Argentina |
| 28 Jun 2003 | versus England XV | 6 – 43 | Vancouver, Canada |
| 21 Jun 2003 | versus England XV | 10 – 36 | Vancouver, Canada |
| 18 Jun 2003 | versus Canada | 16 – 11 | Vancouver, Canada |
| 17 May 2003 | versus Japan | 69 – 27 | San Francisco, U.S. |
| 27 Apr 2003 | versus Spain | 58 – 13 | Fort Lauderdale, U.S. |
| 12 Apr 2003 | versus Spain | 63 – 13 | Madrid, Spain |
| 31 Aug 2002 | versus Uruguay | 9 – 10 | Montevideo, Uruguay |
| 24 Aug 2002 | versus Chile | 13 – 21 | Santiago, Chile |
| 15 Aug 2002 | versus Uruguay | 28 – 24 | San Francisco, U.S. |
| 10 Aug 2002 | versus Chile | 35 – 22 | Salt Lake City, U.S. |
| 13 Jul 2002 | versus Canada | 13 – 36 | Chicago, U.S. |
| 29 Jun 2002 | versus Canada | 9 – 26 | Markham, Canada |
| 22 Jun 2002 | versus Scotland | 23 – 65 | San Francisco, U.S. |
| 01 Dec 2001 | versus South Africa | 20 – 43 | Houston, U.S. |
| 16 Jun 2001 | versus England | 19 – 48 | San Francisco, U.S. |
| 26 May 2001 | versus Uruguay | 31 – 28 | Markham, Canada |
| 23 May 2001 | versus Argentina | 16 – 44 | Hamilton, Canada |
| 19 May 2001 | versus Canada | 10 – 19 | Kingston, Canada |
| 18 Nov 2000 | versus Wales | 11 – 42 | Cardiff, Wales |
| 04 Nov 2000 | versus Scotland | 6 – 53 | Edinburgh, Scotland |
| 15 Jul 2000 | versus Samoa | 12 – 19 | San Francisco, U.S. |
| 07 Jul 2000 | versus Tonga | 6 – 29 | Nuku A'lofa, Tonga |
| 30 Jun 2000 | versus Fiji | 21 – 37 | Apia, Samoa |

| Date | Match | Score | Location |
| --- | --- | --- | --- |
| 10 Jun 2000 | versus Ireland | 3–83 | Manchester, U.S. |
| 03 Jun 2000 | versus Canada | 34–25 | Manchester, U.S. |
| 27 May 2000 | versus Japan | 36–21 | Osaka, Japan |
| 14 Oct 1999 | versus Australia | 19–55 | Limerick, Ireland |
| 09 Oct 1999 | versus Romania | 25–27 | Dublin, Ireland |
| 02 Oct 1999 | versus Ireland | 8–53 | Dublin, Ireland |
| 21 Aug 1999 | versus England | 8–106 | London, England |
| 26 Jun 1999 | versus Samoa | 20–27 | Apia, Samoa |
| 19 Jun 1999 | versus Canada | 18–17 | Toronto, Canada |
| 12 Jun 1999 | versus Japan | 31–47 | Honolulu, U.S. |
| 22 May 1999 | versus Fiji | 25–14 | San Francisco, U.S. |
| 15 May 1999 | versus Tonga | 30–10 | San Francisco, U.S. |
| 22 Aug 1998 | versus Uruguay | 21–16 | Buenos Aires, Argentina |
| 18 Aug 1998 | versus Canada | 14–31 | Buenos Aires, Argentina |
| 15 Aug 1998 | versus Argentina | 24–52 | Buenos Aires, Argentina |
| 25 Jul 1998 | versus Fiji | 9–18 | Suva, Fiji |
| 20 Jun 1998 | versus Hong Kong | 17–27 | San Francisco, U.S. |
| 13 Jun 1998 | versus Japan | 21–25 | San Francisco, U.S. |
| 06 Jun 1998 | versus Canada | 3–37 | Burlington, U.S. |
| 23 May 1998 | versus Canada | 15–17 | Vancouver, Canada |
| 16 May 1998 | versus Hong Kong | 25–43 | Hong Kong |
| 10 May 1998 | versus Japan | 38–27 | Tokyo, Japan |
| 12 Apr 1998 | versus Spain | 49–3 | El Puerto de Santa Maria, Spain |
| 08 Apr 1998 | versus Portugal | 61–5 | Lisbon, Portugal |
| 12 Jul 1997 | versus Wales | 23–28 | San Francisco, U.S. |
| 05 Jul 1997 | versus Wales | 20–30 | Wilmington, U.S. |
| 28 Jun 1997 | versus Canada | 11–22 | San Francisco, U.S. |
| 14 Jun 1997 | versus Hong Kong | 17–14 | San Francisco, U.S. |

*(continued)*

## United States Test Record *(continued)*

| Date | Match | Score | Location |
|------|-------|-------|----------|
| 07 Jun 1997 | versus Japan | 51 – 29 | San Francisco, U.S. |
| 25 May 1997 | versus Japan | 20 – 12 | Osaka, Japan |
| 17 May 1997 | versus Hong Kong | 9 – 46 | Hong Kong |
| 10 May 1997 | versus Canada | 12 – 53 | Vancouver, Canada |
| 11 Jan 1997 | versus Wales | 14 – 34 | Cardiff, Wales |
| 21 Sep 1996 | versus Uruguay | 27 – 13 | Markham, Canada |
| 18 Sep 1996 | versus Canada | 18 – 23 | Hamilton, Canada |
| 14 Sep 1996 | versus Argentina | 26 – 29 | Nepean, Canada |
| 06 Jul 1996 | versus Japan | 74 – 5 | San Francisco, U.S. |
| 29 Jun 1996 | versus Hong Kong | 42 – 23 | San Francisco, U.S. |
| 16 Jun 1996 | versus Japan | 18 – 24 | Tokyo, Japan |
| 08 Jun 1996 | versus Hong Kong | 19 – 22 | Hong Kong |
| 18 May 1996 | versus Canada | 20 – 24 | Vancouver, Canada |
| 11 May 1996 | versus Canada | 19 – 12 | San Francisco, U.S. |
| 06 Jan 1996 | versus Ireland | 18 – 25 | Atlanta, U.S. |
| 09 Sep 1995 | versus Canada | 15 – 14 | Markham, Canada |
| 05 Nov 1994 | versus Ireland | 15 – 26 | Dublin, Ireland |
| 20 Jun 1994 | versus Argentina | 11 – 16 | Buenos Aires, Argentina |
| 28 May 1994 | versus Argentina | 22 – 28 | Long Beach, U.S. |
| 21 May 1994 | versus Canada | 10 – 15 | Long Beach, U.S. |
| 12 Mar 1994 | versus Bermuda | 60 – 3 | Devonshire, Bermuda |
| 02 Oct 1993 | versus Australia XV (non-cap) | 22 – 26 | Riverside, U.S. |
| 19 Jun 1993 | versus Canada | 9 – 20 | Winnipeg, Canada |
| 13 Jun 1992 | versus Canada | 9 – 32 | Denver, U.S. |
| 18 Apr 1992 | versus Hong Kong | 23 – 16 | San Francisco, U.S. |
| 11 Oct 1991 | versus England | 9 – 37 | London, U.S. |
| 08 Oct 1991 | versus New Zealand | 6 – 46 | Gloucester, England |

| Date | Match | Score | Location |
|------|-------|-------|----------|
| 05 Oct 1991 | versus Italy | 9 – 30 | Otley, England |
| 20 Jul 1991 | versus France | 3 – 10 | Colorado Springs, U.S. |
| 13 Jul 1991 | versus France | 9 – 41 | Denver, U.S. |
| 08 Jun 1991 | versus Canada | 15 – 34 | Calgary, Canada |
| 18 May 1991 | versus Scotland XV (non-cap) | 12 – 41 | Hartford, U.S. |
| 04 May 1991 | versus Japan | 27 – 15 | Chicago, U.S. |
| 27 Apr 1991 | versus Japan | 20 – 9 | Blaine, U.S. |
| 23 Sep 1990 | versus Japan | 25 – 15 | Tokyo, Japan |
| 08 Jul 1990 | versus Australia | 9 – 67 | Brisbane, Australia |
| 09 Jun 1990 | versus Canada | 14 – 12 | Seattle, U.S. |
| 07 Apr 1990 | versus Argentina | 6 – 13 | Santa Barbara, U.S. |
| 08 Nov 1989 | versus Argentina | 6 – 23 | Buenos Aires, Argentina |
| 05 Nov 1989 | versus Uruguay | 60 – 6 | Montevideo, Uruguay |
| 23 Sep 1989 | versus Canada | 3 – 21 | Toronto, Canada |
| 09 Sep 1989 | versus Ireland XV (non-cap) | 7 – 32 | New York, U.S. |
| 25 Sep 1988 | versus Soviet Union | 16 – 31 | Moscow, Russia |
| 17 Sep 1988 | versus Romania | 17 – 7 | Moscow, Russia |
| 11 Jun 1988 | versus Canada | 28 – 16 | Saranac Lake, U.S. |
| 14 Nov 1987 | versus Canada | 12 – 20 | Victoria, Canada |
| 07 Nov 1987 | versus Wales | 0 – 46 | Cardiff, Wales |
| 03 Jun 1987 | versus England | 6 – 34 | Sydney, Australia |
| 31 May 1987 | versus Australia | 12 – 47 | Brisbane, Australia |
| 24 May 1987 | versus Japan | 21 – 18 | Brisbane, Australia |
| 10 May 1987 | versus Canada | 9 – 33 | Vancouver, Canada |
| 03 May 1987 | versus Tunisia | 47 – 13 | Pebble Beach, U.S. |
| 08 Nov 1986 | versus Canada | 16 – 27 | Tucson, U.S. |
| 31 May 1986 | versus Japan | 9 – 9 | Torrance, U.S. |

*(continued)*

## United States Test Record *(continued)*

| Date | Match | Score | Location |
|------|-------|-------|----------|
| 16 Nov 1985 | versus Canada | 10 – 21 | Vancouver, Canada |
| 21 Apr 1985 | versus Japan | 16 – 15 | Tokyo, Japan |
| 09 Jun 1984 | versus Canada | 21 – 13 | Chicago, U.S. |
| 09 Jul 1983 | versus Australia | 3 – 49 | Sydney, Australia |
| 11 Jun 1983 | versus Canada | 9 – 15 | Burnaby, Canada |
| 19 Jun 1982 | versus England XV (non-cap) | 0 – 59 | Hartford, U.S. |
| 12 Jun 1982 | versus Canada | 3 – 3 | Albany, U.S. |
| 25 Sep 1981 | versus South Africa | 7 – 38 | Glenville, U.S. |
| 06 Jun 1981 | versus Canada | 3 – 6 | Calgary, Canada |
| 08 Oct 1980 | versus New Zealand XV (non-cap) | 6 – 53 | San Diego, U.S. |
| 08 Jun 1980 | versus Canada | 0 – 16 | Saranac Lake, U.S. |
| 10 May 1980 | versus Wales XV (non-cap) | 18 – 24 | Long Beach, U.S. |
| 09 Jun 1979 | versus Canada | 12 – 19 | Toronto, Canada |
| 28 May 1978 | versus Canada | 12 – 7 | Baltimore, U.S. |
| 15 Oct 1977 | versus England XV (non-cap) | 11 – 37 | London, England |
| 21 May 1977 | versus Canada | 6 – 17 | Burnaby, Canada |
| 12 Jun 1976 | versus France | 14 – 33 | Chicago, U.S. |
| 31 Jan 1976 | versus Australia | 12 – 24 | Anaheim, U.S. |
| 18 May 1924 | versus France | 17 – 3 | Paris, France |
| 10 May 1924 | versus Romania | 37 – 0 | Paris, France |
| 10 Oct 1920 | versus France | 5 – 14 | Paris, France |
| 05 Sep 1920 | versus France XV (non-cap) | 8 – 0 | Anvers, Belgium |
| 01 Jul 1919 | versus Romania | 21 – 0 | Paris, France |
| 15 Nov 1913 | versus New Zealand | 3 – 51 | Berkeley, U.S. |
| 16 Nov 1912 | versus Australia | 8 – 12 | Berkeley, U.S. |

## Canada Test Record

| Date | Match | Score | Location |
|------|-------|-------|----------|
| 19 May 2007 | versus Ireland A | 20 – 39 | Exeter, England |
| 25 Nov 2006 | versus Italy | 6 – 41 | Fontanafredda, Italy |
| 17 Nov 2006 | versus Wales | 24 – 61 | Cardiff, Wales |
| 12 Aug 2006 | versus United States | 56 – 7 | St. John's, Canada |
| 24 Jun 2006 | versus Barbados | 69 – 3 | Bridgetown, Barbados |
| 17 Jun 2006 | versus United States | 33 – 18 | Edmonton, Canada |
| 10 Jun 2006 | versus England Saxons | 11 – 41 | Toronto, Canada |
| 07 Jun 2006 | versus Scotland A | 10 – 15 | Ottawa, Canada |
| 02 Jul 2005 | versus Argentina | 22 – 15 | Calgary, Canada |
| 26 Jun 2005 | versus United States | 19 – 20 | Edmonton, Canada |
| 19 Jun 2005 | versus England A | 5 – 29 | Edmonton, Canada |
| 11 Jun 2005 | versus Wales | 3 – 60 | Toronto, Canada |
| 29 May 2005 | versus Japan | 15 – 10 | Tokyo, Japan |
| 25 May 2005 | versus United States | 30 – 26 | Tokyo, Japan |
| 13 Nov 2004 | versus England | 0 – 70 | London, England |
| 06 Nov 2004 | versus Italy | 6 – 51 | L'Aquila, Italy |
| 10 Jul 2004 | versus France | 13 – 47 | Toronto, Canada |
| 19 Jun 2004 | versus United States | 32 – 29 | Edmonton, Canada |
| 13 Jun 2004 | versus England | 23 – 48 | Calgary, Canada |
| 30 May 2004 | versus Japan | 21 – 34 | Tokyo, Japan |
| 27 May 2004 | versus United States | 23 – 20 | Tokyo, Japan |
| 29 Oct 2003 | versus Tonga | 24 – 7 | Wollongong, Australia |
| 21 Oct 2003 | versus Italy | 14 – 19 | Canberra, Australia |
| 17 Oct 2003 | versus New Zealand | 6 – 68 | Melbourne, Australia |
| 12 Oct 2003 | versus Wales | 10 – 41 | Melbourne, Australia |
| 30 Aug 2003 | versus Argentina | 22 – 62 | Buenos Aires, Argentina |
| 27 Aug 2003 | versus United States | 20 – 35 | Buenos Aires, Argentina |

*(continued)*

## Canada Test Record *(continued)*

| Date | Match | Score | Location |
|------|-------|-------|----------|
| 23 Aug 2003 | versus Uruguay | 21 – 11 | Buenos Aires, Argentina |
| 02 Aug 2003 | versus New Zealand Maori | 9 – 30 | Toronto, Canada |
| 26 Jul 2003 | versus New Zealand Maori | 27 – 65 | Calgary, Canada |
| 18 Jun 2003 | versus United States | 11 – 16 | Vancouver, Canada |
| 14 Jun 2003 | versus England XV (non-cap) | 7 – 43 | Vancouver, Canada |
| 23 Nov 2002 | versus France | 3 – 35 | Paris, France |
| 16 Nov 2002 | versus Wales | 21 – 32 | Cardiff, Wales |
| 31 Aug 2002 | versus Chile | 29 – 11 | Santiago, Chile |
| 24 Aug 2002 | versus Uruguay | 23 – 25 | Montevideo, Uruguay |
| 17 Aug 2002 | versus Chile | 27 – 6 | Calgary, Canada |
| 10 Aug 2002 | versus Uruguay | 51 – 16 | Edmonton, Canada |
| 13 Jul 2002 | versus United States | 36 – 13 | Chicago, U.S. |
| 29 Jun 2002 | versus United States | 26 – 9 | Markham, Canada |
| 15 Jun 2002 | versus Scotland | 26 – 23 | Vancouver, Canada |
| 08 Jul 2001 | versus Japan | 7 – 39 | Tokyo, Japan |
| 03 Jul 2001 | versus Fiji | 23 – 52 | Tokyo, Japan |
| 09 Jun 2001 | versus England | 20 – 59 | Burnaby, Canada |
| 02 Jun 2001 | versus England | 10 – 22 | Markham, Canada |
| 26 May 2001 | versus Argentina | 6 – 20 | Markham, Canada |
| 23 May 2001 | versus Uruguay | 14 – 8 | Hamilton, Canada |
| 19 May 2001 | versus United States | 19 – 10 | Kingston, Canada |
| 11 Nov 2000 | versus Italy | 22 – 17 | Rovigo, Italy |
| 15 Jul 2000 | versus Japan | 62 – 18 | Markham, Canada |
| 07 Jul 2000 | versus Fiji | 11 – 42 | Apia, Samoa |
| 01 Jul 2000 | versus Samoa | 22 – 41 | Apia, Samoa |
| 17 Jun 2000 | versus Ireland | 27 – 27 | Markham, Canada |

| Date | Match | Score | Location |
|------|-------|-------|----------|
| 10 Jun 2000 | versus South Africa | 18–51 | East London, South Africa |
| 03 Jun 2000 | versus United States | 25–34 | Manchester, U.S. |
| 20 May 2000 | versus Tonga | 29–11 | Vancouver, Canada |
| 14 Oct 1999 | versus Namibia | 72–11 | Toulouse, France |
| 09 Oct 1999 | versus Fiji | 22–38 | Bordeaux, France |
| 02 Oct 1999 | versus France | 20–33 | Beziers, France |
| 28 Aug 1999 | versus England | 11–36 | London, England |
| 21 Aug 1999 | versus Wales | 19–33 | Cardiff, Wales |
| 03 Jul 1999 | versus Tonga | 10–18 | Nuku A'lofa, Tonga |
| 19 Jun 1999 | versus United States | 17–18 | Toronto, Canada |
| 29 May 1999 | versus Samoa | 13–17 | Vancouver, Canada |
| 15 May 1999 | versus Fiji | 29–40 | Vancouver, Canada |
| 01 May 1999 | versus Japan | 21–23 | Tokyo, Japan |
| 22 Aug 1998 | versus Argentina | 28–54 | Buenos Aires, Argentina |
| 18 Aug 1998 | versus United States | 31–14 | Buenos Aires, Argentina |
| 15 Aug 1998 | versus Uruguay | 38–15 | Buenos Aires, Argentina |
| 21 Jun 1998 | versus Japan | 34–25 | Vancouver, Canada |
| 13 Jun 1998 | versus Hong Kong | 38–12 | Shawnigan Lake, |
| 06 Jun 1998 | versus United States | 37–3 | Burlington, U.S. |
| 23 May 1998 | versus United States | 17–15 | Vancouver, Canada |
| 09 May 1998 | versus Hong Kong | 17–23 | Hong Kong |
| 03 May 1998 | versus Japan | 30–22 | Tokyo, Japan |
| 30 Nov 1997 | versus Ireland | 11–33 | Dublin, Ireland |
| 19 Jul 1997 | versus Wales | 25–28 | Markham, Canada |
| 28 Jun 1997 | versus United States | 22–11 | San Francisco, U.S. |
| 14 Jun 1997 | versus Japan | 42–18 | Vancouver, Canada |
| 07 Jun 1997 | versus Hong Kong | 17–16 | Vancouver, Canada |
| 24 May 1997 | versus Hong Kong | 35–27 | Hong Kong |

*(continued)*

## Canada Test Record *(continued)*

| Date | Match | Score | Location |
|------|-------|-------|----------|
| 18 May 1997 | versus Japan | 31 – 32 | Tokyo, Japan |
| 10 May 1997 | versus United States | 53 – 12 | Vancouver, Canada |
| 21 Sep 1996 | versus Argentina | 21 – 41 | Markham, Canada |
| 18 Sep 1996 | versus United States | 23 – 18 | Hamilton, Canada |
| 14 Sep 1996 | versus Uruguay | 24 – 18 | Nepean, Canada |
| 13 Jul 1996 | versus Japan | 51 – 30 | Vancouver, Canada |
| 06 Jul 1996 | versus Hong Kong | 57 – 9 | Vancouver, Canada |
| 29 Jun 1996 | versus Australia | 9 – 74 | Brisbane, Australia |
| 09 Jun 1996 | versus Japan | 45 – 18 | Tokyo, Japan |
| 01 Jun 1996 | versus Hong Kong | 18 – 12 | Hong Kong |
| 18 May 1996 | versus United States | 24 – 20 | Vancouver, Canada |
| 11 May 1996 | versus United States | 12 – 19 | San Francisco, U.S. |
| 09 Sep 1995 | versus United States | 14 – 15 | Markham, Canada |
| 03 Jun 1995 | versus South Africa | 0 – 20 | Pt Elizabeth, South Africa |
| 31 May 1995 | versus Australia | 11 – 27 | Pt Elizabeth, South Africa |
| 26 May 1995 | versus Romania | 34 – 3 | Pt Elizabeth, South Africa |
| 22 Apr 1995 | versus New Zealand | 7 – 73 | Auckland, New Zealand |
| 08 Apr 1995 | versus Fiji | 22 – 10 | Nadi, Fiji |
| 10 Mar 1995 | versus Argentina | 26 – 29 | Buenos Aires, Argentina |
| 07 Mar 1995 | versus Uruguay | 28 – 9 | Montevideo, Uruguay |
| 21 Jan 1995 | versus Scotland | 6 – 22 | Edinburgh, Scotland |
| 17 Dec 1994 | versus France | 9 – 28 | Besancon, France |
| 10 Dec 1994 | versus England | 19 – 60 | London, England |
| 11 Jun 1994 | versus Wales | 15 – 33 | Markham, Canada |
| 04 Jun 1994 | versus France | 18 – 16 | Nepean, Canada |
| 21 May 1994 | versus United States | 15 – 10 | Long Beach, U.S. |
| 10 Nov 1993 | versus Wales | 26 – 24 | Cardiff, Wales |
| 09 Oct 1993 | versus Australia | 16 – 43 | Calgary, Canada |

| *Date* | *Match* | *Score* | *Location* |
|--------|---------|---------|------------|
| 19 Jun 1993 | versus United States | 20 – 9 | Winnipeg, Canada |
| 05 Jun 1993 | versus England XV (non-cap) | 14 – 19 | Nepean, |
| 29 May 1993 | versus England XV (non-cap) | 15 – 12 | Burnaby, Canada |
| 17 Oct 1992 | versus England | 13 – 26 | London, England |
| 13 Jun 1992 | versus United States | 32 – 9 | Denver, U.S. |
| 20 Oct 1991 | versus New Zealand | 13 – 29 | Lille, France |
| 13 Oct 1991 | versus France | 13 – 19 | Agen, France |
| 09 Oct 1991 | versus Romania | 19 – 11 | Toulouse, France |
| 05 Oct 1991 | versus Fiji | 13 – 3 | Bayonne, France |
| 08 Jun 1991 | versus United States | 34 – 15 | Calgary, Canada |
| 25 May 1991 | versus Scotland XV (non-cap) | 24 – 19 | Saint John, Canada |
| 11 May 1991 | versus Japan | 49 – 26 | Vancouver, Canada |
| 16 Jun 1990 | versus Argentina | 19 – 15 | Buenos Aires, Argentina |
| 09 Jun 1990 | versus United States | 12 – 14 | Seattle, U.S. |
| 30 Mar 1990 | versus Argentina | 15 – 6 | Burnaby, Canada |
| 23 Sep 1989 | versus United States | 21 – 3 | Toronto, Canada |
| 02 Sep 1989 | versus Ireland XV (non-cap) | 21 – 24 | Victoria, Canada |
| 11 Jun 1988 | versus United States | 16 – 28 | Saranac Lake, U.S. |
| 14 Nov 1987 | versus United States | 20 – 12 | Victoria, Canada |
| 03 Jun 1987 | versus Wales | 9 – 40 | Invercargill, New Zealand |
| 30 May 1987 | versus Ireland | 19 – 46 | Dunedin, New Zealand |
| 24 May 1987 | versus Tonga | 37 – 4 | Napier, New Zealand |
| 10 May 1987 | versus United States | 33 – 9 | Vancouver, Canada |
| 08 Nov 1986 | versus United States | 27 – 16 | Tucson, U.S. |
| 07 Jun 1986 | versus Japan | 21 – 26 | Burnaby, Canada |

*(continued)*

## Canada Test Record *(continued)*

| Date | Match | Score | Location |
|------|-------|-------|----------|
| 16 Nov 1985 | versus United States | 21 – 10 | Vancouver, Canada |
| 23 Jun 1985 | versus Australia | 15 – 43 | Brisbane, Australia |
| 15 Jun 1985 | versus Australia | 3 – 59 | Sydney, Australia |
| 09 Jun 1984 | versus United States | 13 – 21 | Chicago, U.S. |
| 15 Oct 1983 | versus England XV (non-cap) | 0 – 27 | London, England |
| 01 Jul 1983 | versus Italy | 9 – 37 | Toronto, Canada |
| 25 Jun 1983 | versus Italy | 19 – 13 | Burnaby, Canada |
| 11 Jun 1983 | versus United States | 15 – 9 | Burnaby, Canada |
| 12 Jun 1982 | versus United States | 3 – 3 | Albany, U.S. |
| 29 May 1982 | versus England XV (non-cap) | 6 – 43 | Burnaby, Canada |
| 18 Apr 1982 | versus Japan | 6 – 16 | Tokyo, Japan |
| 11 Apr 1982 | versus Japan | 18 – 24 | Osaka, Japan |
| 03 Oct 1981 | versus Argentina | 0 – 35 | Buenos Aires, Argentina |
| 06 Jun 1981 | versus United States | 6 – 3 | Calgary, Canada |
| 11 Oct 1980 | versus New Zealand XV (non-cap) | 10 – 43 | Burnaby, |
| 08 Jun 1980 | versus United States | 16 – 0 | Saranac Lake, U.S. |
| 24 May 1980 | versus Wales XV (non-cap) | 7 – 24 | Burnaby, Canada |
| 29 Sep 1979 | versus France XV (non-cap) | 15 – 34 | Paris, France |
| 09 Jun 1979 | versus United States | 19 – 12 | Toronto, Canada |
| 30 Sep 1978 | versus France XV (non-cap) | 9 – 24 | Calgary, Canada |
| 28 May 1978 | versus United States | 7 – 12 | Baltimore, U.S. |
| 11 Jun 1977 | versus England Under-23 | 9 – 29 | Toronto, Canada |

| Date | Match | Score | Location |
|------|-------|-------|----------|
| 04 Jun 1977 | versus England Under-23 | 13 – 26 | Ottawa, Canada |
| 21 May 1977 | versus United States | 17 – 6 | Burnaby, Canada |
| 12 Jun 1976 | versus Barbarians | 4 – 29 | Toronto, Canada |
| 25 Oct 1974 | versus Tonga | 14 – 40 | Vancouver, Canada |
| 09 Jun 1973 | versus Wales XV (non-cap) | 20 – 58 | Toronto, Canada |
| 02 Oct 1971 | versus Wales XV (non-cap) | 10 – 56 | Cardiff, Wales |
| 28 Nov 1970 | versus Fiji | 17 – 35 | Burnaby, Canada |
| 30 Sep 1967 | versus England XV (non-cap) | 0 – 29 | Vancouver, Canada |
| 17 Sep 1966 | versus British Lions XV (non-cap) | 8 – 19 | Toronto, Canada |
| 01 Dec 1962 | versus Wales Under-23 | 0 – 8 | Cardiff, Wales |
| 17 Nov 1962 | versus Barbarians | 3 – 3 | Gosforth, England |
| 11 Feb 1932 | versus Japan | 5 – 38 | Tokyo, Japan |
| 31 Jan 1932 | versus Japan | 8 – 9 | Osaka, Japan |

# Appendix B

# Glossary

**ACT Brumbies:** Australian Super 14 team based in Canberra in the Australian Capital Territory. In 2001 they became the only non-Kiwi team to win the Super 12 title.

**advantage:** Occurs when a referee allows play to continue even though there has been an infringement. The referee gives the non-offending team the chance to do something positive with the ball. If the team is unable to do so, the referee goes back to the site of the original infraction and restarts play with the appropriate method. The goal of advantage is to minimize stoppages and keep play flowing.

**age-grade rugby:** The term for all rugby from ages 6–18.

**Air New Zealand Cup:** Used to be called the National Provincial Championship (NPC). New Zealand's top domestic competition. Contested by 14 provincial unions in the first division and 12 in the second; called the Heartland Championship.

**ankle tap:** When a defender attempts to stop a ball-carrier by tapping him on the ankle from behind in an attempt to bring him down. This is a last-ditch, desperation tackle.

**back row:** The third line of the scrum, comprising a number 8 and two flankers. These three are known as back-rowers.

**back three:** The fullback and the two wingers.

**backs:** Numbers 9–15; generally faster players.

**ball-carrier:** The player carrying the ball.

**binding:** Firmly grasping another player's body from the shoulder to the hips with the whole arm from hand to shoulder.

**Bledisloe Cup:** Trophy played for by Australia and New Zealand, usually in an annual series. Named after the former Governor General of New Zealand, Lord Bledisloe.

**blindside:** The area between the ball and the closest sideline.

**blindside flanker:** The flanker who binds onto the scrum on the blindside, usually wears number 6, except in South Africa.

**blood bin:** If a player is bleeding, he must leave the field of play until the wound is covered or dressed. While he is being treated he is said to be in the blood bin — but it's not an actual place.

**Blues:** Auckland-based Super 14 team, encompassing the Auckland, North Harbour, and Northland Unions. Three-time champions with titles in 1996, 1997, and 2003. One of five New Zealand franchises in the competition.

**bomb:** A high kick generally aimed at the opposition fullback in the hope that under pressure he'll drop it and lose possession.

**box kick:** A high kick aimed to land in front of the opposition winger, usually taken by the scrumhalf.

**breakaway:** Another name for flankers who wear numbers 6 and 7. They bind on the side of the scrum and break away when the scrum is over. Their primary jobs are to win the ball at rucks and mauls and to make tackles.

**breakdown:** When play transitions from one phase to another, usually because of a tackle and the resultant struggle for possession.

**Bulls:** South African Super 14 team based in Pretoria. Formerly called the Blue Bulls.

**Calcutta Cup:** A trophy crafted from melted Indian silver rupees played for annually by England and Scotland as part of the Six Nations.

**caps:** A term used to denote the number of times an individual has played for his national team in a test match. When someone is said to have 22 caps for the United States, it means that he has played in 22 tests for the Eagles.

**Carisbrook Stadium:** Located in Dunedin, New Zealand. The home of the Highlanders, Otago, and the scene of numerous All Blacks triumphs. Also known as the House of Pain and frequented by Otago University students who are known as Scarfies. Set to be replaced in time for Rugby World Cup 2011.

**centers:** The players wearing number 12 (inside center) and number 13 (outside center). They are the heart and soul of a team's attack. Also called the midfielders.

**channel:** The path a ball takes when coming back through the scrum between the legs of the forwards.

**charge down:** The blocking of a kick by an opposing player.

**Cheetahs:** New South African Super 14 team based in Bloemfontein. Used to be part of the Cats franchise and were awarded their own team when the Super 14 expanded in 2006.

**Chiefs:** New Zealand Super 14 team based in Hamilton in the Waikato region. Also includes the Bay of Plenty, Counties-Manukau, King Country, and Thames Valley unions.

**chip kick:** A short kick, usually directed over the top of the opposition's defensive line, hopefully to be regathered by the kicker or a teammate.

**clearing kick:** A kick aimed to go over the touchline as a way of relieving pressure and gaining territory.

**Colts rugby:** The under-19 age group level before adult rugby.

**conversion:** After a try is scored, the attacking team is given a kick at goal from a spot in line with where the try was touched down. If good, it's worth two points, making a converted try good for seven total.

**counter attack:** An attacking move in response to an opposition attack when the ball has changed possession.

**cross kick:** A kick across the field aimed toward the attacking team's openside winger, who plans to run through the defense and regather the ball.

**crossbar:** The bar joining the two uprights of the goalposts. For a conversion or penalty goal to be successful it has to go over the crossbar.

**Crusaders:** Christchurch-based Super 14 team that is made up mostly of Canterbury players but also includes the provincial unions of Nelson Bays, Marlborough, Buller, West Coast, Mid Canterbury, and South Canterbury. The franchise won three straight championships from 1998–2000, and has now won a total of six titles, including a perfect season in 2002.

**Currie Cup:** The name of the competition and the trophy awarded to the winner of South Africa's premier provincial competition. Originally given by Sir Donald Currie, a Scotsman who donated it as a cricket trophy.

**cut-out pass:** A pass that deliberately misses one or more players and goes to the next player in the attacking line.

**dead:** Means that the ball is out of play. This occurs when the ball has gone outside the playing area and remained there, or when the referee has blown the whistle to indicate a stoppage, or when a conversion kick is being taken.

**dead-ball line:** The farthest lines at the back of the in-goal areas at both ends of the field.

**decoy:** A player who pretends that he is about to receive the ball in an attempt to deceive the opposition's defensive line.

**defense:** Used by one team to stop another when it is attacking.

**dive pass:** Passing the ball while diving toward the person for whom the pass is intended.

**drawing the man:** Making an opponent commit to tackling you just before you pass to a teammate.

**drift defense:** A defensive system that has the defending players drift sideways across the field.

**driving maul:** A maul where the opposition is driven back through sheer force and coordination.

**driving tackle:** When the tackler pushes the ball-carrier backward.

**drop goal:** When a player kicks the ball over the opposition's crossbar during general play. The ball must hit the ground before being kicked. It is worth three points.

**drop kick:** A type of kick where the ball hits the ground first, used for a drop goal or to restart play after a score or at the beginning of a half.

**drop out:** A drop kick used to restart play from a team's 22-meter line.

**Eden Park:** Stadium in Auckland, New Zealand. Home of the Blues, Auckland, and site of the 1987 World Cup final. More All Blacks tests have been played there than any other venue.

**EDF Energy Cup:** The English/Welsh knockout cup, which dates back to 1972 under a variety of sponsors.

**Ellis Park:** Stadium in Johannesburg, South Africa, and scene of many Springbok victories since 1928. Home of the Lions in both the Super 14 and the Currie Cup, and site of the 1995 World Cup Final.

**Ellis, William Webb:** The alleged creator of rugby. In 1823 Ellis, a student at the Rugby School, reportedly picked up a ball and ran with it during a soccer game, thus inspiring a new form of football called rugby. No evidence actually supports the account, similar to Abner Doubleday supposedly founding baseball in Cooperstown.

**European Cup:** A 24-team tournament featuring club and provincial sides from England, France, Ireland, Italy, Scotland, and Wales. Sponsored for many years by Heineken.

**feed:** The placing of the ball into the scrum by the scrumhalf.

**fend:** When an attacking player uses an arm to push away a defender. The same as a straight-arm in American or Canadian football.

**field goal:** Another name for a drop goal.

**five-eighth:** Another name for the flyhalf, used in Australia and New Zealand.

**five-meter scrum:** A scrum that is set 5 meters from the tryline.

**flick pass:** A quick pass to a teammate. The player throwing the ball flicks his wrists to quicken the pace of the ball.

**flyhalf:** The back who wears jersey number 10. The flyhalf is one of the most important players in the team, often dictating the flow of play.

**forward pass:** An illegal pass that travels forward when released.

**foul play:** Play deemed by the referee to be illegal. The offending player is penalized or, in serious cases, given a yellow or red card.

**free kick:** A kick awarded to a team for a minor penalty.

**front row:** The forwards in the first line of the scrum, the loose-head prop, the hooker, and the tight-head prop. These players are called front-rowers.

**fullback:** The back who wears the number 15 jersey, who is the last line of defense.

**fulltime:** The end of the game.

**Garryowen:** A high kick, also known as an up and under, designed to be chased and taken. Named after the Irish club renowned for using the tactic.

**goal:** A successful kick between the goalposts.

**goal kicker:** The designated player in the team who has the task of kicking conversions and penalty goals.

**goal line:** The line that has to be reached for a team to score a try. For this reason, the goal line is often called the tryline.

**Grand Slam:** The term used in the Six Nations when one country beats all its opponents during the tournament. (Also applies to touring sides if they beat all the Home Unions.)

**grubber kick:** A kick that travels along the ground and bounces unpredictably.

**Guinness Premiership:** The English domestic competition, with 12 teams that play home and away.

**halfback:** Another term for scrumhalf.

**halfback pass:** A fast, accurate pass thrown by the halfback.

**halfway line:** Marks the middle of the field where the game is started and also restarted after tries or successful penalty goals.

**halves:** The term used for the scrumhalf and flyhalf.

**Heineken Cup:** Named after its sponsor, this is another name for the European Cup.

**high tackle:** A dangerous tackle that hits the opponent above the line of the shoulders. Punished with either a penalty or a yellow or red card depending upon the severity of the tackle.

**Highlanders:** Dunedin, New Zealand–based Super 14 team made up of the Otago, North Otago, and Southland provincial unions.

**hit and spin:** When the ball-carrier commits himself to being tackled and then spins out of the tackle.

**Home Nations:** England, Ireland, Scotland, Wales.

**hooker:** The forward in the number 2 jersey, who is a central figure. In the front row of the scrum he is supported by the two props and hooks the ball backward. In the line-out he throws the ball in.

**hospital pass:** A badly timed pass that puts the person catching the ball in great danger as it arrives just before he is about to be smashed by an opponent.

**Hurricanes:** Super 14 team based in Wellington, New Zealand. Comprises the East Coast, Poverty Bay, Hawkes Bay, Wairarapa-Bush, Wellington, Horowhenua-Kapiti, Manawatu, Wanganui, and Taranaki provincial unions.

**infringement:** Occurs when a team is guilty of breaking a law, prompting the referee to blow the whistle, or play advantage.

**injury time:** During a match the referee stops the clock whenever play is halted for an injured player. After normal time has finished (40 minutes each half), play continues for the amount of time lost for the injury stoppages.

**inside center:** The back who wears number 12. Also known as the second five-eighth in Australia and New Zealand.

**International Rugby Board (IRB):** The governing body that controls the world game, runs the World Cup, and determines the laws of the game.

**judiciary committee:** A group of officials (usually three) who determine whether a player should be suspended and for how long after serious incidents on the field of play.

**kickoff:** Used to start a game. One team kicks the ball from the center of the halfway line to the opposition.

**knock-on:** A knock-on occurs when a player loses possession of the ball and it goes forward. Or, when a player hits the ball forward with the hand or arm, or when the ball hits the hand or arm and goes forward, and then the ball touches the ground or another player before the original player can catch it.

**Lansdowne Road:** Ireland's national rugby stadium in Dublin. It's the oldest venue in world rugby and a fantastic place to watch a match. Currently being rebuilt.

**lifting:** When a player is helped into the air by his teammates, either to secure a line-out or a restart kick.

**line-out:** How play is restarted when the ball goes into touch, or out of bounds. The two sets of forwards line up in a row beside each other and the team with the ball throws it in. The throw must go straight down the middle of the tunnel formed by the two rows.

**Lions:** Johannesburg–based South African Super 14 team. Used to be called the Cats. They play their home matches at Ellis Park.

**lob pass:** A high, looping pass, aimed to go over the heads of the opposition.

**locks:** The two forwards who wear jerseys number 4 and 5. Usually the tallest players in the team, the locks are charged with providing strength in the scrum and winning the ball in the line-outs. Together they form the second row or the engine room.

**loitering:** Refers to someone who is standing or jogging in an offside position, preventing the opposing team from playing the ball as they wish.

**loop:** When a player runs around a teammate to whom he has just passed in the hope of receiving the ball back from him.

**loose-head prop:** The prop on the left hand side of the scrum, closest to his scrumhalf when his team is putting the ball in the scrum.

**loosie:** A term used for the three members of the back row: the number 8 and the two flankers. So called because they are supposed to be the first to the loose ball.

**Magners League:** An Irish, Scottish, and Welsh competition meant to rival the Guinness Premiership. Twelve teams play in a home-and-away format.

**man-on-man defense:** A form of defense where the tackler takes on the man directly opposite him.

**mark:** A player who catches a kick inside his own 22-meter line while calling "mark" can be awarded a free kick by the referee.

**match ball:** The high-quality rugby ball used in a match.

**maul:** A maul occurs when a player carrying the ball is held by one or more opponents, and one or more of the ball-carrier's teammates bind on the ball-carrier. All the players involved are on their feet and moving toward a goal line. Open play has ended.

**Millennium Stadium:** Welsh national stadium in Cardiff; has a retractable roof. Site of the 1999 World Cup final.

**Murrayfield:** Scottish national rugby stadium located in Edinburgh. Opened in 1925 with a Scotland victory over England.

**Newlands:** Stadium in Cape Town, South Africa. Home to the Stormers and Western Province.

**obstruction:** Unfairly getting in the way of an opposing player.

**offside:** A player is offside if he is in front of a teammate who is carrying the ball or in front of a teammate who last played the ball. Offside means that a player is temporarily out of the game. Such players are liable to be penalized if they take part in the game.

**Olympic Stadium:** Now known as Telstra Stadium, the Sydney venue was the site of the 2003 World Cup final and also holds the world record for a crowd at a test match with 109,874 for an Australia–versus–New Zealand clash in 2000.

**onside:** A player is onside if he is behind a teammate who has the ball. An onside player can participate fully in the match.

**openside:** The area between the ball and the farthest sideline.

**openside flanker:** The flanker who binds on the openside of the scrum and usually wears number 7.

**outside center:** The back who wears jersey number 13.

**overlap:** When a team has more players in an attacking line than the opposition.

**pack:** The term for the entire group of forwards.

**pass:** When a player throws the ball to a teammate.

**peel:** When a forward runs around the front or back of the line-out to take the ball upfield from a catch or tap.

**penalty:** When the referee rules that a team is guilty of an indiscretion or has contravened the laws of the game he awards a penalty to the non-offending team.

**penalty kick:** When a team chooses to kick at goal after it has been awarded a penalty.

**penalty try:** When the referee believes a team would have scored if not for the opposition's illegal play, he can award the try anyway.

**pick-and-go:** A forward charge where the ball is placed on the ground at the tackle and another forward quickly picks it up and continues the attack.

**pill:** Another name for the ball.

**props:** The two forwards who wear jerseys number 1 (loose-head) and number 3 (tight-head). They support the hooker in the scrums and lift the jumpers in the line-out.

**punt kick:** The most common form of kick used in a match.

**pushover try:** A try that happens during a scrum when the pack is able to keep the ball under their feet and push the opposition scrum across the tryline.

**quick throw-in:** When the ball is thrown in before the line-out forms.

**red card:** The card shown to a player when the referee is sending him off for the rest of the match.

**Reds:** Australian Super 14 team based in Brisbane, Queensland. They play at Suncorp Stadium.

**referee:** Person appointed to officiate a match by the organizers. Called "Sir" by the players, but also known as the whistle-blower.

**reserve bench:** The name given to the place where the replacements sit during the match.

**restart kick:** The kick that restarts play at each half and after points have been scored.

**ruck:** When one or more players from each team, who are on their feet and in contact, close around the ball on the ground. Once a ruck has been formed, players cannot use their hands to get the ball but are allowed to use their feet.

**scissors pass:** Passing to a teammate who cuts back in the opposite direction in a bid to disorient the opposition.

**screw punt:** A form of punt where the ball spirals in the air, which increases the distance it travels.

**scrum:** Players from each team come together in a formation, where eight forwards bind in against eight opposing forwards, with the aim of winning the ball which is thrown in between the front rows of the two packs.

**scrum machine:** An apparatus used at training where teams practice their scrummaging skills.

**scrumhalf:** The player wearing jersey number 9, who puts the ball into the scrum and usually distributes it from scrums, rucks, mauls, and line-outs. Also called a halfback.

**second row:** Another name for lock.

**sevens:** An abbreviated form of rugby where just seven players play on a full field for seven minutes a half.

**Sharks:** South African Super 14 team based in Durban with most players coming from Natal province. They play their matches at ABSA Stadium, also called the Shark Tank.

**shortened line-out:** When the team throwing the ball in decides to have fewer than seven players in the line-out.

**shove:** When the players in an attacking scrum push in unison.

**side:** Another name for a team.

**sideline:** The same as the touchline.

**side-on tackle:** A tackle used when a ball-carrier is trying to run in between defenders.

**sidestep:** A way to evade a tackler by stepping to one side and then quickly to the other.

**sin bin:** The referee can send players to the sin bin for ten minutes if they are guilty of foul play, a repeated infringement, or a professional foul. The sin bin is usually a seat on the sideline where the player waits for his time to expire so he can reenter the match.

**Six Nations:** The oldest annual tournament in international rugby, involving England, France, Ireland, Italy, Scotland, and Wales.

**spiral pass:** A pass where the player imparts spin on the ball to improve its trajectory.

**squad:** A group of players who make up a rugby team. A squad usually is made up of 22 team members.

**Stade de France:** New home of the Tricolors in Paris, where France plays their home fixtures.

**Stormers:** Super 14 team made up mostly of players from Western Province in South Africa. They play their matches at Newlands Stadium in Cape Town.

**Super 14:** The annual tournament involving the 14 best provincial teams from South Africa (5), Australia (4), and New Zealand (5). Used to be the Super 12 until 2006, when two teams were added.

**support:** Following the ball-carrier in order to help if he is tackled or needs to pass.

**swerve:** A form of run where the attacking player attempts to swerve past his opponents.

**tackle:** Where a player brings an opponent carrying the ball down to the ground.

**tackle area:** The general area in which a tackle has been made, usually defined as several meters around where the player has been brought to ground.

**television match official (TMO):** During most televised matches, the TMO can be asked by the referee to assist on in-goal decisions.

**throw-in:** When the ball is thrown into the line-out.

**tight five:** The term given to the three front-rowers and the two second-rowers.

**tight-head:** The prop on the right-hand side of the scrum who packs in on the opposite side of where his scrumhalf puts the ball in. This player is the anchor of the scrum. "Winning a tight-head" happens when the team that didn't put the ball in is able to win possession.

**touch judges:** These two officials assist the referee during the course of the game. They patrol either sideline and determine the exact position where line-out throws are taken, check whether teams are offside, watch for foul play, and decide whether penalty goals and conversions are successful.

**touchline:** The two lines situated on either side of the field. A ball is described as going "into touch" when it crosses either of these two lines and goes out of the field of play.

**training ball:** The type of rugby ball used for training purposes.

**Tri Nations:** An annual tournament involving Australia, New Zealand, and South Africa that began in 1996.

**Triple Crown:** The term used in the Six Nations if one of the Home Unions (England, Scotland, Ireland, or Wales) beats all the others during a season.

**try:** The grounding of the ball by an attacking player in the opposition's in-goal area. It is worth five points.

**tryline:** The line marked at either end of the field of play that must be crossed to score a try. Also called the goal line.

**Twickenham:** Home of the Rugby Football Union in London; where England plays their home matches.

**up and under:** A tactical kick that goes high in the air and tests the catching ability of the opposition as defenders run at him. Also called a Garryowen.

**Waratahs:** Sydney-based Australian Super 14 team. They play their home matches at Aussie Stadium.

**Western Force:** New Australian Super 14 team based in Perth. They play their home matches at Subiaco Oval.

**wheel:** When a scrum turns more than 90 degrees.

**wing:** The two attacking players that wear jersey numbers 11 and 14, who play closest to the touchline and are usually the fastest on the team.

**Wooden Spoon:** The term used in many tournaments to designate the last-place team.

**yellow card:** A card shown to a player by the referee if that player is considered guilty of foul play, a professional foul, or a repeated infringement. Results in a ten-minute suspension in the sin bin.

# Index

••••••••••••••••••••••••••••••••••••••••••••••••

## • A •

ABSA Currie Cup, 225
accidentally offside, 88
adaptation, 175, 176
adapting to weather, 175
advantage law, 85–86
agility, 188
Air New Zealand Cup, 224–225
Allied Dunbar Premiership, 225
altitude, 174
amateur rugby. *See* club rugby
amateurism, 11
American Rugby News, 307
Amin, Idi, 328
analyzing the opponent, 172–174
Anitoni, Vaea, 316
ankle tap, 166
annual calendar
  how the game is organized, 213–215
  international calendar, 216–221
  interprovincial and provincial
    competition, 221–226
Argentina, 204, 325
assistant coach, 267–268
athleticism, 54
attacks
  aim of, 63
  attack plans, 177–179
  breaking through, 178–179
  effective attacks, 178
  fullbacks and, 63
  mauls. *See* mauls
  mountaineering, 106
  offensive attacks, 178
  from the ruck, 106
  from the scrum, 123–124
Australia
  1999 World Cup semifinal #1, 206
  2000 test match *vs.* New Zealand, 218
  2003 World Cup final, 205, 320–321
  Bledisloe Cup, 219, 319–320
Australian Wallabies, 161
awarded a penalty. *See* taking penalties

## • B •

Baa-Baas, 220–221
back foot, 126
back line
  centers, 60–61
  described, 29, 58
  flyhalf, 59–60
  fullback, 62–63
  inside center, 60
  outside center, 61
  scrumhalf, 58–59
  wings, 62
back row, 56–58, 117–118
backs, 48
backs coach, 267
balanced diet, 192
ball, 34–35
ball-and-all tackle, 166
ball handling skills, 82
Barbarian Football Club, 220–221, 321–322
Barclays Churchill Cup, 239
barred gear, 43–44
basic skills. *See* skills
basics of rugby
  the field, 19–23
  the players, 29–32
  scoring, 23–27
  terminology, 20
  timekeeping, 27–29
Baugh, Dan, 317
Bautris, Uldis, 202
being match fit. *See* fitness
best rugby moments
  international, 319–323
  North American rugby, 323–325

Bevan, Derek, 284
binding, 121–122
birth of rugby, 9–11
bizarre injuries, 330
Bladen, Hugh, 295
Bledisloe Cup, 161, 219, 319–320
blindside, 124
blindside flanker, 30, 56–57
blocking the advance, 179–181
Bloom, Russ, 252
boots, 38, 39
*Boots 'n All* (Haden), 304
Bray, Gordon, 295
break. *See* flankers
breakaway. *See* flankers
breakdown, 83, 103–104, 177
breaking through, 178–179
British & Irish Lions, 219–220
brought to ground, 102
Bush, George W., 328

● *C* ●

cable companies, 291
calling the play, 132–133
Campese, David, 148
Canada
  *vs.* Argentina, 2005, 325
  birth of Rugby Canada, 236–237
  club rugby, 246–248
  coaching certification, 273
  collegiate rugby, 255
  development of rugby, 235–236
  *vs.* France, 1994, 324
  high school rugby, 256
  National Women's League, 238
  referee, becoming a, 284–285
  Rugby Canada Super League, 238
  sevens rugby, 238
  televised rugby, 291
  *vs.* Wales, 1993, 325
  women's rugby, 237
  youth rugby, 256
Canadian Interuniversity Sport (CIS), 255
Canadian Rugby News, 307
Canterbury Mokos, 39

cap, 301
Capostagno, Andy, 295
cardiovascular endurance, 187
Catcheside, Carston, 328
Celtic League, 223–224
centers, 60–61
*Championship Rugby,* 290
Charron, Al, 313
chip kick, 157–158
Christie, Sommer, 318
Clark, Greg, 294
clearing kick, 155
cleats, 38, 39
Clinton, Bill, 328
club rugby
  Canada, 246–248
  Canadian national championships, 247–248
  coaching, 276–277
  finding the right club to join, 246
  Rugby Canada Super League, 246–247
  spectators, 301–302
  United States, 241–245
  USA club championships, 245
  USA Rugby Super League, 243–245
Coach Development Program (CDP), 271, 272
coaching
  advancement, 274–277
  assistant coach, 267–268
  backs coach, 267
  club rugby, 276–277
  collegiate rugby, 275–276
  communication, 266
  criteria, 265
  defense coach, 268
  described, 16
  fit team, 261
  forwards coach, 267
  head coach, 267
  high school, 275
  improving skill levels, 260–261
  knowledge of laws, 69
  making of a good coach, 260–261
  motivation, 261
  "play to the whistle," 86

requirements, 264–265
roles of the coach, 264
safety, 262–264
self-assessment, 266
support staff, 267–269
three-man coaching structure, 267
tough job of, 264–265
youth players, 274–275
coaching certification
  Canada, 273
  Coach Development Program (CDP),
      271, 272
  International Rugby Academy, 273–274
  United States, 271–272
codes, 133, 134
collapsing, 122
collegiate rugby
  Canada, 255
  coaching, 275–276
  United States, 249–250
commentators, 294–295
communication, 266, 280–281
community coach course, 273
compression shorts, 42
consistency, 280
containing the stars, 173
continuation of play, 85–86
conversion kicks, 25
converting a try, 24–25
Courage Leagues, 225
Crawford, Jen, 315
creating space, 80
crossbar, 22
Crosse, Doug, 307
crouch, 119
the Crusaders, 180
Currie, Sir Donald, 225
Currie Cup, 225
cut-out pass, 152

**• D •**

Dahlgren, Bill, 252
Dallaglio, Lawrence, 220
dash lines, 21
Dawes, John, 266

Dawson, Matt, 205
dead-ball line, 21
defense
  blocking the advance, 179–181
  commitment, 179, 182
  coordinating the defense, 179
  drift defense, 180–181
  goal of, 179
  man-on-man defense, 180
  trust, 182
defense coach, 268
defensive systems, 179–181
developmental coach course, 273
diet, 191–193
dive pass, 154
Dowd, Craig, 161
drawing the defender, 150–151
drift defense, 180–181
driving in and up, 122
driving maul, 110–111
drop kick, 26, 98, 159
drop-kicking goals, 26–27
dropped (drop) goal, 26
dropped goal, 12
droppie, 26
Duff, Tom, 252
dummy, 149
dummying, 123
Dwyer, Bob, 265
dynamic stretch routine, 186

**• E •**

Eales, John, 161, 218
Edwards, Gareth, 266
eight-man push, 173
Elizabeth, Queen of England, 334
Ellis, William Webb, 9, 10–11
energy drinks, 193
engage, 119
engagement, 119–121
engine room, 55
England (2003 World Cup final),
      205, 320–321
English League, 225–226
errors. *See* mistakes

etiquette, 298–299
European Cup, 213
exercise. *See* fitness
exploiting weaknesses, 173

Fall tests, 219
false security, 263–264
feeding, 123
fending off, 147
the field
  dash lines, 21
  dead-ball line, 21
  described, 11–12
  dimensions of playing area, 19–20
  field of play, 20
  5-meter line, 21
  flags, 22–23
  goal lines, 12, 21
  goalposts, 22–23
  halfway line, 12, 20
  illustration, 22f
  in-goal areas, 20
  lines, 20–21
  playing area, 20
  10-meter line, 20
  touch-in-goal line, 21
  touchline, 21
  22-meter lines, 12, 21
field of play, 20
15-meter dash line, 21
finals tournaments, 201–202
first-phase possession, 177
first receiver. *See* flyhalf
fitness. *See also* training
  agility, 188
  cardiovascular endurance, 187
  developing a fitness program, 187–189
  dynamic stretch routine, 186
  interval training, 188
  need for, 183–184
  referees, 282
  sprint training, 187–188
  stamina, 187
  static stretching after training, 186–187

strength, 188–189
stretching for performance, 185–187
stretching routine, 184–185
variation in routines, 189
warming up, 184–185
Zen Theory of Rugby Fitness, 190
Fitzpatrick, Sean, 273
FitzSimons, Peter, 304
5-meter dash line, 21
5-meter line, 21
flags, 22–23
flankers
  blindside flanker, 30, 56–57
  openside flanker, 30, 56, 57
  role of, 56
  in scrum, 117–118
flat pass, 79
Flatley, Elton, 205
flexibility, 184
Florence, Gillian, 315
Flores, Kathy, 317
flyhalf, 30, 59–60
footwear, 38, 39
forming a line-out, 132
forward pass, 82
forwards
  back row, 56–58
  blindside flanker, 56–57
  described, 50
  flankers, 56–57
  front-rowers, 52–55
  hooker, 54–55
  locks, 55–56
  loose-head prop, 52–54
  number 8, 58
  openside flanker, 56, 57
  props, 52–54
  second-rowers, 55–56
  tight five, 51–52
  tight-head prop, 52–54
forwards coach, 267
Foster, Julie, 318
foul play
  identification of, 73
  misconduct, 93

obstruction, 92
parts of foul play law, 92
repeated infringements, 93
taking penalties, 94–95
unfair play, 93
France
  1999 World Cup semifinal #2, 207
  *vs.* Canada, 1994, 324
  Top 14, 226
  *vs.* U.S. Olympians, 324–325
free kicks, 95
front-on driving tackle, 163–164
front row, 52–55, 115–117
full international. *See* test match
full scrum, 121
fullback, 31, 62–63
fundamentals of the game
  advantage law, 85–86
  errors, 81–82
  foul play law, 92–95
  kicking, 79–80
  object of the game, 78
  offside law, 87–92
  passing, 79
  running, 79
  tackle law, 82–84

### • G •

game plan, 168–174, 176–177
gap, 132
Garryowen, 156–157
gear
  "Approved Clothing," 41
  barred gear, 43–44
  finding gear in North America, 40
  kicking tees, 35–36
  kit bag essentials, 33–36
  pads, 36
  rugby ball, 34–35
  rugby boots, 38, 39
  rugby jerseys, 37
  rugby shorts, 37
  rugby socks, 39
  safety gear, 12, 40–44
Georgia Lelos, 204
global differences in position names, 50

goal kicker
  converting a try, 24–25
  round-the-corner style, 160
  specialist goal kicker, 26
goal kicking, 160–161
goal lines, 12, 21
goalposts, 22–23
Godfree, Michael, 114, 276
goose step, 148
Grand Slam, 216
greatest North American players, 311–318
Gregan, George, 218
Gross, Luke, 317
grubber kick, 158
Guevara, Che, 327
Guinness Premiership, 225, 226

### • H •

Haden, Andy, 304
halfback. *See* scrumhalf
halfway dash line, 21
halfway line, 12, 20
Harrison, Miles, 294
head coach, 267
headgear, 41
Heineken Cup, 222–223
Hercus, Mike, 316
high ball, 63
high-performance coach course, 273
high school rugby
  Canada, 256
  coaching, 275
  United States, 252–253
hit-and-spin, 148
Hodges, Dave, 159, 314
hookers, 30, 54–55, 117, 120, 134–135
hooter, 28–29
horn, 28–29
hospital pass, 80

### • I •

information about rugby. *See* learning
  about rugby
in-goal areas, 20
injuries, 28, 263–264, 330

injury prevention, 42–43, 262–263
inside center, 30, 60
inside half. *See* scrumhalf
intentional mistakes, 82
international calendar
  Barbarian Football Club, 220–221
  Barclays Churchill Cup, 239
  British & Irish Lions, 219–220
  Fall tests, 219
  North America 4 (NA4), 239
  North American internationals, 238–239
  SANZAR home tests, 217
  Six Nations, 216–217
  test match, 216
  Tri Nations Series, 217–219
  World Sevens Series, 221
international differences in position
    names, 50
International Rugby Academy (IRANZ),
    273–274
International Rugby Board (IRB)
  assessment of referees, 280
  described, 214
  founding of, 214
  gear standards, 41
  international test schedule, 214
  kicking restarts, 98
  lifting an opponent, 122
  pads, standards for, 36
  safety gear, 43
  structure of, 66
  tackle laws, 83
  test match, 300
  Web sites, 307–308
  World Cup competitions, creation of, 211
  World Cup qualification structure, 201
Internet rugby, 292, 305–308
interprovincial and provincial competition
  ABSA Currie Cup, 225
  Air New Zealand Cup, 224–225
  Celtic League, 223–224
  described, 221–222
  English domestic game, 225–226
  Heineken Cup, 222–223
  Magners League, 223

Super 14, 222
Top 14, 226
interval training, 188
introductory coach course, 273
Irish position names, 50

**• J •**

Jablonski, Dennis, 317
James, Mike, 314
jersey numbers, 30–31, 48–49
jerseys, 37
Jervey, Patty, 315
jewelry removal, 43
jock straps, 42
Johnson, Tony, 295
jumpers, 136

**• K •**

Karvoski, Ellie, 317
Kearns, Phil, 295
Kelly, Bo, 69
kicking. *See also* kicks
  to advance the ball, 79–80
  in field position, 80
  goal kicking, 160–161
  as necessary skill, 14–15
  out of bounds, 129
  skills, 154–161
  through the mark, 95
  for touch, 94
kicking game, 189
kicking tees, 35–36
kickoffs, 98–100, 170
kicks. *See also* kicking
  chip kick, 157–158
  clearing kick, 155
  drop kick, 98, 159
  free kicks, 95
  Garryowen, 156–157
  grubber kick, 158
  high ball, 63
  the kick that won the game, 160, 161
  long kicks, 80
  medium kicks, 80

penalty kick, 94, 129
restart kicks, 100–101
short kicks, 80
spiral punt, 155–156
up and under, 63, 156–157
kit bag essentials, 33–36
Knight, Phaedra, 317
knock-on, 81–82
Kronfeld, Josh, 107

### • *L* •

Laban, Ken, 295
Lacasse, Josée, 318
Larkham, Stephen, 205, 206, 218
late charge, 93
Latvia, 215
law book, 68
laws of the game. *See* rugby laws
lazy runner, 89
learning about rugby
   North American magazines, 303–305
   rugby books, 304
   on the Web, 305–308
letting the ball do the work, 151
lifters, 137
lifting an opponent, 122
lifting in the line-out, 67
line of touch, 132
line-out
   calling the play, 132–133
   codes, 133, 134
   defense, 132
   described, 20, 127
   directly into touch, 129
   element of surprise, 139
   forming a line-out, 132
   indirectly into touch, 129
   jumpers, 136
   lifters, 137
   lifting in the line-out, 67
   line-out law, 140–141
   lining up for, 131–136
   movement in the line-out, 138
   on offense, 132
   offside laws, 90–91
   peeling off, 139

props, 54
quick off the top, 140
receivers, 138
setting up the maul, 140
short line-out, 132
in simplified form, 131
starring roles, 136–138
tactical moves, 139–140
taking it quick, 141–142
taking the throw, 135–136
tap down, 140
throw-in, 130–131, 134–135
throwing to the front, 139
wacky maneuvers, 138
when it occurs, 128
where it takes place, 128–129
winning the line-out, 170
lines on the field, 20–21
Lions tour, 219–220
lob pass, 153
local unions, 215
locks, 30, 55–56, 117
loitering, 89
Lomu, Jonah, 148, 218
long kicks, 80
loose forwards. *See* flankers; number 8
loose-head prop, 30, 52–54, 121–122
loosies. *See* flankers; number 8
Lougheed, Dave, 318
Lowe, Brian, 307
Lundgren, Steve, 252
Lyle, Dan, 223, 312–313

### • *M* •

Maggotfest, 242
the Maggots, 176, 242
Magners League, 223
Mains, Laurie, 273
Mandela, Nelson, 206, 323
man-on-man defense, 180
mark, 157
match ball, 34
match officials
   referees. *See* referees
   reserve touch judge, 72

match officials *(continued)*
  substitution official, 72
  television match official (TMO), 72–73
  touch judges, 71–72
Matfield, Victor, 43
mauls
  described, 48, 109–110
  directing the maul, 111
  driving maul, 110–111
  initiating during line-out, 140
  maul laws, 110–111
  offside law, 91–92
  proper binding, 110
  rolling maul, 111
  speed of, 109
  stopping the maul, 112
  *vs.* tackles, 104
McCaw, Richie, 43, 57
MediaZone Rugby, 292
medium kicks, 80
Melville, Nigel, 231
mental preparation, 190–191
Merrick, Steve, 329
Mexted, Murray, 191, 273, 293, 294
midfield, 60–61
mini rugby. *See* youth rugby
misconduct, 93
mistakes
  forward pass, 82
  intentional mistakes, 82
  knock-on, 81–82
Mortlock, Stirling, 161, 218
motivation, 261
motor home, 112
mountaineering, 106
mouth guards, 41
movement in the line-out, 138
Moyse, Heather, 237, 316
multicultural blunders, 333–334

## • *N* •

National Championship Festival, 248
National Coaching Certification Program
    (NCCP), 273
*National Rugby Post,* 304
national unions, 214–215

National Women's League, 238
Neazor, Paul, 304
Nel, Pieter, 330
New Zealand
  1995 World Cup final, 206
  1999 World Cup semifinal #2, 207
  2000 test match *vs.* Australia, 218
  Air New Zealand Cup, 224–225
  *vs.* Barbarians, 1973, 321–322
  Bledisloe Cup, 219, 319–320
  Lions tour of 2005, 220
  position names, 50
  Ranfurly Shield, 224
  Tri Nations Series, 218
New Zealand All Blacks, 161, 218, 331
New Zealand Black Ferns, 209, 210
New Zealand Rugby Union (NZRU), 215
New Zealand Rugby Union Web site, 308
Nicol, Andy, 330
Nisbett, Grant, 294
non-contact youth rugby, 255
North America
  American collegiate rugby, 249–250
  American high school and youth rugby,
      251–255
  best rugby moments, 323–325
  Canadian collegiate championships, 255
  Canadian high school and youth rugby,
      255–256
  Canadian rugby, 235–238
  club rugby, 241–248
  finding gear in, 40
  internationals, 238–239
  rugby in, 16
  rugby magazines, 303–305
  rugby Web sites, 307
  spectators, 300–302
  televised rugby, 289–291
  ten greatest North American players,
      311–318
  test matches, 300–301
  United States rugby, 227–235
  in the World Cup, 203–204
North America 4 (NA4), 239
Northern Football Union, 11
number 8, 30, 58, 118

# • O •

object of the game, 78
obstruction, 92
Occidental College, 43, 78, 114, 134, 159, 276
O'Driscoll, Brian, 61, 220
offensive scrum, 118
officials. *See* match officials
offside law
  accidentally offside, 88
  crossing the 10-meter line, 89–90
  in general play, 87–90
  mauls, 91–92
  penalty for, 89
  rucks, 91–92
  set pieces, 90–91
  tackles, 91–92
openside flanker, 30, 56, 57
opponent, analyzing, 172–174
Orsini, Candi, 317
outside center, 31, 61
outside half. *See* flyhalf
overseas matches, 302–304
Oxy Olde Boys RFC, 54, 69, 134, 243

# • P •

pack, 29, 48
pack leader, 58
padded vests, 41
Paoli, Fred, 317
passing
  accuracy, 150
  to advance the ball, 79
  cut-out pass, 152
  dive pass, 154
  drawing the defender, 150–151
  flat pass, 79
  forward pass, 82
  goal of, 149
  hospital pass, 80
  letting the ball do the work, 151
  lob pass, 153

  as necessary skill, 14–15
  pop pass, 153
  preparing to make a pass, 150
  receiving a pass on the run, 145
  scrumhalf pass, 154
  skills, 149–154
  spiral pass, 151
  tactical awareness, 150
  throwing the dummy, 149
  velocity, 150
Patrick Parcs boots, 39
Paul, Jeremy, 218
pause, 119
peculiar facts about rugby, 327–335
peeling off, 139
penalties. *See also* taking penalties
  for going offside, 89
  obstruction, 92
  penalty goals, 26
  penalty try, 24
  unfair play, 93
penalty goals, 26
penalty kick, 94, 129
penalty try, 24
Philip, Prince of England, 335
physiotherapist, 269
pick-and-go, 108
Pienaar, Francois, 206, 323
pitch, 175
pivot. *See* flyhalf
Planet Rugby, 306
"play to the whistle," 86
the players, 29–32
playing area, 20
playing the game
  breakdown, 103–104
  the field, 11–12
  gear, 12
  getting started, 98–101
  mauls, 109–112
  positions, 13
  rucks, 104–108
  scoring, 12
  tackle situation, 101–103
pop pass, 153

Portsmouth Victoria, 330
positions
  back line, 58–63
  back row forwards, 56–58
  backs, 48
  blindside flanker, 56–57
  centers, 60–61
  described, 13
  flankers, 56–57
  flyhalf, 59–60
  forwards, 48, 50–58
  front-rowers, 52–55
  fullback, 62–63
  hooker, 54–55
  inside center, 60
  international differences in names, 50
  jersey numbers, 30–31, 48–49
  locks, 55–56
  loose-head prop, 52–54
  number 8, 58
  by the numbers, 30–31
  openside flanker, 56, 57
  outside center, 61
  props, 52–54
  regional variations in names, 50
  reserves, 31–32
  scrumhalf, 58–59
  second-rowers, 55–56
  side, 48
  taking up position, 29
  tight five, 51–52
  tight-head prop, 52–54
  typical scrum attacking formation, 49
  wings, 62
power, 184
Practical Coaching Course, 273
pre-game fuel, 192
props, 52–54, 117, 121–122
protective equipment. *See* safety gear
*Provincial Giants* (Neazor), 304
provincial rugby. *See* interprovincial and
  provincial competition
provincial unions, 215
pushover try, 126
put-in, 120

## • Q •

qualifying for World Cup, 201–202
quality possession, 178
quick tap, 95
quick throws, 141–142

## • R •

rain, 175
Randall clan, 331
Ranfurly Shield, 224
receivers, 138
receiving a pass on the run, 145
red card, 93
Rees, Gareth, 311–312
referees
  in Canada, 284–285
  communication, 280–281
  consistency, 280
  described, 70–71
  examination of gear, 44
  fitness, 282
  free kick signal, 95
  knowledge of laws, 69, 280
  microphones, 73
  responsibilities, 279–282
  role of, 16–17
  at rucktime, 107
  scrum commands, 119
  signals, 73–76
  straight-arm penalty, 95
  temperament, 281–282
  in United States, 282–284
  unofficial calls, 333
  video referee. *See* television match
    official (TMO)
releasing, 121–122
repeated infringements, 93
*repechage* system, 202
replays. *See* television match official
  (TMO)
reserve back, 31
reserve forward, 31
reserve hooker, 31

reserve prop, 31
reserve scrumhalf, 31
reserve touch judge, 72
reserves, 31–32
restart kicks, 100–101, 170
Roberts, Kevin, 231, 232
Robinson, Jason, 205
rolling maul, 111
Roosevelt, Theodore, 229
roots of rugby, 9–11
Ross, Bob, 318
round-the-corner style, 160
rucks
  attacking from the ruck, 106
  common infractions, 106–108
  described, 48, 104–106
  directing the ruck, 108
  form and body position, 105
  listening to referee, 107
  mountaineering, 106
  offside law, 91–92
  pick-and-go, 108
  primary aim, 105
  rucking rules, 106–108
  stamping, 107
  stay on your feet, 108
  *vs.* tackles, 104
  winning the ball, 106
rugby
  advantages of, 10
  essentials of the game, 13–15
  *vs.* football, 82–83
  international aspect, 15–16
  necessary skills, 14–15
  object of the game, 78
  peculiar facts, 327–335
  playing the game. *See* playing the game
  roots of rugby, 9–11
rugby attacks. *See* attacks
rugby ball, 34–35
rugby books, 304
rugby boots, 38, 39
Rugby Canada, 203–204, 210,
    215, 236–237, 238, 285
Rugby Canada Super League, 238, 246–247
Rugby Canada Web site, 308

*The Rugby Club,* 290
rugby etiquette, 298–299
Rugby Football Union (RFU), 11, 214
rugby gear. *See* gear
Rugby Heaven, 306
rugby jerseys, 37
rugby laws
  advantage law, 85–86
  building up your knowledge, 68–69
  described, 14, 65
  dynamic nature of, 67–68
  foul play law, 92–95
  knock-on, 81–82
  law book, 68
  lifting in the line-out, 67
  line-out, 67
  line-out law, 140–141
  maul laws, 110–111
  mistakes, 81–82
  offside law, 87–92
  rucking laws, 106–108
  scrum laws, 121–123
  tackle law, 82–84
  10-meter law, 89–90
*Rugby* magazine, 305
rugby magazines, 303–305
rugby matches. *See* spectators
rugby pitches, 175
rugby shorts, 37
rugby socks, 39
rugby terminology, 20
*The Rugby War* (FitzSimons), 304
rugby Web sites, 305–308
Rugby World Cup
  1987 World Cup (Australia and New
      Zealand), 199
  1991 World Cup (Great Britain, Ireland,
      and France), 199
  1995 World Cup final (South Africa *vs.*
      New Zealand), 206
  1995 World Cup (South Africa), 199–200
  1999 World Cup semifinal #1 (Australia *vs.*
      South Africa), 206
  1999 World Cup semifinal #2 (New
      Zealand *vs.* France), 207

Rugby World Cup *(continued)*
  1999 World Cup (Wales, England,
    Scotland, Ireland, and France), 200
  2003 World Cup (Australia), 200–201
  2003 World Cup final (Australia *vs.*
    England), 205
  2007 World Cup (France, Wales, and
    Scotland), 201
  crown jewel of rugby, 197–198
  described, 15–16
  disparity between nations, 204
  finals tournaments, 201–202
  great World Cup moments, 205–207
  growth of, 198
  history of, 198–201
  North Americans in the World Cup,
    203–204
  origins of, 198–201
  qualification, 201–202
  *repechage* system, 202
  Web site, 308
  William Webb Ellis Cup, 198
rules. *See* rugby laws
running
  to advance the ball, 79
  from everywhere, 172
  fending off, 147
  goose step, 148
  hit-and-spin, 148
  as necessary skill, 14–15
  notable running styles, 148
  practice, 144
  receiving a pass on the run, 145
  side-stepping the tackler, 145–146
  skills, 144–149
  sprint training, 187–188
  swerve, 146
  throwing the dummy, 149
running time, 28
running with the ball, 78

### • S •

safety
  coaching safety, 262–264
  false security, 263–264
  injuries in rugby, 263–264

  injury prevention, 262–263
  keeping players safe, 262–263
  learning how to tackle, 264
safety gear
  barred gear, 43–44
  choosing, 40–42
  permitted, 12
  types of, 41–42
Salut, Jean-Pierre, 330
San Luis Obispo RFC, 69
SANZAR home tests, 217
Sayler, Logan, 252
Schnapp, Dianne, 317
The Score, 291
scoring
  conversion kicks, 25
  converting a try, 24–25
  described, 12, 23
  drop-kicking goals, 26–27
  penalty goals, 26
  penalty try, 24
  try, 23–24
Scrum, 306
scrum. *See also* scrummaging
  after an infraction, 121
  attacking from the scrum, 123–124
  back row, 117–118
  described, 20, 51–52
  formation, 115
  front row, 115–117
  full scrum, 121
  offensive scrum, 118
  offside line, 90–91
  physical domination of opposing pack,
    125–126
  pushover try, 126
  scrumhalf, 118–119
  second row, 117
  sections of the scrum, 115–119
  taking a penalty by choosing scrum, 95
  tunnel, 120
  uncontested scrums, 121
  well-organized, synchronized activity,
    113–114
  wheeling the scrum, 124–125
  winning your own scrums, 170
scrum attacking formation, 49

scrum formation, 95
scrumhalf, 30, 52, 58–59, 108, 111, 118–119
scrumhalf pass, 154
scrummaging. *See also* scrum
  binding and releasing, 121–122
  collapsing, 122
  contest for possession, 120–121
  described, 114
  driving in and up, 122
  engagement, 119–121
  feeding, 123
  laws, 121–123
  *vs.* mayhem, 113–115
  put-in, 120
  repetitive drilling, 115
  strategic scrummaging, 123–126
  throw in, 123
  workouts, 115
second row, 55–56, 117
selecting horses for courses, 174
send-off, 333
Serevi, Waisale, 208
set pieces, 90–91, 169–171, 173
Setanta Sports on DirecTV, 290
sevens rugby, 208, 221, 235, 238
Sevens World Cup, 208
short kicks, 80
short line-out, 132
shorts, 37
shoulder pads, 41
sibling players, 329
side, 29, 48
side-on tackle, 165
side-step, 62, 145–146
Simms Tigers High School Rugby Club, 252
siren, 28–29
Six Nations, 213, 216–217
skills
  coaches' role, 260–261
  kicking, 154–161
  passing, 149–154
  running, 144–149
  tackling, 162–166
Slocock, Noel, 328
sloppy balls, 178
Smith, George, 57

smother tackle, 166
Snow, Rod, 318
socks, 39
Sokolovs, Wilmars, 134, 202
South Africa
  1995 World Cup final, 206, 323
  1999 semifinal #1, 206
  ABSA Currie Cup, 225
  Super 14 win, 322–323
South Africa Baby Boks, 210
South African position names, 50
Southampton Trojans, 330
specialist goal kicker, 26
spectators
  blending in with the crowd, 298–302
  clothes to wear, 299
  club rugby, 301–302
  finding a match to watch, 297–298
  North America, 300–302
  rugby etiquette, 298–299
  sounding like a rugby expert, 302
  test match, 300–301
  touring overseas, 302–304
spiral pass, 151
spiral punt, 155–156
sports bag essentials, 33–36
sports bras, 41
*Sportsworld,* 291
sprint training, 187–188
squad, 29
stamina, 184, 187
stamping, 105, 107
Stanley, Winston, 317
star players, 173
starting the game
  changes in, 98
  drop kick, 98
  kickoffs, 98–100
  restarts after scores and 22s, 100–101
stationary tackle, 166
Stoop, Adrian, 331
stop in play, 85–86
strange locations, 331–332
Stransky, Joel, 295
strategic scrummaging, 123–126

strategies. *See* tactics
stray dogs, 330
strength, 184, 188–189
stretching for performance, 185–187
stretching routine, 184–185
Stuff, 306
substitution official, 72
Super 12 (Super 14), 213
Super 14, 222, 322–323
SuperSport Zone, 306
supplements, 193
suspension, 93
swerve, 146

## • T •

tackle bags, 162
tackle from behind, 165
tackle law
  breakdown, 83
  described, 83
  restrictions, 84
  rugby *vs.* football, 82–83
  tackle situation and continuity, 83
  tackled player, 83–84
  tackler, 84
tackle situation
  breakdown, 103–104
  brought to ground, 102
  and continuity, 83
  described, 101–102
  *vs.* maul, 104
  offsides, 91–92
  *vs.* ruck, 104
  side-stepping the tackler, 145–146
  tackled player, 102
  tackler, 102–103
tackled player, 83–84, 102
tackler, 84, 102–103
tackling skills
  ankle tap, 166
  ball-and-all tackle, 166
  front-on driving tackle, 163–164
  learning, 162–163
  necessity of, 14–15
  and safety, 264

side-on tackle, 165
smother tackle, 166
stationary tackle, 166
tackle from behind, 165
tactical advantage, 86
tactical awareness, 150
tactics
  analyzing the opponent, 172–174
  attack plans, 177–179
  breakdown, 177
  containing the stars, 173
  defense, 179–182
  eight-man push, 173
  exploiting weaknesses, 173
  first-phase possession, 177
  game plan, 168–174, 176–177
  running from everywhere, 172
  selecting horses for courses, 174
  ten-man game, 171–172
  weather conditions, 174–175
  winning the set pieces, 169–171
  your team's strengths and weaknesses,
    168–172
Tahitian 15, 331
taking it quick, 141–142
taking one against the head, 123
taking penalties. *See also* penalties
  described, 94
  forming a scrum, 95
  free kicks, 95
  kicking for touch, 94
  penalty kick, 94
  quick tap, 95
  tap and go, 95
taking the throw, 135–136
taking up position, 29
tap and go, 95
tap down, 140
team doctor, 269
team manager, 268
team trainer, 269
teamwork. *See* tactics
technique, 54
Telecom Virtual Rugby, 307
televised rugby
  best commentators, 294–295
  cable companies, 291

Canada, 291
history of, in North America, 289–290
Internet rugby, 292
jargon glossary, 292–293
Murray Mexted, 293
The Score, 291
Setanta Sports on DirecTV, 290
TV 5, 291
United States, 290–291
Versus, 291
television match official (TMO)
   described, 72–73
   foul play identification, 73
   scoring a try, 73
   and timekeeping, 28
ten-man game, 171–172
10-meter law, 89–90
10-meter line, 20
terminology, 20
test match, 216, 300–301
*Thinking Rugby* (Hodge and McKenzie), 304
Thompson, Randy, 252
throw-in, 130–131, 134–135
throwing the dummy, 149
throwing to the front, 139
tight five, 51–52, 170
tight-head, 123
tight-head prop, 30, 52–54, 121–122
timekeeping
   duration of halves, 27–28
   hooter, 28–29
   injuries, 28
   running time, 28
   TMO, 28
Title IX, 250
TMO. *See* television match official (TMO)
*Total Rugby,* 291
touch, 119
touch judges, 71–72
touch-in-goal line, 21
touchline, 21, 128, 131
touring overseas, 302–304
touring teams, 334–335
training
   diet, 191–193
   fitness, 183–190
   interval training, 188

mental preparation, 190–191
pre-game fuel, 192
sprint training, 187–188
static stretching after training, 186–187
supplements, 193
team trainer, 269
variation in routines, 189
training ball, 35
Tri Nations Series, 213, 217–219
Triple Crown, 216
trust, 182
try
   converting a try, 24–25
   described, 12
   penalty try, 24
   pushover try, 126
   scoring a try, 23–24
tunnel, 120, 132
Tuqiri, Lote, 205
turnover balls, 178
TV 5, 291
22-meter drop-out, 100–101
22-meter lines, 12, 21
Twickenham, 207
two-man cut-out, 152

### • U •

uncontested scrums, 121
Under-19 World Championships, 211
Under-21 Rugby World Cup, 210
unfair play, 93
United Kingdom position names, 50
United States
   club rugby, 241–245
   Coach Development Program (CDP),
      271, 272
   coaching certification, 271–272
   collegiate rugby, 249–250
   formation and reformation of USA rugby,
      229–231
   governance model, 230–231
   growth trends in rugby, 251–252
   high school championships, 252–253
   misperceptions, 227–228
   Olympic gold, 228–229
   origins, 228–229

United States *(continued)*
  referee, becoming a, 282–284
  sevens rugby, 235
  televised rugby, 290–291
  U.S. Olympians *vs.* France, 324–325
  USA Eagles, 232–233
  women's rugby, 234, 254
  youth rugby, 253–255
unorthodox plays, 332–333
up and under, 63, 156–157
USA club championships, 245
USA Eagles, 203, 209, 229–230, 232–233, 234
USA Rugby, 215, 229–231
USA Rugby Super League, 243–245
USA Rugby Web site, 308

## • *V* •

Versus, 291
vests, 41
video referee. *See* television match
    official (TMO)
visualization, 191
Vizard, Brian, 314–315

## • *W* •

Wales, 325
warming up, 184–185
warnings, 93
watching a match. *See* spectators
Watson, Andre, 89
weather conditions, 174–175, 331–332
wheeling the scrum, 124–125
Wilkinson, Jonny, 26, 205
William Webb Ellis Cup, 198
Williams clan, 331

Wilson, Stu, 295
wing forward. *See* flankers
wings, 30, 62
winning the set pieces, 169–171
women's rugby
  Canada, 237
  as emerging sport, 250
  growth of, 254
  United States, 234
  Women's Rugby World Cup, 209–210
Women's Rugby World Cup, 209–210,
    237, 324
Woodward, Clive, 220
World Cup. *See* Rugby World Cup
World Sevens Series, 221
World War II, 335
WorldRugbyShop.com, 40

## • *X* •

XANZAR/UAR Under-21 tournament, 210

## • *Y* •

Yahoo Xtra NZ, 307
yellow card, 93
Youth & High School Strategic Plan, 254
youth rugby
  Canada, 256
  coaches, need for, 274–275
  United States, 253–255

## • *Z* •

Zen Theory of Rugby Fitness, 190
The Zone, 191
Zurich Premiership, 225